Gretchen Bitterlin
Dennis Johnson
Donna Price
Sylvia Ramirez
K. Lynn Savage, Series Editor

Ventures 2
TEACHER'S EDITION

with **Becky Tarver Chase**

CAMBRIDGE UNIVERSITY PRESS
Cambridge, New York, Melbourne, Madrid, Cape Town, Singapore, São Paulo, Delhi, Dubai, Tokyo

Cambridge University Press
32 Avenue of the Americas, New York, NY 10013–2473, USA

www.cambridge.org
Information on this title: www.cambridge.org/9780521690805

© Cambridge University Press 2008

This publication is in copyright. Subject to statutory exception
and to the provisions of relevant collective licensing agreements,
no reproduction of any part may take place without the written
permission of Cambridge University Press.

First published 2008
3rd printing 2010

Printed in the United States of America

A catalog record for this publication is available from the British Library.

ISBN 978-0-521-54839-7 pack consisting of Student's Book and Audio CD
ISBN 978-0-521-67959-6 Workbook
ISBN 978-0-521-69080-5 pack consisting of Teacher's Edition and Teacher's Toolkit Audio CD / CD-ROM
ISBN 978-0-521-67728-8 CDs (Audio)
ISBN 978-0-521-67729-5 Cassettes
ISBN 978-0-521-67584-0 Add Ventures

Copyright
It is normally necessary for written permission for copying to be obtained in advance
from a publisher. The tests in this book are designed to be copied and distributed
in class. The normal requirements are waived here and it is not necessary to write to
Cambridge University Press for permission for an individual teacher to make copies
for use within his or her own classroom. Only those pages which carry the wording
"© Cambridge University Press" may be copied.

Cambridge University Press has no responsibility for
the persistence or accuracy of URLs for external or
third-party Internet Web sites referred to in this publication
and does not guarantee that any content on such
Web sites is, or will remain, accurate or appropriate.

Art direction, book design, photo research, and layout services: Adventure House, NYC
Layout services: Page Designs International
Audio production: Richard LePage & Associates

Contents

Introduction

To the teacher	iv
Scope and sequence	vi
Correlations	x
Features of the Student's Book	xiv
Features of the Teacher's Edition	xviii
Class time guidelines	xx
Meet the Ventures author team	xxi

Teaching Notes

Welcome unit	2
Unit 1 Personal information	6
Unit 2 At school	18
Review: Units 1 and 2	30
Unit 3 Friends and family	32
Unit 4 Health	44
Review: Units 3 and 4	56
Unit 5 Around town	58
Unit 6 Time	70
Review: Units 5 and 6	82
Unit 7 Shopping	84
Unit 8 Work	96
Review: Units 7 and 8	108
Unit 9 Daily living	110
Unit 10 Leisure	122
Review: Units 9 and 10	134

Additional Resources

Projects	T-136
Self-assessments	T-141
Reference: Grammar charts	146
Class audio script	T-151
Tests	T-164
Tests audio script	T-193
Tests answer key	T-195
Teacher's Toolkit Audio CD / CD-ROM	T-197
Games	T-198
Multilevel classroom management	T-201
Acknowledgments	202
Art credits	203

To the teacher

What is *Ventures*?

Ventures is a five-level, standards-based, integrated-skills series for adult students. The five levels, which are Basic through Level Four, are for low-beginning literacy to high-intermediate students.

The *Ventures* series is flexible enough to be used in open enrollment, managed enrollment, and traditional programs. Its multilevel features support teachers who work with multilevel classes.

What components does *Ventures* have?

Student's Book with Self-study Audio CD

Each **Student's Book** contains a Welcome Unit and ten topic-focused units, plus five review units, one after every two units. Each unit has six skill-focused lessons. Projects, self-assessments, and a reference section are included at the back of the Student's Book.

- **Lessons** are self-contained, allowing for completion within a one-hour class period.
- **Review lessons** recycle, reinforce, and consolidate the materials presented in the previous two units and include a pronunciation activity.
- **Projects** offer community-building opportunities for students to work together, using the Internet or completing a task, such as making a poster or a book.
- **Self-assessments** are an important part of students' learning and success. They give students an opportunity to evaluate and reflect on their learning as well as a tool to support learner persistence.
- The **Self-study Audio CD** is included at the back of the Student's Book. The material on the CD is indicated in the Student's Book by an icon.

Teacher's Edition with Teacher's Toolkit Audio CD/CD-ROM

The interleaved **Teacher's Edition** walks instructors step-by-step through the stages of a lesson.

- Included are learner-persistence and community-building tasks as well as teaching tips, expansion activities, and ways to expand a lesson to two or three instructional hours.
- The Student's Book answer key is included on the interleaved pages in the Teacher's Edition.
- The **Teacher's Toolkit Audio CD/CD-ROM** contains additional reproducible material for teacher support. Included are picture dictionary cards and worksheets, tests with audio, and student self-assessments for portfolio assessment. Reproducible sheets also include cooperative learning activities. These activities reinforce the materials presented in the Student's Book and develop social skills, including those identified by SCANS[1] as being highly valued by employers.
- The unit, midterm, and final tests are found on both the Teacher's Toolkit Audio CD/CD-ROM and in the Teacher's Edition. The tests include listening, vocabulary, grammar, reading, and writing sections.

Audio Program

The *Ventures* series includes the ***Class Audio*** and the ***Student Self-study Audio***. The Class Audio contains all the listening materials in the Student's Book and is available on CD or audiocassette. The Student Self-study Audio CD contains all the unit conversations, readings, and picture dictionary words from the Student's Book.

Workbook

The **Workbook** has two pages of activities for each lesson in the Student's Book.

- The exercises are designed so learners can complete them in class or independently. Students can check their own answers with the answer key in the back of the Workbook. Workbook exercises can be assigned in class, for homework, or as student support when a class is missed.
- Grammar charts at the back of the Workbook allow students to use the Workbook for self-study.
- If used in class, the Workbook can extend classroom instructional time by 30 minutes per lesson.

Add Ventures

Add Ventures is a book of reproducible worksheets designed for use in multilevel classrooms. The worksheets give students 15–30 minutes additional practice with each lesson and can be used with homogeneous or heterogeneous groupings. These worksheets can

---

[1] The Secretary's Commission on Achieving Necessary Skills, which produced a document that identifies skills for success in the workplace. For more information, see wdr.doleta.gov/SCANS.

also be used as targeted homework practice at the level of individual students, ensuring learner success.

There are three tiered worksheets for each lesson.

- **Tier 1 Worksheets** provide additional practice for those who are at a level slightly below the Student's Book or who require more controlled practice.
- **Tier 2 Worksheets** provide additional practice for those who are on the level of the Student's Book.
- **Tier 3 Worksheets** provide additional practice that gradually expands beyond the text. These multilevel worksheets are all keyed to the same answers for ease of classroom management.

Unit organization

Within each unit there are six lessons:

LESSON A Get ready The opening lesson focuses students on the topic of the unit. The initial exercise, *Talk about the picture*, involves one "big" picture. The visuals create student interest in the topic and activate prior knowledge. They help the teacher assess what learners already know and serve as a prompt for the key vocabulary of each unit. Next is *Listening*, which is based on short conversations. The accompanying exercises give learners the opportunity to relate vocabulary to meaning and to relate the spoken and written forms of new theme-related vocabulary. The lesson concludes with an opportunity for students to practice language related to the theme in a communicative activity, either orally with a partner or individually in a writing activity.

LESSONS B and C focus on grammar. The sections move from a *Grammar focus* that presents the grammar point in chart form; to *Practice* exercises that check comprehension of the grammar point and provide guided practice; and, finally, to *Communicate* exercises that guide learners as they generate original answers and conversations. The sections on these pages are sometimes accompanied by a *Culture note*, which provides information directly related to the conversation practice (such as the use of titles with last names), or a *Useful language* note, which provides several expressions that can be used interchangeably to accomplish a specific language function (such as greetings).

LESSON D Reading develops reading skills and expands vocabulary. The lesson opens with a *Before you read* exercise, whose purpose is to activate prior knowledge and encourage learners to make predictions. A *Reading tip*, which focuses learners on a specific reading skill, accompanies the **Read** exercise. The reading section of the lesson concludes with *After you read* exercises that check students' understanding. In the Basic Student's Book and Student's Books 1 and 2, the vocabulary expansion portion of the lesson is a **Picture dictionary**. It includes a *word bank*, pictures to identify, and a conversation for practicing the new words. The words are intended to expand vocabulary related to the unit topic. In Student's Books 3 and 4, the vocabulary expansion portion of the lesson occurs in **Check your understanding**.

LESSON E Writing provides writing practice within the context of the unit. There are three kinds of exercises in the lesson: prewriting, writing, and postwriting. *Before you write* exercises provide warm-up activities to activate the language students will need for the writing and one or more exercises that provide a model for students to follow when they write. A *Writing tip*, which presents information about punctuation or organization directly related to the writing assignment, accompanies the **Write** exercise. The Write exercise sets goals for the student writing. In the *After you write* exercise, students share with a partner using guided questions and the steps of the writing process.

LESSON F Another view has three sections.

- **Life-skills reading** develops the scanning and skimming skills that are used with documents such as forms, charts, schedules, announcements, and ads. Multiple-choice questions that follow the document develop test-taking skills similar to CASAS[2] and BEST.[3] This section concludes with an exercise that encourages student communication by providing questions that focus on some aspect of information in the document.
- **Fun with language** provides exercises that review and sometimes expand the topic, vocabulary, or grammar of the unit. They are interactive activities for partner or group work.
- **Wrap up** refers students to the self-assessment page in the back of the book, where they can check their knowledge and evaluate their progress.

The Author Team
Gretchen Bitterlin Sylvia Ramirez
Dennis Johnson K. Lynn Savage
Donna Price

---

[2] The Comprehensive Adult Student Assessment System. For more information, see www.casas.org.
[3] The Basic English Skills Test. For more information, see www.cal.org/BEST.

Scope and sequence

UNIT TITLE / TOPIC	FUNCTIONS	LISTENING AND SPEAKING	VOCABULARY	GRAMMAR FOCUS
Welcome Unit pages 2–5	• Giving personal information – name, address, telephone number, and date of birth • Introducing a classmate • Clarifying spelling • Describing work and life skills	• Asking and answering questions about personal information • Introducing a classmate	• Review of time words	• Review of simple present, present continuous, simple past, and future with *be going to*
Unit 1 **Personal information** pages 6–17 Topic: **Describing people**	• Describing height, hair, and eyes • Describing clothing • Describing habitual actions • Describing actions in the present	• Describing what people look like • Asking and describing what people are wearing • Asking and describing what people are doing at the present time • Asking and describing people's habitual actions	• Accessories • Adjectives of size, color, and pattern	• Adjective order • Present continuous vs. simple present
Unit 2 **At school** pages 18–29 Topic: **School services**	• Offering advice • Describing wants • Describing future plans	• Asking and describing what people want and need • Asking about and describing future plans	• Computer terms • Vocational courses	• *want* and *need* • Future with *will*
Review: Units 1 and 2 pages 30–31		• Understanding a narrative		
Unit 3 **Friends and family** pages 32–43 Topic: **Friends**	• Describing past actions • Describing daily activities • Responding to good and bad news	• Asking and answering questions about past actions • Asking and answering questions about daily habits	• Parts of a car • Daily activities	• Review of simple past with regular and irregular verbs • Simple present vs. simple past
Unit 4 **Health** pages 44–55 Topic: **Accidents**	• Identifying appropriate action after an accident • Asking for and giving advice • Expressing necessity • Showing understanding	• Asking for and giving advice • Clarifying meaning	• Health problems • Accidents • Terms on medicine packaging	• *have to* + verb • *should*
Review: Units 3 and 4 pages 56–57		• Understanding a narrative		
Unit 5 **Around town** pages 58–69 Topic: **Transportation**	• Identifying methods of transportation • Describing number of times • Describing length of time	• Asking and answering questions about train and bus schedules • Asking and answering questions about personal transportation habits • Describing personal habits	• Train station terms • Travel activities • Adverbs of frequency	• *How often* and *How long* questions • Adverbs of frequency

STUDENT'S BOOK 2

READING	WRITING	LIFE SKILLS	PRONUNCIATION
• Reading a story about someone's day	• Filling out a library card application	• Reading a library card application • Talking about work skills and life skills	• Pronouncing key vocabulary
• Reading an e-mail about a family member • Scanning to find the answers to questions	• Writing a descriptive paragraph about a classmate • Using a comma after time phrases at the beginning of a sentence	• Reading an order form	• Pronouncing key vocabulary
• Reading a short essay on an application form • Skimming for the main idea	• Writing an expository paragraph about goals • Using *First*, *Second*, and *Third* to organize ideas	• Reading course descriptions • Setting short-term goals	• Pronouncing key vocabulary
			• Recognizing and pronouncing strong syllables
• Reading a personal journal entry • Scanning for *First*, *Next*, and *Finally* to order events	• Writing a personal journal entry about the events of a day • Using a comma after sequence words	• Reading a cell phone calling-plan brochure	• Pronouncing key vocabulary
• Reading a warning label • Understanding a bulleted list	• Filling out an accident report form • Using cursive writing for a signature	• Reading medicine labels	• Pronouncing key vocabulary
			• Recognizing and emphasizing important words
• Reading a personal letter • Scanning for capital letters to determine names of cities and places	• Writing a personal letter about a trip • Spelling out hours and minutes from one to ten in writing	• Reading a bus schedule • Reading a train schedule	• Pronouncing key vocabulary

Scope and sequence

UNIT TITLE TOPIC	FUNCTIONS	LISTENING AND SPEAKING	VOCABULARY	GRAMMAR FOCUS
Unit 6 **Time** pages 70–81 Topic: **Time lines and major events**	• Describing major events in the past • Inquiring about life events	• Asking and answering questions about major life events in the past • Ordering events in the past	• Life events	• *When* questions and simple past • Time phrases
Review: Units 5 and 6 pages 82–83		• Understanding a conversation		
Unit 7 **Shopping** pages 84–95 Topic: **Comparison shopping**	• Comparing price and quality • Comparing two things • Comparing three or more things	• Asking and answering questions to compare furniture, appliances, and stores	• Furniture • Descriptive adjectives	• Comparatives • Superlatives
Unit 8 **Work** pages 96–107 Topic: **Work history and job skills**	• Identifying job duties • Describing work history	• Asking and answering questions about completed actions • Connecting ideas • Beginning and ending conversations	• Hospital terms • Job duties	• *What* and *Where* questions and simple past • Conjunctions *and, or, but*
Review: Units 7 and 8 pages 108–109		• Understanding a narrative		
Unit 9 **Daily living** pages 110–121 Topic: **Solving common problems**	• Asking for recommendations • Requesting help politely • Agreeing to a request • Refusing a request politely	• Asking for and making recommendations • Explaining choices • Making polite requests • Agreeing to and refusing requests politely	• Home problems • Descriptive adjectives	• *Which* questions and simple present • Requests with *Can, Could, Will, Would*
Unit 10 **Leisure** pages 122–133 Topic: **Special occasions**	• Making offers politely • Responding to offers politely	• Making offers politely • Responding to offers politely • Asking and answering questions involving direct and indirect objects	• Celebrations • Party food • Gifts	• *Would you like . . . ?* • Direct and indirect objects
Review: Units 9 and 10 pages 134–135		• Understanding a conversation		

Projects pages 136–140
Self-assessments pages 141–145
Reference pages 146–154
   Grammar charts pages 146–150
   Useful lists pages 151–153
   Map of North America page 154
Self-study audio script pages 155–161

READING	WRITING	LIFE SKILLS	PRONUNCIATION
• Reading a magazine interview • Scanning interview questions to determine what an article is about	• Writing a narrative paragraph about important life events • Using a comma after a time phrase at the beginning of a sentence	• Reading an application for a marriage license • Describing important life events in sequence	• Pronouncing key vocabulary
			• Pronouncing intonation in questions
• Reading a short newspaper article • Guessing the meaning of new words from other words nearby	• Writing a descriptive paragraph about a gift • Using *because* to answer *Why* and to give a reason	• Reading a sales receipt	• Pronouncing key vocabulary
• Reading a letter of recommendation • Scanning text for names and dates	• Writing a summary paragraph about employment history • Capitalizing the names of businesses	• Reading a time sheet	• Pronouncing key vocabulary
			• Pronouncing the *-s* ending in the simple present
• Reading a notice on a notice board • Determining if new words are positive or negative in meaning	• Writing a letter of complaint • Identifying the parts of a letter	• Reading a customer invoice for service and repairs	• Pronouncing key vocabulary
• Reading a narrative paragraph about a party • Looking for examples of the main idea while reading	• Writing a thank-you note for a gift • Indenting paragraphs in an informal note	• Reading a formal invitation to a party	• Pronouncing key vocabulary
			• Pronouncing reduced forms of *Could you* and *Would you*

Correlations

UNIT/PAGES	CASAS	EFF
Unit 1 **Personal information** pages 6–17	0.1.2, 0.1.4, 0.1.5, 0.1.6, 0.2.1, 0.2.3, 0.2.4, 1.1.6, 1.1.9, 1.2.1, 1.2.5, 1.3.1, 1.3.3, 1.3.4, 1.3.9, 1.6.4, 2.4.2, 2.6.1, 4.8.1, 4.8.2, 4.8.3, 6.0.2, 7.2.1, 7.4.7, 7.5.1, 8.1.2, 8.1.4	Most EFF standards are met, with particular focus on: • Conveying ideas in writing • Interacting with others in positive ways • Monitoring comprehension • Reading with understanding • Speaking so others can understand • Understanding and working with pictures
Unit 2 **At school** pages 18–29	0.1.2, 0.1.4, 0.1.5, 0.2.1, 0.2.4, 1.2.1, 1.9.6, 2.3.2, 2.5.5, 4.1.4, 4.1.6, 4.1.7, 4.1.8, 4.1.9, 4.4.2, 4.4.5, 4.8.1, 4.8.2, 7.1.1, 7.1.4, 7.2.2, 7.2.6, 7.3.1, 7.3.2, 7.3.4, 7.4.2, 7.4.7, 7.4.8, 7.5.1, 7.5.7, 8.3.2	Most EFF standards are met, with particular focus on: • Conveying ideas in writing • Guiding others • Listening actively • Paying attention to the conventions of written English • Seeking input from others • Solving problems and making decisions
Unit 3 **Friends and family** pages 32–43	0.1.2, 0.1.4, 0.1.5, 0.2.1, 0.2.4, 1.2.1, 1.2.2, 1.2.4, 1.2.5, 1.5.2, 2.1.4, 2.6.1, 4.8.1, 4.8.2, 4.8.4, 6.0.1, 6.0.2, 6.0.3, 6.0.4, 6.1.1, 6.1.3, 6.2.3, 6.5.1, 6.6.6, 7.1.4, 7.2.1, 7.2.7, 7.3.2, 7.4.2, 7.4.3, 7.4.7, 7.5.1, 8.1.2, 8.2.1, 8.2.2, 8.2.3, 8.2.4	Most EFF standards are met, with particular focus on: • Attending to oral information • Organizing and presenting written information • Paying attention to the conventions of spoken English • Selecting appropriate reading strategies • Solving problems using appropriate quantitative procedures • Speaking so others can understand
Unit 4 **Health** pages 44–55	0.1.2, 0.1.4, 0.1.5, 0.2.1, 1.2.5, 3.1.1, 3.2.1, 3.3.1, 3.3.2, 3.4.1, 3.4.2, 3.4.3, 3.5.9, 4.3.3, 4.8.1, 7.1.4, 7.2.1, 7.3.2, 7.4.2, 7.4.7	Most EFF standards are met, with particular focus on: • Conveying ideas in writing • Offering clear input • Seeking input from others • Speaking so others can understand • Taking stock of where one is • Understanding and working with numbers
Unit 5 **Around town** pages 58–69	0.1.2, 0.1.4, 0.1.5, 0.1.6, 0.2.1, 0.2.4, 2.2.1, 2.2.3, 2.2.4, 2.3.1, 4.8.1, 6.0.1, 6.0.2, 6.0.3, 6.0.4, 6.1.2, 6.6.6, 7.1.1, 7.4.2, 7.4.7	Most EFF standards are met, with particular focus on: • Conveying ideas in writing • Listening actively • Offering clear input • Organizing and presenting written information • Selecting appropriate reading strategies • Understanding and working with numbers and pictures

SCANS	BEST Plus Form A	BEST Form B
Most SCANS standards are met, with particular focus on: • Acquiring and evaluating information • Improving basic skills • Interpreting and communicating information • Participating as a member of a team • Practicing self-management	Overall test preparation is supported, with particular impact on the following items: Locator: W1, W7 Level 1: 4.2 Level 3: 4.1	Overall test preparation is supported, with particular impact on the following areas: • Oral interview • Personal information • Money and shopping • Writing notes
Most SCANS standards are met, with particular focus on: • Acquiring and evaluating information • Improving basic skills • Organizing and maintaining information • Solving problems • Teaching others	Overall test preparation is supported, with particular impact on the following items: Locator: W5 Level 1: 4.2 Level 2: 4.2 Level 3: 2.2, 2.3, 5.2	Overall test preparation is supported, with particular impact on the following areas: • Calendar • Employment and training • Oral interview • Personal information • Reading passages • Reading signs, ads, and notices • Writing notes
Most SCANS standards are met, with particular focus on: • Allocating money • Improving basic skills • Interpreting and communicating information • Participating as a member of a team • Practicing self-management	Overall test preparation is supported, with particular impact on the following items: Locator: W6 Level 1: 4 Level 3: 4	Overall test preparation is supported, with particular impact on the following areas: • Money and shopping • Numbers • Personal information • Reading signs, ads, and notices • Reading passages • Time • Writing notes
Most SCANS standards are met, with particular focus on: • Acquiring and evaluating information • Organizing and maintaining information • Practicing reasoning • Practicing self-management • Seeing things in the mind's eye	Overall test preparation is supported, with particular impact on the following items: Level 3: 1.2, 1.3	Overall test preparation is supported, with particular impact on the following areas: • Emergencies and safety • Health and parts of the body • Labels • Oral interview • Personal information • Reading signs, ads, and notices • Reading passages • Writing notes
Most SCANS standards are met, with particular focus on: • Improving basic skills • Interpreting and communicating information • Knowing how to learn • Participating as a member of a team • Teaching others	Overall test preparation is supported, with particular impact on the following items: Locator: W6, W7 Level 1: 3.1, 3.2, 3.3 Level 2: 2.1	Overall test preparation is supported, with particular impact on the following areas: • Oral interview • Personal information • Reading passages • Time/Numbers • Train schedule • Writing notes

UNIT/PAGES	CASAS	EFF
Unit 6 **Time** pages 70–81	0.1.2, 0.1.4, 0.1.5, 0.2.1, 0.2.3, 0.2.4, 2.3.1, 2.3.2, 2.7.2, 4.8.1, 5.3.1, 5.3.6, 6.0.1, 7.1.1, 7.2.1, 7.2.4, 7.2.7, 7.4.2, 7.4.3, 7.4.7, 7.4.8, 7.5.1	Most EFF standards are met, with particular focus on: • Conveying ideas in writing • Cooperating with others • Paying attention to the conventions of spoken English • Reading with understanding • Reflecting and evaluating • Understanding and working with numbers and pictures
Unit 7 **Shopping** pages 84–95	0.1.2, 0.1.4, 0.1.5, 0.2.1, 1.1.6, 1.2.1, 1.2.2, 1.4.1, 1.6.3, 4.8.1, 6.0.1, 6.0.2, 7.1.1, 7.2.3, 7.4.2, 7.4.7, 7.5.1, 8.1.4	Most EFF standards are met, with particular focus on: • Attending to oral information • Attending to visual sources of information • Identifying strengths and weaknesses as a learner • Making inferences, predictions, or judgments • Seeking feedback and revising accordingly • Taking responsibility for learning
Unit 8 **Work** pages 96–107	0.1.2, 0.1.4, 0.1.5, 0.2.1, 1.1.6, 2.3.1, 2.3.2, 4.1.2, 4.1.6, 4.1.8, 4.2.1, 4.4.3, 4.5.1, 4.8.1, 4.8.2, 6.0.1, 7.1.1, 7.1.4, 7.2.1, 7.2.3, 7.4.7, 7.5.1	Most EFF standards are met, with particular focus on: • Listening actively • Monitoring comprehension and adjusting reading strategies • Organizing and presenting written information • Setting and prioritizing goals • Speaking so others can understand • Testing out new learning in real-life applications
Unit 9 **Daily living** pages 110–121	0.1.2, 0.1.4, 0.1.5, 0.2.1, 0.2.3, 1.1.6, 1.4.1, 1.4.5, 1.4.7, 1.6.3, 1.7.4, 1.7.5, 4.1.8, 4.8.1, 4.8.6, 6.0.1, 7.1.1, 7.1.2, 7.2.1, 7.2.2, 7.3.2, 7.3.4, 7.4.2, 7.4.7, 7.5.1, 7.5.6, 8.1.4, 8.2.6, 8.3.1, 8.3.2	Most EFF standards are met, with particular focus on: • Anticipating and identifying problems • Conveying ideas in writing • Engaging parties in trying to reach agreement • Reading with understanding • Setting and prioritizing goals • Speaking so others can understand
Unit 10 **Leisure** pages 122–133	0.1.2, 0.1.4, 0.1.5, 0.2.1, 0.2.3, 0.2.4, 2.3.1, 2.3.2, 2.6.1, 2.7.1, 2.7.2, 4.8.1, 4.8.3, 7.1.1, 7.2.1, 7.4.7, 7.5.1, 7.5.6	Most EFF standards are met, with particular focus on: • Cooperating with others • Identifying strengths and weaknesses as a learner • Paying attention to the conventions of spoken English • Reflecting and evaluating • Testing out new learning in real-life applications • Understanding and working with pictures and numbers

SCANS	BEST Plus Form A	BEST Form B
Most SCANS standards are met, with particular focus on: • Improving basic skills • Interpreting and communicating information • Knowing how to learn • Organizing and maintaining information • Participating as a member of a team	Overall test preparation is supported, with particular impact on the following items: Level 1: 4.1, 4.2 Level 3: 4.1	Overall test preparation is supported, with particular impact on the following areas: • Calendar • Oral interview • Personal information • Reading passages • Time/Numbers • Writing notes
Most SCANS standards are met, with particular focus on: • Acquiring and evaluating information • Interpreting and communicating information • Knowing how to learn • Participating as a member of a team • Practicing self-management	Overall test preparation is supported, with particular impact on the following items: Level 1: 2.1, 2.3 Level 2: 3.2 Level 3: 2.2	Overall test preparation is supported, with particular impact on the following areas: • Money and shopping • Oral interview • Personal information • Reading signs, ads, and notices • Reading passages • Writing notes
Most SCANS standards are met, with particular focus on: • Acquiring and evaluating information • Improving basic skills • Knowing how to learn • Practicing reasoning • Teaching others	Overall test preparation is supported, with particular impact on the following items: Locator: W5, W6	Overall test preparation is supported, with particular impact on the following areas: • Calendar • Employment and training • Oral interview • Personal information • Reading passages • Time/Numbers • Writing notes
Most SCANS standards are met, with particular focus on: • Improving basic skills • Practicing negotiation • Seeing things in the mind's eye • Serving clients and customers • Understanding systems	Overall test preparation is supported, with particular impact on the following items: Locator: W2 Level 1: 2.1, 2.2, 2.3 Level 2: 1.1, 3.1, 3.2 Level 3: 2.2, 2.3	Overall test preparation is supported, with particular impact on the following areas: • Emergencies and safety • Housing • Oral interview • Personal information • Reading signs, ads, and notices • Reading passages • Time/Numbers • Writing notes
Most SCANS standards are met, with particular focus on: • Improving basic skills • Knowing how to learn • Participating as a member of a team • Practicing sociability • Teaching others • Working with diversity	Overall test preparation is supported, with particular impact on the following items: Locator: W7 Level 1: 4.1, 4.2 Level 3: 1.1, 4.1	Overall test preparation is supported, with particular impact on the following areas: • Calendar • Oral interview • Personal information • Reading passages • Time/Numbers • Writing notes

Features of the Student's Book

The *Ventures* Student's Book is based on high-interest topics that reinforce the vocabulary and language adult language learners need in their daily lives. Not only are skills integrated throughout a lesson, but *Ventures* also teaches listening, speaking, reading, and writing individually in every unit.

To encourage learner persistence, the *Ventures* series is designed so that the one-hour lessons in the Student's Book are self-contained; each lesson moves from presentation to guided practice to communicative activities.

The self-study audio CD at the back of the Student's Book provides a way for students to practice at home.

The core philosophy of *Ventures* is:
Hear it before you say it.
Say it before you read it.
Read it before you write it.

Before producing language, students need input that can be internalized and understood. This holistic approach is essential to successful language acquisition and is the foundation of the *Ventures* series.

The Student's Book, combined with the *Workbook*, *Teacher's Edition Toolkit Audio CD / CD-ROM*, and *Add Ventures*, offers maximum flexibility of use in multilevel classrooms, classes of various duration, and classes that encourage independent learning.

The "Big" Picture

- Introduces the unit topic
- Activates students' prior knowledge
- Previews unit grammar and vocabulary

Listening

- Provides guided listening and structured speaking practice
- Expands topic vocabulary
- Encourages learner persistence and autonomy with self-study audio CD

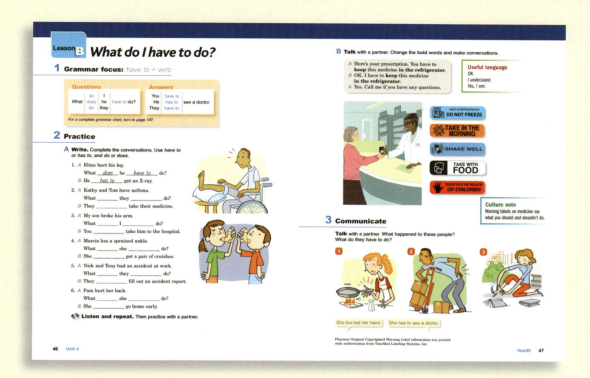

Grammar

- Builds fluency through two grammar lessons
- Moves from guided practice to communicative activities
- Includes *Useful language* notes
- Includes audio to check comprehension and practice pronunciation

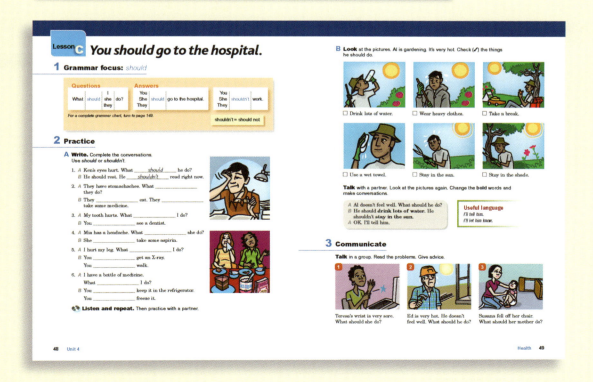

Features of the Student's Book　xv

Reading

- Features three-step approach to reading: **Before you read**, **Read**, **After you read**
- Highlights reading strategies and skills
- Contextualizes unit vocabulary and grammar
- Integrates four skills: speaking, listening, reading, writing
- Presents a variety of reading texts on audio

Picture dictionary

- Expands topic-related vocabulary
- Practices pronunciation of new vocabulary
- Reinforces vocabulary through writing and conversation

Writing

- Includes a process approach to writing: prewriting, writing, and peer review
- Contextualizes unit vocabulary and grammar
- Features integrated skills: speaking, listening, reading, writing
- Moves from guided practice to personalized writing

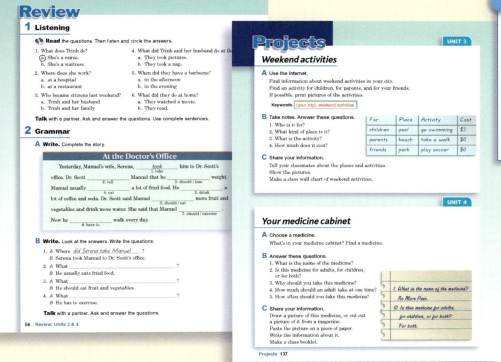

Assessment and consolidation

- Concludes unit with practical and playful practice
- Familiarizes students with real-life documents
- Reviews unit content
- Provides test-taking practice and self-assessment
- Motivates students as they see progress

Review unit

- Reinforces language of previous two units
- Focuses on listening, grammar, and pronunciation

Project

- Builds community among students
- Enhances learner persistence
- Exposes students to simple Internet searches
- Reinforces the theme of the unit

Features of the Student's Book   xvii

Features of the Teacher's Edition

Introduction

Ventures Teacher's Edition includes step-by-step teaching notes for each lesson. The teaching notes divide the lesson into six stages. Each lesson begins with a warm-up and review followed by a presentation stage. The practice, comprehension, application, and evaluation stages do not follow a strict sequence in the Teacher's Edition. They vary depending on the content of the lesson being presented.

Stages of a lesson

Warm-up and review Each lesson begins with a review of previous material and connects that material to the present lesson. Quick review activities prompt students' memory. Warm-up activities at the beginning of class introduce the new lesson. These activities may take many forms, but they are quick, focused, and connected to the new material to be introduced. A warm-up also helps teachers ascertain what students already know about the topic and what they are able to say.

Presentation During this stage of the lesson, the teacher presents new information, but it should not be a one-way delivery. Rather, it is a dynamic process of student input and interaction – a give-and-take between the teacher and students as well as students and students. The teacher may give examples rather than rules, model rather than tell, and relate the material to students' experiences.

Practice It is important that students have enough time to practice. A comfortable classroom environment needs to be created so that students are not afraid to take risks. The practice needs to be varied and interesting. There should be a progression from guided to independent practice. In the *Ventures* grammar lessons, for example, practice begins with mechanical aspects such as form, moves to a focus on meaning, and ends with communicative interactions.

Comprehension check Asking, "Do you understand?" is not enough to ascertain whether students are following the lesson. The teacher must ask concrete questions and have students demonstrate that they understand. In this stage, students are asked to repeat information in their own words. Students are also invited to come to the board or to interact with other students in some way.

Application A teacher must provide opportunities for students to practice newly acquired language in more realistic situations. These situations could be in class or out of class. The important point is that students use what they have learned in new ways. In the grammar lessons, for example, the *Communicate* section asks students to role-play, interview, share information, or ask questions.

Evaluation An ongoing part of the lesson is to determine whether students are meeting the lesson objectives. This can be done formally at the end of a unit by giving a unit test and having students complete the self-assessment, but it can also be done informally toward the end of the lesson. Each lesson in the Teacher's Edition ends with a review and verification of understanding of the lesson objectives. Any in-class assignment or task can serve as an evaluation tool as long as it assesses the objectives. Having students complete **Add Ventures** worksheets or **Workbook** pages can also serve as an informal evaluation to gauge where students may be having difficulty.

The following chart presents the most common order of each stage and suggests how long each stage could take within a one-hour class period.

Stages of the lesson	Approximate time range
Warm-up and review	5–10 minutes
Presentation	10–20 minutes
Practice	15–20 minutes
Comprehension check	5–10 minutes
Application	15–20 minutes
Evaluation	10–15 minutes

The Teacher's Edition includes:

- Interleaved Student's Book pages with answers
- Lesson objectives and step-by-step teaching instructions
- Expansion activities, extra teaching tips, and culture notes
- Activities to encourage learner persistence and community building
- Tests, games, self-assessments, and projects
- Ideas for multilevel classroom management
- **Teacher's Toolkit Audio CD / CD-ROM** with a wealth of supplemental materials for teachers and students
- Class audio listening scripts

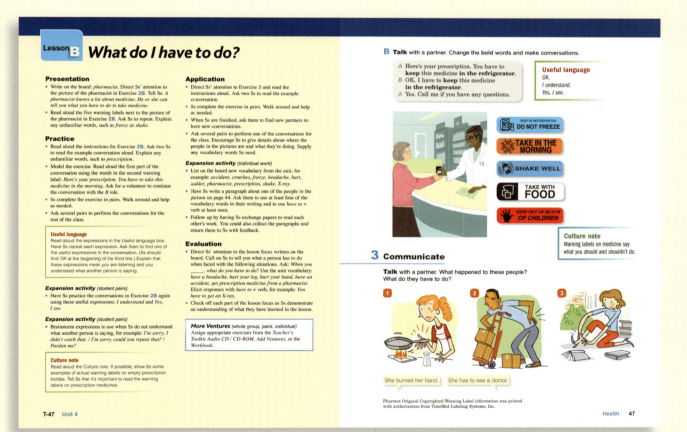

Class time guidelines

Class time varies in different educational settings. The flexibility of the *Ventures* series provides for the expansion of a one-hour class into a two- or three-hour class. For longer class periods, the expansion activities, teaching tips, culture notes, and community building and learner persistence activities in the Teacher's Edition offer ample material to expand the lesson. The Projects at the back of the Student's Book as well as the Games suggested in the Teacher's Edition offer further ways to enrich the two- or three-hour class. In addition, the materials on the *Teacher's Toolkit Audio CD / CD-ROM* as well as in the other components of the series can be used in class or as homework to satisfy the needs of the longer class period.

The chart below illustrates how the *Ventures* series might be used in a one-hour, two-hour, and three-hour class.

A one-hour class

Follow *Teacher's Edition* step-by-step lessons for the *Student's Book*.

Assign *Workbook* for homework.

Assign appropriate level *Add Ventures* worksheets for homework.

Optional: Projects and Games; Collaborative Activities on the *Teacher's Toolkit Audio CD / CD-ROM*

A two-hour class

Follow *Teacher's Edition* step-by-step lessons for the *Student's Book*.

Assign *Workbook* for homework.

Use appropriate level *Add Ventures* worksheets as an in-class activity.

Optional: Projects and Games; Collaborative Activities and Picture Dictionary Cards on the *Teacher's Toolkit Audio CD / CD-ROM*

A three-hour class

Follow *Teacher's Edition* step-by-step lessons for the *Student's Book*.

Use *Workbook* as an in-class activity.

Use appropriate level *Add Ventures* worksheets as an in-class activity.

Optional: Projects and Games; Collaborative Activities, Picture Dictionary Cards, and Picture Dictionary worksheets on the *Teacher's Toolkit Audio CD / CD-ROM*

Meet the *Ventures* author team

Gretchen Bitterlin has been an ESL instructor and ESL department instructional leader with the Continuing Education Program, San Diego Community College District. She now coordinates that agency's large noncredit ESL program. She was also an ESL Teacher Institute Trainer and Chair of the TESOL Task Force on Adult Education Program Standards. She is a co-author of *English for Adult Competency*.

Dennis Johnson has been an ESL instructor at City College of San Francisco, teaching all levels of ESL, since 1977. As ESL Site Coordinator, he has provided guidance to faculty in selecting textbooks. He is the author of *Get Up and Go* and co-author of *The Immigrant Experience*.

Donna Price is Associate Professor of ESL and Vocational ESL/Technology Resource Instructor for the Continuing Education Program, San Diego Community College District. She has taught all levels of ESL for 20 years and is a former recipient of the TESOL Newbury House Award for Excellence in Teaching. She is also the author of *Skills for Success*.

Sylvia Ramirez is a professor at MiraCosta College, where she coordinates the large noncredit ESL program. She has more than 30 years of experience in adult ESL, including multilevel ESL, vocational ESL, family literacy, and distance learning. She has represented the California State Department of Education in providing technical assistance to local ESL programs.

K. Lynn Savage, Series Editor, is a retired ESL teacher and Vocational ESL Resource teacher from City College of San Francisco, who trains teachers for adult education programs around the country. She chaired the committee that developed *ESL Model Standards for Adult Education Programs* (California, 1992) and is the author, co-author, and editor of many ESL materials, including *Teacher Training through Video*, *Parenting for Academic Success: A Curriculum for Families Learning English*, *Crossroads Café*, *Building Life Skills*, *Picture Stories*, *May I Help You?*, and *English That Works*.

Welcome

1 Meet your classmates

A Look at the picture. What do you see?
B What are the people doing?

Lesson objectives
- Greet and introduce people
- Use the alphabet and numbers
- Give personal information

Warm-up
- Before class. Write today's lesson focus on the board.
  Welcome unit:
  Names and introductions
  Personal information: name, address, date of birth
  The alphabet and numbers
- Begin class. Books closed. Say: *Welcome to English class.*
- Write your name on the board. Point to it. Say: *My name is _____*. Ask a S: *What's your name?* If the S doesn't answer, ask different Ss until someone can answer you.
- As Ss respond, repeat their names as you say: *Nice to meet you, _____.*

▼ **Teaching tip**
It takes time to learn everyone's name. Take attendance regularly using the names Ss want to be called by in class, or have Ss sign in when they arrive. Then, look at the sign-in sheet and greet each S by name.

Expansion activity *(whole group)*
- Bring to class self-stick name tags or pieces of paper and tape, along with dark-colored markers.
- Say: *My name is _____*. Write your name on a name tag and put it on.
- Distribute blank name tags and markers for Ss to fill out and wear.
- Write on the board: *Hi, I'm _____, and this is _____.* Use this sentence to introduce yourself and one S by the name written on his or her name tag.
- Tell the S you introduced: *Now it's your turn.* Indicate that the S should say the sentence written on the board and introduce the next S.
- Continue until all Ss have introduced themselves and another S.

Presentation
- Books open. Hold up the Student's Book. Direct Ss to the big picture on page 2. Ask Ss: *Where is this?* (a library) *What do you see?* Elicit and write on the board as much vocabulary about the picture as possible (people, calendar, books, etc.).

- Ask Ss the question in Exercise **1B**: *What are the people doing?* Point to the men at the table and ask: *What are they doing?* (reading, studying) Point to the two women near the back of the library and ask: *What are they doing?* (shaking hands, introducing themselves)
- Ask Ss what they think people in the picture might be saying. Point to the librarian and ask: *What is she saying?* Elicit an appropriate response, for example: *English classes start next week.* Point to the two women shaking hands and ask: *What are they saying?* Elicit expressions for introducing oneself, for example: *Hi, my name is Teresa.*

▼ **Teaching tip**
Don't worry if some Ss in your class don't understand all the words or can't answer all of these questions. Talking about the picture in this way will help you assess your Ss' current language level.

- Review the names of Ss in the class by standing near them and asking their classmates: *What's his / her name?* If Ss don't remember some names, ask the S you're standing near: *What's your name?*

Expansion activity *(student pairs)*
- Bring to class copies of a page from a calendar or draw a calendar page on the board. In the numbered squares, write the words for the ordinal numbers, for example: *first, third, fifth.* Leave some squares blank.
- Direct Ss' attention to the sign at the back of the library in the big picture. Ask: *When do English classes start?* (Monday, September seventeenth) If a S says the date correctly, ask that S to repeat it. Explain that we use ordinal numbers such as *seventeenth* for dates in English.
- Ss in pairs. Ask Ss to write the missing words on the calendar page, or if you're using the board, ask for volunteers to complete the calendar there. Supply any numbers Ss don't know, or direct them to the list of ordinal numbers on page 152.
- Practice saying the ordinal numbers. Then, point to specific dates and call on Ss to say them.

Welcome

Presentation

- Books open. Direct Ss' attention to the word bank in Exercise **2A**. Tell Ss: *These are words for giving personal information.* Read each word aloud and ask Ss to repeat. Explain any words Ss don't know.
- Read aloud the instructions for Exercise **2A**. Ss complete the exercise individually. Walk around and help as needed.

Practice

- Direct Ss' attention to the second part of the instructions in Exercise **2A** and read them aloud.
- [Class Audio CD1 track 2] Play or read the audio program (see audio script, page T-151). Ss listen and repeat as they check their answers. Repeat the audio program as needed.
- Have pairs of Ss practice saying the questions and answers. Help with pronunciation as needed.

▼ **Teaching tip**
Ss may be unfamiliar with the word *initial* or with the concept of a *middle name*. Write a full English name, such as "Mary Louise Burnson," on the board and point out the middle name "Louise." Then write the same name using the middle initial. Discuss the ways your Ss' names follow or differ from this pattern.

Expansion activity (whole group)

- Brainstorm times when people ask for and give personal information, for example, when someone is signing up for a class.
- Discuss when it's safe or not safe to give out personal information. For instance, it's generally not a good idea to give out personal information to someone in an e-mail or to a stranger who calls you on the phone. However, if you have contacted someone to get information or to place an order, you can expect to be asked for personal information.

Learner persistence (individual work)

- [Self-Study Audio CD track 2] Exercise **2A** is recorded on the Ss' self-study CD at the back of the Student's Book. Ss can listen to the CD at home for reinforcement and review. They can also listen to the CD for self-directed learning when class attendance is not possible.

Application

- Direct Ss' attention to Exercise **2B**. Say: *This is a library card application.* Show Ss your own library card and explain that you can use it to borrow books from the library.
- Read the instructions aloud. Ask two Ss to read aloud the example question and answer.
- Model the exercise. Hold up the Student's Book. Point to the library card application. Ask a S: *What's your first name?* Write the name in your book. Repeat with *middle initial* and *last name*.
- Tell Ss that they can use their real addresses and phone numbers or invented information.
- Ss complete the application form in pairs. Walk around and help as needed.
- When Ss are finished filling out the form, have them check their partner's application form for accuracy.

▼ **Teaching tip**
Ss may not be familiar with American conventions for writing dates. Write on the board: *mm / dd / yyyy*. Tell Ss that the letters stand for *month, day,* and *year*. Write several dates on the board, including today's date, using this convention.

Comprehension check

- Read aloud the second part of the instructions for Exercise **2B**. Ask a S to read the example introduction aloud. As a class, read aloud the response: *Nice to meet you, Ben*.
- Model the exercise. Borrow and hold up one S's book. Use the information written on the application to introduce the S's partner. Have the class respond: *Nice to meet you, _____*.
- Ss introduce their partners to the class. After each introduction, be sure to encourage the rest of the class to say: *Nice to meet you, _____*.

Community building (whole group)

- Distribute brochures or other information from your community's public library. Ask Ss to find out the library's address, its days and hours of operation, and how to get a library card.

Evaluation

- Direct Ss' attention to the lesson focus written on the board. Ask Ss to introduce themselves and a classmate. Have Ss spell their first and last names, give their addresses and zip codes, and say their birth dates, if they feel comfortable doing that.
- Check off each part of the lesson focus as Ss demonstrate an understanding of what they have learned in the lesson.

2 Greetings and introductions

A Read the conversations. Complete the sentences with words from the box.

address	date of birth	last name	name
apartment	home phone	middle initial	zip code

1. **A** What's your _____name_____?
   B Ben Navarro.
2. **A** How do you spell your _____last name_____?
   B N-A-V-A-R-R-O.
3. **A** Do you have a _____middle initial_____?
   B Yes. It's J.
4. **A** What's your _____address_____?
   B 1737 Van Dam Street, Brooklyn, New York.

5. **A** What's your _____zip code_____?
   B It's 11222.
6. **A** Do you have an _____apartment_____ number?
   B Yes. It's 3A.
7. **A** What's your _____home phone_____ number?
   B 718-555-5983.
8. **A** What's your _____date of birth_____?
   B January 18th, 1982.

 Listen and check your answers. Then practice with a partner.

B Talk with a partner. Ask questions. Write your partner's answers.

What's your first name? Ben.

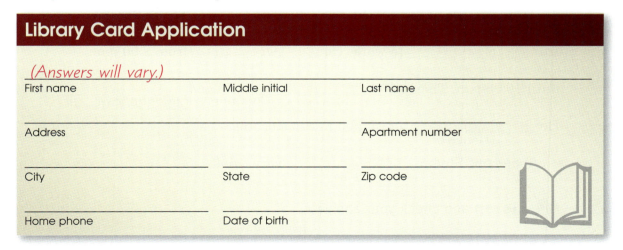

Library Card Application

(Answers will vary.)

First name   Middle initial   Last name

Address   Apartment number

City   State   Zip code

Home phone   Date of birth

Talk with your class. Introduce your partner.

This is my classmate Ben Navarro. His birthday is January 18th.

Nice to meet you, Ben.

3 Verb tense review

A **Listen** to each sentence. Complete the chart. Check (✓) the time words.

	Now	Every day	Yesterday	Tomorrow
1.		✓		
2.			✓	
3.	✓			
4.				✓
5.				✓

Listen again. Check your answers.

B **Read** about Stefan's day. Complete the story. Use the correct verb tense.

Right now it's 11:30 p.m., but Stefan ___isn't sleeping___ .
　　　　　　　　　　　　　　　　　　　1. not / sleep

He ___'s studying___ for an English test.
　　2. study

Stefan ___goes___ to school every
　　　　3. go

morning from 9:00 to 12:00. After class, he

usually ___meets___ Armin in the library,
　　　　　4. meet

and they ___study___ together.
　　　　　5. study

Yesterday was different. Stefan ___didn't go___ to the library.
　　　　　　　　　　　　　　　　　　　6. not / go

He ___went___ to work. He ___worked___ from 2:00 p.m.
　　　7. go　　　　　　　　　　8. work

until 10:00 p.m. Then he ___came___ home and ___started___ studying.
　　　　　　　　　　　　　9. come　　　　　　　　　10. start

He ___studied___ until 2:00 in the morning.
　　　11. study

Tomorrow Stefan ___is going to be___ very tired!
　　　　　　　　　　　12. be

Listen and check your answers.

C **Talk** with a partner. Ask about your partner's day.

> What did you do before class?

> I ate lunch.

Welcome

Lesson objectives
- Review basic verb tenses and time words
- Talk about skills and abilities

Warm-up
- Before class. Write today's lesson focus on the board.
  Welcome unit:
  Verb tenses and time words
  Work skills and life skills
- Before class. Write on the board: *Now, Every day, Yesterday, Tomorrow.* Also write the days of the week on the board in a horizontal line.
- Begin class. Books closed. Review names and introductions. Stand next to a S and introduce him or her, for example: *Everyone, this is Fatima.* Elicit from the class: *Nice to meet you, Fatima.*
- Assess Ss' knowledge of verb tenses and time words. Point to the time words on the board. Say them aloud and ask Ss to repeat. Ask Ss a variety of questions using the time words, for example: *What time is it now? Are you watching TV now? Do you go to English class every day? Yesterday, did you go to work? What did you do yesterday? Tomorrow, are you going to go to the library?*
- Point to the days of the week on the board. Say them aloud and ask Ss to repeat.
- Point to the current day and write down the current time. Ask a S: *What are you doing now?* Point to the previous day and ask: *Yesterday, what did you do?* Continue in this manner with *Every day* and *Tomorrow*. Emphasize the connection between the time words and the correct verb tenses by repeating correct answers and writing Ss' verb phrases under the corresponding time words on the board.

Practice
- Books open. Direct Ss' attention to the chart in Exercise **3A**. Read the instructions aloud.
- [Class Audio CD1 track 3] Model the exercise. Play or read the first sentence of the audio program (see audio script, page T-151). Point to where *Every day* is checked in the chart.
- [Class Audio CD1 track 3] Play or read the rest of the audio program (see audio script, page T-151). Ss listen and check off the time words after they hear them. Repeat the audio program as needed.

Comprehension check
- Read aloud the second part of the instructions in Exercise **3A**.
- [Class Audio CD1 track 3] Play or read the audio program again (see audio script, page T-151). Pause the audio program after each sentence. Ask: *What time word did you hear?* As Ss answer, point to the correct time word in the book or in the list on the board.

Learner persistence (individual work)
- [Self-Study Audio CD track 3] Exercise **3A** is recorded on the Ss' self-study CD at the back of the Student's Book. Ss can listen to the CD at home for reinforcement and review. They can also listen to the CD for self-directed learning when class attendance is not possible.

Practice
- Direct Ss' attention to Exercise **3B** and read the instructions aloud.
- Model the exercise. Point to the example sentence and read it aloud. Ask: *What's the time word?* Elicit: *now* or *right now*. Make sure Ss understand the connection between the time word and the verb tense.
- Ss complete the exercise individually. Walk around and help as needed.
- Read aloud the second part of the instructions in Exercise **3B**.
- [Class Audio CD1 track 4] Play or read the audio program (see audio script, page T-151). Ss listen and check their answers. Repeat the audio program as needed.

Learner persistence (individual work)
- [Self-Study Audio CD track 4] Exercise **3B** is recorded on the Ss' self-study CD at the back of the Student's Book. Ss can listen to the CD at home for reinforcement and review. They can also listen to the CD for self-directed learning when class attendance is not possible.

Application
- Direct Ss' attention to Exercise **3C** and read the instructions aloud. Ask two Ss to read aloud the example question and answer.
- Ss complete the activity in pairs. Walk around and help as needed.

Welcome T-4

Presentation

- Books closed. Write on the board: *Yes, I can. / No, I can't.*
- Direct Ss' attention to the list of skills in Exercise **4A**. Read the verb phrases aloud and ask Ss to repeat.
- Ask several Ss about the skills, for example: *Marisol, can you use a computer?* Point to the possible answers on the board.

Practice

- Direct Ss' attention to Exercise **4A** and read the instructions aloud.
- 🎧 [Class Audio CD1 track 5] Play or read the audio program (see audio script, page T-151). Ss listen and check off the work skills. Repeat the audio program as needed.

Comprehension check

- Write the six work skills from Exercise **4A** on the board.
- 🎧 [Class Audio CD1 track 5] Play or read the audio program again (see audio script, page T-151). Pause the program after each skill is mentioned, and call on Ss to tell you if it's something Soon Mi can or can't do.

Application

- Read aloud the second part of the instructions in Exercise **4A**. Ask two Ss to read the example sentences.
- Ss complete the exercise in pairs. Walk around and help as needed.
- Ask each S to tell you one thing his or her partner can do.

Learner persistence (individual work)

- 🎧 [Self-Study Audio CD track 5] Exercise **4A** is recorded on the Ss' self-study CD at the back of the Student's Book. Ss can listen to the CD at home for reinforcement and review. They can also listen to the CD for self-directed learning when class attendance is not possible.

Practice

- Direct Ss' attention to the chart in Exercise **4B**. Read the instructions aloud and ask two Ss to read the example question and answer.

- Model the exercise. Take your Student's Book and walk up to different Ss. Ask about the skills in the chart and fill in your chart with the names of Ss who answer, *Yes, I can.*
- Ask Ss to stand up, walk around, and talk to as many classmates as possible as they complete the chart.

> **Useful language**
> Read the tip box aloud and ask Ss to repeat. As they complete the chart, have Ss use the useful language for each S's name they may have difficulty spelling.

- Read aloud the second part of the instructions for Exercise **4B**. Ask three Ss to read aloud the example question and answers.
- Call on different Ss to ask the class about work and life skills. Correct pronunciation as needed.

> ▼ **Teaching tip**
> Urge Ss to participate in class discussions early in the course. This lets Ss know that you want and expect their active participation in class.

Application

- Direct Ss' attention to Exercise **4C** and read the instructions aloud. Ss complete the exercise individually.
- Read aloud the second part of the instructions for Exercise **4C**. Have Ss talk about the list in pairs.
- When Ss are finished, ask the class which skills are easy for them to do in English, and which are difficult.
- Ask for volunteers to talk about the two skills they added to the list. Write the skills on the board.

Community building (whole group)

- Ask Ss about the things they need to do using English in their daily lives. This will give Ss a chance to get better acquainted with one another as they talk about their jobs, their interests, and their home lives.

Evaluation

- Direct Ss' attention to the lesson focus written on the board. Ask Ss to say sentences using the time words and to tell you some of the skills they have.
- Check off each part of the lesson focus as Ss demonstrate an understanding of what they have learned in the lesson.

4 Work skills and life skills

A **Listen.** Soon Mi is at the library. She is talking about her work skills. Check (✓) the things Soon Mi can do.

- ✓ use a computer
- ✓ read to children
- ✓ write in English
- ✓ speak English
- ___ speak Spanish
- ✓ speak Korean

Talk with a partner. What work skills do you have? What work skills are you going to learn?

> I can use a computer.

> I can't use a computer, but I'm going to learn.

B **Talk** about life skills with your classmates. Complete the chart.

> Armin, can you swim?

> Yes, I can.

Find a classmate who can:	Classmate's name
swim	Armin
iron a shirt	(Answers will vary.)
cook	
drive a truck	
paint a house	
speak three languages	

Useful language
How do you spell that?

Talk with your class. Ask and answer questions.

> Who can swim?

> Armin can.

> Ali can, too.

C **Read** the list. Check (✓) the things you can do. Add two more skills.

Things I can do in English

- ☐ introduce myself
- ☐ say my address and telephone number
- ☐ register for a class
- ☐ make an appointment with a doctor
- ☐ give directions
- ☐ write a shopping list
- ☐ ask about prices
- ☐ help my child with homework
- ☐ read to my child
- ☐ read a class schedule
- ☐ read a television schedule
- ☐ talk about my weekend
- _____
- _____

Talk with a partner. Share your information.

Welcome 5

Lesson A Get ready

1 Talk about the picture

A Look at the picture. What do you see?

B Point to: long brown hair • straight hair • black shoes • a soccer uniform
curly blond hair • short black hair • a red shirt • a striped skirt

C Describe the people. What are they doing?

Personal information

UNIT 1

Lesson objectives
- Introduce Ss to the topic
- Find out what Ss know about the topic
- Preview the unit by talking about the picture
- Practice key vocabulary
- Practice listening skills

Warm-up and review

- Before class. Write today's lesson focus on the board. *Lesson A: Describing people*
- Begin class. Books closed. Point to the words *Describing people* on the board. Say the words. Ask Ss to repeat.
- Give a brief description of yourself. Say, for example: *My name is _____. I have short brown hair. I'm wearing a red sweater today. I'm standing in front of the class right now.*
- Ask Ss questions about people's appearance, for example: *Does anyone else in the class have short brown hair? Oh, yes. Tanya has short brown hair. Does anyone in the class have black hair?*
- Ask Ss questions about what people in the class are wearing, for example: *Is anyone in the class wearing a dress today? No? OK, is anyone in the class wearing a blue shirt today? Right, Alex and Derrick are both wearing blue shirts.*
- Ask Ss questions about what people in the class are doing, for example: *Is anyone in the class drinking coffee right now? Alicia, you're drinking coffee. Is anyone in the class talking on the phone right now? Good! Nobody is talking on the phone in class. Is anyone in the class studying English? Oh, everyone is studying English!*

Presentation

- Books open. Set the scene. Direct Ss' attention to the picture on page 6. Ask: *Where is this?* (downtown, a shopping center, a mall, etc.) Ask the question from Exercise **1A**: *What do you see?* Elicit and write on the board as much vocabulary about the picture as possible (people, shops, ice cream, etc.).
- Direct Ss' attention to the key words in Exercise **1B**. Read each word aloud while pointing to a person in the picture who matches the description. Ask the class to repeat and point.
- Listen to Ss' pronunciation and repeat the words as needed.

> **Teaching tip**
> The key words are intended to help students talk about the picture and learn some of the vocabulary in the unit.

Comprehension check

- Ask Ss *Yes / No* questions about the picture. Say: *Listen to the questions. Answer "Yes" or "No."*
  Point to the big picture. Ask: *Are people shopping here?* (Yes.)
  Point to Shoko in the lower left part of the picture. Ask: *Does this woman have photos?* (Yes.)
  Point to the woman sitting next to Shoko. Ask: *Does this woman have black hair?* (No.)
  Point to the man with the ice-cream cone. Ask: *Is the man wearing a soccer uniform?* (No.)
  Point to the tall blond woman. Ask: *Is she wearing a skirt?* (Yes.)
  Point to the same woman again. Ask: *Does she have straight hair?* (No.)
  Point to the shorter woman next to her. Ask: *Did she buy something?* (Yes.)

Practice

- Direct Ss' attention to Exercise **1B**. Model the exercise. Hold up the Student's Book. Say to a S: *Point to a red shirt*. The S points to the appropriate part of the picture.
- Ss in pairs. Say to one S: *Say the words in Exercise* **1B**. Say to his or her partner: *Point to the correct part of the picture*.
- When pairs finish, have them change roles.
- Ask several pairs to perform the exercise for the rest of the class to check Ss' understanding.
- Direct Ss' attention to Exercise **1C** and read the instructions aloud.
- Model the exercise. Hold up the Student's Book. Say to a S: *Point to a person in the picture*. Describe the person the S indicates by saying what he or she looks like, what he or she is wearing, and what he or she is doing. For example, if the S points to the tall woman standing in front of the earrings store, say: *She is tall. She has blond hair. She is wearing a striped skirt and a white shirt. She is looking at earrings.*
- Ss in pairs. Say to one S: *Point to a person in the picture*. Say to his or her partner: *Describe the person. Say what the person is doing.*
- Walk around and help as needed. Make sure both Ss in each pair have a chance to describe people in the picture.
- Ask several pairs to perform the exercise for the rest of the class.

Lesson A T-6

Lesson A Get ready

Presentation
- Books open. Direct Ss' attention to the pictures in Exercise **2A**. For each picture, ask Ss: *Where is this?* (an office, a soccer field, a bedroom)

Practice
- Read aloud the instructions for Exercise **2A**.
- 🔊 [Class Audio CD1 track 6] Play or read the audio program (see audio script, page T-151). Pause the audio program after the first conversation and ask Ss: *Which picture shows conversation A?* (Picture 2) Hold up the Student's Book and point to the letter *a* next to number 2. Make sure Ss understand the exercise.
- 🔊 [Class Audio CD1 track 6] Play or read the rest of the audio program and repeat as needed.
- Check answers. Ask Ss which picture shows each conversation.
- Direct Ss' attention to Exercise **2B**.
- 🔊 [Class Audio CD1 track 6] Model the exercise. Say: *Listen to conversation A*. Play or read the first two sentences of conversation A. Direct Ss to the example sentence. Read it and point to where the letter *T* (True) is written. Make sure Ss understand the exercise.
- 🔊 [Class Audio CD1 track 6] Read aloud each group of sentences before listening to the corresponding conversation. Read aloud the three sentences for conversation A. Then, play or read conversation A on the audio program (see audio script, page T-151). Do the same for conversations B and C.
- Ss complete the exercise individually. When Ss are finished writing their answers, play or read the complete audio program once more to allow Ss to check answers.

Comprehension check
- Check answers. Write the numbers *2–9* on the board. Ask a few Ss to come to the board and write the correct answers to Exercise **2B** next to the numbers. Point to each answer and ask: *Is this correct?* If Ss are not sure about an answer, play or read the appropriate part of the audio program again.

Learner persistence *(individual work)*
- 🔊 [Self-Study Audio CD track 6] Exercises **2A** and **2B** are recorded on the Ss' self-study CD at the back of the Student's Book. Ss can listen to the CD at home for reinforcement and review. They can also listen for self-directed learning when class attendance is not possible.

▼ **Culture tip**
Although the rest of the world calls it football, Americans call the sport that Victoria plays soccer. When Americans use the word *football*, they're referring to the sport that requires helmets and heavy pads and which culminates professionally in the Super Bowl each year.

Expansion activity *(whole group)*
- After Ss have completed Exercises **2A** and **2B**, write the names *Victoria, Eddie,* and *Mark* across the top of the board. For each name, ask Ss: *How can we describe her / him?* Write Ss' responses on the board under the corresponding name. Encourage Ss to supply as much information about each person as possible.

Application
- Direct Ss' attention to Exercise **2C** and read the instructions aloud. Ask two Ss to read the example sentences. If Ss don't want to describe a family member, they can describe a friend or a co-worker.
- Ss complete the exercise in pairs. Help as needed.

Expansion activity *(individual students)*
- Bring to class large pieces of paper and colored markers.
- Write on the board: *What does she / he look like? What is she / he wearing? What is she / he doing?* Read each question aloud and ask Ss to repeat.
- Model the activity. Draw a picture on the board of one of your friends or family members similar to the pictures in Exercise **2A**. Talk about the person in your picture and answer the questions on the board.
- Ask Ss to draw their own picture of a friend or a family member. Encourage Ss to use the questions on the board as they think about and draw their pictures.
- Ask individual Ss to stand up, show the class their drawing, and talk about the person in the picture.

Evaluation
- Direct Ss' attention to the lesson focus written on the board. Go back to the big picture on page 6 and ask Ss to describe some of the people.
- Check off each part of the lesson focus as Ss demonstrate an understanding of what they have learned in the lesson.

More Ventures *(whole group, pairs, individual)*
Assign appropriate exercises from the *Teacher's Toolkit Audio CD / CD-ROM, Add Ventures,* or the *Workbook.*

UNIT 1

2 Listening

A **Listen.** Who is Shoko talking about? Write the letter of the conversation.

1. _c_

2. _a_

3. _b_

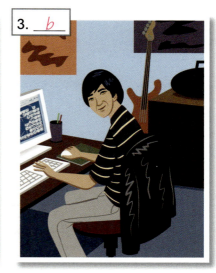

B **Listen again.** Write *T* (true) or *F* (false).

Conversation A

1. Victoria is Shoko's daughter.   _T_
2. Victoria plays soccer every day.   _T_
3. Victoria looks like her mother.   _F_

Conversation B

4. Eddie is Shoko's brother.   _F_
5. Eddie is playing computer games.   _T_
6. Eddie is a very quiet boy.   _T_

Conversation C

7. Mark is Shoko's husband.   _T_
8. Mark wears small shirts and pants.   _F_
9. Mark studies Spanish.   _F_

Listen again. Check your answers.

C **Talk** with a partner. Describe someone in your family.

> My mother has long blond hair.

> My mother has curly brown hair.

Personal information   7

Lesson B She's wearing a short plaid skirt.

1 Grammar focus: adjective order

Question
What's she wearing?

Answers
She's wearing a short plaid skirt.
She's wearing a long black and white coat.

Adjective order

Size	Color		Pattern
small	black	purple	checked
large	blue	red	plaid
short	brown	yellow	striped
long	green	white	

2 Practice

A Write. Complete the conversations. Write the words in the correct order.

1. **A** What's Amy wearing?
   B She's wearing a ___long___ ___black___ dress.
   (black / long)

2. **A** What's she wearing?
   B She's wearing ___black and white___ ___checked___ pants.
   (black and white / checked)

3. **A** What does he take to school?
   B He takes a ___large___ ___red___ backpack.
   (large / red)

4. **A** What do you usually wear to work?
   B I wear a ___blue and white___ ___striped___ uniform.
   (blue and white / striped)

5. **A** What's he wearing today?
   B He's wearing a ___red and yellow___ ___plaid___ sweater.
   (plaid / red and yellow)

6. **A** What are they wearing?
   B They're wearing ___short___ ___green___ skirts.
   (green / short)

🔘 **Listen and repeat.** Then practice with a partner.

8 Unit 1

Lesson objectives
- Introduce adjective order
- Talk about what people are wearing

Warm-up and review
- Before class. Write today's lesson focus on the board.
  Lesson B:
  Adjective order
  What are people wearing?
- Begin class. Books open. Review the language for describing people Ss learned in Lesson A. Direct Ss' attention to the big picture on page 6. Point to some of the people in the picture and ask: *What's he / she wearing?* Write Ss' responses on the board.
- Hold up the big picture and ask: *Who has long hair?* (e.g., the woman at the top of the page) *Who has short hair?* (e.g., the man with the ice-cream cone) *Who has straight hair?* (e.g., the woman who is showing the photos) *Who has curly hair?* (e.g., the woman looking at the photos)

Presentation
- Books open. Direct Ss' attention to the grammar chart in Exercise **1**. Read the question and the answers aloud. Ask Ss to repeat.

> **Contractions**
> Point to *What's* and *She's* in the grammar chart. Say: *These are contractions.* Hold up two fingers and say: *What is.* Hold up one finger and say: *What's.* Repeat with *She is* and *She's.* Explain that a contraction is a short way to say two words.

- Point to *adjective order* in the lesson focus on the board. Explain that an adjective is a word that tells about a noun – a person, a place, or a thing. Write these key words from Lesson A on the board: *a red shirt, a striped skirt.* Explain that a "shirt" is a noun (a thing) and that "red" (an adjective) tells something about the shirt. The word "skirt" is also a noun, and "striped" is an adjective.
- Ask Ss: *Which word is first, the adjective or the noun?* (the adjective) Write several adjectives and several clothing items in random places on the board, for example: *blue; long; dress; jacket; brown; shoes.* Ask Ss to tell you possible combinations of the words. Write correct responses on the board, for example: *blue jacket.*

- Erase the words on the board except for *long, dress, brown.* Say: *Now there are two adjectives and one noun. How can we say it?* If some Ss know that it's a *long brown dress,* ask them to explain why. If your Ss are like most English speakers, they won't be able to explain. This is your chance to turn Ss' attention to the second part of the grammar chart. Explain that when we describe clothes, adjectives for size come first, then color, then patterns, such as striped or plaid.
- Turn Ss' attention back to the answers in the first part of the grammar chart. Ask for volunteers to explain how the sentences follow the adjective order pattern. Write an example on the board that uses all three types of adjectives, for example: *a short black and red striped dress.*

> ▼ **Teaching tip**
> In many languages, adjectives come after nouns, so students sometimes make errors, such as "a shirt red." In some languages, adjectives show singular / plural agreement, so you might also hear "some shoes browns." Listen for errors such as these. Explain that adjectives usually come before nouns in English, and they are always "singular."

Practice
- Books open. Direct Ss' attention to Exercise **2A** and read the instructions aloud. Read the example aloud and make sure Ss understand the exercise.
- Ss complete the sentences individually. Walk around and help as needed.

Comprehension check
- [Class Audio CD1 track 7] Read aloud the second part of the instructions for Exercise **2A**. Play or read the audio program (see audio script, page T-151). Have students check their answers as they listen and repeat.
- Ss practice the conversations in pairs. Correct pronunciation as needed.
- Call on different pairs to read one of the conversations to the class.

Lesson B She's wearing a short plaid skirt.

Presentation

- Books closed. Make a chart on the board with three columns labeled: *size, color, pattern*. Ask for volunteers to write examples of each type of adjective in the appropriate column.
- Books open. Direct Ss' attention to Exercise **2B** and read the instruction line aloud.
- Read aloud all the possible answers and ask Ss to repeat.
- Direct Ss' attention to the people pictured in Exercise **2B**. Point out the handwritten letter *g* next to number 1. Say: *Lisa is wearing a long yellow shirt.*
- Ss complete the exercise individually. Walk around and help as needed.

Practice

- Read aloud the second part of the instructions for Exercise **2B**. Ask two Ss to read the example conversation to the class.
- Model the exercise. Point to the name *Lisa* in the conversation. Ask a different S the example question substituting *Nick* for *Lisa*. Make sure students understand the task.
- Ss complete the exercise in pairs. Walk around and help with pronunciation as needed.

> **Useful language**
> Read aloud the vocabulary from the tip box. Ask Ss to repeat. Encourage Ss to practice the conversation using the useful language.

Application

- Direct Ss' attention to Exercise **3** and read the instructions aloud. Ask two Ss to read the example aloud.
- Model the exercise. Ask a S what someone in the class is wearing.
- Ss complete the exercise in pairs, taking turns asking and answering. When they finish, ask Ss to switch partners and have different conversations. Walk around and help as needed.

Expansion activity *(small groups)*

- Clip from a magazine pictures of people wearing a wide variety of clothing. Bring to class large poster paper, colored markers, and tape.

- Have each small group of Ss choose three pictures to include on a poster. (Demonstrate that Ss will tape the pictures to the poster paper.) Tell Ss that they will need to describe the clothing in the pictures.
- Write on the board: *He / She is wearing _____.* Explain that Ss will write a sentence next to each picture on the poster. Encourage Ss to use more than one adjective to describe the clothing.
- Give Ss time to make the posters, offering help and adjectives as needed. Tape the posters to the walls and let Ss walk around the room and talk about their classmates' work.

Community building *(small groups)*

- Write on the board categories of clothing that your Ss might need to shop for, for example: *women's clothes; work clothes; children's clothes; shoes; men's clothes.*
- Ss in small groups. Ask Ss to talk about the best places in your community to shop for clothes. Ss will enjoy sharing their knowledge, and they may learn about new clothing stores.
- When the groups are finished, point to and say each category written on the board. Ask Ss to report on their group's discussion.
- Write on the board the stores that Ss name. If other Ss in the class don't know about a certain store, ask the S who suggested that place to talk about where it is and why he or she likes to shop there.

Evaluation

- Direct Ss' attention to the lesson focus written on the board.
- Ask Ss to use adjectives to describe what they're wearing.
- Check off each part of the lesson focus as Ss demonstrate an understanding of what they have learned in the lesson.

> **More Ventures** *(whole group, pairs, individual)*
> Assign appropriate exercises from the *Teacher's Toolkit Audio CD / CD-ROM*, *Add Ventures*, or the *Workbook*.

B **Write** the letter. What are the people wearing?

a. blue plaid pants
b. a long purple coat
c. small red shoes
d. a blue checked skirt
e. a short striped dress
f. long black boots
g. a long yellow shirt
h. red and white striped socks
i. a big brown sweater
j. a green plaid suit

Talk with a partner. Change the **bold** words and make conversations.

A What's **Lisa** wearing?
B **She's** wearing **a long yellow shirt**.

Useful language
Some clothing items are always plural:
jeans, pants, shorts

3 Communicate

Talk with a partner about your classmates.

What's Maya wearing?   She's wearing jeans and a long green sweater.

Personal information 9

Lesson C What are you doing right now?

1 Grammar focus: present continuous and simple present

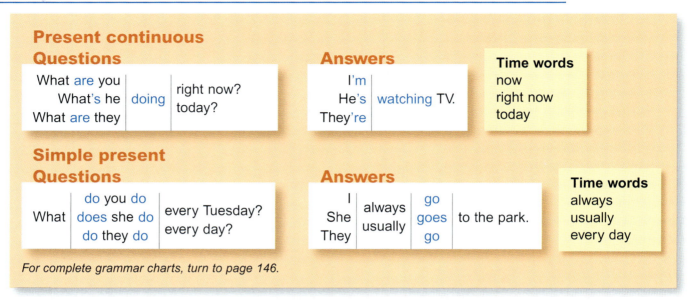

2 Practice

A Write. Complete the conversations. Use the correct form of the verb.

1. **A** What ___does___ Ed ___do___ every night?
   (do)
   B He ___relaxes___ .
   (relax)
   A What ___'s___ Ed ___doing___ right now?
   (do)
   B He ___'s watching___ TV.
   (watch)

2. **A** What ___'s___ Mary ___doing___ right now?
   (do)
   B She ___'s teaching___ .
   (teach)
   A What ___does___ Mary ___do___ every Tuesday?
   (do)
   B She ___teaches___ .
   (teach)

3. **A** What ___'s___ Isaac ___doing___ right now?
   (do)
   B He ___'s studying___ .
   (study)
   A What ___does___ Isaac ___do___ every day?
   (do)
   B He ___goes___ to class.
   (go)

Listen and repeat. Then practice with a partner.

Lesson objective
- Introduce the present continuous and the simple present verb tenses

Warm-up and review
- Before class. Write today's lesson focus on the board.
  Lesson C:
  Present continuous
  Simple present
- Begin class. Books closed. Review vocabulary from Lesson B. Ask individual Ss questions, such as: *Karl, what color shirt are you wearing?* Elicit, for example: *I'm wearing a blue and white striped shirt.* Ask, for example: *Mimi, what are you wearing today?* Elicit, for example: *I'm wearing a short black skirt and a yellow blouse.* Ask, for example: *Soo Jin, are you wearing checked pants today?* Elicit, for example: *No, I'm wearing plaid pants.*
- Preview the present continuous. Write the following words in random places on the board: *sitting, writing, walking, counting, reading, standing, borrowing, waving.*
- Act out each word. For example, walk back and forth in front of the board and ask Ss: *What am I doing right now?* (walking) Walk up to a S and ask to use her pen. Ask Ss: *What am I doing right now?* (borrowing) As Ss answer, cross out each word on the board.
- Preview the simple present. Ask Ss *Yes / No* questions about their habits, for example: *Sam, do you usually work in the morning?* Elicit, for example: *No, I sleep in the morning. I work at night.* Ask, for example: *Raquel, do you have English class every Wednesday?* Elicit, for example: *Yes.* Ask, for example: *Po Hua, do you ride your bicycle every day?* Elicit, for example: *No, only when the weather is good.*

Presentation
- Books open. Direct Ss' attention to the grammar chart in Exercise **1**. Read aloud the present continuous questions and answers in the top part of the chart. Ask Ss to repeat.
- Ss in pairs. Ask Ss to practice asking and answering the present continuous questions in the top part of the grammar chart.
- Direct Ss' attention to the time words in the top part of the grammar chart. Say the words aloud and ask Ss to repeat. Emphasize the connection between the time words and the present continuous verb tense by writing on the board: *Lisa is wearing a long yellow shirt today.*
- Repeat the process with the bottom part of the grammar chart. Read the questions and answers aloud and have Ss repeat. Ask Ss to practice in pairs. Read the time words aloud. Then write on the board: *Lisa plays soccer every day.*

- Make sure Ss understand that the present continuous is used with things that are happening now, while the simple present is used with things that usually or always happen.

Expansion activity *(whole group)*
- You can expand the grammar presentation by using the grammar chart on page 146. Practice asking and answering *Wh-* questions in the present continuous and simple present. Practice using the subject pronouns that are not emphasized in the lesson, including *it, we,* and *you* (plural).

Practice
- Directs Ss' attention to Exercise **2A** and read the instructions aloud. Then, read the example question and answer. Point out the verbs in parentheses under the blanks.
- Ss complete the activity individually. Walk around and help as needed.

> **Teaching tip**
> It might be helpful to remind Ss that we use an *-s* or *-es* ending after simple present verbs when the subject is a singular person or thing.

Comprehension check
- Read aloud the second part of the instructions for Exercise **2A**.
- [Class Audio CD1 track 8] Play or read the audio program (see audio script, page T-152). Ss listen and repeat as they check their answers. Repeat the audio program as needed.
- Ss in pairs. Have Ss practice the conversations. Correct pronunciation as needed.
- Ask pairs to perform the conversations for the class.

Learner persistence *(whole group)*
- Make sure Ss know how to contact you if they can't come to class. Give them your office phone number or e-mail address. Ask students for reasons they may not be able to attend class. Practice conversations. Help Ss by writing some examples on the board, such as: *I'm working an extra shift today; My daughter is sick today.*

Lesson C   **T-10**

Lesson C — What are you doing right now?

Presentation

- Write on the board: *What's he doing? What's she doing? What are they doing?*
- Books open. Direct Ss' attention to the picture in Exercise **2B**. Point to Henry. Ask: *What's he doing?* Elicit: *He's talking on the telephone*. Point to Betty and ask: *What's she doing?* Elicit: *She's leaving* or *She's walking out*. Point to Yan and Ling and ask: *What are they doing?* Elicit: *They're drinking (coffee or tea)*.

Practice

- Direct Ss' attention to Exercise **2B** and read the instructions aloud. Ask two Ss to read the example conversation aloud.
- Model the exercise. Point to number 2 and say to a different S: *Look! Henry is calling his wife!* Elicit: *Of course. He calls his wife every night.*
- Ss complete Exercise **2B** in pairs. Then, ask Ss to switch partners to form new pairs for further practice.
- Ask several pairs to perform their conversations for the class.

Expansion activity (student pairs)

- Challenge Ss by expanding the substitution exercise in **2B** to include negative questions and statements.
- Write this example conversation on the board:
  A: *Look! Betty isn't wearing a coat!*
  B: *Of course not. She never wears a coat.*
- Write these substitution phrases on the board. Ss complete the activity in pairs.
  1. Betty / wear a coat
  2. Henry / drink coffee
  3. Antonio / wear glasses
  4. Olga and Yuri / leave early
  5. Yan and Ling / eat cookies
  6. Jin Ho / sit in the front

Application

- Direct Ss' attention to Exercise **3A** and read the instructions aloud. Explain that habits are things you always or usually do. As an example, you could ask Ss what time they usually get up in the morning.
- Remind Ss that we use the simple present to talk about habits.
- Model the exercise. Ask a S to read the first example question. Read aloud the answer yourself. Then, ask the same S the second example question. The S should respond with the example answer.

- Write on the board several time expressions Ss can use as they make conversations, for example: *always; usually; every day; every Saturday; on the weekend; during the week.*
- Ss complete the exercise in pairs. Walk around and help as needed.
- Ask each pair to perform one of their conversations for the class.
- Read aloud the instructions for Exercise **3B** and ask two Ss to read the example conversation aloud.
- Remind Ss that we use the present continuous to talk about what is happening right now.
- Ss complete the exercise in small groups. Ask each group to perform one of its conversations for the class.

▼ **Teaching tip**
Ss may need some help with open-ended activities such as the ones in Exercises **3A** and **3B**. The teacher's challenge in this situation is to circulate and be available without taking control of the exercise. Listen carefully to what Ss are saying and make quick corrections or suggestions. Then, move to another group. This lets Ss know that you are available, but that the exercise is still theirs to do.

Expansion activity (whole group)

- Refer Ss to the grammar charts on page 146. Have students make present continuous statements with *I'm, we're, you're,* and *it's*. Then have Ss make negative statements in the simple present.

Evaluation

- Direct Ss' attention to the lesson focus written on the board. Ask Ss when we use the present continuous. Ask for some examples. Then ask Ss when we use the simple present and ask for examples.
- Check off each part of the lesson focus as Ss demonstrate an understanding of what they have learned in the lesson.

More Ventures (whole group, pairs, individual)
Assign appropriate exercises from the *Teacher's Toolkit Audio CD / CD-ROM, Add Ventures,* or the *Workbook.*

B Talk with a partner. Change the **bold** words and make conversations.

A Look! **Betty is leaving early!**
B Of course. **She leaves early** every night.

1. Betty / leave early
2. Henry / call his wife
3. Jin Ho / study alone
4. Olga and Yuri / speak English
5. Yan and Ling / drink coffee
6. Antonio / wear jeans and a tie

3 Communicate

A Talk with a partner. Ask and answer questions about your habits.

A What do you do on the weekend?
B I always do things with my children.

A What do you do every night?
B I usually study English.

B Talk in a group. Ask and answer questions about your classmates right now.

A What's Sara doing right now?
B She's talking to Samuel and Kwan.

Lesson D Reading

1 Before you read

Look at the picture. Answer the questions.

1. Who is the girl?
2. What is she wearing?
3. What is she doing?

2 Read

 Read Shoko's e-mail. Listen and read again.

Hi Karin,

How are you doing? Guess what! Today is my daughter's birthday. The last time you saw Victoria, she was three years old. Now she's 17! She's tall and very athletic. She likes sports. She plays soccer every afternoon. Here is her photo. She's wearing her red and white striped soccer uniform. She usually wears jeans and a T-shirt. Victoria is also a very good student. She has lots of friends and goes with them to the mall every weekend. How are your daughters? Please send a photo!
Let's stay in touch.

Shoko

Look for a key word or words in the question, and read quickly to find the answer.
How **old** is Victoria?

3 After you read

A Write. Answer the questions about Victoria.

1. How old is Victoria? *She's 17.*
2. When does she go to the mall? *She goes to the mall every weekend.*
3. What sport does she play? *She plays soccer.*
4. What kind of student is Victoria? *She's a very good student.*
5. What does she usually wear? *She usually wears jeans and a T-shirt.*

B Write. Complete the sentences about Victoria.

1. Victoria is very *athletic* .
2. She likes *sports* .
3. She has lots of *friends* .
4. She's wearing *her red and white striped soccer uniform* .

Lesson objectives
- Introduce and read an e-mail message
- Practice using new topic-related words

Warm-up and review
- Before class. Write today's lesson focus on the board.
  Lesson D:
  Read and understand Shoko's e-mail
  Look for key words
  Learn vocabulary for accessories
- Begin class. Books closed. Point to the first item in the lesson focus on the board and read it aloud. Say: *The reading today is an e-mail message.* Ask: *Do you send e-mail messages? Who do you send them to?* Get answers from several Ss. Find out if everyone in the class uses e-mail, and whether they use it at work or to stay in touch with family and friends.

Presentation
- Books open. Direct Ss' attention to Exercise **1** and read the instructions aloud. Ask Ss the three questions and remind them that Victoria was featured in Lesson A. Elicit appropriate answers.

Practice
- Direct Ss' attention to Exercise **2** and read the instructions aloud. Ss read the e-mail silently.

> Read the tip box aloud. Explain that key words are words that give important information. Read the question aloud and emphasize the key word *old*. Have Ss look over the reading and quickly find the answer. (Victoria is 17.) Ask a S to read aloud the sentence that answers the question.

- [Class Audio CD1 track 9] Play or read the audio program and ask Ss to read along (see audio script, page T-152). Repeat the audio program as needed.

Learner persistence *(individual work)*
- [Self-Study Audio CD track 7] Exercise **2** is recorded on the Ss' self-study CD at the back of the Student's Book. Ss can listen to the CD at home for reinforcement and review. They can also listen to the CD for self-directed learning when class attendance is not possible.

Comprehension check
- Read aloud the instructions in Exercise **3A**. Ask a S to read the example question and answer aloud.

- Ask Ss: *What is the key word in number 2?* Elicit: *mall*. Have Ss scan the reading to find out when Victoria goes to the mall.
- Continue in this manner, having Ss identify the key word in each question and then scan the reading passage for the answer. (Key words are: *sport*, *student*, and *wear*.)
- Direct Ss' attention to Exercise **3B** and read the instructions aloud. Read the beginning of the example sentence and sustain the word *very* . . . until Ss supply the answer: *athletic*.
- Ss complete the exercise individually. Walk around and help as needed.
- Check answers with the class. Ask Ss to write their answers on the board. Then ask different Ss to read the answers aloud. Ask: *Are the sentences correct?* Make any necessary corrections on the board.

Expansion activity *(student pairs)*
- Give pairs of Ss time to practice reading to each other the e-mail in Exercise **2**.
- Ask Ss which words in the reading were difficult to say. Write the words on the board and practice the pronunciation of each one.

Community building *(whole group)*
- Ask Ss who have e-mail addresses and who are comfortable sharing them with the class to write their addresses, along with their names, on a piece of paper. Type the list and make copies for everyone. Suggest that Ss e-mail each other to ask about homework assignments or other aspects of their lives.
- If everyone in the class uses e-mail, assign pairs of Ss to be e-mail "buddies." Give periodic assignments such as: *Send an e-mail about your favorite TV show to your buddy*. These simple assignments help Ss establish a rapport and openness in the classroom.
- If your Ss don't use e-mail or don't want to share their personal information, consider having class "buddies" write and exchange more traditional letters in class.

Expansion activity *(individual students)*
- Have Ss write their own e-mail message about a friend or a family member using the descriptive vocabulary from the unit. Ss can exchange and read the messages in pairs.

Lesson D   T-12

Lesson D Reading

Warm-up and review

- Books closed. Write *Accessories* on the board. Point to your watch if you're wearing one. Ask: *What is this?* Elicit: *It's a watch*. Write the word *watch* on the board, and continue with any other available accessories, for example: *gloves; a ring; a tie; a bracelet; a purse*.
- Draw a picture of a head on the board with a *hat, scarf, earrings,* and *necklace*. For each item, ask Ss: *What is this?* Have the S who answers label the item on the board. Try to use all the words in the word bank in Exercise **4A**.

▼ **Teaching tip**
Ss will probably already know some of these words, but not all of them. If Ss don't know the answer, say the word and write it on the board. Ask Ss to repeat.

Presentation

- Books open. Direct Ss' attention to the picture dictionary in Exercise **4**. Ask: *What do you see?* (three models, a fashion show) Ask: *What are they wearing?* (Accept all correct answers.)
- Recycle vocabulary from the e-mail on page 12. Write on the board: *tall, athletic, jeans, T-shirt*. Ask Ss questions about the models in the picture, for example: *Is anyone in the picture tall? Do you think Sally is athletic? Is Ben wearing jeans?* (no, a suit) *Is anyone in the picture wearing jeans?* (Angie) *Is Angie wearing a T-shirt with her jeans?* (no, a sweater)
- Direct Ss' attention to the word bank. Say each word in the word bank aloud and ask Ss to repeat. Listen to Ss' pronunciation. Correct pronunciation as needed.
- Read aloud the instructions for Exercise **4A**. Point to the first example, which has been done. Make sure Ss understand the exercise.
- Ss complete the exercise individually. Walk around and help as needed.

Comprehension check

- [Class Audio CD1 track 10] Say: *Listen and repeat.* Play or read the audio program (see audio script, page T-152). Ss listen and repeat as they check their answers. Repeat the audio program if necessary.

Learner persistence *(individual work)*

- [Self-Study Audio CD track 8] Exercise **4A** is recorded on the Ss' self-study CD at the back of the Student's Book. Ss can listen to the CD at home for reinforcement and review. They can also listen to the CD for self-directed learning when class attendance is not possible.

Practice

- Read aloud the instructions for Exercise **4B**. Model the example conversations with Ss.
- Make sure Ss understand that they are to use the language in the picture dictionary. Ss complete the exercise in pairs. Walk around and help as needed.
- Ask several pairs to perform their conversations for the class.
- Elicit other types of jewelry, for example: *a pin*. Look for a S in the class who is wearing *a belt* and bring it to Ss' attention. List Ss' responses on the board, and encourage Ss to write down the new vocabulary next to the word bank in the Student's Book.

Expansion activity *(whole group)*

- On the board, draw a generic outline of a person. Ask a S to come to the board. Read one of the vocabulary words aloud. Ask the S to draw the item on the person. Ask another S to write the word next to the item on the board. Continue with different Ss until all the accessories have been drawn and labeled. (This may become funny as the person accumulates a ridiculous number of accessories.)

Evaluation

- Direct Ss' attention to the lesson focus written on the board.
- Ask Ss some questions about Shoko's e-mail such as: *Who is Shoko's daughter?* (Victoria) *How old is Shoko's daughter?* (17) *Does Shoko's friend Karin have any children?* (Yes, she has daughters.)
- Ask Ss to tell you the words they learned for fashion accessories. Check off each part of the lesson focus as Ss demonstrate an understanding of what they have learned in the lesson.

More Ventures *(whole group, pairs, individual)*
Assign appropriate exercises from the *Teacher's Toolkit Audio CD / CD-ROM, Add Ventures,* or the *Workbook.*

4 Picture dictionary   Accessories

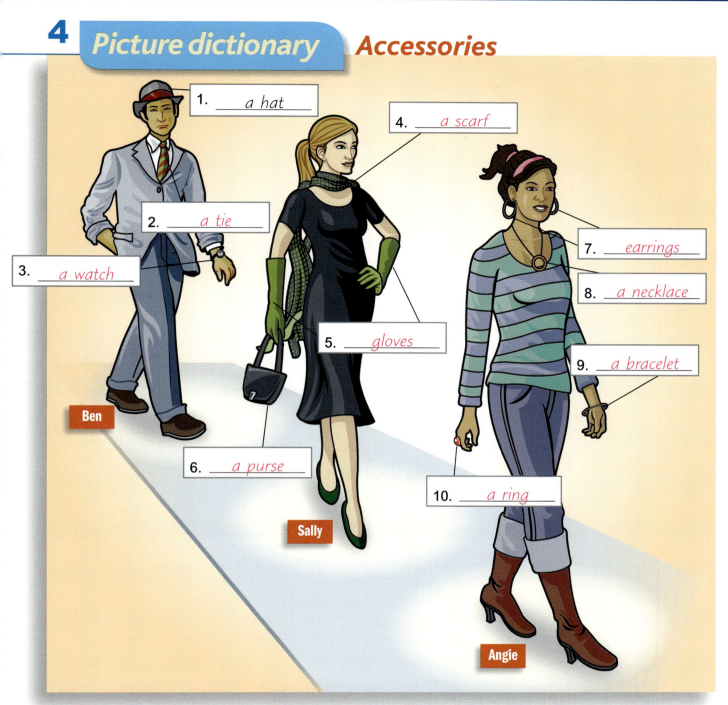

 A **Write** the words in the picture dictionary. Then listen and repeat.

| a bracelet | gloves | a necklace | a ring | a tie |
| earrings | a hat | a purse | a scarf | a watch |

B **Talk** with a partner. Change the **bold** words and make conversations.

A What's Ben wearing?
B He's wearing **a red and green striped tie**.

A What's Sally wearing?
B She's wearing **a green and black checked scarf**.

Personal information 13

Lesson E Writing

1 Before you write

A Write. Answer the questions about yourself.

1. What's your name? _____(Answers will vary.)_____
2. What color is your hair? _____
3. What color are your eyes? _____
4. What are you wearing? _____
5. What do you do after class? _____
6. What do you do on the weekend? _____

B Read about a new classmate.

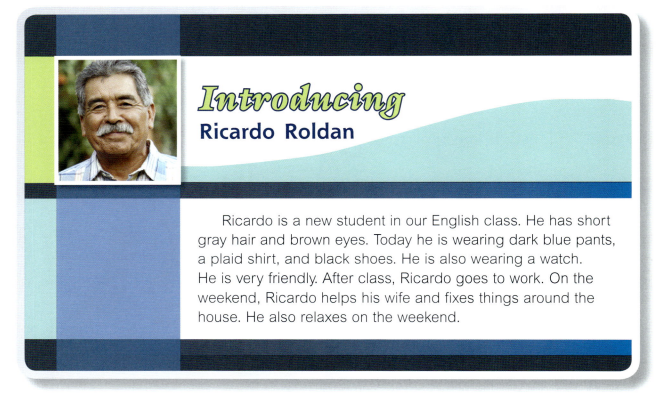

Ricardo is a new student in our English class. He has short gray hair and brown eyes. Today he is wearing dark blue pants, a plaid shirt, and black shoes. He is also wearing a watch. He is very friendly. After class, Ricardo goes to work. On the weekend, Ricardo helps his wife and fixes things around the house. He also relaxes on the weekend.

C Write. Answer the questions about Ricardo.

1. Does Ricardo have gray hair or brown hair? _Gray hair._
2. Is his hair long or short? _Short._
3. What is he wearing? _Dark blue pants, a plaid shirt, and black shoes._
4. What does he do on the weekend? _He helps his wife and fixes things around the house. He also relaxes._

Lesson objectives
- Write a descriptive paragraph about a classmate
- Use time phrases

Warm-up and review
- Before class. Write today's lesson focus on the board.
Lesson E:
Write a paragraph about a classmate
Use time phrases
- Begin class. Books closed. Ask Ss: *What are some ways we describe a person?* Write Ss' responses on the board, for example: *by hair color; size (tall or short); age; clothes; accessories.*
- Books open. Direct Ss' attention to the big picture on page 6. Choose one of the people in the picture you haven't talked much about before. As a class, brainstorm sentences to describe him or her. Write Ss' ideas on the board. Encourage the use of the simple present and the present continuous.

Presentation
- Direct Ss' attention to Exercise **1A** and read the instructions aloud. Ask Ss to write complete sentences about themselves.
- Model the exercise. Read the first question aloud. Write on the board: *My name is _____ .*
- Ss in pairs. Ask Ss to read their partner's sentences. Then ask: *Are there any mistakes in your partner's sentences? Please tell your partner if you see any mistakes.*
- Write the numbers 2–6 on the board. Ask for Ss to come to the board to write one of their sentences. Go over each sentence and ask the class: *Is this sentence correct?* Make corrections on the board.

Practice
- Direct Ss' attention to the paragraph in Exercise **1B**. Read the instructions aloud. Ss read the paragraph silently. Explain any words Ss don't know.
- Ask Ss: *What is the new student's name?* (Ricardo Roldan) Ask: *What color is Ricardo's hair?* (gray) Ask: *Is Ricardo wearing any accessories today?* (Yes, he's wearing a watch.)
- Read the paragraph aloud or have pairs read it to each other.

> **Teaching tip**
> It might be helpful to remind Ss of the structural features of a paragraph: a paragraph indent at the beginning of the first sentence, a capital letter at the beginning of the first word of a sentence, and a period, question mark, or exclamation point at the end of a sentence. You can also point out that new sentences do not begin on a new line.

Comprehension check
- Direct Ss' attention to Exercise **1C** and read the instructions aloud. Say: *Now you will write sentences about Ricardo.* Ss complete the activity individually. Walk around and help as needed.
- Check answers. Ask for volunteers to write their sentences on the board. Ask: *Are the sentences correct?* Have the Ss come back to the board to correct any errors.

Expansion activity (small groups)
- Have Ss work in small groups to do a brainstorming activity. Ask each group to choose a secretary who will write the group's ideas on paper. Say: *Your group will make a list. When do we need to describe someone? Think of as many ideas as possible.*
- Set a time limit, and when time is up, ask each group how many ideas it has. Ask the group with the most ideas to write its list on the board, and read the ideas to the class. Ask other groups to add ideas to the list on the board. Examples of when we might need to describe someone might include: *when we tell our families about people at work; when we tell our boss about a customer with a problem; when we tell the police about a criminal.*

Lesson E Writing

Warm-up and review

- Review the use of commas with time phrases. Write sentences without commas on the board:
  Every weekend Victoria plays soccer.
  Right now Lisa is leaving for school.
  Mary goes to the park every Saturday.
  Isaac is studying English right now.
- Point to each sentence and read it aloud. Ask Ss to repeat.
- Ask a volunteer to come to the board. Point to each sentence again and ask the class: *Does this sentence need a comma? Tell (S's name) where to put a comma.* (The first sentence needs a comma after *Every weekend* and the second sentence needs a comma after *Right now*.)

Practice

- Books open. Direct Ss' attention to Exercise **1D** and read the instructions aloud.
- Read aloud the example sentence and ask a S to read the revised version. Point out the comma in the first sentence. Make sure Ss understand the exercise. Ss write the sentences individually.
- Write the numbers *2–5* on the board. Call on individual Ss to come to the board to write one of their sentences. Go over each sentence and ask the class: *Is this sentence correct?* Make any necessary corrections on the board.

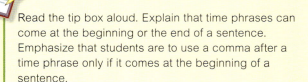

Read the tip box aloud. Explain that time phrases can come at the beginning or the end of a sentence. Emphasize that students are to use a comma after a time phrase only if it comes at the beginning of a sentence.

Expansion activity *(whole group)*

- Give some additional practice with time phrases. Write three columns on the board with the headings: *Before, After, In.* Make the columns as far apart as possible.
- In the first column, write time phrases, such as: *Before work, Before class, Before dinner.* In the second column, write time phrases, such as: *After breakfast, After the soccer game, After a big meal.* In the third column, write time phrases, such as: *In the morning, In the afternoon, In October.*
- Ask Ss what they do before work, before class, and so on. Write sentences on the board using the time phrases, commas after the time phrases, and Ss' ideas.
- **Option** Have Ss come to the board and write the sentences.

Application

- Tell Ss that they will write a paragraph, such as the one on page 14, about their partner. First, they will need information about their partner, so they will need to ask him or her some questions.
- Direct Ss' attention to Exercise **1E**, and read the instructions aloud. Say to Ss: *This is the information you need about your partner.* Read the items in the chart aloud, and ask Ss to repeat.
- Turn Ss' attention back to Exercise **1A** on page 14. Say to Ss: *Ask your partner these questions. Then write the answers in the chart on page 15.* You may want to write the questions from Exercise **1A** on the board for Ss to refer to.
- Ss complete the activity in pairs.
- Direct Ss' attention to Exercise **2** and read the instructions aloud. Point to Exercises **1B** (on page 14) and **1E** (on page 15) to show Ss where to look for help.
- Ss write their paragraphs individually. Walk around and help as needed.

Comprehension check

- Direct Ss' attention to Exercise **3A** and read the instructions aloud.
- Ss in pairs. Ss read their sentences aloud, and then trade papers.
- Read the instructions for Exercise **3B**. Say: *Now check your partner's work. Is everything correct?*
- Ss complete the exercise individually. Walk around and help as needed. Ask individual Ss: *Are your partner's sentences correct? Are there any time phrases?*

Evaluation

- Direct Ss' attention to the lesson focus written on the board.
- Ask Ss to tell you some of the things they wrote in their paragraphs. Ask for a volunteer to come to the board and write a sentence with a time phrase. Ask another S to write the same sentence in a different way, reversing the position of the time phrase.
- Check off each part of the lesson focus as Ss demonstrate an understanding of what they have learned in the lesson.

More Ventures *(whole group, pairs, individual)*
Assign appropriate exercises from the *Teacher's Toolkit Audio CD / CD-ROM, Add Ventures,* or the *Workbook.*

D Write each sentence in a different way.

1. After class, Ricardo goes to work.
   Ricardo goes to work after class.
2. Tanya goes shopping on the weekend.
   On the weekend, Tanya goes shopping.
3. Victoria plays soccer every Tuesday.
   Every Tuesday, Victoria plays soccer.
4. After work, Henry watches TV.
   Henry watches TV after work.
5. On the weekend, Yan studies English.
   Yan studies English on the weekend.

> Time phrases like *after class* or *on the weekend* can come at the beginning or end of a sentence. Use a comma if they are at the beginning.

E Talk with a partner. Complete the chart. Use the questions in Exercise 1A.

Partner's name:	_(Answers will vary.)_
Hair color:	
Eye color:	
Clothing:	
Accessories:	
After-class activities:	
Weekend activities:	

2 Write

Write a paragraph about your partner. Use Exercises 1B and 1E to help you.

3 After you write

A Read your paragraph to your partner.

B Check your partner's paragraph.
- What did your partner write about you?
- Is the information correct?
- Are the time phrases correct?

Lesson F Another view

1 Life-skills reading

ORDER FORM

ITEM NUMBER	QUANTITY	SIZE	COLOR	ITEM NAME	PRICE
105B	1	L	RED	SWEATER	$29.00
265A	1	M	PURPLE	COAT	$69.00
350G	2	XS	WHITE	T-SHIRT	$18.00
670F	1	8	BLACK	SHOES	$59.00

METHOD OF PAYMENT:
- ☐ Global Express
- ☑ MasterCharge
- ☐ Vista
- ☐ Discovery
- ☐ Personal check

CREDIT CARD ACCOUNT NUMBER: 123-1234-123

EXPIRATION DATE: 12/2010

SIGNATURE: Phong Nguyen

SUBTOTAL $175.00
SHIPPING AND HANDLING $15.00
Under $50.........$5.00
$50–$100.........$10.00
Over $100.........$15.00
EXPRESS DELIVERY
(ADD $5.00)

TOTAL $190.00

Useful language
- XS extra small
- S small
- M medium
- L large
- XL extra large

A Read the questions. Look at the order form. Circle the answers.

1. How much is the large red sweater?
   a. $18.00
   b. $29.00 (circled)
   c. $59.00
   d. $69.00

2. What color are the shoes?
   a. black (circled)
   b. purple
   c. red
   d. white

3. What is the method of payment?
   a. Discovery
   b. Global Express
   c. MasterCharge (circled)
   d. Vista

4. How much is shipping and handling?
   a. $5.00
   b. $10.00
   c. $15.00 (circled)
   d. $150.00

B Talk in a group. Ask and answer the questions.

1. Where do you shop for clothing?
2. What clothes do you usually buy?
3. How do you usually pay?

Lesson objectives
- Practice reading an order form
- Review unit vocabulary
- Introduce the project
- Complete the project and self-assessment

Warm-up and review
- Before class. Write today's lesson focus on the board.
  Lesson F:
  Read an order form
  Review topic vocabulary
  Complete the project and the self-assessment
- Bring to class a few clothing catalogs or other catalogs with order forms.
- Begin class. Books closed. Ask Ss: *Where do you usually buy clothes in* (your town or city)? Write Ss' responses on the board.
- Ask Ss: *Do you ever use a catalog for shopping?* Show Ss some clothing catalogs. Ask whether any Ss shop online.

Practice
- Books open. Direct Ss' attention to the order form in Exercise **1A**. Say: *This is an order form. It is inside a catalog. It shows the clothes you want to buy.* Show Ss the real order forms inside the catalogs you brought.
- Read aloud the instructions for Exercise **1A**. This exercise helps prepare Ss for standardized-type tests they may have to take. Make sure Ss understand the exercise. Have Ss individually scan for and circle the correct answers. Walk around and help as needed.

Comprehension check
- Check the answers to Exercise **1A**. Make sure Ss followed the instructions and circled their answers.

Expansion activity (whole group)
- Go over the order form and explain vocabulary Ss do not know.

Community building (whole group)
- Ask Ss if they think the clothes on the order form are expensive or inexpensive. Have a class discussion about how much clothing for adults or children usually costs.

Practice
- Ss in groups. Say: *Ask and answer the questions in Exercise 1B.*
- Walk around and listen to Ss' pronunciation. Write difficult words on the board. When Ss are finished, say the words aloud. Ask Ss to repeat.

> **Useful language**
> Point out the abbreviations for sizes in the Useful language box. Write *XS, S, M, L, XL* on the board, and tell Ss what each abbreviation stands for. This will make Ss more confident when they shop.

Community building (whole group)
- Discuss the shoe size 8 on the order form and ask Ss about the system they use for shoe sizes and clothing sizes in their countries. Ss will be interested to hear about other cultures.

Expansion activity (student pairs)
- If you brought catalogs with order forms to class, distribute them to pairs of Ss. Ask Ss to find a few items in the catalog that they like and to fill out the order form for the items. Draw a large "credit card" on the board with fake numbers and your name. Tell Ss they can use your credit card!
- Walk around and answer any questions the pairs have about their order forms.
- **Option** Have Ss compare the order form in the Student's Book to the order form in the catalog. Ask Ss: *How are the order forms the same? How are they different?* Ask each pair to tell the class something about the catalog. Answer any questions Ss may have about vocabulary from the catalog.

Lesson F Another view

Warm-up and review
- Books closed. Review order of adjectives. Write three columns on the board: *size, color, pattern*.
- Start by asking about Ss in the class, for example: *What is Sai wearing?* Write any adjectives Ss say in the appropriate column on the board.
- Then, ask Ss to call out imagined items of clothing. Encourage Ss to use as many adjectives as possible. Write Ss' ideas in the columns on the board.
- Review vocabulary for accessories. Give clues such as: *You wear these on your hand.* (gloves) If Ss have trouble guessing the word, write the first letter on the board. Continue writing letters until Ss can say the word.

Presentation
- Books open. Direct Ss' attention to Exercise **2A** and read the instructions aloud.
- Say to Ss: *Look at Bob and Louise. Are they alike? Are they very different?* (They're very different.) Point out the two examples written in the chart and read them aloud.

Practice
- Ss complete the exercise in small groups. Walk around and help with vocabulary as needed. Encourage Ss to fill in the chart with complete sentences in the present continuous and the simple present verb tenses.
- Divide the board into halves. Label one side *Bob* and the other *Louise*. Have groups take turns sending someone to the board to write one of the differences they found. Continue until Ss have written all their sentences.
- Read aloud the instructions for Exercise **2B**. Ask two Ss to read the example aloud.
- Ss complete the exercise in small groups. Walk around and help as needed.
- When groups are finished, have them say some of their clues for the rest of the class to guess.

Expansion activity *(small groups)*
- If Ss need more practice with the unit vocabulary, have them make their own "concentration" game.
- Ss in small groups. Give each group an even number of index cards – perhaps 20 or 24.
- Ask Ss to choose half as many vocabulary words to practice as they have cards; for example, 12 vocabulary words from the unit. Ss write one word per card. On the remaining 12 cards, they draw pictures of the corresponding clothes, accessories, curly hair, and so on.
- Ss shuffle the cards and arrange them face-down in a grid; for example, four rows of six cards. They then take turns turning over two cards and saying any words aloud. If Ss have a matching pair, they keep the cards. Otherwise, they turn the cards face-down again. The S with the most cards at the end wins.

Community building *(student pairs)*
- Divide the class into pairs and give Ss time to talk about English class. Say: *Tell your partner things you like about the class. Talk about things in the class that are difficult, too.*
- Conduct a brief informal discussion about the course so far. Encourage Ss to say what has been useful to them or what they believe will be useful. Let Ss take the lead by asking open questions such as: *What did you and your partner talk about? What are the most useful words you have learned in this book?* This will give Ss a chance to reflect, and it will give you feedback about what Ss are learning.

> ***More Ventures*** *(whole group, pairs, individual)*
> Assign appropriate exercises from the *Teacher's Toolkit Audio CD / CD-ROM, Add Ventures,* or the *Workbook.*

Application
Community building
- **Project** Ask Ss to turn to page 136 in their Student's Book to complete the project for Unit 1.

Evaluation
- Before asking Ss to turn to the self-assessment on page 141, do a quick review of the unit. Have Ss turn to Lesson A. Ask the class to talk about what they remember about this lesson. Prompt Ss, if necessary, with questions. For example, *What are the conversations about on this page? What vocabulary is in the big picture?* Continue in this manner to review each lesson quickly.
- **Self-assessment** Read the instructions for Exercise **3**. Ask Ss to turn to the self-assessment page to complete the unit self-assessment.
- If Ss are ready, administer the unit test on pages T-165–T-166 of this *Teacher's Edition* (or on the *Teacher's Toolkit Audio CD / CD-ROM*). The audio and audio script for the tests are on the *Teacher's Toolkit Audio CD / CD-ROM.*

2 Fun with language

A Work in a group. Talk about the ways Bob and Louise are different. Write your ideas in the chart.

Bob

He has blue eyes.
(Answers will vary.)

Louise

She has green eyes.
(Answers will vary.)

B Work in a group. Play a game. Sit in a circle. One person describes a student. Everyone tries to guess who it is.

> She's wearing blue pants and a striped shirt.

> Is it Soon Mi?

3 Wrap up

Complete the **Self-assessment** on page 141.

Personal information

Lesson A *Get ready*

1 Talk about the picture

A Look at the picture. What do you see?

B Point to: an English teacher • a computer lab • a hall • a monitor
a lab instructor • an ESL classroom • a keyboard • a mouse

C Look at the people. What are they doing?

At school

UNIT 2

Lesson objectives
- Introduce Ss to the topic
- Find out what Ss know about the topic
- Preview the unit by talking about the picture
- Practice key vocabulary
- Practice listening skills

Warm-up and review

- Before class. Write today's lesson focus on the board. *Lesson A: School services*
- Begin class. Books closed. Review the present continuous by asking questions about what Ss are wearing and what is happening in the classroom, for example: *Kim, what are you wearing today? What is Bea doing right now? Bea, are you drinking coffee or tea?*
- Direct Ss' attention to the lesson focus you wrote on the board. Ask: *How do schools help students?* Write Ss' responses on the board, for example: *classes; counselors; child-care; job skills.* Tell Ss: *These are things schools do to help students. They are school services.*

Presentation

- Books open. Set the scene. Direct Ss' attention to the picture on page 18. Ask: *Where is this?* (a school, a classroom) Ask the question from Exercise **1A**: *What do you see?* Elicit and write on the board as much vocabulary about the picture as possible (tables, computers, a computer lab, books, chairs, etc.).
- Direct Ss' attention to the key words in Exercise **1B**. Read each word aloud while pointing to the item in the picture. Ask the class to repeat and point.
- Listen to Ss' pronunciation and correct as needed.

Comprehension check

- Ask Ss *Yes / No* questions about the picture. Recycle questions in the present continuous. Say: *Listen to the questions. Answer "Yes" or "No."*
Point to the big picture. Ask: *Is this a school?* (Yes.)
Point to the man and woman at the bottom of the picture. Ask: *Are they using computers?* (Yes.)
Point to the woman wearing the red sweater. Ask: *Is she reading a book?* (No.)
Point to the man next to her wearing a green sweater. Ask: *Is he wearing a blue sweater?* (No.)
Point to the woman standing near the table. Ask: *Is the English teacher talking to a student?* (Yes.)
Point to the man in the computer lab. Ask: *Is he working in the computer lab?* (Yes.)
Point to the "Registration Office" sign in the hall. Ask: *Is the Registration Office down the hall?* (Yes.)

> **Teaching tip**
> Don't insist on complete sentences at this point. These *Yes / No* comprehension questions give Ss a chance to warm up and engage with English receptively before they are asked to produce the language themselves.

Practice

- Direct Ss' attention to Exercise **1B**. Model the exercise. Hold up the Student's Book. Say to a S: *Point to an English teacher.* The S points to the appropriate person in the picture.
- Ss in pairs. Say to one S: *Say the words in Exercise 1B.* Say to his or her partner: *Point to the picture.*
- Ss complete the exercise in pairs. Help as needed. When Ss finish, have them change roles.
- Ask several pairs to perform the exercise for the class to check Ss' understanding.
- Direct Ss' attention to Exercise **1C** and read aloud the instructions and the question.
- Model the exercise. Point to the man at the top left of the picture. Ask a S: *What is he doing?* Elicit an appropriate response, for example: *He is sitting at a table* or *He is talking to the teacher.*
- Ss complete the exercise in pairs. Help as needed.

Expansion activity *(student pairs)*

- Review classroom vocabulary. In pairs, have Ss make a list of words they know for items pictured in the classroom on page 18, for example: *globe; bulletin board.*
- Call on a S from each pair to come to the board to write one of the words from the list.
- Read each word aloud and ask Ss to repeat. Explain any words Ss don't know.

Learner persistence *(whole group)*

- Create a matching exercise on the board of school services in one column and places where Ss can find the services in random order in the other. School services might include: *learn computer skills; find child care; ask questions about English homework.* Places in the school might be: *my office, computer lab, office of student services.*
- Read aloud the school services and make sure Ss understand what they are. Draw a line between the service and the place it can be found.

Lesson A

Lesson A Get ready

Presentation
- Direct Ss' attention to the big picture on page 18. Point to one of the computer keyboards. Ask Ss: *What is this?* (a keyboard) Write *keyboard* on the board.
- Write the word *keyboarding* on the board. Ask Ss: *What does this mean?* (using a keyboard)
- Ask Ss: *Does anyone in the class do keyboarding at work?* If some Ss answer "yes," find out what they do at work that requires keyboarding. If nobody answers "yes," ask Ss to think of some jobs that require the use of a keyboard, for example: *data entry clerk; office manager; accountant.*
- Direct Ss' attention to the big picture again and point to Joseph. Tell Ss: *You will hear Joseph talking to three different people about a keyboarding class.*

Practice
- Read aloud the instructions for Exercise **2A**.
- [Class Audio CD1 track 11] Play or read the audio program (see audio script, page T-152). Pause the audio program after the first conversation and ask Ss: *Who is Joseph talking to in conversation A?* (Picture 3) Hold up the Student's Book and write the letter *a* next to number 3. Make sure Ss understand the task.
- [Class Audio CD1 track 11] Play the rest of the audio program and repeat as needed.
- Check answers. Ask Ss which picture shows the person Joseph is talking to in the other conversations.
- Direct Ss' attention to Exercise **2B** and read the instructions aloud.
- [Class Audio CD1 track 11] Model the exercise. Say: *Listen to conversation A.* Play or read conversation A (see audio script, page T-152). Direct Ss' attention to the example sentence. Read it aloud and point to where the letter *F* (False) is written. Make sure Ss understand the task.
- [Class Audio CD1 track 11] Read aloud each group of sentences before listening to the corresponding conversation. Read aloud the three sentences for conversation A. Then, play or read conversation A on the audio program (see audio script, page T-152). Do the same for conversations B and C.
- Ss complete the exercise individually. When Ss are finished writing their answers, play the complete audio program once more to allow Ss to check the answers they wrote.

Comprehension check
- Check answers. Write the numbers *2–9* on the board and ask volunteers to come to the board and write the correct answers to Exercise **2B** next to each number.
- [Class Audio CD1 track 11] Play or read the audio program again (see audio script, page T-152). Pause the program after each conversation. Point to each answer on the board. Ask: *Is this correct?* Make any necessary corrections on the board.

Expansion activity *(small groups)*
- In the audio program, Joseph says that he wants to open his own business someday. Divide the class into small groups and have Ss in each group choose a secretary to write down its ideas. Ask groups to list at least five skills besides keyboarding that Joseph will need to have in order to be a small business owner.
- Consolidate Ss' ideas on the board.

Learner persistence *(individual work)*
- [Self-Study Audio CD track 9] Exercises **2A** and **2B** are recorded on the Ss' self-study CD at the back of the Student's Book. Ss can listen to the CD at home for reinforcement and review. They can also listen to the CD for self-directed learning when class attendance is not possible.

Application
- Direct Ss' attention to Exercise **2C** and read the instructions aloud. Ss complete the exercise in pairs. Walk around and help as needed.
- Ask pairs to tell you which skills they talked about. Compile a list of skills on the board.
- Ask for volunteers to tell the class about which skills they want to learn, and why.

Evaluation
- Direct Ss' attention to the lesson focus written on the board. Ask questions about the key vocabulary from page 18, for example: *Is this a computer lab?* Elicit *Yes / No* answers.
- Ask Ss to tell you some job skills they can learn at a school. Check off each part of the lesson focus as Ss demonstrate an understanding of what they have learned in the lesson.

More Ventures *(whole group, pairs, individual)*
Assign appropriate exercises from the *Teacher's Toolkit Audio CD / CD-ROM*, *Add Ventures,* or the *Workbook.*

UNIT 2

2 Listening

  A **Listen.** Who is Joseph talking to? Write the letter of the conversation.

1. _c_

2. _b_

3. _a_

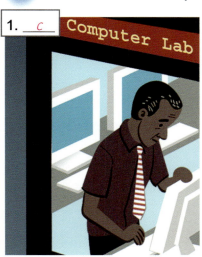

  B **Listen again.** Write *T* (true) or *F* (false).

Conversation A

1. Eva and Joseph are in the computer lab.   _F_
2. Mrs. Lee helped Eva.   _T_
3. Joseph is taking a keyboarding class.   _F_

Conversation B

4. Joseph needs to use a computer at work.   _F_
5. The computer lab is next door to Joseph's classroom.   _F_
6. Mrs. Lee is the lab instructor.   _F_

Conversation C

7. Joseph needs to register for a keyboarding class.   _T_
8. Mrs. Smith works in the computer lab.   _F_
9. Joseph needs to register next month.   _F_

Listen again. Check your answers.

C **Talk** with a partner. Ask and answer the questions.

1. What are some important skills?
2. What new skills do you want to learn?

At school   19

Lesson B — What do you want to do?

1 Grammar focus: *want* and *need*

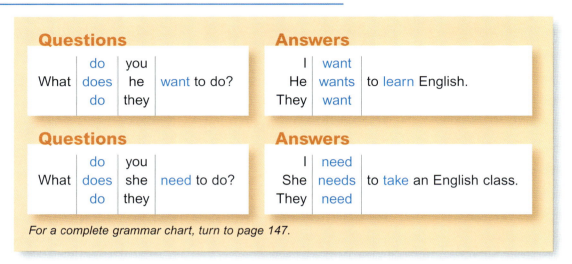

For a complete grammar chart, turn to page 147.

2 Practice

A Write. Complete the conversations.

1. **A** What do you want to do now?

   B I ____*want to get*____ my GED.
   (want / get)

2. **A** What do you need to do?

   B I ____*need to take*____ a GED class.
   (need / take)

3. **A** What does Sandra want to do this year?

   B She ____*wants to learn*____ about computers.
   (want / learn)

4. **A** What does Ali want to do this year?

   B He ____*wants to make*____ more money.
   (want / make)

5. **A** What does Celia need to do tonight?

   B She ____*needs to do*____ her homework.
   (need / do)

6. **A** What do Sergio and Elena want to do next year?

   B They ____*want to become*____ citizens.
   (want / become)

Culture note
The GED (General Equivalency Diploma) is a certificate. It is equal to a high school diploma.

🔊 **Listen and repeat.** Then practice with a partner.

Lesson objectives
- Introduce the verbs *want* and *need*
- Talk about goals and ways of reaching them

Warm-up and review
- Before class. Write today's lesson focus on the board. *Lesson B: Questions and answers with want and need*
- Begin class. Books closed. Point to the word *want* on the board. Ask Ss *Yes / No* questions with *want*, for example: *Do you want to study English now? Do you want to visit the computer lab today? Do you want to get a better job next year?*
- Point to the word *need* on the board. Ask Ss *Yes / No* questions with *need*, for example: *Do you need to leave early today? Do you need to take a keyboarding class? Do you need to talk to me after class?*

Presentation
- Books open. Direct Ss' attention to the grammar chart in Exercise **1**. Read each question and answer aloud. Ask Ss to repeat the questions and answers.
- Ss in pairs. Have students practice reading the grammar chart to each other while pointing to an appropriate person or persons in the class (I, you, he, she, they).

Comprehension check
- Point to various people in the class and ask Ss the questions in the grammar chart. Call on individual Ss to answer the questions using the answers in the grammar chart.

> ▼ **Teaching tip**
> If Ss are unsure about the difference between *want* and *need*, provide a few examples using *want* to express a goal and *need* as a necessary step in achieving the goal. For example, tell Ss that your friend *wants* to visit her mother in the Philippines, but she really can't afford to go. She *needs* to work overtime or find a second job so that she can save the money for the trip.

Practice
- Books open. Direct Ss' attention to Exercise **2A** and read the instructions aloud. Read the example aloud and make sure Ss understand the exercise.
- Ss complete the sentences individually. Walk around and help as needed.
- Check answers. Write the numbers *2–6* on the board and ask volunteers to come to the board and write the correct answer to Exercise **2A** next to each number. Ask the class: *Are these answers correct?* Make any corrections on the board.

> **Culture note**
> Read the Culture note aloud. Tell Ss that the GED is an option for people in the United States and Canada who have not received a high school diploma. These people complete five multiple-choice tests and write a timed essay in order to receive their GED.

Comprehension check
- [Class Audio CD1 track 12] Read aloud the second part of the instructions for Exercise **2A**. Play or read the audio program (see audio script, page T-152). Have Ss check their answers as they listen and repeat.
- Ss practice the conversations in pairs. Correct pronunciation as needed.
- Call on different pairs to each read one of the conversations aloud to the class.

Expansion activity (whole group)
- If you want to expand the grammar presentation, turn to the grammar charts on page 147. Practice asking questions and giving answers using the pronouns *I*, *we*, and *it*.

Learner persistence (whole group)
- If some Ss regularly arrive late for class or are frequently absent, try to find out why this is happening. If Ss are having problems with transportation or child care, try to connect them with a school counselor or classmates who might be able to help them with these issues. Encourage Ss to attend class regularly and on time.

Lesson B What do you want to do?

Presentation

- Books closed. Draw a vertical line down the middle of the board. On the left side, write *wants to*. On the right side, write *needs to*. Under *wants to*, write several goals that Ss in your class might have, for example: *get a promotion at work; make new friends; learn to cut hair.* In random order under *needs to*, write several possible ways to meet the goals, for example: *volunteer at a neighborhood center; take an English course; go to beauty school.*
- Conduct a class discussion about what someone needs to do in order to meet the goals you wrote on the board. Use the *needs to* column to get the discussion started, and use Ss in the class as examples. Say: *Let's imagine that Elena wants to get a promotion at work. What does she need to do to get a promotion?* Encourage any reasonable answers, including ideas that are not on the board.

▼ **Teaching tip**
Don't worry too much about moments of silence in the classroom. Ss may need time to formulate an answer. Teachers who try to fill silences with a lot of "teacher talk" can be overwhelming, and Ss may tune out rather than try to understand every word.

Practice

- Books open. Direct Ss' attention to the pictures in Exercise **2B**. Go over the goals and solutions under each picture, and add them to the list on the board if they are not already there. Explain words the Ss don't understand.
- Read aloud the instructions for Exercise **2B**. Point to the phrases in number 1. Then ask two Ss to read the example conversation aloud. Ss complete the exercise in pairs.

▼ **Teaching tip**
It might be helpful to remind Ss to use *wants* and *needs* only with *he* and *she*. The other subjects in Exercise **2B** require *want* and *need*.

Useful language
Read the Useful language box aloud. Ask Ss to repeat the suggestions. Have them use the useful language to make the conversations in Exercise **2B**.

Application

- Direct Ss' attention to Exercise **3** and read the instructions aloud. Ask two Ss to read the example conversation aloud.
- Ss complete the exercise in pairs. Walk around and help as needed.
- Ask pairs to perform their conversations for the class.

Expansion activity (small groups)

- Before class. Prepare an index card for every S with a situation or minor problem that requires a solution, for example: *I have a bad cold; My son is not doing well in math class; I want to find a bigger apartment.* On the board, write: *Why don't you . . . ?* and *You could . . .*
- Have Ss take turns reading their situation cards aloud in small groups. Ask the other Ss in the group to give advice using the useful language.
- When the groups are finished, have Ss read their cards to the class and talk about the best advice they got from their classmates.

Community building (small groups)

- Ask Ss to work in small groups to make a list of places in your community where they can accomplish some of the goals you've talked about in Lesson B. For example, is there a technical college where someone could study auto mechanics?
- When the groups are finished, compile a class list of ideas on the board. If there are places that some Ss haven't heard of, ask the Ss who suggested those places to explain what and where they are.

Evaluation

- Direct Ss' attention to the lesson focus written on the board. Elicit questions and answers with *want* and *need*.
- Check off each part of the lesson focus as Ss demonstrate an understanding of what they have learned in the lesson.

More Ventures (whole group, pairs, individual)
Assign appropriate exercises from the *Teacher's Toolkit Audio CD / CD-ROM, Add Ventures,* or the *Workbook*.

B Talk with a partner. Change the **bold** words and make conversations.

> A **She wants** to **fix cars**. What **does she** need to do?
> B **She needs** to **study auto mechanics**.
> A That's a good idea.

1. she / fix cars
study auto mechanics

2. they / learn computer skills
take a computer class

3. he / make more money
get a second job

4. he / get a driver's license
take driving lessons

5. they / become citizens
take a citizenship class

6. she / go to college
talk to a counselor

3 Communicate

Talk with your classmates. Ask about their goals. Give advice.

What do you want to do?

I want to get a good job.

Why don't you take a computer class?

Useful language
Why don't you take a computer class?
You could take a computer class.

At school   21

Lesson C   What will you do?

1 Grammar focus: future with will

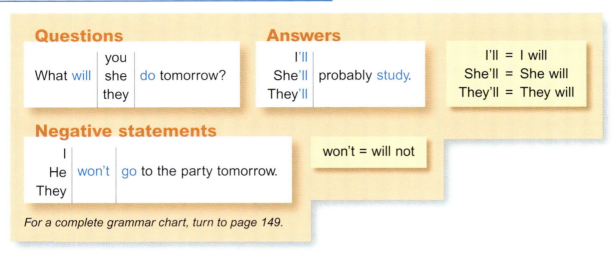

2 Practice

A Write. Complete the sentences. Use *will* or *won't*.

1
~~Emily's party tonight 7:30 p.m.~~
Study for test.

2
Volunteer in Tom's class on ~~Tuesday~~, 10:00 a.m.
Wednesday

3
Work on ~~Wednesday~~ afternoon.
Thursday

4
Talk to college counselor on ~~Thursday~~.
Friday

1. Sue has a test tomorrow. She __will__ study tonight. She __won't__ go to the party.
2. She __will__ volunteer in Tom's class on Wednesday. She __won't__ volunteer on Tuesday.
3. She __won't__ work on Wednesday afternoon. She __will__ work on Thursday.
4. She __won't__ talk to a counselor on Thursday. She __will__ talk to a counselor on Friday.

Listen and repeat. Check your answers.

Lesson objectives
- Introduce the future with *will*
- Talk about future plans

Warm-up and review
- Before class. Write today's lesson focus on the board. *Lesson C: The future with will*
- Begin class. Books closed. Write on the board: *today*. Ask Ss questions such as: *How are you today? What is Gabriel wearing today? What are we studying today?*
- Write on the board: *every day*. Ask Ss questions such as: *Do you come to English class every day? What do you do every day? What time do you get up every day?*
- Write on the board: *tomorrow*. Ask Ss: *What will you do tomorrow?* Write Ss' responses on the board using *will*, for example: *Olga will call her grandchildren tomorrow.*

Presentation
- Books open. Direct Ss' attention to the grammar chart in Exercise **1**. Read each question and answer aloud. Ask Ss to repeat the questions and answers.
- Read the negative statements aloud and ask Ss to repeat.

> **Contractions**
> Direct Ss' attention to the boxes with contractions. Explain that *I'll* has the same meaning as *I will*. Do the same for *she'll* and *they'll*. Point out that *won't* is a negative expression with the same meaning as *will not*. Have pairs of students practice reading the grammar chart to each other while pointing to an appropriate person in the class (I, you, he, she, they).

Expansion activity *(whole group)*
- You can expand the grammar presentation by using the grammar chart on page 149. Practice asking Wh- questions with *What*, and practice making affirmative and negative statements. Add the pronouns *it, we, he,* and *you (plural)* to the lesson.

Practice
- Direct Ss' attention to the notes in Exercise **2A** and read the instructions aloud.
- Model the exercise. Point to the note in number 1. Ask: *What's happening tonight at 7:30?* (Emily's party) *What will the person who wrote this note do tonight? Will she go to Emily's party?* (No.) *Oh, she won't go to Emily's party. What will she do tonight?* (study for a test)
- Read aloud the example sentences in number 1. Make sure Ss understand the exercise.
- Ss complete the exercise individually. Walk around and help as needed.

Comprehension check
- Read aloud the second part of the instructions for Exercise **2A**.
- [Class Audio CD1 track 13] Play or read aloud the audio program (see audio script, page T-152. Ss listen and repeat as they check their answers. Repeat the audio program as needed.
- Ss in pairs. Have Ss practice the sentences. Correct pronunciation as needed.
- Call on individual Ss to read the sentences to the rest of the class. Clarify any confusion about the grammar and vocabulary.

Expansion activity *(small groups)*
- Give Ss practice saying sentences with *will* and *won't*.
- Write on the board: *heads = will; tails = won't*
- Make sure Ss understand the idea of flipping a coin and which side is which. It's likely that at least one person in each group can explain it to the others if necessary.
- Point to the words written on the board. Tell Ss: *If you get heads, you will say a sentence with "will." If you get tails, you will say a sentence with "won't."*
- Model the activity. Flip a coin and say, for example: *Heads.* Point to *heads = will* on the board. Then say a sentence with *will*, for example: *I will drive my son to school tomorrow.* Do the same for *tails = won't*.
- Give each group a coin or have Ss take out a coin. Ss take turns flipping the coin and making a sentence about something they will do or won't do tomorrow.

Lesson C What will you do?

Presentation

- Books open. Direct Ss' attention to the pictures in Exercise **2B**. Read aloud the verb phrase under each picture and ask Ss to repeat. Explain any words Ss don't know.
- Point to the picture in number 1. Then point to the example conversation. Ask two Ss to read the example conversation aloud.
- Read aloud the instructions for Exercise **2B**. Explain that Ss will use the verb phrase under each picture to change the sample conversation. Make sure Ss understand the exercise.

> **Useful language**
> Read aloud the Useful language box. Ask Ss to repeat each sentence. Encourage Ss to use the useful language in Exercise **2B**.

Practice

- Ss complete Exercise **2B** in pairs. Walk around and help as needed.
- Ask different pairs to perform the conversations for each picture.

Expansion activity (whole group)

- Ask the class questions about the goals pictured in Exercise **2B**, for example:
  1. Does anyone in the class want to open a business? What kind of business do you want to open?
  2. What is a vocational course? Can you give me an example?
  3. Why do these people want to start business school?
  4. Why does this young man want to go to college?
  5. How long does it take to learn a new language?
  6. Is it easy or difficult to buy a new house? How much do new houses cost?

Application

- Read aloud the instructions for Exercise **3**. Model the example with a S.
- Ss complete the exercise in pairs. When they are finished, ask Ss to find a new partner and have new conversations.
- Ask different pairs to perform their conversations for the class.

Expansion activity (small groups)

- Before class, make sets of index cards with the goals from Lessons B and C and others that you think of, for example: *take a computer class; talk to a counselor; open a business; buy a house.*
- Write on the board:
  I'll probably . . .   I probably won't . . .
  I'll most likely . . .   I most likely won't . . .
  Maybe I'll . . .   Maybe I won't . . .
- Model the activity. Choose one of the cards and read it aloud. Then, use one of the phrases on the board and explain why it is or isn't likely that you'll do the action on the card someday. Talk for at least a minute.
- Give one set of cards to each group and ask Ss to take turns choosing and reading the cards aloud. Have Ss use the phrases on the board to talk about whether or not they'll probably do the task on the card.

Learner persistence (whole group)

- Brainstorm different ways of keeping up with English lessons when Ss miss a class. Write ideas on the board, for example: *Practice the last lesson. Do Workbook exercises. Call a classmate and ask about class. Listen and repeat exercises on the Student Self-Study Audio CD. Call or e-mail your teacher for help.*

Evaluation

- Direct Ss' attention to the lesson focus written on the board. Ask Ss to tell you something they plan to do *tomorrow, next year,* and *in the next five years.*
- Check off each part of the lesson focus as Ss demonstrate an understanding of what they have learned in the lesson.

> **More Ventures** (whole group, pairs, individual)
> Assign appropriate exercises from the *Teacher's Toolkit Audio CD / CD-ROM, Add Ventures,* or the *Workbook.*

B **Talk** with a partner. Change the **bold** words and make conversations.

A What will you do in the next five years?
B Maybe I'll **open a business**.
A That's great!

Useful language
Maybe I'll open a business.
I'll probably open a business.
I'll most likely open a business.

open a business

take a vocational course

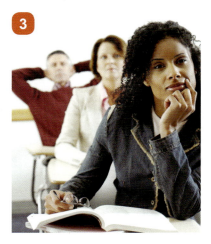
start business school

go to college

learn a new language

buy a house

3 Communicate

Talk with your classmates. Ask and answer questions about future plans.

A Ming, what will you do next year?
B I'll probably take a vocational course.
A What will you do after that?
B Maybe I'll get a new job. I want to make more money.

Lesson D Reading

1 Before you read

Look at the picture. Answer the questions.

1. Who is the man?
2. Where is he?

2 Read

  Read Joseph's application. Listen and read again.

What are your future goals? What steps do you need to take?

I want to open my own electronics store. I need to take three steps to reach my goal. First, I need to learn keyboarding. Second, I need to take business classes. Third, I need to work in an electronics store. I will probably open my store in a couple of years.

> First, read quickly to get the main idea. Ask yourself *What is it about?*

3 After you read

A Write. Answer the questions about Joseph.

1. What is Joseph's goal? *He wants to open his own electronics store.*
2. What does he need to do first? *First, he needs to learn keyboarding.*
3. What does he need to do second? *Second, he needs to take business classes.*
4. What does he need to do after that? *After that, he needs to work in an electronics store.*
5. When will he open his business? *He will probably open his business in a couple of years.*

B Write. Complete the sentences.

| business | electronics | goal | learn | steps |

1. Joseph wants to have his own store. That is his _____*goal*_____.
2. Joseph wants to have his own _____*electronics*_____ store.
3. He needs to take three _____*steps*_____ to reach his goal.
4. He needs to _____*learn*_____ keyboarding and take _____*business*_____ classes.

Lesson objectives
- Introduce and read Joseph's application
- Practice using new topic-related words

Warm-up and review

- Before class. Write today's lesson focus on the board.
  Lesson D:
  Read and understand the reading
  Read quickly to get the main idea
  Learn vocabulary for vocational courses
- Begin class. Books open. Direct Ss' attention to the picture in Exercise **1**. Ask: *Who is the man?* (Joseph from page 18) Ask: *Where is he?* (at the Registration Office)

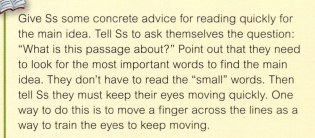

Give Ss some concrete advice for reading quickly for the main idea. Tell Ss to ask themselves the question: "What is this passage about?" Point out that they need to look for the most important words to find the main idea. They don't have to read the "small" words. Then tell Ss they must keep their eyes moving quickly. One way to do this is to move a finger across the lines as a way to train the eyes to keep moving.

Presentation

- [Class Audio CD1 track 14] Direct Ss' attention to Exercise **2** and read the instructions aloud. Play or read the audio program and ask Ss to read along (see audio script, page T-153). Repeat as needed, or give Ss time to read the passage silently.
- Answer any questions Ss have about the reading.

▼ **Teaching tip**
You can vary the presentation of the reading by pausing the audio program after each sentence and asking Ss to repeat the sentence. Give additional speaking practice by having Ss read the passage to each other in pairs.

Learner persistence (individual work)

- [Self-Study Audio CD track 10] Exercise **2** is recorded on the Ss' self-study CD at the back of the Student's Book. Ss can listen to the CD at home for reinforcement and review. They can also listen to the CD for self-directed learning when class attendance is not possible.

Comprehension check

- Read the instructions for Exercise **3A** aloud. Read the question in number 1 and call on a S to read the answer.
- Ss complete the exercise individually. Walk around and help as needed.
- Check answers with the class. Ask Ss to read the questions and answers aloud.

Practice

- Direct Ss' attention to the word bank in Exercise **3B**. Ask Ss about each word, for example: *Does Joseph want to open his own business?* (Yes.) *What kind of business does he want to open?* (an electronics store) Continue in this manner with the other vocabulary words.
- Read aloud the instructions and the example for Exercise **3B**. Ss complete the exercise individually.
- Check answers with the class. Ask Ss to read their sentences aloud.

Expansion activity (individual work)

- Have Ss write their own answers to the two questions in the application in Exercise **2**.
- Direct Ss' attention to the reading passage in Exercise **2**. Tell Ss: *This is Joseph's goal. Now write about your goal.* Have Ss write about their goal, the necessary steps to reach the goal, and when they think they'll reach it.
- Ask pairs to exchange and read each other's paragraphs. You could also collect the paragraphs and return them to Ss with individual feedback.

Lesson D   **T-24**

Lesson D Reading

Warm-up and review
- Books closed. Write *Vocational courses* on the board. Ask: *What are vocational courses?* If Ss don't know the answer, tell them that vocational courses are classes that teach job skills. Remind Ss of the keyboarding class Joseph wanted to take in Lesson A.
- Ask Ss to name some vocational courses they know about. You could also find a course schedule for a vocational school in your area and write sample course offerings on the board.

Presentation
- Books open. Direct Ss' attention to the pictures in the picture dictionary in Exercise **4**. For each picture, ask: *Where is he / she? What is he / she doing?* If Ss don't know the answer, give them hints.
- Direct Ss' attention to the word bank in Exercise **4A**. Say each word in the word bank and ask Ss to repeat. Listen to Ss' pronunciation. Correct pronunciation as needed.
- Read aloud the instructions for Exercise **4A**. Point to the first example, which has been done. Make sure Ss understand the exercise.
- Ss complete the exercise individually. Walk around and help as needed.

Comprehension check
- [Class Audio CD1 track 15] Say: *Listen and repeat*. Play or read the audio program (see audio script, page T-153). Ss listen and repeat as they check their answers. Repeat the audio program as needed.

Learner persistence *(individual work)*
- [Self-Study Audio CD track 11] Exercise **4A** is recorded on the Ss' self-study CD at the back of the Student's Book. Ss can listen to the CD at home for reinforcement and review. They can also listen to the CD for self-directed learning when class attendance is not possible.

Practice
- Read aloud the instructions for Exercise **4B**. Model the example conversations with two different Ss. (You ask the questions.) Point to the appropriate pictures in the picture dictionary as you ask the questions.
- Ss practice the conversations in pairs.
- Call on several pairs to perform one of their conversations for the rest of the class.

Expansion activity *(small groups)*
- Brainstorm ideas about what people who have completed the vocational courses in the picture dictionary do at work every day.
- Divide the vocations from the word bank in Exercise **4A** among small groups of Ss.
- Write on the board: *What does this person do at work?* Ask each group to answer this question about the vocation or vocations. Encourage Ss to use the picture dictionary to get ideas.
- Have the groups report to the class. On the board, list the vocations and Ss' ideas about them.

Community building
- Many vocational schools offer community outreach advisors who would be happy to visit your class. Request a visit from an advisor and ask for brochures, posters, or a slide presentation about vocational courses. Allow time for Ss to ask questions, and if they're interested, to talk to the advisor one-on-one.

Expansion activity *(small groups)*
- Before class, find and print out information about average salaries for the occupations in the picture dictionary. Bring copies of the information to class, along with large paper, tape, and markers.
- Ask Ss to work in small groups to create an advertising poster for a vocational school. The poster should include the vocational courses from the picture dictionary, along with salary information.
- Tape the posters to the classroom walls, and if the class is small enough, have each group do a short presentation about its vocational school.

Evaluation
- Direct Ss' attention to the lesson focus written on the board. Ask what Joseph (from the reading) wants and needs to do. Ask Ss to explain how to read quickly to get the main idea. Finally, ask questions about some of the vocational courses in the picture dictionary.
- Check off each part of the lesson focus as Ss demonstrate an understanding of what they have learned in the lesson.

> **More Ventures** *(whole group, pairs, individual)*
> Assign appropriate exercises from the *Teacher's Toolkit Audio CD / CD-ROM, Add Ventures,* or the *Workbook*.

4 Picture dictionary — Vocational courses

1. automotive repair

2. computer technology

3. accounting

4. nursing

5. counseling

6. hotel management

7. culinary arts

8. home health care

9. landscape design

A **Write** the words in the picture dictionary. Then listen and repeat.

accounting	counseling	hotel management
automotive repair	culinary arts	landscape design
computer technology	home health care	nursing

B **Talk** with a partner. Ask and answer questions.

Do you want to study automotive repair?

Yes, I do.

Do you want to study computer technology?

No, I don't.

Lesson E Writing

1 Before you write

A Talk with a partner. Ask and answer the questions.

1. What are your goals this year?
2. What is your most important goal? Why?
3. What do you need to do to reach your goal?

B Read about Angela's goal.

My Goal for Next Year

I have a big goal. I want to help my grandchildren with their homework. There are three steps I need to take to reach my goal. First, I need to learn to speak, read, and write English well. Second, I need to volunteer in my grandchildren's school. Third, I need to talk with their teachers and learn more about their homework assignments. Maybe I'll be ready to help my grandchildren with their homework in a few months.

C Write. Complete the chart about Angela's goal.

Angela's goal

She wants to:
help her grandchildren with their homework
She needs to:
1. learn to speak, read, and write English well
2. volunteer in her grandchildren's school
3. talk with their teachers and learn more about their homework assignments
She will probably reach her goal in:
a few months

Lesson objectives
- Read and talk about personal goals
- List the steps to take to achieve a goal

Warm-up and review
- Before class. Write today's lesson focus on the board.
Lesson E:
Read and write about Angela's goal
Write about goals and things you need to do to achieve them
- Begin class. Books closed. Review the use of *want* and *need*. Ask individual Ss: *What do you want to do in your life?* Follow up on Ss' answers by asking: *What do you need to do to (achieve X)?*
- Write the word *goal* on the board. Say: *A goal is something you want to achieve in your life. A goal is something you need to work toward.*
- If you know some Ss' goals, ask those Ss, for example: *Marco, do you want to open a business?* (Yes.) *That is Marco's goal. He wants to open a business.* Repeat with other Ss' goals.
- Ask other Ss about their goals using unit vocabulary. Ask, for example: *Does anyone in the class want to buy a house?* (S raises hand.) *OK, Izumi's goal is to buy a house. Does anyone want to study nursing?*
- Books open. Direct Ss' attention to Exercise **1A** and read the instructions aloud. Ask three Ss to read the questions aloud.
- Ss complete the exercise in pairs. Ask for volunteers to share their answers with the class.

Practice
- Direct Ss' attention to the paragraph in Exercise **1B**. Read the instructions aloud. Ask: *Who wrote this?* (Angela) Ask: *What is the title?* (My Goal for Next Year)
- Ss read the paragraph silently. Help Ss with vocabulary as needed.
- Read the paragraph aloud or have pairs read it to each other.

> **Culture tip**
> You may want to discuss volunteering, which is not common in some cultures. Talk about why Angela wants to volunteer at her grandchildren's school. Perhaps she wants to practice English or learn more about American schools. List a few places in which people in the United States volunteer, for example: in hospitals and nursing homes; schools; parks; and animal shelters.

Comprehension check
- Direct Ss' attention to Exercise **1C** and read the instructions aloud. Read the first part of the chart: *She wants to . . .* Elicit: *help her grandchildren with their homework*. Point to the space for that answer in the chart.
- Ss complete the exercise individually. Walk around and help as needed.
- Check answers with the class. Ask for volunteers to write their answers on the board. Ask: *Are these answers correct?* Ask other Ss to come to the board and correct any errors.

Expansion activity *(whole group)*
- Angela thinks she might be able to reach her goal in a few months. Conduct a class discussion about whether or not she is being realistic.
- Point to the three steps written on the board that Angela needs to take. Ask Ss how long each step might take. It might be especially interesting to discuss how long it takes "to learn to speak, read, and write English well."

Lesson E

Lesson E Writing

Presentation

- Direct Ss' attention to Exercise **1D**. Point to the chart and ask: *Who wrote this chart?* (Donald) *What does Donald want to do?* (get a job as a landscape designer)
- Read aloud the instructions for Exercise **1D**. Make sure Ss understand the exercise.
- Check answers as a class. Read aloud each question and call on Ss to read their answers.

Application

- Direct Ss' attention to the chart in Exercise **1E**. Say: *Now it's your turn! You will write about your goal.* Hold up the Student's Book and point to the first space at the top of the chart. Ask: *What will you write here?* (my goal; what I want to do) Ask: *What will you write next?* (three things I need to do)
- Ss complete the chart individually.
- Direct Ss' attention to Exercise **2** and read the instructions aloud. Ss complete the paragraph individually.
- Direct Ss' attention back to the paragraph on page 26. Tell Ss that their paragraph will look like this. Ask Ss to take out a piece of paper.

Read the tip box aloud. Ask Ss to find the words *First, Second,* and *Third* in Angela's paragraph on page 26. Have Ss use the words in their own paragraph to sequence the steps they will take.

▼ **Teaching tip**
It might be helpful to explain that *First, Second,* and *Third* are ordinal numbers, which can be used to show the sequence of events in writing. If your Ss are not very familiar with ordinal numbers, refer them to the list on page 152.

▼ **Teaching tip**
While Ss are doing in-class writing, be prepared to help with vocabulary. If you think Ss have prior knowledge of an appropriate word, it's fine to give hints to help them retrieve the word themselves. Remember that Ss at this level have a fairly limited vocabulary. There's nothing wrong with taking advantage of "teachable moments" and suggesting a suitable word or words.

Comprehension check

- Direct Ss' attention to Exercise **3A** and read the instructions to the class. Have pairs read their paragraphs aloud.
- Help with pronunciation as needed.
- Read aloud the instructions in Exercise **3B**. Read the questions aloud. Tell Ss they will read their partner's paragraph to look for the answers to the questions.
- To check comprehension, have Ss tell their partners the answer to each question in Exercise **3B**. When they are finished, ask Ss: *Did your partner find your goal in your paragraph? And the three steps? Did everyone use the words* First, Second, *and* Third?

Evaluation

- Direct Ss' attention to the lesson focus written on the board. Point to the paragraph on page 26 and ask Ss: *What is Angela's goal? What does she need to do?*
- Point to page 27 and ask Ss: *What did you learn to do in this writing lesson?* Elicit, for example: *We learned how to use a chart to organize ideas. We learned how to use* First, Second, *and* Third *to show order in our writing.*
- Check off each part of the lesson focus as Ss demonstrate an understanding of what they have learned in the lesson.

> **More Ventures** *(whole group, pairs, individual)*
> Assign appropriate exercises from the *Teacher's Toolkit Audio CD / CD-ROM, Add Ventures,* or the *Workbook.*

D Read Donald's chart. Talk with a partner. Ask and answer.

1. What does Donald want to do?
2. First, what does he need to do?
3. Second, what does he need to do?
4. Third, what does he need to do?
5. When will he probably reach his goal?

Donald's goal

I want to:
get a job as a landscape designer
I need to:
1. work in people's gardens
2. take a course in landscape design
3. look for jobs in the newspaper
I will probably reach my goal in:
two years

E Write. Complete the chart about your goal.

My goal

I want to:
(Answers will vary.)
I need to:
1.
2.
3.
I will probably reach my goal in:

2 Write

Write a paragraph about your goal. Write about the steps you need to take. Use Exercises 1B, 1D, and 1E to help you.

3 After you write

A Read your paragraph to a partner.

B Check your partner's paragraph.
- What is your partner's goal?
- What are the three steps?
- Did your partner use the words *First*, *Second*, and *Third*?

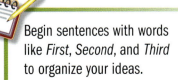
Begin sentences with words like *First*, *Second*, and *Third* to organize your ideas.

At school 27

Lesson F Another view

1 Life-skills reading

COURSE CATALOG

General Equivalency Diploma (GED)

Do you want to get your GED? Then you need to practice your reading, writing, and math skills. Classes are in English or Spanish. No fee.

Instructor: Mr. Chen (English)
　　　　　　Ms. Lopez (Spanish)
Days/Times: Mon, Wed 6:00 p.m.–8:00 p.m.

TV and DVD Repair

This class will teach you how to repair TVs and DVD players. You will also learn about opening your own repair shop. Fee: $85

Instructor: Mr. Stern
Days/Times: Mon, Tues 6:00 p.m. – 8:00 p.m.

Introduction to Computers

This class is for adults who want to learn about computers and the Internet. You will learn about keyboarding, e-mail, and computer jobs. Fee: $75

Instructor: Mrs. Gates
Days/Times: Mon, Wed 7:00 p.m.–9:00 p.m.

Citizenship

Do you want to be an American citizen? First, you need to learn about American history and civics. This class will prepare you for the U.S. citizenship test. Requirements: Legal resident. No fee.

Instructor: Ms. Cuevas
Days/Times: Thurs 7:00 p.m.–9:00 p.m.

A **Read** the questions. Look at the course catalog. Circle the answers.

1. How much will the GED class cost?
   a. $35
   b. $75
   c. $85
   (d.) no fee

2. When is the computer class?
   a. Monday and Tuesday
   (b.) Monday and Wednesday
   c. Tuesday and Thursday
   d. Wednesday and Friday

3. Who will teach TV and DVD Repair?
   a. Mr. Chen
   b. Ms. Cuevas
   c. Mrs. Gates
   (d.) Mr. Stern

4. Which class is in English or Spanish?
   a. Citizenship
   (b.) GED
   c. Introduction to Computers
   d. TV and DVD Repair

B **Talk** with a partner. Ask and answer the questions.

1. What do you want to learn about this year?
2. What classes will you take?

Lesson objectives
- Read a course catalog
- Review unit vocabulary
- Introduce the project
- Complete the project and self-assessment

Warm-up and review
- Before class. Write today's lesson focus on the board.
  Lesson F:
  Read a course catalog
  Review topic vocabulary
  Complete the project and the self-assessment
- Begin class. Books closed. Review school services by asking Ss: *How can schools help Ss with their goals?* Write Ss' responses on the board. If Ss have trouble answering, have them look through the unit for ideas.

Practice
- Books open. Direct Ss' attention to the course catalog above Exercise **1A**. Read aloud the instructions for Exercise **1A**. This exercise helps prepare Ss for standardized-type tests they may have to take. Make sure Ss understand the exercise. Have Ss individually scan for the answers and circle the correct letters. Walk around and help as needed.

Comprehension check
- Go over the answers to Exercise **1A** together. Make sure that Ss followed the instructions and circled their answers.

Expansion activity (whole group)
- Go over the course catalog and explain any vocabulary Ss do not know.
- Discuss how each of the vocational courses could help people reach their goals.

▼ Culture tip
On the course catalog, legal residency is required for the citizenship course. You might want to explain the difference between being a legal resident of the United States and being a citizen. Legal residents can live and work in the U.S., but they do not have the right of U.S. citizens to vote or run for a political office.

▼ Culture tip
Explain the use of personal titles in the course catalog. Write on the board: *Mr., Miss, Ms.,* and *Mrs.* Tell Ss that the only title for men is *Mr.,* while women have three options: *Miss, Ms.,* or *Mrs.* In the catalog, one female teacher has chosen to identify herself as married with the title *Mrs.,* while two other female teachers have chosen the title *Ms.,* which doesn't reveal a woman's marital status.

Expansion activity (whole group)
- Bring in a real course catalog from your school or another institution. You can also cut and paste selections from the catalog and make photocopies if the size of the real catalog is overwhelming.
- Prepare several questions about the information in the catalog. Write the questions on the board and ask Ss to look for the answers in the catalog. For example, you might ask questions such as: *Can anyone take Computer Repair II? How long does it take to finish the program in culinary arts? What do students learn in Automotive Skills I?*
- When Ss are finished, have partners compare their answers. Clear up any confusion about the questions you asked, unfamiliar vocabulary, or the courses themselves.

Practice
- Read aloud the instructions for Exercise **1B**. Ss complete the exercise in pairs.
- Walk around and listen to Ss' pronunciation. Write difficult words on the board. When Ss are finished, say the words aloud. Ask Ss to repeat the words.
- When Ss are finished, ask for volunteers to tell the class about their academic plans.

Lesson F Another view

Presentation

- Books open. Direct Ss' attention to the word bank in Exercise **2A**. Say each vocation aloud and ask Ss to repeat. Review the meaning of the vocabulary by asking Ss, for example: *What do people in accounting do? What do people in automotive repair do?*

Practice

- Read aloud the instructions for Exercise **2A**.
- Model the exercise. Point to the calculator in the first picture and ask: *Who could use this?* Elicit: *an accountant; a person who does accounting.* Point to where *accounting* has been written for number 1.
- Ss complete the exercise in pairs. Walk around and help as needed.
- Check answers together. Write the numbers 2–6 on the board and ask volunteers to come to the board and write the correct answer to Exercise **2A** next to each number. Make any necessary corrections.

Expansion activity (whole group)

- Go over each item pictured in Exercise **2A**. Ask Ss: *What is this?* Ss may know some of the words, but be prepared to help with this vocabulary: *a calculator, a chef's hat, a blood pressure gauge, tools / a wrench set, a shrub or small tree, a luggage cart.*
- Write the words on the board. Say each word and ask Ss to repeat. Encourage Ss to write the words next to the pictures in the Student's Book.

Expansion activity (whole group)

- Use realia to review additional unit vocabulary.
- Direct Ss' attention to the picture dictionary on page 25. Ask Ss to tell you which of the vocational courses in the word bank were not included in Exercise **2A** in Lesson F (computer technology, counseling, home health care). Write the three courses on the board.
- Hold up a computer keyboard or a mouse and ask: *Which vocational course?* (computer technology) Hold up a box of bandages or a medicine container to elicit *home health care*. Finally, point to a pair of students to elicit *counseling*. Explain to Ss that they can talk to a counselor at the school about questions or problems they might have.

Practice

- Direct Ss' attention to Exercise **2B** and read the instructions aloud.
- Make sure Ss understand the exercise. Point to the illustrations. Ask two Ss to read the example sentences. Point out the verb forms *want* and *wants* in the examples.
- Ss complete the exercise in small groups. Walk around and help as needed.
- When groups are finished, ask for volunteers to try to remember and report the goals of everyone in their group.

> **More Ventures** *(whole group, pairs, individual)*
> Assign appropriate exercises from the *Teacher's Toolkit Audio CD / CD-ROM, Add Ventures,* or the *Workbook.*

Application

Community building

- **Project** Ask Ss to turn to page 136 to complete the project for Unit 2.

Evaluation

- Before asking Ss to turn to the self-assessment on page 141, do a quick review of the unit. Have Ss turn to Lesson A. Ask the class to talk about what they remember about this lesson. Prompt Ss, if necessary, with questions, for example: *What are the conversations about on this page? What vocabulary is in the big picture?* Continue in this manner to review each lesson quickly.
- **Self-assessment** Read the instructions for Exercise **3**. Ask Ss to turn to the self-assessment page and complete the unit self-assessment.
- If Ss are ready, administer the unit test on pages T-167–T-168 of this *Teacher's Edition* (or on the *Teacher's Toolkit Audio CD / CD-ROM*). The audio and audio script for the tests are on the *Teacher's Toolkit Audio CD / CD-ROM.*

2 Fun with language

A Work with a partner. Match the courses with the pictures.

accounting	culinary arts	landscape design
automotive repair	hotel management	nursing

1. _accounting_   2. _culinary arts_   3. _nursing_

4. _automotive repair_   5. _landscape design_   6. _hotel management_

B Work in a group. Play a game. Sit in a circle. The first person says one goal. The next person repeats the first goal and adds another goal. Continue until everyone has a chance to speak.

3 Wrap up

Complete the **Self-assessment** on page 141.

At school

Review

1 Listening

Read the questions. Then listen and circle the answers.

1. How old is Fernando?
   a. 25
   (b.) 35

2. What color is his hair?
   (a.) brown
   b. black

3. Where does he go in the morning?
   (a.) to school
   b. to work

4. What does he do at Green's Grocery Store?
   (a.) He's a cashier.
   b. He's a computer technician.

5. When does Fernando play soccer?
   (a.) on Saturday
   b. on Sunday

6. What does Fernando want to study?
   a. computer repair
   (b.) computer technology

Talk with a partner. Ask and answer the questions. Use complete sentences.

2 Grammar

A Write. Complete the story.

An Important Day

Tan Nguyen __is__ 45 years old. He is a home health assistant.
         1. be

He __wants to be__ a nurse. He __works__ from 8:00 a.m. to 4:00 p.m.,
      2. want / be   3. work

but today he __isn't working__. This afternoon, he and his wife __became__
              4. not / work   5. become

United States citizens. Every day at work, Tan __wears__ a uniform.
                                                 6. wear

Today he __is wearing__ a new blue suit, a white shirt, and a red and white
           7. wear

striped tie. Tan is very excited.

B Write. Look at the answers. Write the questions.

1. **A** How old _is Tan_ ?
   B Tan is 45 years old.
2. **A** What _does he do_ ?
   B He is a home health assistant.
3. **A** When _does he work_ ?
   B He usually works from 8:00 a.m. to 4:00 p.m.
4. **A** What _is he wearing today_ ?
   B Today he is wearing a blue suit, a white shirt, and a striped tie.

Talk with a partner. Ask and answer the questions.

Lesson objectives
- Review vocabulary and grammar from Units 1 and 2
- Introduce the pronunciation of strong syllables

UNITS 1 & 2

Warm-up and review
- Before class. Write today's lesson focus on the board.
  Review unit:
  Review vocabulary from Units 1 and 2
  Review adjective order; present continuous vs. simple present; want and need; and the future with will
  Pronounce strong syllables
- Begin class. Books closed. Review language for describing people. Ask individual Ss:
  What are you wearing today?
  What do you usually do on the weekend?
  What does your best friend look like?
  What's (classmate's name) doing right now?
  What do you want to do in the future?
  What will you do after class?

Practice
- Books open. Direct Ss' attention to Exercise **1** and read the instructions aloud. Read the question and answer choices in number 1 and point to where the answer *b* has been circled.
- Ask individual Ss to read aloud the remaining questions and answers. Say: *Now listen and circle the correct answers.*
- [Class Audio CD1 track 16] Play or read the audio program (see audio script, page T-153). Ss listen and circle the answers to the questions. Repeat the audio program as needed.
- Check answers. Read each question aloud and call on different Ss to answer.
- Read aloud the second part of the instructions for Exercise **1**. Emphasize that answers need to be in complete sentences.
- Ss complete the exercise in pairs. Walk around and help as needed.
- Ask several pairs to ask and answer the questions for the rest of the class.
- Direct Ss' attention to Exercise **2A**. Ask Ss: *What is the title of this story?* (An Important Day)
- Have Ss skim the reading quickly to get the main idea. Encourage Ss to ask themselves the question *What is the story about?* while they're skimming.
- Read aloud the instructions for Exercise **2A**. Ask a S to read aloud the first sentence in the paragraph. Point to where *is* has been written for number 1.
- Ss complete the exercise individually. Walk around and help as needed.

- Write the numbers 2–7 on the board. Ask a few Ss to come to the board to write the correct answer next to each number.
- Read the story aloud using Ss' answers. If there is an error, say to Ss: *There's a problem here. Does anyone have a different answer?* Elicit the correct answer.
- Discuss the use of the simple present or the present continuous in each sentence of the story.

Presentation
- Books closed. Write on the board:
  What's your name? / My name is (your name).
  _____ ? / I'm (your age) *years old.*
- Point to the first question and answer. Tell Ss: *This is the question. This is the answer.* Point to the blank in the second set and ask: *What's the question?* (How old are you?)

Practice
- Books open. Direct Ss' attention to Exercise **2B**. Read the instructions aloud. Ask two Ss to read aloud the example question and answer.
- Ss write the questions individually. Walk around and help as needed.
- Check answers. Ask for volunteers to read aloud their questions. If there are minor errors, encourage other Ss to supply the corrections. Write the correct questions on the board.
- Read aloud the second part of the instructions for Exercise **2B**.
- Ss ask and answer the questions in pairs. Walk around and help as needed.
- Ask several pairs to ask and answer the questions for the rest of the class.

Expansion activity *(whole group)*
- If the class is not too large, have each S write a question and answer similar to the items in Exercise **2B**. Encourage Ss to use the language they learned in Units 1 and 2.
- Ask individual Ss to write only their answer on the board. Have the rest of the class guess the question.

Review: Units 1 & 2   T-30

Warm-up and review

- Books closed. Write the word *syllable* on the board. Point to the word. Say it aloud. Ask Ss to repeat.
- Underline the syllables in the word *syllable* (syl - la - ble). Clap while you say the word, emphasizing each syllable. Say: *These are syllables.*
- Draw a circle around the first syllable in the word *syllable*. Say the word again and clap each syllable, but this time put extra emphasis on the first syllable. Say: *Words in English have a strong syllable.* Point to the circled first syllable on the board and say the word again, emphasizing the first syllable.

Presentation

- Direct Ss' attention to Exercise **3A**. Read the instructions.
- [Class Audio CD1 track 17] Play or read the audio program (see audio script, page T-153). Ss just listen.
- Direct Ss' attention to Exercise **3B** and read the instructions aloud.
- [Class Audio CD1 track 18] Play or read the audio program (see audio script, page T-153). Ss listen and repeat each word. Clap and say the words along with Ss. Exaggerate the strong syllables.

▼ **Teaching tip**
Ss may feel self-conscious clapping out syllables, but if you make it fun, they will join you.

Practice

- Read aloud the second part of the instructions for Exercise **3B**.
- Model the exercise. Point to the word *necklace* in the Student's Book. Say the word. Ask a S to clap the syllables after you say the word. Then, have the same S say *nursing* while you clap the syllables.
- Ss complete the exercise in pairs. Correct pronunciation.
- Ask several pairs to say the words aloud and clap the syllables for the rest of the class.
- Direct Ss' attention to Exercise **3C** and read the instructions aloud.
- [Class Audio CD1 track 19] Model the exercise. Play or read the first word on the audio program. Ask: *Which syllable is strong?* (the second one) Point to the circle over the second syllable in *instructor*.
- [Class Audio CD1 track 19] Play or read the audio program (see audio script, page T-153). Ss listen and draw a circle over the strong syllable in each word. Repeat the audio program as needed.

- Check answers. Say each word and clap out the syllables. Call on individual Ss to say which syllable is strong (first, second, third, or fourth).

▼ **Teaching tip**
If Ss have trouble saying *first, second, third,* and *fourth,* ask them to review and practice saying the ordinal numbers they used for dates in the Welcome unit; have them refer to the Useful lists section on page 152.

Community building (whole group)

- Ask Ss to write their names on the board and draw a circle over the strong syllable.
- Go over the names, one by one. Check that Ss have correctly identified the strong syllable, and make sure everyone in the class can pronounce the name.
- Discuss any obvious differences between pronunciation patterns in Ss' native languages and English. For example, speakers of some Asian languages don't stress a particular syllable strongly, while Spanish speakers always stress the second-to-last syllable except when words have special stress markers.

Practice

- Direct Ss' attention to the chart in Exercise **3D** and read the instructions aloud.
- Model the exercise. Look through Units 1 and 2 in the Student's Book. Write a word on the board that isn't in Exercise **3B**. Say: *Find other words to write in the chart.*
- After Ss have written their eight words, point to the word you wrote on the board. Say it aloud. Ask a S to tell you which syllable is the strong syllable. Draw a circle over that syllable.
- Ss complete the exercise individually. Help as needed.
- Read aloud the second part of the instructions in Exercise **3D**.
- Ss complete the exercise in pairs. Correct pronunciation.

Evaluation

- Direct Ss' attention to the lesson focus on the board.
- Ask Ss to describe the clothing they're wearing using multiple adjectives, and have them identify the strong syllable in several vocabulary words from the units.
- Call on individual Ss to tell what they're doing right now. Ask other Ss what they usually do on the weekend.
- Ask Ss about their goals and plans using *want* and *need,* and the future with *will.*
- Check off each part of the lesson focus as Ss demonstrate an understanding of what they have learned in the lesson.

UNITS 1 & 2

3 Pronunciation: strong syllables

A 💿 **Listen** to the syllables in these words.

p**a**per   r**e**staurant   comp**u**ter

B 💿 **Listen and repeat.** Clap for each syllable. Clap loudly for the strong syllable.

● ●	● ●	● ● ●	● ● ●	● ● ● ●
necklace	cashier	medium	mechanic	television
nursing	career	counselor	accounting	citizenship
bracelet	repair	uniform	tomorrow	usually
sweater	achieve	manager	computer	
jacket		citizen	eraser	

Talk with a partner. Take turns. Say each word. Your partner claps for each syllable.

C 💿 **Listen** for the strong syllable in each word. Put a circle over the strong syllable.

1. instr**u**ctor   4. d**i**ctionary   7. man**a**gement
2. **u**niform   5. b**u**siness   8. l**a**ndscape
3. sw**e**atshirt   6. enr**o**ll   9. des**i**gn

D **Write** eight words from Units 1 and 2. Put a circle over the strong syllable in each word.

1. *(Answers will vary.)*	5.
2.	6.
3.	7.
4.	8.

Talk with a partner. Read the words.

Review: Units 1 & 2   31

Lesson A Get ready

1 Talk about the picture

A Look at the picture. What do you see?

B Point to: a broken-down car • smoke • groceries • a trunk
a cell phone • an engine • a supermarket • a hood

C Look at the people. What happened?

UNIT 3

Lesson objectives
- Introduce Ss to the topic
- Find out what Ss know about the topic
- Preview the unit by talking about the picture
- Practice key vocabulary
- Practice listening skills

Warm-up and review

- Before class. Write today's lesson focus on the board. *Lesson A: Friends and family*
- Begin class. Books closed. Draw a line down the middle of the board and write *friends* on one side and *family* on the other.
- Point to the word *friends*. Ask the class: *What are friends?* List Ss' responses on the board. If necessary, suggest a few sample definitions that recycle the simple present, for example: *Friends do things together after work. Friends help you with your problems. Friends spend time together.*

▼ **Teaching tip**
Ss' responses may be single words or phrases, which is fine at this point in the lesson. You can write on the board exactly what Ss say, or you can write complete sentences using Ss' ideas.

- Point to the word *family* on the board. Ask the class: *Who is in a family?* Ss should respond with words they know, such as: *mother; brother; husband; aunt; children; grandparents; daughter.* List responses on the board. Tell Ss: *Unit 3 is about friends and family.*

Presentation

- Books open. Set the scene. Direct Ss' attention to the picture on page 32. Ask: *Where is this?* (a street / road / highway) Ask the question from Exercise **1A**: *What do you see?* Elicit and write on the board as much vocabulary about the picture as possible (cars, a family, a store, buildings, trees, bags, an electronic game, etc.).
- Direct Ss' attention to the key words in Exercise **1B**. Read each word aloud while pointing to the corresponding item in the picture. Ask the class to repeat and point.
- Listen to Ss' pronunciation and repeat the words as needed.

Comprehension check

- Ask Ss *Yes / No* questions about the picture. Recycle questions in the simple present and the present continuous. Say: *Listen to the questions. Answer "Yes" or "No."*
Point to the red car. Ask: *Is this a broken-down car?* (Yes.)

Point to the SaveMore store. Ask: *Is this a supermarket?* (Yes.)
Point to the woman in the foreground. Ask: *Is she talking on a cell phone?* (Yes.)
Point to the trunk of the red car. Ask: *Does the family need to buy groceries now?* (No.)
Point to the children. Ask: *Are the children reading a book?* (No.)
Point to the hood of the red car. Ask: *Is the hood of the car open?* (Yes.)

Practice

- Direct Ss' attention to Exercise **1B**. Model the exercise. Hold up the Student's Book. Say to a S: *Point to the cell phone*. The S points to the appropriate part of the picture.
- Ss in pairs. Say to one S: *Say the words in Exercise 1B.* Say to his or her partner: *Point to the correct part of the picture.*
- Ss complete the exercise in pairs. Walk around and help as needed. When Ss finish, have them change roles. If time allows, have Ss repeat the exercise with new partners.
- Ask several pairs to perform the exercise for the class to check Ss' understanding.
- Direct Ss' attention to Exercise **1C** and read the instructions aloud. Tell Ss: *Talk about the picture.* Ss complete the exercise in pairs.

▼ **Teaching tip**
Here are two other ways to present Exercise **1C**:
- Ask Ss the question in the instruction line and list their responses on the board.
- Give Ss a small piece of paper and ask them to write two or three sentences about what happened to the people in the picture. Then collect the papers and read aloud some of the Ss' responses.

Expansion activity (student pairs)

- Ask pairs of Ss to imagine and write down the woman's telephone conversation from the big picture. Then have them practice the conversation.
- Ask each pair to tell the class who the woman might be talking to and then perform the conversation for the class.

Lesson A T-32

Lesson A   Get ready

Presentation
- Books open. Direct Ss' attention to the pictures in Exercise **2A**. Tell Ss that these are the people Rosa is calling on her cell phone in the picture on page 32. For each picture, ask Ss: *Where is this?* (auto repair shop, dry cleaner's, restaurant) *Do you think this person is a friend or a family member?*

Practice
- Read aloud the instructions for Exercise **2A**.
- [Class Audio CD1 track 20] Play or read the audio program (see audio script, page T-153). Pause the audio program after the first conversation and ask Ss: *Which picture shows the person from conversation A?* (Picture 3) Hold up the Student's Book and write the letter *a* next to number 3.
- [Class Audio CD1 track 20] Play or read the rest of the audio program and repeat as needed.
- Check answers. Ask Ss which picture shows each conversation.
- Direct Ss' attention to Exercise **2B** and read the instructions aloud.
- [Class Audio CD1 track 20] Model the exercise. Say: *Listen to conversation A.* Play or read the first four lines of conversation A. Direct Ss' attention to the example sentence. Read it aloud, and point to where the letter *F* (False) is written. Lead Ss to see that the answer is false because Rosa went to the supermarket with her children.
- [Class Audio CD1 track 20] Read aloud each group of sentences before listening to the corresponding conversation. Read aloud the three sentences for conversation A. Then, play or read conversation A on the audio program (see audio script, page T-153). Do the same for conversations B and C.
- Ss complete the exercise individually. When Ss are finished writing their answers, play or read the complete audio program once more to allow Ss to check answers.

Comprehension check
- Check answers. Write the numbers 2–9 on the board. Ask for a few Ss to come to the board to write the correct answers to Exercise **2B** next to the numbers. Point to each answer and ask: *Is this correct?*

Learner persistence *(individual work)*
- [Self-Study Audio CD track 12] Exercises **2A** and **2B** are recorded on the Ss' self-study CD at the back of the Student's Book. Ss can listen to the CD at home for reinforcement and review. They can also listen for self-directed learning when class attendance is not possible.

Expansion activity *(whole group)*
- After Ss have completed Exercises **2A** and **2B**, write the names *Daniel, Mike,* and *Ling* across the top of the board. For each name, ask Ss: *Who is this?* Write Ss' responses under the corresponding name. Encourage Ss to say whether each person is a friend, a family member, or something else, such as an acquaintance or a classmate. This could be a good follow-up to the warm-up question, *What are friends?*

▼ **Culture tip**
The definition of the word *friend* can vary from culture to culture. Americans might consider a classmate a friend even if they only spend time with that person for one semester. Other cultures might reserve the word for people they have been very close to for a long time. It might be interesting to ask Ss to describe the ideas about friendship in their own cultures.

Application
- Direct Ss' attention to Exercise **2C** and read the instructions aloud. Ss complete the exercise in pairs.
- Ask for volunteers to tell the class about a time when they asked for help or when friends or family asked them for help. Discuss Ss' ideas about whether people should or shouldn't ask for help, and whether they think it's easy or difficult to ask for help.
- Ask Ss if they think it was easy or difficult for Rosa to ask for help.

Evaluation
- Direct Ss to the lesson focus on the board. Ask Ss to tell about Rosa's family (her husband is Daniel, and they have two children, a son and a daughter). Have Ss tell why Rosa needed to ask for help (she went to the supermarket and her car broke down). Ask Ss to say the names of two of Rosa's friends (Mike and Ling).
- Check off each part of the lesson focus as Ss demonstrate an understanding of what they have learned in the lesson.

More Ventures *(whole group, pairs, individual)*
Assign appropriate exercises from the *Teacher's Toolkit Audio CD / CD-ROM, Add Ventures,* or the *Workbook*.

UNIT 3

2 Listening

A **Listen.** Who is Rosa talking to? Write the letter of the conversation.

1. _b_
2. _c_
3. _a_

B **Listen again.** Write *T* (true) or *F* (false).

Conversation A
1. Rosa went to the supermarket with her friends. _F_
2. Rosa's car broke down. _T_
3. Rosa opened the hood of the car. _T_

Conversation B
4. Mike works at a coffee shop. _F_
5. Rosa bought groceries for a picnic. _T_
6. Mike will pick up Rosa and her children. _F_

Conversation C
7. Ling needs a ride to school tonight. _F_
8. Rosa usually leaves her house at 7:00. _T_
9. Ling will pick up Rosa at 8:00. _F_

Listen again. Check your answers.

C **Talk** with a partner. Ask and answer the questions.

1. Did you ever ask a friend for help?
2. Did a friend or family member ever ask you for help?
3. What happened?

Friends and family

Lesson B What did you do last weekend?

1 Grammar focus: simple past with regular and irregular verbs

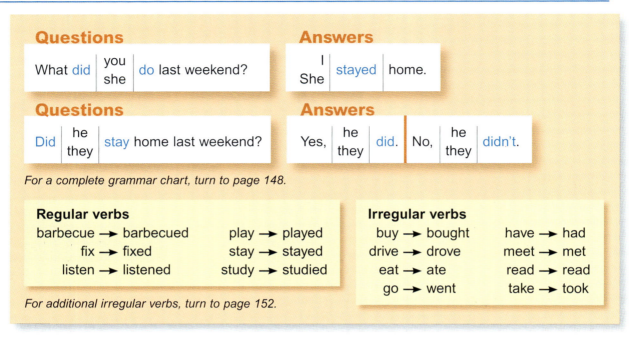

For a complete grammar chart, turn to page 148.

Regular verbs
barbecue → barbecued
fix → fixed
listen → listened
play → played
stay → stayed
study → studied

Irregular verbs
buy → bought
drive → drove
eat → ate
go → went
have → had
meet → met
read → read
take → took

For additional irregular verbs, turn to page 152.

2 Practice

A Write. Complete the conversations. Use the simple past.

1. **A** What did Dahlia and her friends do on Sunday?
   B They ___barbecued___ hamburgers.
          (barbecue)
2. **A** What did the children do on Thursday?
   B They ___took___ a walk in the park.
          (take)
3. **A** What did your family do last weekend?
   B We ___drove___ to the beach.
         (drive)
4. **A** What did Sarah do Monday night?
   B She ___went___ to the movies.
          (go)
5. **A** What did Nikos do Saturday morning?
   B He ___fixed___ the car.
         (fix)
6. **A** What did Carlos do Wednesday morning?
   B He ___bought___ groceries.
         (buy)

Listen and repeat. Then practice with a partner.

34 Unit 3

Lesson objectives
- Introduce the simple past with regular and irregular verbs
- Ask and answer questions about past actions

Warm-up and review

- **Before class.** Write today's lesson focus on the board. *Lesson B: Simple past with regular and irregular verbs*
- **Before class.** Write the key words from page 32 on the board.
- **Begin class.** Books closed. Review the key words Ss learned in Lesson A. Point to and say each of the key words and ask Ss to repeat. Call on Ss to answer specific questions about each key word: *Can you drive a broken-down car?* (No.) *Is there any smoke in this classroom?* (No.) *What are groceries? Give me some examples.* (fruit, milk, vegetables, etc.) *Does anyone in the class have a cell phone? Please show us your cell phone.* (a S who has a cell phone shows it to the class) *What can you buy at a supermarket? Give me some examples.* (food, shampoo, cleaning supplies, etc.)
- Draw on the board a quick sketch of a car with its hood open. Make sure Ss can identify the front end of the car by including a steering wheel. Ask: *Where is the trunk? Where is the hood? Where is the engine?* (Call on Ss to come to the board to point to each.)
- Books open. Direct Ss' attention to the big picture on page 32. Ask Ss: *Do you remember this? What happened to Rosa and her children?* Point to the key words on the board and ask Ss to use them as they tell the story. Elicit, for example: *They went to the supermarket and bought a lot of groceries. Then, their car broke down. Rosa called her husband and some friends on her cell phone and asked for help.*
- As Ss recount the story from Lesson A, write on the board verb phrases in the simple past that Ss use.

Presentation

- Hold up the Student's Book. Point to the grammar chart in Exercise **1**. Read aloud the questions and answers. Ask Ss to repeat.
- Ss in pairs. Have Ss practice reading the top part of the grammar chart (Questions and Answers) to each other while pointing to the appropriate person in the class (I, you, she, he, they).
- Point to the box with regular verbs. Read aloud the present and past forms of each verb and ask Ss to repeat. Ask Ss: *How do we form the simple past with regular verbs?* (add -ed)
- Point to the box with irregular verbs. Read aloud the present and past forms of each verb and ask Ss to repeat. Ask Ss: *How do we form the simple past with irregular verbs?* (in many different ways)

Expansion activity *(whole group)*

- If you want to expand the grammar presentation, turn to the grammar charts on page 148. Practice asking questions and giving affirmative and negative answers with regular and irregular verbs. Add the subject pronouns *it, we,* and *you (plural)* to the presentation.

Practice

- Direct Ss' attention to the picture in Exercise **2A**. Ask: *What are the people doing?* Elicit appropriate answers, for example: *eating; spending time with their friends.*
- Point to number 1 and read the question aloud. Call on a S to read the example answer aloud. Make sure Ss understand that the past tense of the verbs in parentheses can be found in the grammar chart.
- [Class Audio CD1 track 21] Read aloud the second part of the instructions for Exercise **2A**. Play or read the audio program (see audio script, page T-154). Have Ss check their answers as they listen and repeat. Correct pronunciation as needed.
- Ask Ss to come to the board and write the sentences with the past tense verbs. Ask different Ss to read the sentences aloud. Make corrections on the board as needed.
- Have pairs practice the questions and answers.

Expansion activity *(student pairs)*

- Have Ss make quizzes for each other. Write the numbers *1–5* in a column on the board.
- Ask Ss to take out a piece of paper and number it as you've done on the board.
- Books open. Direct Ss' attention to the list of past tense irregular verbs on page 152. Have Ss choose any five irregular verbs and write the present tense of those verbs.
- Ss in pairs. Books closed. Have Ss exchange papers and write the simple past tense form of the verbs their partner gave them. When Ss are finished, ask them to use the list on page 152 to check their answers.
- **Option** After finishing the "quiz," ask Ss to work together to write sentences using their verbs. Collect the sentences or walk around and give Ss oral feedback about their work.

Lesson B What did you do last weekend?

Presentation

- Books closed. Write on the board: *What did you do last weekend?* Ask Ss the question. Write on the board the name of each S who answers, and under the name, write what that S did, for example:

Marta	Sami	Nabil
took her son to the zoo	worked a double shift	cooked dinner for his family

- Ask Ss what these people did last weekend, for example: *What did Marta do last weekend?* Elicit: *She took her son to the zoo.*

Practice

- Books open. Direct Ss' attention to the pictures in Exercise **2B**. Read aloud the verb phrases as you point to each picture. Explain any unfamiliar words.
- Read aloud the instructions in Exercise **2B**. Point to the name *Alicia* above the first two pictures and the phrase *go shopping* in number 1. Then, ask two Ss to read aloud the example conversation.
- Ss complete the activity in pairs. Walk around and help as needed.

Presentation

- Books closed. Turn Ss' attention back to the names and information you wrote on the board.
- Ask Ss *Yes / No* questions, for example: *Did Marta take her husband to the zoo last weekend?* Elicit: *No, she didn't. She took her son to the zoo.* Or, for example: *Did Sami work a long time last weekend?* Elicit: *Yes, he did.*

Practice

- Books open. Direct Ss' attention to Exercise **2C** and read the instructions aloud.
- Ask two Ss to read aloud the first example conversation. Ask two different Ss to read aloud the second example conversation. Make sure Ss understand the exercise.
- Ss complete the exercise in pairs. Walk around and help as needed.
- Ask several pairs to perform the conversations for the class.

Application

- Read aloud the instructions for Exercise **3**. Ask two Ss to read the example conversations aloud, with one S reading role *A* and the other role *B*.

- Divide the class into small groups. Encourage Ss to ask both *Wh-* and *Yes / No* questions.
- Walk around and help as needed.
- Ask volunteers from each group to perform a conversation for the class.

Expansion activity (small groups)

- Bring to class enough dice so that each small group has one die.
- Write the numbers *1–6* on the board. After each number, write a past-time expression, for example: *yesterday; last weekend; this morning; last night; on Saturday night; on Sunday afternoon*. Make sure the expressions make sense for your class, for example: If you meet in the evening, then "this morning" is a past-time expression.
- Model the activity. Call on a S to come to the front of the room. Roll one of the dice, call out the number, and read aloud the corresponding time expression from the board, such as: *on Sunday afternoon*. Then, ask the S: (S's name), *what did you do on Sunday afternoon?* Elicit an appropriate response, for example: *I went to the beach on Sunday afternoon.* Then, ask a follow-up *Yes / No* question, for example: *Did you barbecue hamburgers at the beach?* Elicit: *Yes, I did. / No, I didn't.*
- Ss in small groups. Write the steps on the board:
  1. *Roll the dice.*
  2. *Find your time word on the board.*
  3. *Ask a person in your group: What did you do (time word)?*
  4. *Listen to the answer. Then, ask a question with Did: (Did you _____ ?).*

Evaluation

- Direct Ss' attention to the lesson focus written on the board. Elicit questions and answers with regular and irregular verbs in the simple past.
- Check off each part of the lesson focus as Ss demonstrate an understanding of what they have learned in the lesson.

> **More Ventures** (whole group, pairs, individual)
> Assign appropriate exercises from the *Teacher's Toolkit Audio CD / CD-ROM, Add Ventures,* or the *Workbook.*

B **Talk** with a partner. Change the **bold** words and make conversations.

> **A** What did **Alicia** do last weekend?
> **B** **She went shopping** and **read a book**.

C **Talk** with a partner. Change the **bold** words and make conversations. Look at the pictures in Exercise B.

> **A** Did **Alicia go shopping** last weekend?
> **B** **Yes, she did.**

> **A** Did **John play soccer** last weekend?
> **B** **No, he didn't. He listened to music.**

1. Alicia / go shopping
2. John / play soccer
3. Sam and Lisa / read a book
4. John / eat in a restaurant
5. Alicia / have a picnic
6. Sam and Lisa / play soccer

3 Communicate

Talk with your classmates. Ask and answer questions about last weekend.

> **A** Karen, did you go to the beach last weekend?
> **B** No, I didn't. I stayed home.

> **A** Marco, what did you do last weekend?
> **B** I studied for a test.

Friends and family

Lesson C — When do you usually play soccer?

1 Grammar focus: simple present vs. simple past

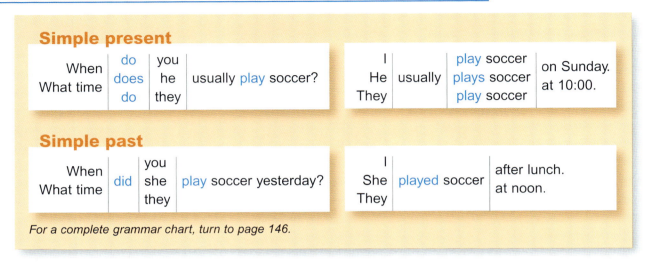

For a complete grammar chart, turn to page 146.

2 Practice

A Write. Complete the conversations. Use the simple present or the simple past.

1. **A** When does Sharon usually meet her friends?
   B She usually __meets__ her friends after work.
   A When did Sharon meet her friends yesterday?
   B Yesterday, she __met__ them at noon for lunch.

2. **A** What time do Roberto and Selma usually eat dinner?
   B They usually __eat__ dinner at 7:00.
   A When did they eat dinner last night?
   B They __ate__ dinner at 8:00.

3. **A** When do Irma and Ron usually study?
   B They usually __study__ on Saturday.
   A When did they study last weekend?
   B They __studied__ on Friday night.

4. **A** When do you usually watch movies?
   B I usually __watch__ movies after dinner.
   A What time did you watch a movie last night?
   B I __watched__ a movie at 6:00.

Listen and repeat. Then practice with a partner.

Lesson objectives
- Introduce the simple present vs. the simple past
- Ask and answer *Wh-* questions with *When* about daily activities

Warm-up and review
- Before class. Write today's lesson focus on the board. *Lesson C:*
The simple present tense and the simple past tense Questions with When
- Begin class. Books closed. Write on the board: *usually.* Ask Ss questions such as: *What do you usually do on the weekend? Do you usually work at night? What do you usually bring to this class?*
- Write on the board: *yesterday.* Ask Ss questions such as: *What did you do yesterday? Did you watch TV yesterday? What TV shows did you watch yesterday?*

▼ **Teaching tip**
Accept incomplete sentences as responses to these warm-up questions. The questions will reveal which Ss understand the grammar and will give Ss a chance to make the transition from their daily lives to English class.

Presentation
- Books open. Direct Ss' attention to the grammar chart in Exercise **1**. Read aloud the questions and answers in the simple present and ask Ss to repeat. Do the same with questions and answers in the simple past tense.
- Ss in pairs. Have students practice reading the grammar chart to each other while pointing to an appropriate person or persons in the class (I, he, she, they).

Expansion activity (whole group)
- Practice the simple present tense. Write on the board: *I usually go to bed at _____.*
- Ask a S: *When do you usually go to bed?* Point to the sentence on the board and elicit, for example: *I usually go to bed at eleven o'clock.*
- Tell Ss: *(S's name) usually goes to bed at eleven o'clock.*
- Continue to ask Ss when they usually go to bed. After each answer, call on a different S and ask, for example: *Kimiko, what time does Hillary go to bed?* Make sure that Ss answer using the third-person singular form *goes.*

▼ **Teaching tip**
Ss usually appreciate a quick, understandable explanation of the grammar points. For this lesson, tell Ss that the simple present tense is often used with words such as *usually* and *always* to talk about things that happen regularly or things we do regularly. The simple past tense is used with words such as *yesterday* and *last week* to talk about completed actions or situations in the past.

Practice
- Direct Ss' attention to Exercise **2A** and read the instructions aloud. Ask two Ss to read the example conversation to the class.
- Direct Ss' attention to the picture in Exercise **2A**. Ask Ss: *Who are these people?* Elicit: *Sharon and her friends.*
- Ss complete the exercise individually. Walk around and help as needed.

Comprehension check
- Read aloud the second part of the instructions for Exercise **2A**.
- [Class Audio CD1 track 22] Play or read the audio program (see audio script, page T-154). Ss listen and repeat as they check their answers. Repeat the audio program as needed.
- Ss in pairs. Have Ss practice the conversations from Exercise **2A**.
- Walk around and listen to Ss' pronunciation. Write difficult words on the board. When Ss are finished, say the words aloud. Ask Ss to repeat.
- Call on pairs to read the conversations to the class. Answer any questions about the grammar and vocabulary.

Learner persistence
- If you have any Ss who are absent, ask Ss in the class to call or e-mail the absent Ss and tell them what happened in class that day. If no one knows the Ss' contact information, ask Ss to explain today's lesson briefly to the absent Ss before class begins next time.

Lesson C T-36

Lesson C: When do you usually play soccer?

Practice

- Direct Ss' attention to the picture of the man sitting in an English class in Exercise **2B**. Ask the class: *Where is this?* (English class, English 101, a school, etc.)
- Point to number 1 and read aloud the time and the verb phrase. Ask two Ss to read the example conversation aloud.
- Read aloud the instructions for Exercise **2B**. Have Ss use the times and actions in items 1–4 to change the example conversation. Make sure Ss understand the exercise.
- Ss complete Exercise **2B** in pairs. Walk around and help as needed.
- Call on different pairs to perform the conversations for each picture.

▼ **Teaching tip**
It might be a good idea to teach Ss the spelling rules for singular subjects in the simple present tense. Verbs that end in a vowel, such as *go*, usually have an *-es* ending (*go / goes*). Two-syllable verbs that end in *-y*, such as *study*, drop the *-y* and add *-ies* (*study / studies*).

- Direct Ss' attention to Exercise **2C**. Read the instructions aloud.
- Point to number 1 and ask two students to read aloud the example conversation.
- Ss complete the exercise in pairs. Walk around and help as needed.
- When Ss are finished, have them switch partners and repeat the conversations.
- Ask several pairs to perform the conversations for the rest of the class.

Expansion activity (student pairs)

- Give Ss controlled practice answering questions with *When*.
- Before class, create a handout for each S. In the top half of the handout, Ss answer questions about when they usually do things. Type the heading: *When do you usually . . . ?* Then, list several endings to the question, for example: *get up in the morning; go to work; shop for groceries; eat lunch; practice speaking English*. Leave space for Ss to write answers.
- In the bottom half of the handout, Ss answer questions about when they did things in the past. Type the heading: *When did you . . . ?* Then, list several endings to the question, for example: *get up this morning; shop for groceries last week; come to the United States; come to this school for the first time*. Make sure that the questions apply to your group of Ss. Leave space for Ss to write answers.
- Ask Ss to write complete sentences to answer the questions. Then, have pairs practice asking and answering the questions.

Application

- Read aloud the instructions in Exercise **3**. Ask Ss: *What are some daily activities?* List Ss' responses on the board, for example: *go shopping, eat breakfast, go to work*.
- Model the exercise by reading aloud the questions in the examples. Call on two different Ss to answer.
- Ss complete the exercise in pairs. Encourage Ss to ask both *Wh-* and *Yes / No* questions.
- Ask several pairs to perform their conversations for the class.

Community building (small groups)

- Bring to class information about activities in your community for the upcoming weekend. For example, bring the calendar pages from a local weekly newspaper. If possible, make copies of the information for each S in the class.
- Ask small groups to scan the information for activities in which they and their families might be interested. Then, have Ss discuss the activities with their group members.
- When the groups are finished, ask Ss whether they found something they think they'll attend. Encourage Ss who are interested in the same activities to make arrangements to go together or to meet at the event.

Evaluation

- Direct Ss' attention to the lesson focus written on the board. Ask Ss to tell you something they usually do. Ask different Ss to tell what they did last weekend.
- Write on the board: *When do you _____? When did you _____?* Call on individual Ss to ask a classmate questions using the question prompts. Listen to Ss' questions and answers to evaluate whether Ss are using the simple present and the simple past correctly.
- Check off each part of the lesson focus as Ss demonstrate an understanding of what they have learned in the lesson.

> **More Ventures** (whole group, pairs, individual)
> Assign appropriate exercises from the *Teacher's Toolkit Audio CD / CD-ROM*, *Add Ventures*, or the *Workbook*.

B **Talk** with a partner. Change the **bold** words and make conversations.

> **A** When does Karim usually **go to English class**?
> **B** He usually **goes to English class** at **8:00 a.m.**

1. 8:00 a.m. / go to English class
2. 11:30 a.m. / go to the gym
3. 2:00 p.m. / go to work
4. 9:00 p.m. / study

C **Talk** with a partner. Change the **bold** words and make conversations.

> **A** When did Maria **go shopping** last Saturday?
> **B** She **went shopping** at **10:00 a.m.**

1. 10:00 a.m. / go shopping
2. 1:00 p.m. / go to her citizenship class
3. 6:00 p.m. / clean her apartment
4. 7:30 p.m. / go to the movies

3 Communicate

Talk with your classmates. Ask and answer questions about daily activities.

When do you usually get up?   I usually get up at 7:00 a.m.

When did you get up this morning?   I got up at 7:30 a.m.

Friends and family   37

Lesson D  Reading

1 Before you read

Look at the picture. Answer the questions.

1. Who is the woman?
2. What is she thinking about?

2 Read

  Read Rosa's journal. Listen and read again.

> Thursday, June 20th
>
> Today was a bad day! On Thursday, my children and I usually go to the park for a picnic, but today we had a problem. We drove to the store to buy groceries, and then the car broke down. I checked the engine, and there was a lot of smoke. Luckily, I had my cell phone! First, I called my husband at work. He left early, picked us up, and took us home. Next, I called the mechanic. Finally, I called Ling and asked for a ride to school tonight. In the end, we didn't go to the park because it was too late. Instead, we had a picnic in our backyard. Then, Ling drove me to school.

Look for these words: *First, Next, Finally.* They tell the order of events.

3 After you read

A Write. Answer the questions about Rosa's day.

1. Where do Rosa and her children go on Thursday? <u>They go to the park.</u>
2. Why did they go to the store? <u>They went to the store to buy groceries.</u>
3. Who did Rosa call first? <u>She called her husband first.</u>
4. Who picked up Rosa and the children? <u>Her husband picked them up.</u>
5. What did Ling do? <u>She drove Rosa to school.</u>

B Number the sentences in the correct order.

<u>5</u> Ling drove Rosa to school.
<u>3</u> Rosa called her husband at work.
<u>4</u> Rosa's husband took them home.
<u>1</u> Rosa went to the store.
<u>2</u> The car broke down.

Lesson objectives
- Introduce and read Rosa's journal
- Practice using new topic-related words

Warm-up and review

- Before class. Write today's lesson focus on the board.
  Lesson D:
  Read and understand Rosa's journal
  Use <u>First</u>, <u>Next</u>, and <u>Finally</u> to show the order of events
- Begin class. Books closed. Ask a S: *Where do you usually buy groceries?* (Elicit the name of a store such as *Miller's Market*.) Ask the same S: *Did you buy groceries at Miller's Market last week?* (Elicit: *Yes, I did. / No, I didn't.*) Ask a different S: *What do you usually do on the weekend?* (Elicit some activity, for example: *I volunteer at the hospital on Saturday.*) Ask the same S: *Did you volunteer at the hospital last Saturday?* (Elicit: *Yes, I did. / No, I didn't.*) If Ss answer "No," find out why they didn't follow their usual routine.
- Books open. Direct Ss' attention to Exercise **1** and read the instructions aloud. Point to the picture of the woman and ask: *Who is the woman?* (Rosa) Point to the thought bubble. Ask: *What is she thinking about?* (Elicit appropriate responses, such as: *Her broken-down car* or *Her problem with her car.*)

Presentation

- [Class Audio CD1 track 23] Direct Ss' attention to Exercise **2** and read the instructions aloud. Make sure Ss understand the word *journal*. Play or read the audio program and ask Ss to read along (see audio script, page T-154). Repeat as needed.

▼ **Teaching tip**
You can vary the presentation of the reading by asking Ss to close their eyes and listen to the audio program. Then have Ss open their eyes and read along with the audio program. Finally, have Ss read the journal entry silently.

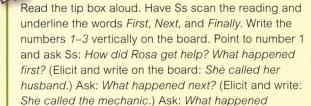

Read the tip box aloud. Have Ss scan the reading and underline the words *First, Next,* and *Finally*. Write the numbers *1–3* vertically on the board. Point to number 1 and ask Ss: *How did Rosa get help? What happened first?* (Elicit and write on the board: *She called her husband.*) Ask: *What happened next?* (Elicit and write: *She called the mechanic.*) Ask: *What happened finally?* (Elicit and write: *She called Ling.*)

Learner persistence (individual work)
- [Self-Study Audio CD track 13] Exercise **2** is recorded on the Ss' self-study CD at the back of the Student's Book. Ss can listen to the CD at home for reinforcement and review. They can also listen to the CD for self-directed learning when class attendance is not possible.

Comprehension check

- Read aloud the instructions for Exercise **3A**. Read the example question aloud and call on a S to read the answer. Point to the second sentence in the reading and say: *Right. On Thursday, they go to the park.*
- Ss complete the exercise individually. Walk around and help as needed.
- Check answers with the class. Ask Ss to read the questions and their answers aloud.
- Read aloud the instructions for Exercise **3B**.
- Model the exercise of putting the sentences in order. Read all the sentences aloud. Then, ask Ss: *What happened first?* Point to where the number 1 is written.
- Ss complete the exercise individually. Walk around and help as needed.
- Check answers with the class. Write the numbers *1–5* on the board. Write the sentence *Rosa went to the store* next to number 1.
- Call on Ss to write the number 2 sentence on the board, the number 3 sentence, and so on. Then, ask a different S to read all five sentences aloud. Ask: *Are the sentences in the correct order?* Make any necessary corrections on the board.

Lesson D Reading

Warm-up and review

- Before class, draw a large picture of a person on the board and give the person a name, for example, *Pat*. The picture does not need to be artistic, but Ss will enjoy it more if the person has some character, for example, a funny hairstyle or large feet.
- Begin class. Books closed. Write *Daily activities* on the board. Make three columns on the board with the headings *every morning, every afternoon, every night*.
- Point to the picture you drew. Tell Ss: *This is Pat. Let's talk about Pat's daily activities. For example, what do you think Pat does every morning?* Elicit and write on the board in the appropriate column responses, such as: *gets up; gets dressed; eats breakfast; waits for the bus*.
- Do the same with *every afternoon* and *every night*.

Presentation

- Books open. Direct Ss' attention to the word bank in Exercise **4A**. Say each vocabulary phrase in the word bank aloud and ask Ss to repeat. Listen to Ss' pronunciation. Correct pronunciation as needed.
- For "Pat's" daily activities that are the same as phrases from the word bank, direct Ss' attention to those phrases and underline them on the board.
- Say: *Write the words in the picture dictionary*. Point to the first example, which has been done. Make sure Ss understand the exercise.
- Ss complete the exercise individually. Walk around and help as needed.

Comprehension check

- [Class Audio CD1 track 24] Say: *Listen and repeat*. Play or read the audio program (see audio script, page T-154). Ss listen and repeat as they check their answers. Listen to Ss' pronunciation and make any necessary corrections. Repeat the audio program if necessary.

Learner persistence *(individual work)*

- [Self-Study Audio CD track 14] Exercise **4A** is recorded on the Ss' self-study CD at the back of the Student's Book. Ss can listen to the CD at home for reinforcement and review. They can also listen to the CD for self-directed learning when class attendance is not possible.

Practice

- Read aloud the instructions in Exercise **4B**. Model the example conversations with two different Ss (you ask the questions). Point to the appropriate pictures in the picture dictionary as you ask the questions.
- Ss practice the conversations in pairs.
- Call on several pairs to perform one of the conversations for the class.

Expansion activity *(whole group)*

- Play a pantomime game using the Picture dictionary cards. Print out the cards from the *Teacher's Toolkit Audio CD / CD-ROM*.
- Place all the cards face-down on a desk or table in the front of the classroom. Tell the class: *Look at one Picture dictionary card. Do not show your classmates the card. Do the activity on the card*.
- Model the activity. Pick up and look at one card. Pantomime the activity on the card, for example: If you pick up the card "do homework," you might sit down at a desk, open your Student's Book, and begin to read and take notes. Ask the class: *What is the daily activity?* or *What am I doing?*
- Ask for volunteers to come to the front of the classroom, one at a time, and perform one of the daily activities. Have Ss call out the vocabulary phrase. Collect each card after it has been used.

Evaluation

- Direct Ss' attention to the lesson focus written on the board. Ask Ss some questions about Rosa's journal, such as: *What do Rosa and her children usually do on Thursday? What happened today? Who did Rosa call first? Who did she call next?*
- Pantomime one of the actions from the picture dictionary. Ask Ss: *What am I doing?* Then, call on a S to come to the front of the class. Point to one of the activities in your book for that S to pantomime. The rest of the class guesses which activity the S is doing. Repeat with several of the daily activities.
- Check off each part of the lesson focus as Ss demonstrate an understanding of what they have learned in the lesson.

> **More Ventures** *(whole group, pairs, individual)*
> Assign appropriate exercises from the *Teacher's Toolkit Audio CD / CD-ROM*, *Add Ventures*, or the *Workbook*.

4 Picture dictionary Daily activities

1. make lunch

2. take a bath

3. do the dishes

4. do the laundry

5. get up

6. do homework

7. take a nap

8. make the bed

9. get dressed

A Write the words in the picture dictionary. Then listen and repeat.

do homework	get dressed	make the bed
do the dishes	get up	take a bath
do the laundry	make lunch	take a nap

B Talk with a partner. Change the **bold** words and make conversations.

A Did you **do the laundry** yesterday?
B Yes, I did.

A Did you **make the bed** this morning?
B No, I didn't. I **got up late**.

Friends and family 39

Lesson E Writing

1 Before you write

A Write. Think about a day last week. Draw three pictures about that day. Write a sentence about each picture.

| 1 | 2 | 3 |

1. _(Answers will vary.)_
2. _____
3. _____

Talk with a partner. Share your pictures and sentences.

B Read Tina's journal.

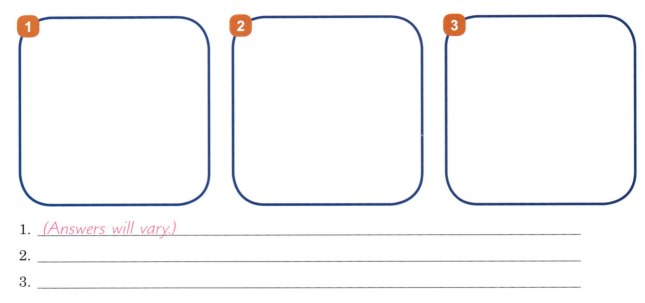

Tuesday, September 1

Last Saturday, I went shopping. I bought five bags of food. I put the groceries in the trunk of my car. Then, I drove home. When I got home, I didn't have my purse. It wasn't in the car, and it wasn't in the trunk. First, I drove back to the store. Next, I looked for my purse outside by the shopping carts, but I didn't find it. Finally, I went inside and asked the manager about my purse. He looked and found my purse in the Lost and Found. I was very happy. In the end, it was a good day.

Culture note
Many places have a *Lost and Found*. Go there to find lost things.

C Write. Answer the questions about Tina's day. Write complete sentences.

1. When did Tina go shopping? _She went shopping last Saturday._
2. Where did she put the groceries? _She put the groceries in the trunk of her car._
3. Where did she first look for her purse? _She looked for her purse outside by the shopping carts._
4. Where was her purse? _Her purse was in the Lost and Found._

Lesson objectives
- Write a personal journal entry
- Introduce the use of a comma after a sequence word

Warm-up and review

- Before class. Write today's lesson focus on the board.
  Lesson E:
  Write a page in a journal
  Use a comma after a sequence word
- Begin class. Books closed. Point to the first part of the lesson focus. Say: *Today, you will write a page in a journal*.
- Ask Ss: *Is a journal different from a letter or an e-mail?* (Yes, we write letters and e-mails to other people. We write in journals just for ourselves.) Ask Ss whether they write in a journal or a diary.
- Books open. Direct Ss' attention to the big picture on page 32. Ask: *What did Rosa write in her journal in Lesson D?* (She wrote about the incident in the picture.) Review the unit vocabulary by asking Ss to describe what happened that day and what Rosa did.

Presentation

- Direct Ss' attention to Exercise **1A** and read the instructions aloud. Make sure Ss understand the exercise.

Teaching tip
Some Ss may feel uncertain about their drawing skills. Reassure them that it's fine to draw simple pictures or even stick figures in this exercise. Explain that the pictures will help them get ideas for their writing.

- Walk around and ask Ss questions about their pictures, for example: *What are you doing in this picture?* Help with vocabulary and grammar as needed.
- Read aloud the second part of the instructions in Exercise **1A**.
- Ss complete the exercise in pairs. When pairs are finished, ask Ss to find a new partner with whom to share their pictures and sentences.

Practice

- Direct Ss' attention to the journal page in Exercise **1B**. Read the instructions aloud. Ss read the journal entry silently. Explain any words Ss don't know.
- Ask Ss: *What did Tina buy?* (five bags of food / groceries) Ask: *When did Tina know she didn't have her purse?* (when she got home) Ask: *Where did Tina look for her purse first?* (outside by the shopping carts) Ask: *Did Tina find her purse? Where?* (Yes, she found it in the Lost and Found.)

Culture note
Read the Culture note aloud. Ask Ss if they have ever used a Lost and Found. A Lost and Found enables people to return something without knowing who the lost item belongs to. It might be interesting for the class to discuss whether this same system is used in Ss' native countries.

Teaching tip
Point out the date at the top of Tina's journal page. Explain that many people write the date in a journal so that they can remember when something happened. You might also mention that personal and business letters also have the date at the top of the page.

Comprehension check

- Direct Ss' attention to Exercise **1C** and read the instructions aloud. Ask two Ss to read the example question and answer to the class.
- Check answers. Ask for volunteers to write their answers on the board. Ask: *Are these answers correct?* Have Ss return to the board to correct any errors.

Learner persistence (whole group)

- Do your Ss have their own Student's Books and Workbooks? Do they ever worry about losing them? Take a few minutes and have Ss write their names and phone numbers or e-mail addresses inside their books. They might want to identify their notebooks, day planners, or address books in the same way. Then, if these things are ever lost, it will be much easier for the finder to return them, and much easier for your Ss to keep up with their English studies.

Lesson E Writing

Presentation

- Direct Ss' attention to the reading passage on page 38 of Lesson D. Remind Ss of the words in the tip box, *First, Next,* and *Finally,* which can be used to show the order of events. Write the words on the board.
- Ask Ss: *Do you remember Rosa? What happened to Rosa on Thursday?* (Her car broke down.) Ask: *What did Rosa do first?* (Have Ss scan the reading for the answer: She called her husband.) Point to the word *First* on the board and tell Ss: *That's right.* <u>First</u>, *Rosa called her husband.*
- Repeat with *Next* and *Finally,* having Ss scan the reading for the answer and then pointing to the word on the board as you repeat what the Ss tell you.

Practice

- Direct Ss' attention to Exercise **1D** and read the instructions aloud. Read aloud the example sentence in number 1. Ask Ss: *What did I do first?* Elicit: *You washed the dirty clothes.* Point to the word *First* in the example and tell Ss: *That's right.* <u>First</u>, *I washed the dirty clothes.*
- Make sure Ss understand the exercise. Ss complete the exercise individually.
- Ask pairs to compare their answers. Then, call on Ss to read the sentences in order.

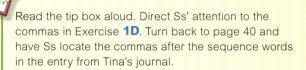

Read the tip box aloud. Direct Ss' attention to the commas in Exercise **1D**. Turn back to page 40 and have Ss locate the commas after the sequence words in the entry from Tina's journal.

- Direct Ss' attention to Exercise **1E**. Read aloud the instructions and the example, and remind Ss to use commas after the sequence words.
- Ss complete the task individually. Walk around and help as needed.
- Ask three volunteers to write on the board their "mini-paragraphs" from Exercise **1E**. Read each one aloud and ask Ss: *Is this correct?* Make any corrections on the board.

Expansion activity *(student pairs)*

- Before class, find one or more comic strips with pictures that clearly show a sequence of events. Use correction fluid to get rid of any words in the comic strips. (If time is limited, do this with just one comic strip and then make photocopies.)

- Ss in pairs. Give each pair a comic strip and ask Ss to talk about what is happening in the pictures.
- Next, have Ss fill in the speech and thought bubbles in the comic strip. Walk around and help with vocabulary and common expressions.
- Finally, ask Ss to take out a piece of paper and write the story using the sequence words *First, Next,* and *Finally.*
- Have each pair join another pair to form small groups. Ask Ss to explain what they think is happening in their comic strip. Then have them read aloud their story using the sequence words.

Application

- Direct Ss' attention to Exercise **2**.
- Have Ss look at Exercises **1A** and **1B** on page 40. Tell Ss that they will write a journal page about the day they drew in Exercise **1A**. The journal page will look like the page in Exercise **1B**.
- Ss complete the journal page individually. Tell Ss to include the date. Help as needed.

Evaluation

- Ss in pairs. Read aloud the instructions for Exercise **3A**. Partners take turns reading their journal entries to each other. Walk around and help with pronunciation.
- Direct Ss' attention to Exercise **3B** and read the instructions aloud. Ask a S to read the three questions to the class.
- Ask Ss to take out a piece of paper and write the three questions from Exercise **3B**.
- Have Ss exchange journal pages to peer-correct each other's writing and offer feedback. Tell Ss: *Read your partner's journal page. Write answers to the three questions.*
- When Ss are finished, have them share their answers and discuss their journal pages in a peer review.
- Direct Ss' attention to the lesson focus written on the board. Ask Ss if they can write a page in a journal now. Have a S to come to the board and write a sentence with a sequence word.
- Check off each part of the lesson focus as Ss demonstrate an understanding of what they have learned in the lesson.

More Ventures *(whole group, pairs, individual)*
Assign appropriate exercises from the *Teacher's Toolkit Audio CD / CD-ROM, Add Ventures,* or the *Workbook.*

D Write. Read the sentences. Write *First, Next,* or *Finally* on the correct line.

1. Last Saturday, I did the laundry.
   _____Next_____ , I dried the clothes in the dryer.
   _____Finally_____ , I folded the clean clothes.
   _____First_____ , I washed the dirty clothes.

> Use a comma after sequence words.
> **First,** I washed the dirty clothes.

2. Last night, I stayed home.
   _____Next_____ , I washed the dishes.
   _____First_____ , I cooked dinner.
   _____Finally_____ , I went to bed.

3. Last Thursday, my family had a picnic.
   _____Next_____ , we ate breakfast.
   _____First_____ , we woke up early.
   _____Finally_____ , we went to the park.

E Write the sentences from Exercise D in the correct order.

1. Last Saturday, I did the laundry. First, I washed the dirty clothes. Next, I dried the clothes in the dryer. Finally, I folded the clean clothes.

2. Last night, I stayed home. First, I cooked dinner. Next, I washed the dishes. Finally, I went to bed.

3. Last Thursday, my family had a picnic. First, we woke up early. Next, we ate breakfast. Finally, we went to the park.

2 Write

Write a journal entry about a day in your life. Use Exercises 1A, 1B, and 1E to help you.

3 After you write

A Read your journal entry to a partner.

B Check your partner's journal entry.
- What kind of day did your partner have?
- What happened first?
- Are there commas after the sequence words (*First, Next, Finally*)?

Friends and family

Lesson F **Another view**

1 Life-skills reading

A Read the questions. Look at the cell phone calling plans. Circle the answers.

1. Which plan costs $79.00 a month?
   a. Plan A
   (b.) Plan B
   c. Plan C
   d. E-Z Plan

2. How much is Plan C every month?
   a. $45.00
   b. $59.00
   c. $79.00
   (d.) $149.00

3. How much are additional minutes with Plan A?
   a. $0.20
   b. $0.30
   (c.) $0.45
   d. $0.59

4. How many monthly minutes come with Plan C?
   a. 149
   b. 700
   c. 1,500
   (d.) 3,000

B Talk with a partner. Ask and answer the questions.

1. Do you have a cell phone? If so, how long do you talk on it each day?
2. When do you usually call your friends? What do you talk about?
3. Sue usually talks on the phone about 15 hours a month. Which plan should she choose?

Lesson objectives
- Practice reading a chart
- Review unit grammar
- Introduce the project
- Complete the project and self-assessment

Warm-up and review
- Before class. Write today's lesson focus on the board.
  Lesson F:
  Read a chart
  Review the simple past tense
  Complete the project and the self-assessment
- Begin class. Books open. Direct Ss' attention to the big picture on page 32. Ask Ss questions to review unit vocabulary and grammar, for example: *Who is the woman? What happened to her?* Be sure to elicit the fact that Rosa used her cell phone to solve her problem.
- Tell Ss: *Rosa used her cell phone to call friends and family.* Ask Ss: *Who in this class has a cell phone? Please raise your hand.*
- Write on the board the names of three or more Ss who raised their hands. Then, ask these Ss: *How much time do you talk on your cell phone each month? How many minutes?* Next to each name, write an approximate number of minutes per month for each S.

Presentation
- Direct Ss' attention to Lesson F and to the chart above Exercise **1A**. Read aloud the chart title. Ask Ss: *What is a calling plan?* Elicit, for example: *The cost per month to use a cell phone.*
- Read aloud each column in the chart. Ask a few comprehension questions, for example: *Why is Plan C so expensive?* (It comes with 3,000 minutes.) *What are "additional minutes"?* (more minutes than the plan's monthly minutes)
- Turn Ss' attention back to the information about Ss' telephone usage that you wrote on the board. Ask Ss which plan they think is the best for each person listed on the board. Encourage Ss to use information from the chart as they give their opinions.

Practice
- Read aloud the instructions for Exercise **1A**. This exercise helps prepare Ss for standardized-type tests they may have to take. Make sure Ss understand the exercise. Have Ss individually scan for and circle the answers.

▼ **Teaching tip**
Point out that *E-Z*, the name of the cell phone company in the chart, sounds like the word *easy*.

Comprehension check
- Go over the answers to **1A** together. Make sure that Ss followed the instructions and circled their answers.

Application
- Read aloud the instructions for Exercise **1B**. Ss complete the exercise in pairs.
- When pairs are finished, call on several Ss to tell the class about their partner's cell phone use.

Expansion activity
- Bring to class self-stick name tags or pieces of paper and tape, along with dark-colored markers.
- Ask Ss to write on their name tag the name of a famous person that everyone in the class has heard of.
- Model the activity. Put on a name tag with a famous person's name. Walk up to a S, read his or her name tag, and pretend to call the "famous person" on the phone. Ask the person something appropriate, for example: *Hello, is this Lance Armstrong? Hi, Lance! Listen, I'm thinking about entering a bicycle race. What should I do to get ready for the race?* When you're finished with the first conversation, have the S "call" the famous person written on your name tag.
- Ask Ss to stand up, walk around the room, and have mock "telephone conversations."
- Ask for volunteers to perform one of their conversations for the class.

Community building *(whole class)*
- Make a class telephone directory. Pass around a sign-up sheet with columns for Ss' names and phone numbers. Be sure to tell Ss that signing the sheet is voluntary. If they don't have a phone, or if they don't want their number distributed to the class, they can simply pass the sign-up sheet to the next person.
- Type the list and distribute it to the class. Brainstorm times Ss might want to call a classmate, for example: when they want to ask about homework or when they need a ride to class.

Lesson F Another view

Presentation

- Books closed. Model Exercise **2A**. Write on the board three things you did last week. Two items should be true, and one should be false. For example: *I saw a movie last week. I met my brother for lunch last week. I played tennis last week.* Read each sentence to the class.
- Next, tell Ss that two of the sentences are true and one sentence is false. Encourage them to make guesses and explain the reasons for their guesses. Don't give anything away yet! The idea is to encourage as much discussion as possible.
- When several Ss have made guesses, reveal which two sentences are true and which one is false by talking about what you did last week.

Practice

- Books open. Direct Ss' attention to Exercise **2A** and read aloud the instructions and the example sentence.
- When Ss have finished writing their sentences, read aloud the second part of the instructions for Exercise **2A**. Ss complete the exercise in small groups.
- When groups have finished, ask for volunteers to read their sentences aloud or write them on the board for the rest of the class to make guesses about.

Expansion activity (small groups)

- Play the "two truths and a lie" game again, but this time have Ss write negative sentences, for example: *I didn't take the bus last week.*

Practice

- Direct Ss' attention to Exercise **2B** and read the instructions aloud.
- Model the exercise. Point to the chart. Read aloud the first prompt as a complete sentence: *Find someone who went to a party last weekend.* Tell Ss: *I need to find someone who went to a party last weekend.* Point to the example conversations. Tell one S: *You are Pablo.* Read aloud the example question and elicit the example answer from "Pablo." Point to where "Pablo" has been written in the chart.
- Ss walk around the room. If you have enough Ss in the class, tell Ss they can use each classmate's name only once.

Comprehension check

- When Ss have completed the chart in Exercise **2B**, call on individual Ss and ask, for example: *Lucia, who in the class visited a friend last week?* (Lucia responds with a classmate's name, for example, *Hee-Jin*.) Ask that S a follow-up question, for example: *Hee-Jin, who did you visit last week?*

> ***More Ventures*** *(whole group, pairs, individual)*
> Assign appropriate exercises from the *Teacher's Toolkit Audio CD / CD-ROM*, *Add Ventures*, or the *Workbook*.

Application

Community building

- **Project** Ask Ss to turn to page 137 in their Student's Book to complete the project for Unit 3.

Evaluation

- Before asking Ss to turn to the self-assessment on page 142, do a quick review of the unit. Have Ss turn to Lesson A. Ask the class to call out what they remember about this lesson. Prompt Ss, if necessary, with questions. For example: *What are the conversations about on this page? What vocabulary is in the big picture?* Continue in this manner to review each lesson quickly.
- **Self-assessment** Read the instructions for Exercise **3**. Ask Ss to turn to the self-assessment page and complete the unit self-assessment.
- If Ss are ready, administer the unit test on pages T-169–T-170 of this *Teacher's Edition* (or on the *Teacher's Toolkit Audio CD / CD-ROM*). The audio and audio script for the tests are on the *Teacher's Toolkit Audio CD / CD-ROM*.

2 Fun with language

A Work in a group. Play a game. Write two true sentences about last week. Write one false sentence about last week.

> I cooked dinner.
> 1. *(Answers will vary.)*
> 2.
> 3.

Talk to your classmates. Read your three sentences out loud. Mix up the order. Your classmates guess which sentence is false.

> I think you didn't cook dinner.

B Work in a group. Ask questions about the past. Complete the chart.

> Pablo, did you go to a party last weekend?   Yes, I did.

Find someone who:	
went to a party last weekend	*Pablo*
visited a friend last week	*(Answers will vary.)*
called a friend last weekend	
had a party last year	
took a trip last summer	
played soccer last Saturday	
cooked breakfast yesterday	
went to the movies last month	
helped a friend yesterday	
got up late this morning	
did the dishes last night	

3 Wrap up

Complete the **Self-assessment** on page 142.

Health

Lesson A Get ready

1 Talk about the picture

A Look at the picture. What do you see?

B Point to a person who: has a headache • is holding an X-ray • hurt his leg
hurt her hand • is taking medicine • is on crutches

C Where are these people? What happened to them?

Lesson objectives
- Introduce Ss to the topic
- Find out what Ss know about the topic
- Preview the unit by talking about the picture
- Practice key vocabulary
- Practice listening skills

UNIT 4

Warm-up and review

- Before class. Write today's lesson focus on the board. *Lesson A: Accidents*
- Before class. On a large piece of paper, draw a picture of a person with his or her leg in a cast and walking on crutches, similar to the young woman in the picture on page 44. As an option, find a full-page picture from a magazine (but nothing too gruesome) that shows the aftermath of any type of accident.
- Begin class. Books closed. Point to the word *Accidents* on the board. Say the word. Ask Ss to repeat.
- Ask the class questions about the picture. For example, if you drew a man on crutches, ask Ss: *Did he have an accident?* (Yes.) *What happened? Did he fall?* (Yes. / No. / Maybe.) *Did he hurt his leg?* (Yes.) Pantomime walking on crutches and ask: *Is he on crutches?* (Yes.)
- Tell Ss: *This unit is about accidents and other health problems.*

Presentation

- Books open. Set the scene. Direct Ss' attention to the picture on page 44. Ask: *Where is this?* (a hospital / clinic / waiting room) Ask the question from Exercise **1A**: *What do you see?* Elicit and write on the board as much vocabulary about the picture as possible (chairs, computer, bandage, crutches, ladder, X-ray, etc.).
- Direct Ss' attention to the key words in Exercise **1B**. Read each phrase aloud while pointing to the corresponding part of the picture. Say: *This person (has a headache;* etc.). Ask the class to repeat and point to the picture.
- Listen to Ss' pronunciation and correct pronunciation as needed.

Comprehension check

- Ask Ss *Yes / No* questions about the picture. Recycle questions in the simple present, the simple past, and the present continuous. Say: *Listen to the questions. Answer "Yes" or "No."*
  Point to the big picture. Ask: *Is this a clinic?* (Yes.)
  Point to the man wearing a cap. Ask: *Does he have a headache?* (Yes.)
  Point to the woman seated in the foreground. Ask: *Is the woman sitting?* (Yes.)
  Point to the man looking at the X-rays. Ask: *Is he taking medicine?* (No.)
  Point to the young woman on crutches. Ask: *Did she hurt her hand?* (No.)
  Point to the man with the cell phone. Ask: *Did he hurt his leg?* (Yes.)
  Point to the girl with the green striped shirt. Ask: *Is the girl taking medicine?* (Yes.)

Practice

- Direct Ss' attention to Exercise **1B**. Model the exercise. Hold up the Student's Book. Say to a S: *Point to a person who is on crutches.* The S points to the appropriate part of the picture.
- Ss in pairs. Say to one S: *Say the vocabulary phrases in Exercise 1B.* Say to his or her partner: *Point to the correct part of the picture.*
- Walk around and help as needed. When pairs finish, have them switch roles. Then, ask Ss to repeat the exercise with new partners.
- Ask several pairs to perform the exercise for the class to check Ss' understanding.
- Direct Ss' attention to Exercise **1C** and read the questions aloud. Ask the class: *Where are these people?* Write Ss' responses on the board (a hospital / clinic / waiting room).
- Model the exercise. Point to the woman seated in the foreground. Ask a S: *What happened to her?* (She hurt her hand.)
- Ss complete the exercise in pairs. Help as needed. Ask several pairs to perform the exercise for the class.

Expansion activity *(whole group)*

- Direct Ss' attention to the sign on the front of the desk in the big picture. Ask the class: *What does this mean: "No Cell Phones"?* Elicit an appropriate response, for example: *It's a rule. They don't want people to use cell phones in the clinic.* Ask: *Why is the receptionist pointing to the sign?* Elicit an appropriate response, for example: *The man who hurt his leg is talking on a cell phone.*
- As a class, brainstorm and list on the board other similar expressions. For example, ask the class: *Can we smoke in this classroom?* Elicit: *No! There's no smoking in the school.* Other expressions might include: *no parking, no talking, no dogs, no trucks, no left turn.*

▼ **Teaching tip**
Ss of English may be confused by the term *smoke-free,* as in: "This is a smoke-free workplace." They might think the expression means that people are free to smoke, the opposite of the actual meaning.

Lesson A **T-44**

Lesson A Get ready

Presentation

- Books closed. Direct Ss' attention to the word *Accidents* written on the board. Say the word and ask Ss to repeat. Ask Ss: *Has anyone in the class ever had an accident? What happened?* Encourage Ss to talk about their experiences.
- Books open. Direct Ss' attention to the big picture on page 44. Point to the woman who hurt her hand and ask: *Do you think she had an accident? What happened?* Elicit possible scenarios. Do the same for the man who hurt his leg and the woman who hurt her foot or ankle. Encourage Ss to think of accidents the people in the picture might have had.
- Direct Ss' attention to the man who hurt his leg. Ask Ss: *What is his name?* (Hamid) Ask: *Who do you think Hamid is talking to on his cell phone?* Elicit, for example: *his wife; his friend; his brother.*

Practice

- Direct Ss' attention to the pictures in Exercise **2A**. Tell Ss: *These are the people Hamid is talking to on his cell phone.* Ask Ss to guess who the people in the pictures might be.
- Read aloud the instructions in Exercise **2A**.
- [Class Audio CD1 track 25] Play or read the audio program (see audio script, page T-154). Pause the audio program after the first conversation and ask Ss: *Who is Hamid talking to in conversation A?* (Lily, Picture 3) Hold up the Student's Book and write the letter *a* next to number 3. Make sure Ss understand the task.
- [Class Audio CD1 track 25] Play or read the rest of the audio program and repeat as needed.
- Check answers. Ask Ss which picture shows the person Hamid is talking to in the other conversations. (Chris, Picture 1; Mr. Jackson, Picture 2)
- Direct Ss' attention to Exercise **2B** and read the instructions aloud.
- [Class Audio CD1 track 25] Read aloud each group of sentences before listening to the corresponding conversation. Read aloud the three sentences for conversation A. Then, play or read conversation A on the audio program (see audio script, page T-154). Do the same for conversations B and C.
- Ss complete the exercise individually. When Ss are finished writing their answers, play or read the complete audio program once more to allow Ss to check the answers they wrote.

Comprehension check

- Check answers. Write the numbers *2–9* on the board. Ask for a few Ss to come to the board and write the correct answers to Exercise **2B** next to the numbers.
- [Class Audio CD1 track 25] Play or read the audio program again. Pause the program after each conversation. Point to each answer on the board. Ask: *Is this correct?*

Learner persistence *(individual work)*

- [Self-Study Audio CD track 15] Exercises **2A** and **2B** are recorded on the Ss' self-study CD at the back of the Student's Book. Ss can listen to the CD at home for reinforcement and review. They can also listen for self-directed learning when class attendance is not possible.

Expansion activity *(student pairs)*

- Have pairs practice the telephone conversations from Exercise **2B**. Ask Ss to turn to the Self-study audio script on page 157 in the Student's Book.
- Ask Ss to choose role *A* or *B* and read the conversations aloud. Three Ss will need to read conversation C.
- [Class Audio CD1 track 25] After Ss have practiced the conversations, ask them to close their books, relax, and listen to the audio program again.

Application

- Direct Ss' attention to Exercise **2C** and read the instructions aloud. Ss complete the exercise in pairs.
- On the board compile a list of dangerous jobs. Ask for volunteers to tell about accidents they've had at work.

Evaluation

- Direct Ss' attention to the lesson focus written on the board. Ask Ss to tell you about Hamid's accident.
- Pretend to have a hurt leg and a hurt hand. Ask Ss: *What happened to me?* Elicit: *You hurt your leg. You hurt your hand.* Pantomime and ask Ss to say the vocabulary for the actions of taking medicine, walking on crutches, and looking at an X-ray.
- Check off each part of the lesson focus as Ss demonstrate an understanding of what they have learned in the lesson.

> **More Ventures** *(whole group, pairs, individual)*
> Assign appropriate exercises from the *Teacher's Toolkit Audio CD / CD-ROM*, *Add Ventures*, or the *Workbook*.

UNIT 4

2 Listening

 A **Listen.** Who is Hamid talking to? Write the letter of the conversation.

1. _b_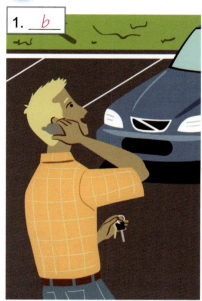
2. _c_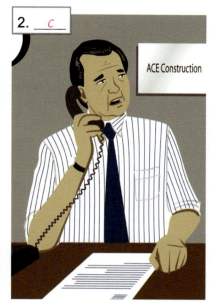
3. _a_

 B **Listen again.** Write *T* (true) or *F* (false).

Conversation A

1. Hamid had an accident at home.   _F_
2. Hamid is at the hospital.   _T_
3. Hamid will pick up his children.   _F_

Conversation B

4. Hamid hurt his leg.   _T_
5. Hamid had to get an X-ray.   _T_
6. The hospital is on 53rd Street.   _F_

Conversation C

7. Hamid works at Ace Construction.   _T_
8. Hamid has to finish the paint job.   _F_
9. Hamid will stay home tomorrow.   _T_

Listen again. Check your answers.

C **Talk** with a partner. Ask and answer the questions.

1. What jobs are dangerous? Why?
2. Did you ever have an accident at work? What happened?
3. Did you ever have an accident at home? What happened?

Health 45

Lesson B *What do I have to do?*

1 Grammar focus: have to + verb

Questions					Answers			
What	do does do	I he they	have to do?		You He They	have to has to have to	see a doctor.

For a complete grammar chart, turn to page 147.

2 Practice

A Write. Complete the conversations. Use *have to* or *has to*, and *do* or *does*.

1. **A** Elian hurt his leg.
   What __does__ he __have to__ do?
   B He __has to__ get an X-ray.

2. **A** Kathy and Tom have asthma.
   What __do__ they __have to__ do?
   B They __have to__ take their medicine.

3. **A** My son broke his arm.
   What __do__ I __have to__ do?
   B You __have to__ take him to the hospital.

4. **A** Marcia has a sprained ankle.
   What __does__ she __have to__ do?
   B She __has to__ get a pair of crutches.

5. **A** Nick and Tony had an accident at work.
   What __do__ they __have to__ do?
   B They __have to__ fill out an accident report.

6. **A** Pam hurt her back.
   What __does__ she __have to__ do?
   B She __has to__ go home early.

Listen and repeat. Then practice with a partner.

46 Unit 4

Lesson objectives
- Introduce *have to* + verb
- Practice expressing necessity
- Identify appropriate action after an accident
- Introduce terms on medicine packaging

Warm-up and review

- Before class. Write today's lesson focus on the board.
  Lesson B:
  <u>have to</u> + verb
  After an accident: What do you have to do?
- Begin class. Books open. Recycle vocabulary from Lesson A as you assess Ss' prior knowledge of *have to* + verb. Direct Ss' attention to page 45. Ask the class: *Do you remember Hamid? What happened to him?* (He had an accident. He fell off a ladder.) *Was Hamid hurt?* (Yes, he hurt his leg.) *Where did he have to go after the accident?* (to the hospital) *Did he have to get an X-ray at the hospital?* (Yes.) *Who did Hamid have to call after the accident?* (his wife, his friend, and his boss)

Presentation

- Direct Ss' attention to the grammar chart in Exercise **1**. Read the questions and answers aloud. Ask Ss to repeat.
- Ss in pairs. Have Ss practice reading the grammar chart to each other while pointing to an appropriate person or persons in the class (I, you, he, they).

Comprehension check

- Call on individual Ss to answer the questions from the chart. Use people in the class as subjects, for example: *What do I have to do?* (You have to see a doctor.) *What does Elly have to do?* (She has to see a doctor.) *What do Tomoko and Larry have to do?* (They have to see a doctor.)

Expansion activity *(whole group)*

- If you want to expand the grammar presentation, turn to the grammar charts on page 147. Practice asking questions and giving answers using *have to* + verb and the pronouns *we, it,* and *you (plural)*.

Practice

- Direct Ss' attention to the pictures in Exercise **2A**. Point to the boy in the wheelchair. Ask: *What happened to him?* Elicit: *He hurt his leg.* Point to the two children with inhalers. Ask: *What are they doing?* Elicit: *They're taking medicine.*
- Read aloud the instructions in Exercise **2A**. Ask two Ss to read the example sentences. Remind Ss to use the grammar chart as they do the exercise.
- Ss complete the sentences individually. Walk around and help as needed.

▼ **Teaching tip**
Remind Ss that the auxiliary forms *does* and *has* are used with *he* and *she*, and the forms *do* and *have* are used with *I, you,* and *they*.

Comprehension check

- Check answers with the class. Ask Ss to write their answers on the board. Ask different Ss to read the answers aloud. Ask Ss: *Are these answers correct?* Make corrections on the board.
- Read aloud the second part of the instructions in Exercise **2A**.
- [Class Audio CD1 track 26] Play or read the audio program (see audio script, page T-155). Listen to Ss' pronunciation as they repeat the questions and answers. Correct pronunciation as needed.
- Have pairs practice the questions and answers in Exercise **2A**. Listen for any words Ss have trouble pronouncing. Write those words on the board; then, say the words several times for the class to repeat.

Expansion activity *(whole group)*

- Brainstorm different ways of taking medicine. The children in Exercise **2A** are using inhalers, but "taking medicine" can also mean swallowing capsules or tablets. People with health problems also take liquids or syrups, use eye drops, get injections, or wear a skin patch to take their medicine.
- Discuss this vocabulary and use pantomime and the board to show the various forms of taking medication.

Lesson B

Lesson B   What do I have to do?

Presentation

- Write on the board: *pharmacist*. Direct Ss' attention to the picture of the pharmacist in Exercise **2B**. Tell Ss: *A pharmacist knows a lot about medicine. He or she can tell you what you have to do to take medicine.*
- Read aloud the five warning labels next to the picture of the pharmacist in Exercise **2B**. Ask Ss to repeat. Explain any unfamiliar words, such as *freeze* or *shake*.

Practice

- Read aloud the instructions for Exercise **2B**. Ask two Ss to read the example conversation aloud. Explain any unfamiliar words, such as *prescription*.
- Model the exercise. Read aloud the first part of the conversation using the words in the second warning label: *Here's your prescription. You have to take this medicine in the morning.* Ask for a volunteer to continue the conversation with the *B* role.
- Ss complete the exercise in pairs. Walk around and help as needed.
- Ask several pairs to perform the conversations for the rest of the class.

> **Useful language**
> Read aloud the expressions in the Useful language box. Have Ss repeat each expression. Ask them to find one of the useful expressions in the conversation. (Ss should find *OK* at the beginning of the third line.) Explain that these expressions mean you are listening and you understand what another person is saying.

Expansion activity (student pairs)

- Have Ss practice the conversations in Exercise **2B** again using these useful expressions: *I understand* and *Yes, I see.*

Expansion activity (student pairs)

- Brainstorm expressions to use when Ss do not understand what another person is saying, for example: *I'm sorry, I didn't catch that. / I'm sorry, could you repeat that? / Pardon me?*

> **Culture note**
> Read aloud the Culture note. If possible, show Ss some examples of actual warning labels on empty prescription bottles. Tell Ss that it's important to read the warning labels on prescription medicines.

Application

- Direct Ss' attention to Exercise **3** and read the instructions aloud. Ask two Ss to read the example conversation.
- Ss complete the exercise in pairs. Walk around and help as needed.
- When Ss are finished, ask them to find new partners to have new conversations.
- Ask several pairs to perform one of the conversations for the class. Encourage Ss to give details about where the people in the pictures are and what they're doing. Supply any vocabulary words Ss need.

Expansion activity (individual work)

- List on the board new vocabulary from the unit, for example: *accident, crutches, freeze, headache, hurt, ladder, pharmacist, prescription, shake, X-ray.*
- Have Ss write a paragraph about one of the people in the picture on page 44. Ask them to use at least four of the vocabulary words in their writing and to use *have to* + verb at least once.
- Follow up by having Ss exchange papers to read each other's work. You could also collect the paragraphs and return them to Ss with feedback.

Evaluation

- Direct Ss' attention to the lesson focus written on the board. Call on Ss to tell you what a person has to do when faced with the following situations. Ask: *When you _____, what do you have to do?* Use the unit vocabulary: *have a headache, hurt your leg, hurt your hand, have an accident, get prescription medicine from a pharmacist.* Elicit responses with *have to* + verb, for example: *You have to get an X-ray.*
- Check off each part of the lesson focus as Ss demonstrate an understanding of what they have learned in the lesson.

> **More Ventures** (whole group, pairs, individual)
> Assign appropriate exercises from the *Teacher's Toolkit Audio CD / CD-ROM, Add Ventures,* or the *Workbook.*

B Talk with a partner. Change the **bold** words and make conversations.

A Here's your prescription. You have to **keep** this medicine **in the refrigerator**.
B OK. I have to **keep** this medicine **in the refrigerator**.
A Yes. Call me if you have any questions.

Useful language
OK.
I understand.
Yes, I see.

Culture note
Warning labels on medicine say what you should and shouldn't do.

3 Communicate

Talk with a partner. What happened to these people? What do they have to do?

She burned her hand.   She has to see a doctor.

Pharmex Original Copyrighted Warning Label information was printed with authorization from TimeMed Labeling Systems, Inc.

Health 47

Lesson C You should go to the hospital.

1 Grammar focus: should

Questions

| What | should | I / she / they | do? |

Answers

| You / She / They | should | go to the hospital. |

| You / She / They | shouldn't | work. |

For a complete grammar chart, turn to page 149.

shouldn't = should not

2 Practice

A Write. Complete the conversations. Use *should* or *shouldn't*.

1. **A** Ken's eyes hurt. What ___should___ he do?
   B He should rest. He ___shouldn't___ read right now.

2. **A** They have stomachaches. What ___should___ they do?
   B They ___shouldn't___ eat. They ___should___ take some medicine.

3. **A** My tooth hurts. What ___should___ I do?
   B You ___should___ see a dentist.

4. **A** Mia has a headache. What ___should___ she do?
   B She ___should___ take some aspirin.

5. **A** I hurt my leg. What ___should___ I do?
   B You ___should___ get an X-ray.
   You ___shouldn't___ walk.

6. **A** I have a bottle of medicine. What ___should___ I do?
   B You ___should___ keep it in the refrigerator.
   You ___shouldn't___ freeze it.

🎧 **Listen and repeat.** Then practice with a partner.

Lesson objectives
- Introduce *should*
- Practice giving advice about health problems

Warm-up and review
- Before class. Write today's lesson focus on the board.
  Lesson C:
  Should
  Giving advice about health problems
- Before class. Write on the board some of the actions from Lesson B: *go to the hospital, get a pair of crutches, take your medicine, fill out an accident report, get an X-ray.*
- Begin class. Books closed. Ask the class to read aloud the actions written on the board. Explain any words Ss don't know.
- Say and, when possible, act out some of the health problems from the unit. Ask Ss what you have to do in each case, for example:
  I hurt my foot. What do I have to do?
  I have asthma. What do I have to do?
  I had an accident here at the school. What do I have to do?
  I fell and broke my arm. What do I have to do?
- Accept any logical responses using *have to* + the verb phrases written on the board, or any others.

Presentation
- Books open. Direct Ss' attention to the grammar chart in Exercise **1**. Read each question aloud. After each question, read aloud both the affirmative and the negative answers. Ask Ss to repeat the questions and answers.
- Explain that *should* is used for giving advice – a helpful idea one person gives another. *Should* recommends that someone act in a certain way in a given situation. *Should* is different from *have to* because it only suggests a course of action. *Have to* is stronger. It means that there is no other choice.
- Have pairs of students practice reading the grammar chart to each other while pointing to an appropriate person in the class (I, you, she, they).

Contractions
Direct Ss' attention to the word *shouldn't* in the grammar chart. Say the word and ask Ss to repeat. Explain that *shouldn't* has the same meaning as the two words *should not*.

▼ **Teaching tip**
The word *shouldn't* may be difficult for some Ss to pronounce. You can help by clapping the two syllables in the word and explaining that the first syllable is the strong syllable. It might also be helpful to practice the vowel sound in the context of a list of familiar words, such as *book, put,* and *good*.

Comprehension check
- Call on Ss to answer the questions from the chart. Preface the questions with a health problem, for example, a hurt back. Use people in the class as subjects, for example: *I hurt my back! What should I do?* (You should go to the hospital.) *Martina hurt her back! What should she do?* (She should go to the hospital.) *Ron and Lee hurt their backs! What should they do?* (They should go to the hospital.)

Expansion activity *(whole group)*
- Expand the grammar presentation by using the grammar charts on page 149. Practice asking questions and giving affirmative and negative answers using *should* and the pronouns *he, we, it,* and *you* (plural).

Practice
- Direct Ss' attention to the pictures in Exercise **2A**. Ask Ss: *What happened to him? / What happened to them?* Elicit sentences about the situations in the simple past, for example: *He read too many books* or *They ate a lot of desserts.*
- Read aloud the instructions for Exercise **2A**. Ask two Ss to read the example question and answer. Remind Ss to use the grammar chart as they do the exercise.
- Ss complete the questions and answers individually. Walk around and help as needed.

Comprehension check
- Check answers. Ask Ss to write their answers on the board. Ask different Ss to read the answers.
- Read aloud the second part of the instructions for Exercise **2A**.
- [Class Audio CD1 track 27] Play or read the audio program (see audio script, page T-155). Listen to Ss' pronunciation as they repeat the questions and answers. Correct pronunciation as needed.
- Have Ss practice the conversations in pairs. Walk around and help as needed.

Lesson C   **T-48**

Lesson C You should go to the hospital.

Practice
- Books open. Direct Ss' attention to Exercise **2B** and read the instructions aloud.
- Read aloud the verb phrases under each picture and ask Ss to repeat. Explain any words Ss don't know.
- Ss complete the exercise individually.

Comprehension check
- Check answers as a class. Go over each action and ask Ss, for example: *Should Al drink lots of water?* When the answer is "yes," make a check mark on the board to indicate that Ss should have checked that answer in their books.
- Read aloud the second part of the instructions in Exercise **2B**. Ask two Ss to read the example conversation aloud. Make sure Ss understand that they can use any combination of the actions in the exercise to talk about what Al should and shouldn't do.

> **Useful language**
> Read the expressions in the Useful language box. Ask Ss to repeat and to find one of the expressions in the example conversation (it's in the last line). Encourage Ss to use both expressions as they practice the conversations in Exercise **2B**.

- Have pairs practice the conversations in Exercise **2B**. Walk around and help as needed.
- Ask several pairs to perform one of the possible conversations.

▼ **Teaching tip**
Teachers have a good opportunity to listen carefully to individual Ss' pronunciation while Ss are practicing conversations in pairs. Use your discretion as to whether it's better to interrupt a conversation to make corrections or give praise, or to make a note of what you hear and go over the pronunciation point with the whole class when the conversations are finished.

Application
- Direct Ss' attention to Exercise **3** and read the instructions aloud.
- Point to each picture and talk about the problem. Say, for example: *Teresa has a problem. Her wrist is very sore.* Explain any words Ss don't know.
- Ss complete the exercise in small groups. Ask each group to choose one person to be the discussion leader. Explain the role of the discussion leader and write it on the board:
  1. *For each picture, read aloud the situation and the question.*
  2. *Ask every person in your group to talk and give advice.*
- When Ss are finished, ask each group to share some of its ideas with the class.

Expansion activity *(whole group)*
- Ask the class questions about the pictures on page 49 that elicit new vocabulary, for example: *What is he wearing?* (a hat) *What is she doing?* (She's holding her wrist.) *Where are they sitting?* (on the floor) Write correct responses on the board and ask Ss to repeat. Supply vocabulary Ss don't know.
- Be sure to ask questions about pictures with objects the Ss might be interested in. Ask: *What is this?* Elicit, for example: *a water bottle; a lawn mower; a hammer.*

Community building *(whole group)*
- Have a class discussion about the different kinds of places in your community that offer health-care services. Make sure Ss know about the Emergency Room (ER) at a hospital, urgent care centers, clinics, or doctors' offices. If possible, bring to class information about these places with addresses and phone numbers and the types of health problems each one treats. Ss need to know that most clinics or doctors' offices require appointments and treat only non-urgent problems. Urgent care centers may be the most affordable places to go for minor emergencies, and the ER is the place to go for more serious situations.

Evaluation
- Direct Ss' attention to the lesson focus written on the board. Ask one S to say a health problem, for example: *I hurt my leg.* Ask another S to give advice using *should,* for example: *You should get an X-ray.* Ask a third S to give advice using *shouldn't,* for example: *You shouldn't walk.* Repeat the process.
- Check off each part of the lesson focus as Ss demonstrate an understanding of what they learned in the lesson.

> **More Ventures** *(whole group, pairs, individual)*
> Assign appropriate exercises from the *Teacher's Toolkit Audio CD / CD-ROM, Add Ventures,* or the *Workbook.*

B Look at the pictures. Al is gardening. It's very hot. Check (✓) the things he should do.

☑ Drink lots of water. ☐ Wear heavy clothes. ☑ Take a break.

☑ Use a wet towel. ☐ Stay in the sun. ☑ Stay in the shade.

Talk with a partner. Look at the pictures again. Change the **bold** words and make conversations.

> A Al doesn't feel well. What should he do?
> B He should **drink lots of water**. He shouldn't **stay in the sun**.
> A OK. I'll tell him.

Useful language
I'll tell him.
I'll let him know.

3 Communicate

Talk in a group. Read the problems. Give advice.

Teresa's wrist is very sore. What should she do?

Ed is very hot. He doesn't feel well. What should he do?

Susana fell off her chair. What should her mother do?

Lesson D Reading

1 Before you read

Look at the picture. Answer the questions.

1. Who is the man?
2. What is he doing?
3. What should he do?

2 Read

Read the warning label. Listen and read again.

- Face the ladder when climbing up and down.
- Don't carry a lot of equipment while climbing a ladder – wear a tool belt.
- Never stand on the shelf of the ladder – stand on the steps.
- Never stand on the top step of a ladder.
- Be safe! Always read and follow the safety stickers.

Lists often begin with a number or bullet (•). Each numbered or bulleted item is a new idea.

3 After you read

A Write. Complete the sentences. Use *should* or *shouldn't*.

1. You ___shouldn't___ carry a lot of equipment while climbing a ladder.
2. You ___should___ read and follow the safety stickers.
3. You ___should___ face the ladder when climbing up or down.
4. You ___shouldn't___ stand on the shelf of the ladder.

B Write. Complete the paragraph.

| accidents | ladder | safe | safety | tool belt |

Culture note
In emergencies, dial 911 for help.

Be Careful in the Workplace!

Don't have ___accidents___ at work. Always read the ___safety___
    1   2
stickers on your tools and equipment. When you climb a ___ladder___, wear
                                                           3
a ___tool belt___. When you carry heavy items, ask someone to help you.
     4
We want our workers to be ___safe___ and healthy.
                              5

50 Unit 4

Lesson objectives
- Introduce and read a warning label
- Understand a bulleted list
- Practice using new topic-related words

Warm-up and review

- Before class. Write today's lesson focus on the board.
  Lesson D:
  Read and understand a warning label
  Read and understand a bulleted list
  Learn vocabulary for health problems
- Begin class. Books closed. Review the use of *should* and *shouldn't*.
- Fan yourself as if it's very hot in your classroom. Say to the class: *It's very hot today! What should I do?* Elicit responses, for example: *You should drink lots of water. You should take a break. You should stay in the shade.* Repeat the advice Ss give you, emphasizing *should* (e.g., *I should drink lots of water*).
- Ask Ss: *What shouldn't I do?* Elicit responses such as: *You shouldn't stay in the sun* or *You shouldn't wear heavy clothes*. This time, emphasize *shouldn't* as you repeat Ss' responses (e.g., *Right, I shouldn't stay in the sun today*.)

Presentation

- Books open. Direct Ss' attention to Exercise **1** and read the instructions aloud. Point to the picture of the man and ask Ss: *Who is the man?* (Hamid, the man who had an accident) Ask: *What is happening in the picture?* (He is painting. He is standing on the shelf of a ladder. He is going to fall, etc.)
- Ask the class the remaining questions in Exercise **1**. Discuss Ss' ideas about what Hamid is doing wrong and what he should do instead.

Read the tip box aloud. Ask Ss how many bullets they see in the reading in Exercise **2** (five). Write a numbered list on the board so that Ss can see what that type of list looks like.

Practice

- Read aloud the instructions for Exercise **2**. Ask Ss to read the warning label silently.
- [Class Audio CD1 track 28] Play or read the audio program and ask Ss to read along (see audio script, page T-155). Repeat the audio program as needed.
- Answer any questions Ss have about the reading.

Comprehension check

- Ask Ss *True / False* questions about the warning label by using *should* and *shouldn't*. Tell Ss: *Listen to the sentence. Say "True" or "False."*
  Say: *You should read the warning label to prevent accidents.* (True.)
  Say: *You should face the ladder when you climb up and down.* (True.)
  Say: *You should carry a lot of equipment when you climb a ladder.* (False.)
  Say: *You shouldn't stand on the shelf of a ladder.* (True.)
  Say: *You shouldn't read safety stickers.* (False.)

Learner persistence (individual work)

- [Self-Study Audio CD track 16] Exercise **2** is recorded on the Ss' self-study CD at the back of the Student's Book. Ss can listen to the CD at home for reinforcement and review. They can also listen to the CD for self-directed learning when class attendance is not possible.

Practice

- Direct Ss' attention to Exercise **3A** and read the instructions aloud. Ask a S to read the example sentence.
- Ss complete the exercise individually. Walk around and help as needed.
- Check answers with the class. Explain any words Ss don't know.
- Read aloud the words in the word bank in Exercise **3B**. Ask Ss to repeat. If Ss are still not sure about the meaning of words, such as *tool belt* or *safety stickers*, point out those items in the picture at the top of the page.
- Read aloud the instructions for Exercise **3B**. Ask a S to read the example sentence aloud.
- Ss complete the exercise individually. Walk around and help as needed.
- Go over answers with the class. Write the numbers *2–5* on the board. Ask a few Ss to come to the board and write the correct answers to Exercise **3B** next to the numbers.
- Call on individual Ss to each read aloud one sentence of the paragraph.

Culture note
Read the Culture note aloud. Find out whether Ss have any questions about calling 911.

Lesson D   T-50

Lesson D Reading

Warm-up and review
- Write on the board: *Health problems*. Direct Ss' attention to the big picture on page 44 in Lesson A. Ask Ss: *What health problems do these people have?* Elicit unit vocabulary: *headache, a hurt leg, asthma,* etc.

Presentation
- Direct Ss' attention to the pictures in the picture dictionary in Exercise 4. Tell Ss: *These people have health problems, too.* Ask the class: *Do you know the words for any of these health problems?* Elicit any vocabulary Ss already know, for example: *high blood pressure; allergies; a cut; a rash.*

▼ **Teaching tip**
Don't worry if Ss don't know the vocabulary in the picture dictionary yet. Assessing prior knowledge tells you how much time you'll need to spend on new material.

- Direct Ss' attention to the word bank. Say each word in the word bank and ask Ss to repeat. Listen to Ss' pronunciation. Correct pronunciation as needed.

Practice
- Tell Ss: *Write the words in the picture dictionary.* Point to the first example, which has been done. Make sure Ss understand the exercise.
- Ss complete the exercise individually. Walk around and help as needed.

Comprehension check
- 💿 [Class Audio CD1 track 29] Say: *Listen and repeat.* Play or read the audio program (see audio script, page T-155). Ss should check their answers and repeat the words after they hear them. Repeat the audio program if necessary.

Learner persistence (individual work)
- 💿 [Self-Study Audio CD track 17] Exercises 4A and 4B are recorded on the Ss' self-study CD at the back of the Student's Book. Ss can listen to the CD at home for reinforcement and review. They can also listen to the CD for self-directed learning when class attendance is not possible.

Expansion activity (student pairs)
- Write on the board: *What happened to this person?* Ask Ss to look at the nine pictures in the picture dictionary and for each picture, to answer the question on the board.

- Model the activity: Point to the first picture or hold up the picture dictionary card from the *Teacher's Toolkit Audio CD / CD-ROM.* Say: *The woman has chills. I think she went to a party. She met a lot of people and shook hands. After that, she got sick.*
- Ss complete the activity in pairs. When Ss are finished, write the numbers 2–9 on the board, leaving some space around each number. For each number, ask Ss: *What happened to this person?* List Ss' ideas.

Practice
- Direct Ss to Exercise 4B and read the instructions aloud. Model the example conversation with a S. Point to the first picture and read aloud the *A* role in the conversation. Have the S read the *B* role.
- Ss practice the conversation in pairs. Make sure Ss understand that they should use the health problems in the picture dictionary, along with any good advice they can think of.
- Help with vocabulary and pronunciation as needed.
- Ask several pairs to say one of their conversations for the class. Write Ss' advice on the board and explain any words that might be new to some Ss.

Expansion activity (whole group)
- Write the nine words from the picture dictionary on the board, leaving some space around each one.
- Compile a class list of advice. Point to each health problem and ask Ss what a person with that problem should and shouldn't do. Write Ss' responses on the board.

Evaluation
- Direct Ss' attention to the lesson focus written on the board. Ask a S to come to the board and write a bulleted list. Ask other Ss to tell you about ladder safety. Act out some of the health problems from the picture dictionary and have Ss call out the correct vocabulary.
- Check off each part of the lesson focus as Ss demonstrate an understanding of what they have learned in the lesson.

> **More Ventures** *(whole group, pairs, individual)*
> Assign appropriate exercises from the *Teacher's Toolkit Audio CD / CD-ROM, Add Ventures,* or the *Workbook.*

4 Picture dictionary — Health problems

 1. _chills_

 2. _a sprained wrist_

 3. _chest pains_

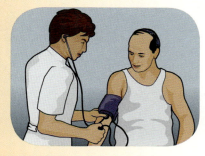 4. _high blood pressure_

 5. _allergies_

 6. _a swollen knee_

 7. _a bad cut_

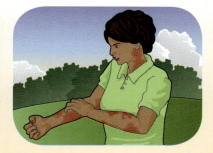 8. _a rash_

 9. _a stiff neck_

A Write the words in the picture dictionary. Then listen and repeat.

allergies	chills	a sprained wrist
a bad cut	high blood pressure	a stiff neck
chest pains	a rash	a swollen knee

B Talk with a partner. Change the **bold** words and make conversations.

A **She** has **chills**. What should **she** do?
B **She** should **stay in bed and rest**.

Health

Lesson E Writing

1 Before you write

A Talk with a partner. What happened to this woman?

B Read the accident report.

ACCIDENT REPORT FORM

Employee name: *Komiko Yanaka*

Date of accident: *January 13, 2008*   Time: *9:00 p.m.*

Type of injury: *cut foot*

How did the accident happen? *Every night, I cut vegetables in the kitchen. Last night, the knife slipped and cut my foot. I have to go to the doctor tomorrow.*

Signature: *Komiko Yanaka*   Date: *1/14/08*

C Write. Answer the questions about the accident report.

1. Who had an accident? *Komiko Yanaka.*
2. When did the accident happen? *January 13, 2008.*
3. What was the injury? *A cut foot.*
4. How did the injury happen? *The knife slipped and cut her foot.*
5. When did she complete the form? *January 14, 2008.*

> **Lesson objectives**
> - Write an accident report form
> - Use cursive writing in a signature

Warm-up and review

- Before class. Write today's lesson focus on the board.
  Lesson E:
  Complete an accident report form
  Use cursive writing in a signature
- Begin class. Books open. Point to the first part of the lesson focus. Say: *Today, you will fill out an accident report form.*
- Direct Ss' attention back to page 46 in Lesson B. Point to Exercise **2** on that page and ask Ss: *Who had to fill out an accident report?* Elicit: *Nick and Tony in number 5.* Ask two Ss to read the conversation in number 5 for the class.
- Ask Ss: *When do people write accident reports?* (after they have had an accident at work) Ask Ss: *Who reads an accident report?* (a person's boss or supervisor)

Practice

- Direct Ss' attention to the pictures in Exercise **1A** on page 52. Ask Ss: *Where is this woman?* (in a restaurant kitchen) Ask Ss: *What is her job?* (She is a cook or chef.)
- Read aloud the instructions in Exercise **1A**. Ss talk in pairs about what happened to the woman.
- Call on several Ss to explain what happened to the woman.
- Direct Ss' attention to the accident report in Exercise **1B**. Read the instructions aloud. Ss read the report silently. Explain any words Ss don't know.

Comprehension check

- Direct Ss' attention to Exercise **1C**. Read the instructions aloud and ask a S to read the example question aloud. Ask the class: *What is the woman's name?* (Komiko Yanaka) Point to where the name has been written in the example.
- Ss complete the exercise individually. When Ss are finished, have them compare answers with a partner. Clear up any confusion about the accident report form.

▼ Culture tip
Ss might be interested to know why employers want a formal report after a workplace accident. Tell Ss that in the United States, employers are required to have insurance in case employees are hurt or become ill at work. Explain that an employer's workers' compensation insurance pays for necessary medical care. Accident reports are a way for the employer to provide information to the insurance company about the employee's accident or illness.

Expansion activity *(whole group)*

- Conduct a class discussion about what Komiko Yanaka "should" or "shouldn't" do in the future.
- Ask Ss: *What should Komiko Yanaka do so that she doesn't cut her foot again?* Write Ss' advice on the board, for example: *She should be very careful with the knife. She shouldn't cut vegetables with wet hands. She should wear shoes instead of sandals at work.*

Community building *(small groups)*

- Have Ss talk to their classmates about their workplaces. Ask Ss to describe their jobs as well as any accidents that have happened at their place of work.
- Write on the board:
  Describe your workplace.
  Describe what you do at work.
  Is your workplace safe or dangerous? Why?
  Describe any accidents that have happened at your workplace.
- Ask each group to choose one person to be the discussion leader. Explain that the discussion leader will make sure that everyone in the group talks about all the topics listed on the board.
- If you have Ss who do not work or who work at home, ask them to talk about past workplaces or accidents and safety in the home.
- Ss will gain new respect for their classmates when they learn about one another's life experiences.

Lesson E   T-52

Lesson E Writing

Practice

- Direct Ss' attention to Exercise **1D** and read the instructions aloud.
- Model the exercise. Read aloud the sentence, *Yesterday, I cut my foot*. Ask Ss: *What happened first?* Elicit: *I was in the kitchen*. Point to where the number 1 has been written.
- If you think Ss may still be unsure about the exercise, ask: *What happened next?* and *What happened then?* Point to where Ss should write number 2 and number 3.
- Ss complete the exercise individually. Walk around and help as needed.
- Ask Ss to compare their answers with those of a partner. Then, call on Ss to read the sentences in order. Ask: *Is that correct?* If there is an error, ask other Ss to explain the problem.

Application

- Direct Ss' attention to Exercise **2** and read the instructions aloud. Point to Exercise **1B** on page 52 and Exercise **1D** on page 53 so that Ss know where to look for ideas for completing the accident report.
- Ss complete the accident report form individually. Walk around and help with vocabulary, grammar, and punctuation.

Read the tip box aloud. Ask for volunteers to write their signatures on the board using cursive writing.

▼ **Teaching tip**
Remind Ss to use the sequence words *First*, *Next*, and *Then* or other sequence words they know in order to make their writing clear.

Comprehension check

- Ss in pairs. Direct Ss' attention to Exercise **3A** and read the instructions aloud.
- Have pairs take turns reading their accident reports to each other. Help with pronunciation as needed.
- Direct Ss' attention to Exercise **3B** and read the instructions aloud. Ask a S to read the three questions to the class.
- Ask Ss to take out a piece of paper and to write the three questions from Exercise **3B**.
- Have Ss exchange accident reports. Tell Ss: *Read your partner's accident report. Write answers to the three questions.*
- When Ss are finished, have pairs share their answers and discuss their accident report forms.

Expansion activity *(individual students)*

- Give Ss practice filling out real accident report forms.
- Request accident report forms from your school and workplaces in your community. Choose a report form that matches your Ss' English level fairly well.
- Make enough photocopies of the form for everyone in the class.
- Have Ss complete the form individually. Walk around and help as needed.
- Collect the forms and give Ss individual feedback, or have partners engage in peer-assessment.

▼ **Teaching tip**
Many Ss do not learn cursive writing when they learn the English alphabet, so they may have trouble writing or even reading cursive script. The Internet has many educational Web sites where you can find resources ranging from handouts with traceable letters to samples of different cursive styles.

Evaluation

- Direct Ss' attention to the lesson focus written on the board. Ask Ss if they can fill out an accident report form now. Ask a S to come to the board and sign his or her name using cursive writing.
- Check off each part of the lesson focus as Ss demonstrate an understanding of what they have learned in the lesson.

More Ventures *(whole group, pairs, individual)*
Assign appropriate exercises from the *Teacher's Toolkit Audio CD / CD-ROM*, *Add Ventures*, or the *Workbook*.

D Write. Work with a partner. Read the sentences. Number the sentences in the correct order.

1. Yesterday, I cut my foot.
   - _3_ It fell on my foot.
   - _2_ The knife slipped.
   - _1_ I was in the kitchen.

2. Yesterday, I sprained my ankle.
   - _1_ There was water on the floor.
   - _3_ I have to fill out an accident report.
   - _2_ I slipped.

3. Yesterday, I broke my leg.
   - _2_ I fell.
   - _3_ I went to the hospital.
   - _1_ I was at the top of a ladder.

4. Yesterday, I hurt my back.
   - _2_ I felt a terrible pain in my back.
   - _1_ I picked up a heavy box.
   - _3_ I have to see a doctor tomorrow.

2 Write

Complete the accident report form. Use your imagination or write about a real accident. Use Exercises 1B and 1D to help you.

ACCIDENT REPORT FORM

Employee name: _(Answers will vary.)_____

Date of accident: _____   Time: _____

Type of injury: _____

How did the accident happen? _____

_____

_____

_____

Signature: _____   Date: _____

Your signature on a form makes it official. For a signature, use cursive writing. Don't print.

Carl Staley
~~Carl Staley~~

3 After you write

A Read your form to a partner.

B Check your partner's form.
- What was the injury?
- What was the date of the accident?
- Is there a signature on the form?

Health 53

Lesson F Another view

1 Life-skills reading

Drug facts	
Active ingredient (in each tablet)	**Purpose**
Acetaminophen 325 mg . . . . Pain reliever	
Uses Temporary relief of minor aches and pains	
Warnings	
Ask a doctor or pharmacist before use if you are taking a prescription drug.	
Ask a doctor before use if you have liver or kidney disease.	
When using this product, do not take more than directed.	
Can cause drowsiness.	
Keep out of reach of children.	
Directions	
Adults and children 12 years and over: Take 2 tablets every 4 to 6 hours as needed. Do not take more than 8 tablets in 24 hours.	
Children under 12 years of age: Ask a doctor.	

A Read the questions. Look at the medicine label. Circle the answers.

1. Why should you take this medicine?
   a. **for aches and pains** ✓
   b. for drowsiness
   c. for kidney disease
   d. for liver disease

2. How many tablets should children under 12 take at one time?
   a. 2 tablets
   b. 4 tablets
   c. no tablets
   d. **none of the above** ✓

3. How many tablets should an adult take at one time?
   a. **2 tablets** ✓
   b. 4 tablets
   c. 6 tablets
   d. 8 tablets

4. How many tablets can an adult take in one day?
   a. **8 tablets** ✓
   b. 12 tablets
   c. 24 tablets
   d. none of the above

B Talk with a partner. Ask and answer the questions.

1. Your father has a headache. How many tablets should you give him?
2. Your son is four years old. Should you give him any tablets?
3. Jane has kidney disease. She wants to take a tablet. What does she have to do first?
4. Paul is taking a prescription drug. He wants to take this medicine. What should he do?

Lesson objectives
- Practice reading a medicine label
- Review unit vocabulary
- Introduce the project
- Complete the project and self-assessment

Warm-up and review

- Before class. Write today's lesson focus on the board.
  Lesson F:
  Read a medicine label
  Review topic vocabulary
  Complete the project and the self-assessment

- Begin class. Books open. Direct Ss' attention to the big picture on page 44 at the beginning of the unit. Ask Ss questions to review unit vocabulary and grammar, for example: *What health problem does this girl have?* (asthma) *What is she doing?* (taking her medicine) *What happened to this man?* (He hurt his leg.) *What does he have to do?* (get an X-ray)

- Point to the man with a headache. Ask Ss: *What should he do?* Ss may answer: *He should take some aspirin.* If Ss don't suggest aspirin or some other pain reliever, you can suggest it. Then, ask Ss: *How many aspirin should he take?* (Ss will probably say different numbers.) Ask: *How do we know how much medicine to take?* Elicit logical responses; if *from information on the medicine package or bottle* is not one of the responses, mention it yourself.

Presentation

- Direct Ss' attention to Lesson F and to the medicine label above Exercise **1A**. Tell Ss: *This is a medicine label.* If possible, show Ss some real over-the-counter medicine packages or bottles with labels.

- Read aloud the major sections of the label: *Drug facts, Active Ingredient, Uses, Warnings, Directions.* Ask Ss to repeat.

- Ask a few comprehension questions to encourage Ss to preview and think about the label, for example: *What is an ingredient?* (something in the medicine) *Why do people take this medicine?* (temporary relief of minor aches and pains) *Why are there warnings on the label?* (The medicine could be dangerous for some people; so people know if the medicine is safe; etc.)

Practice

- Read aloud the instructions for Exercise **1A**. This exercise prepares Ss for standardized-type tests they may have to take. Make sure Ss understand the exercise. Have Ss individually scan for and circle the correct answers. Walk around and help as needed.

Comprehension check

- Check the answers to Exercise **1A** with the class. Make sure Ss followed the instructions and circled their answers.

- Ss in pairs. Tell Ss: *Ask and answer the questions in Exercise 1A.* Encourage Ss to use complete sentences.

Application

- Read aloud the instructions for Exercise **1B**. Have pairs ask and answer the questions.

- Go over each question and ask for volunteers to give their answers. As Ss answer the questions, refer back to the medicine label; for example: *That's right. The directions say your father should take two tablets because he is an adult.*

Expansion activity *(whole group)*

- Go over the medicine label in detail and discuss any words Ss don't know, for example: *minor aches and pains; prescription drug; liver or kidney disease; drowsiness,* etc.

▼ **Teaching tip**
Emphasize the importance of reading labels on any kind of medicine package. Ss may feel intimidated by the somewhat technical language on labels, but knowing where to look for important information such as the dosage and the warnings can be reassuring.

Lesson F Another view

Presentation

- Books closed. Model Exercise **2A**. Write on the board: *Last year, I sprained my ankle, so I needed _ _ _ _ _ _ _ _ to help me walk.* Read the sentence aloud, and act out walking on crutches.
- Point to the blanks on the board and ask Ss: *What word is this?* Elicit: *crutches*. Write the word on the board, with one letter for each blank.

Practice

- Books open. Direct Ss' attention to the word bank in Exercise **2A**. Read each word aloud and ask Ss to repeat.
- Read aloud the instructions for Exercise **2A**. Start to read the example sentence aloud, but when you get to the answer, let your voice trail off so that Ss say, *hurt your back*. Point to where *hurt* has been written with one letter for each blank. Tell Ss not to worry about the circles yet.
- Have pairs of Ss use the words in the word bank to complete the sentences.
- Check answers as a class. Call on Ss to read sentences 2–7 aloud. After each sentence, ask the class: *Is that correct?* Have other Ss correct any errors.
- Read aloud the second part of the instructions for Exercise **2A**. Ss complete the task individually.
- Read aloud the third part of the instructions for Exercise **2A**. If Ss don't know the meaning of "unscramble," write the letters of your name on the board in random order. Tell Ss: *This is my name.* Ask a S to come to the board and unscramble the letters to spell your name.
- Ask the class the question, *Where should you go if you are hurt?* Check to see that everyone wrote the word "hospital."

Application

- Direct Ss' attention to Exercise **2B** and read the instructions aloud. Read each of the three sayings and ask Ss to repeat.
- In small groups, Ss discuss the meanings of the sayings.
- Walk around and explain the saying if Ss can't figure it out themselves.

> ▼ **Teaching tip**
> Here are some possible ways to explain the sayings in Exercise **2B**:
> - "Laughter is the best medicine" means that having a good sense of humor keeps people healthy or even helps sick people get well.
> - "An apple a day keeps the doctor away" means that eating healthy foods every day prevents illness.
> - "Health is better than wealth" means that being healthy is more important than having money. If you don't have your health, you can't enjoy the things your money can buy.

Expansion activity (whole group)

- Ask Ss to think of sayings in their native languages about health or health problems.
- Have volunteers each write a saying on the board, translating it into English.
- Read aloud each saying on the board and ask Ss to make guesses about its meaning. Ask the S who wrote the saying to tell the class how accurate the guesses were.

> *More Ventures* (whole group, pairs, individual)
> Assign appropriate exercises from the *Teacher's Toolkit Audio CD / CD-ROM, Add Ventures*, or the *Workbook*.

Application

Community building

- **Project** Ask Ss to turn to page 137 in their Student's Book to complete the project for Unit 4.

Evaluation

- Before asking Ss to turn to the self-assessment on page 142, do a quick review of the unit. Have Ss turn to Lesson A. Ask the class to talk about what they remember about this lesson. Prompt Ss, if necessary, with questions. For example: *What are the conversations about on this page? What vocabulary is in the big picture?* Continue in this manner to review each lesson quickly.
- **Self-assessment** Read the instructions for Exercise **3**. Ask Ss to turn to the self-assessment page and complete the unit self-assessment.
- If Ss are ready, administer the unit test on pages T-171–T-172 of this *Teacher's Edition* (or on the *Teacher's Toolkit Audio CD / CD-ROM*). The audio and audio script for the tests are on the *Teacher's Toolkit Audio CD / CD-ROM*.

2 Fun with language

A Work with a partner. Complete the sentences.

| accident | blood pressure | hurt | medicine |
| aspirin | fell off | label | |

1. Be careful. Those boxes are heavy. Don't (h) u r t your back.
2. Rosa needs to see a doctor. She has high b l o o d (p) r e s (s) u r e .
3. I have asthma. I have to take m e d (i) c i n e .
4. Always read the warning l a b e (l) .
5. He has a headache. He should take some (a) s p i r i n .
6. Ray f e l l (o) f f the ladder.
7. Todd sprained his ankle at work. He has to fill out an a c c i d e n (t) report.

Write the circled letters from the sentences.
h p s i l a o t

Write. Unscramble the letters to answer the question.

Where should you go if you are hurt?
h o s p i t a l

B Work in a group. Look at the sayings. What do they mean?

1. Laughter is the best medicine.
2. An apple a day keeps the doctor away.
3. Health is better than wealth.

Share your answers with another group.

3 Wrap up

Complete the **Self-assessment** on page 142.

Health 55

Review

1 Listening

Read the questions. Then listen and circle the answers.

1. What does Trinh do?
   a. She's a nurse.
   b. She's a waitress.

2. Where does she work?
   a. at a hospital
   b. at a restaurant

3. Who became citizens last weekend?
   a. Trinh and her husband
   b. Trinh and her family

4. What did Trinh and her husband do at the beach?
   a. They took pictures.
   b. They took a nap.

5. When did they have a barbecue?
   a. in the afternoon
   b. in the evening

6. What did they do at home?
   a. They watched a movie.
   b. They read.

Talk with a partner. Ask and answer the questions. Use complete sentences.

2 Grammar

A Write. Complete the story.

At the Doctor's Office

Yesterday, Manuel's wife, Serena, ___took___ him to Dr. Scott's
                                   1. take
office. Dr. Scott ___told___ Manuel that he ___should lose___ weight.
                  2. tell   3. should / lose
Manuel usually ___eats___ a lot of fried food. He ___drinks___ a
               4. eat   5. drink
lot of coffee and soda. Dr. Scott said Manuel ___should eat___ more fruit and
                                              6. should / eat
vegetables and drink more water. She said that Manuel ___should exercise___ .
                                                       7. should / exercise
Now he ___has to___ walk every day.
       8. have to

B Write. Look at the answers. Write the questions.

1. **A** Where _did Serena take Manuel_ ?
   B Serena took Manuel to Dr. Scott's office.
2. **A** What _does he usually eat_ ?
   B He usually eats fried food.
3. **A** What _should he eat_ ?
   B He should eat fruit and vegetables.
4. **A** What _does he have to do_ ?
   B He has to exercise.

Talk with a partner. Ask and answer the questions.

Lesson objectives
- Review vocabulary and grammar from Units 3 and 4
- Introduce the pronunciation of important words

UNITS 3 & 4

Warm-up and review
- Before class. Write today's lesson focus on the board.
  Review unit:
  Review vocabulary from Units 3 and 4
  Review simple present vs. simple past
  Review should and shouldn't
  Emphasize important words
- Begin class. Books closed. Review the simple present vs. the simple past. Ask several Ss what they usually do and then what they did recently, for example:
  What do you usually do on the weekend? Did you (S's answer) *last weekend?*
  What do you usually do in the morning? Did you (S's answer) *this morning?*

Practice
- Books open. Direct Ss' attention to Exercise **1** and read the instructions aloud.
- Call on a S to read aloud the example question. Call on another S to read the example answer choices. Continue until Ss have read aloud all the questions and the answer choices. Say: *Now listen and circle the correct answers.*
- [Class Audio CD1 track 30] Play or read the audio program (see audio script, page T-155). Ss listen and circle the answers to the questions. Repeat the audio program as needed.
- Check answers. Read each question aloud and call on different Ss to answer.
- Read aloud the second part of the instructions for Exercise **1**. Emphasize that answers need to be in complete sentences.
- Ss complete the exercise in pairs. Walk around and help as needed.
- Ask several pairs to ask and answer the questions for the rest of the class.

> **Teaching tip**
> The audio program can be divided into two parts. The first part is about what Trinh usually does. The second part is about what Trinh and her family did on their special weekend. After Ss listen to the audio program for information, play it again so that Ss can focus their attention on the verbs and verb tenses they hear.

- Direct Ss' attention to Exercise **2A** and read the instructions aloud.
- Ask Ss: *What is the title of this story?* (At the Doctor's Office)
- Ask a S to read aloud the first sentence of the paragraph. Point to where the word *took* has been written for number 1.
- Ss complete the exercise individually. Walk around and help as needed.
- Check answers as a class. Write the numbers *2–8* on the board. Ask a few Ss to come to the board and write the correct answers to Exercise **2A** next to the numbers. Call on individual Ss to read aloud one sentence of the story.
- Direct Ss' attention to Exercise **2B** and read the instructions aloud. Ask two Ss to read the example question and answer.
- Ss write the questions individually. Walk around and help as needed.
- Check answers as a class. Write the numbers *2–4* on the board. Ask a few Ss to come to the board and write the correct question to Exercise **2B** next to each number.
- Read aloud the second part of the instructions for Exercise **2B**.
- Ss ask and answer the questions in pairs. Walk around and help as needed.

Expansion activity *(student pairs)*
- Ask Ss to work together in pairs to write sentences about Manuel's new way of life.
- Tell Ss that it's 11:00 at night. Manuel saw Dr. Scott yesterday. Today, he did things differently from the way he usually does.
- Write on the board: *Manuel usually _____. Today, he _____.*
- Have pairs use the information in the story "At the Doctor's Office," along with their imagination, to write four things Manuel usually does and four things he did today. For example, Ss might write: *Manuel usually eats donuts and fried chicken. Today, he ate fruit and baked fish.*
- Help with grammar and vocabulary. Make sure Ss use the simple present tense for things Manuel usually does and the simple past for things he did today.
- Ask for volunteers to read their sentences aloud.

Review

Warm-up and review
- Books closed. Write the word *emphasize* on the board. Point to the word. Say it aloud. Ask Ss to repeat.
- Underline the syllables in the word *emphasize*. Clap while you say the word, emphasizing the first syllable. Ask Ss: *Which syllable is the strong syllable?* (the first syllable)
- Draw a circle around the first syllable in the word *emphasize*. Say: *"Emphasize" means to say something strongly. In pronunciation, we emphasize the strong syllable in a word.*

Presentation
- Write on the board: *I'm teaching right now*. Read the sentence aloud, placing extra emphasis on the word *teaching*. Ask Ss to repeat.
- Tell Ss: *"Teaching" is an important word in this sentence. When we say the sentence, we emphasize the important word.*
- Again, ask Ss to repeat the sentence: *I'm teaching right now.*

Practice
- Direct Ss' attention to Exercise **3A**. Read the instructions aloud.
- [Class Audio CD1 track 31] Play or read the audio program (see audio script, page T-155). Ss just listen. Repeat the audio program as needed, making sure Ss can hear the emphasis on the important words.
- Direct Ss' attention to Exercise **3B** and read the instructions aloud.
- [Class Audio CD1 track 32] Play or read the audio program (see audio script, page T-155). Ss listen, repeat, and clap for each word. Clap and say the words along with Ss, emphasizing important words.

▼ **Teaching tip**
It may not feel natural for Ss from some language backgrounds to put emphasis on strong syllables or important words. Therefore, it might be helpful to teach the components of stress or emphasis in English: extra volume, higher pitch, and longer duration. Explain that stressed syllables or words are louder, higher, and longer. Ask Ss to practice these three elements of stress in strong syllables and important words.

- Direct Ss' attention to Exercise **3C** and read the instructions aloud.
- [Class Audio CD1 track 33] Model the exercise. Play or read only the first sentence on the audio program. Ask: *Which word is emphasized?* (arm) Point to where *arm* is underlined in number 1.
- [Class Audio CD1 track 33] Play or read the audio program (see audio script, page T-156). Ss listen and underline the important word in each sentence. Repeat the audio program as needed.
- Read aloud the second part of the instructions in Exercise **3C**. Have pairs compare their answers.
- Check answers as a class. Say each sentence and clap for each word. Call on individual Ss to say which word they underlined. Correct as needed.
- Direct Ss' attention to Exercise **3D** and read the instructions aloud.
- Model the exercise. Look through Units 3 and 4 in the Student's Book. Write a sentence on the board from one of the units. Say: *Find four sentences to write in the chart*. Ss find sentences individually.
- When Ss have written their four sentences, point to the sentence you wrote on the board. Read the sentence aloud, emphasizing the most important content word.
- Ask Ss to repeat and tell you which word should be emphasized. Underline that word on the board. Ss work in pairs to find and underline the important words in their partner's sentences.
- Read aloud the last part of the first set of instructions in Exercise **3D**. Ask Ss to take turns reading aloud their partners' sentences as well as their own.
- Walk around and listen to pronunciation. Correct as needed.

Evaluation
- Direct Ss' attention to the lesson focus written on the board. Go around the room. Ask Ss questions to evaluate the simple present vs. the simple past. For example: Ask Ss about what they usually eat for lunch and what they ate for lunch yesterday.
- Pretend to have a headache and ask Ss for some advice about what you should and shouldn't do for a headache.
- Finally, ask Ss to say a sentence from the chart in Exercise **3D**, emphasizing the important word.
- Check off each part of the lesson focus as Ss demonstrate an understanding of what they have learned in the lesson.

T-57 Review: Units 3 & 4

UNITS 3 & 4

3 Pronunciation: important words

A 🎧 **Listen** to the important words in these sentences.

Tina's **car** broke down.
Oscar has to take his **medicine**.

B 🎧 **Listen and repeat.** Clap for each word. Clap loudly for the important word.

1. His **wife** had to do it.
2. Van has a **headache**.
3. I played **soccer** last night.
4. They went to the **library** yesterday.
5. Eliza **works** in the afternoon.
6. **Sam** made breakfast.

C 🎧 **Listen** for the important word in each sentence. Underline the important word.

1. Ali cut his <u>arm</u>.
2. He went to the <u>hospital</u>.
3. His <u>sister</u> took him.
4. He saw the <u>doctor</u>.
5. He has to take some <u>medicine</u>.
6. He <u>shouldn't</u> carry heavy items.

Talk with a partner. Compare your answers.

D **Write** four sentences from Units 3 and 4. Then work with a partner. Underline the important words in your partner's sentences.

1. *(Answers will vary.)*
2.
3.
4.

Talk with a partner. Read the sentences.

Review: Units 3 & 4

Around town

Lesson A Get ready

1 Talk about the picture

A Look at the picture. What do you see?

B Point to: an information desk • a departure board • a track number
a ticket booth • a suitcase • a waiting area

C Where are these people? What are they doing?

UNIT 5

Lesson objectives
- Introduce Ss to the topic
- Find out what Ss know about the topic
- Preview the unit by talking about the picture
- Practice key vocabulary
- Practice listening skills

Warm-up and review

- Before class. Write today's lesson focus on the board. *Lesson A: Transportation*
- Begin class. Books closed. Ask Ss: *How do you get to class? How many people drive a car to class?* Raise your hand to show that Ss who drive a car to class should raise their hands.
- Continue in this manner, asking about different forms of transportation your Ss might use, for example: *How many people take the bus / ride a bicycle to class?*
- Tell Ss: *These ways to get to class are forms of transportation*. Point to the word *Transportation* written on the board. Say the word aloud and ask Ss to repeat.

Presentation

- Books open. Set the scene. Direct Ss' attention to the picture on page 58. Ask: *Where is this?* (a train station) Ask: *What do you see?* Elicit and write on the board as much vocabulary about the picture as possible (an information desk, a map, a ticket window, etc.).
- Direct Ss' attention to the key words in Exercise **1B**. Read each phrase aloud while pointing to the corresponding part of the picture. Have the class repeat and point.
- Listen to Ss' pronunciation. Correct as needed.

Comprehension check

- Ask Ss *Yes / No* questions about the picture. Recycle questions in the simple present and the present continuous. Say: *Listen to the questions. Answer "Yes" or "No."*
  Point to the people sitting near the escalator. Ask: *Is this a waiting area?* (Yes.)
  Point to Binh's suitcase. Ask: *Is this a track number?* (No.)
  Point to the man with crutches at the information desk. Ask: *Is he asking for information?* (Yes.)
  Point to the departure board. Ask: *Is this a ticket booth?* (No.)
  Point to the children playing with the ball. Ask: *Are they sitting in the waiting area?* (No.)
  Point to the sign that says Track 1. Ask: *Is this a departure board?* (Yes.)

Practice

- Direct Ss' attention to Exercise **1B**. Model the exercise. Hold up the Student's Book. Say to a S: *Point to the information desk*. Have the S point to the appropriate part of the picture.
- Ss in pairs. Say to one S: *Say the words in Exercise 1B*. Say to his or her partner: *Point to the correct part of the picture*.
- Ask several pairs to perform the exercise for the class to check Ss' understanding.

Presentation

- Ask questions about the picture. Write Ss' responses on the board and help with vocabulary as needed. Tell Ss: *Listen to the questions. What are the people in the picture doing?*
  Point to the woman at the ticket booth. Ask: *What is the woman doing?* (buying a ticket / getting a ticket)
  Point to the two children. Ask: *What are the children doing?* (playing with a ball / throwing a ball)
  Point to the people in the waiting area. Ask: *What are the people doing?* (sitting / waiting / reading)

Practice

- Direct Ss' attention to Exercise **1C** and read aloud the questions. Ss complete Exercise **1C** in pairs.

Expansion activity *(student pairs)*

- Direct Ss' attention to the scene at the ticket booth in the big picture. Ask Ss: *What is the man doing?* Elicit: *He is giving the woman a ticket*.
- Tell pairs of Ss: *Write what happened <u>before</u> the man gave the woman a ticket*. Model the activity. Ask Ss: *What happened first?* Elicit an appropriate response and write it on the board. For example: *The woman went to the ticket booth*. Then, ask Ss: *What did the woman say?* Elicit a response and write it on the board, along with quotation marks and a reporting phrase. For example: *The woman said, "I need to go to Washington, D.C."*
- Have Ss write at least eight sentences about what happened and what the two people said.
- Ask each pair to be sure the sentences are in sequential order.
- Invite each pair to read its sentences to the class.

▼ **Teaching tip**
Don't try to teach the complexities of reported speech in the Expansion activity. Instead, write a model on the board and tell Ss to write their sentences in the same way.

Lesson A   T-58

Lesson A Get ready

Presentation

- Books open. Turn Ss' attention back to the big picture on page 58. Point to the picture of Binh and ask: *Who is the man?* (Binh) Point to the woman next to Binh and ask: *Who is the woman?* (Binh's mother)
- Direct Ss' attention to the pictures in Exercise **2A**. For each picture, ask Ss: *What is this?* (an information desk, a waiting area, a departure board)

Practice

- Read aloud the instructions in Exercise **2A**. Tell Ss: *Binh and his mother are talking. Listen to the conversations.*
- [Class Audio CD1 track 34] Play or read the complete audio program (see audio script, page T-156). Have Ss listen, look at the pictures, and decide which picture each conversation is about. Repeat the audio program as needed.
- Check answers. Ask Ss which picture shows each conversation.
- Direct Ss' attention to Exercise **2B** and read the instructions aloud.
- [Class Audio CD1 track 34] Model the exercise. Say: *Listen to conversation A.* Play or read the first part of conversation A, including the information about trains to Washington, D.C. Direct Ss' attention to the example sentence. Read it aloud and point to where the letter *T* (True) is written. Make sure Ss understand the exercise.
- [Class Audio CD1 track 34] Read aloud each group of sentences before listening to the corresponding conversation. Read aloud the three sentences for conversation A. Then, play or read conversation A of the audio program (see audio script, page T-156). Do the same for conversations B and C.

Comprehension check

- Check answers. Write the numbers 2–9 on the board. Ask a few Ss to come to the board and write the correct answers to Exercise **2B** next to the numbers. Point to each answer and ask: *Is this correct?* If Ss are not sure about an answer, play or read the appropriate part of the audio program again.

Learner persistence *(individual work)*

- [Self-Study Audio CD track 18] Exercises **2A** and **2B** are recorded on the Ss' self-study CD at the back of the Student's Book. Ss can listen to the CD at home for reinforcement and review. They can also listen to the CD for self-directed learning when class attendance is not possible.

Expansion activity *(whole group)*

- Turn Ss' attention back to the big picture on page 58. Discuss what the people waiting in line at the information desk are saying or thinking. Start with the man with crutches at the front of the line. Ask Ss what they think he and the woman at the desk are saying to each other. Ask Ss what they think the man with the spilled briefcase is thinking, and what the two people with the map of Philadelphia are looking for on the map. List Ss' responses on the board. This activity will give Ss a chance to relate their own life experiences to the situation in the big picture.

Application

- Direct Ss' attention to Exercise **2C** and read the instructions aloud. Ask two Ss to read the example sentences.
- As a class, brainstorm and list on the board as many forms of transportation as possible.

▼ **Teaching tip**
Ss may need help with the collocations used with different forms of transportation. Write on the board the expressions in these three columns:

I drive.	I take the bus.	I go by bus.
I get a ride.	I take the train.	I go by train.
I walk.	I take a taxi.	I go by car.

Add other expressions that your Ss might find useful. Read aloud each phrase and ask Ss to repeat.

- Ss complete the exercise in pairs.
- Ask for volunteers to tell the class how they get to work or school. Encourage Ss to give details such as how long their commute takes, whether or not they enjoy the various forms of transportation they take and how much it costs to get from place to place.

Evaluation

- Direct Ss' attention to the lesson focus written on the board. Have Ss focus on the big picture on page 58. Ask Ss to say as many of the vocabulary words as possible for things they see.
- Check off each part of the lesson focus as Ss demonstrate an understanding of what they have learned in the lesson.

More Ventures *(whole group, pairs, individual)*
Assign appropriate exercises from the *Teacher's Toolkit Audio CD / CD-ROM*, *Add Ventures*, or the *Workbook*.

UNIT 5

2 Listening

 A Listen. What is Binh talking about? Write the letter of the conversation.

1. _b_

2. _c_

3. _a_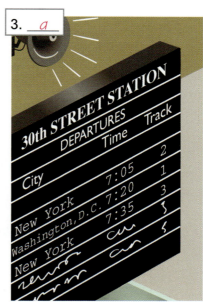

 B Listen again. Write *T* (true) or *F* (false).

Conversation A
1. Trains for Washington, D.C., leave every hour. _T_
2. The next train to Washington, D.C., will leave at 8:00. _F_
3. The next train to Washington, D.C., will leave from Track 1. _T_

Conversation B
4. Trains to New York leave every hour. _F_
5. The next train to New York will leave at 7:35. _T_
6. Binh and his mother need to buy tickets. _T_

Conversation C
7. Binh never travels by train. _F_
8. It takes about two hours to drive to New York. _T_
9. It takes two and a half hours to get to New York by train. _F_

Listen again. Check your answers.

C Talk with a partner. How do you get to work? How do you get to school?

> I go to work by bus, and I walk to school.

> I take the train to work, and I drive to school.

Around town 59

Lesson B — How often? How long?

1 Grammar focus: *How often?* and *How long?*

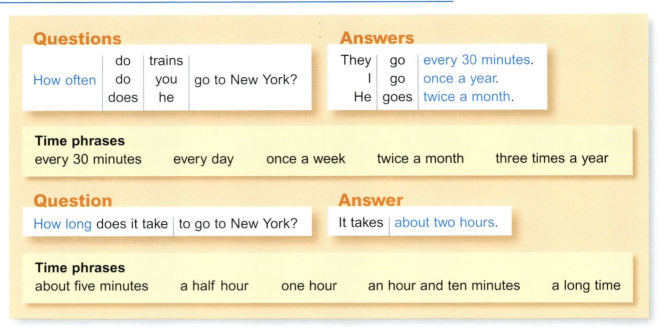

2 Practice

A Write. Circle the correct answers.

1. **A** How often does Binh go to New York?
   B 30 minutes. / (Twice a month.)

2. **A** How long does it take to fly to Mexico?
   B (A long time.) / Once a month.

3. **A** How often do you study?
   B Three hours. / (Twice a week.)

4. **A** How long does it take to drive to Toronto?
   B (Seven hours.) / Once a day.

5. **A** How long does it take to walk to school?
   B Twice a week. / (20 minutes.)

6. **A** How often does Sandra cook dinner?
   B Two hours. / (Three times a week.)

7. **A** How often does the bus go to Springfield?
   B (Once a day.) / A long time.

8. **A** How often do they go on vacation?
   B A long time. / (Once a year.)

9. **A** How long does it take to drive to the airport?
   B (One hour.) / Twice a year.

10. **A** How long does it take to walk to the library?
    B Every 30 minutes. / (25 minutes.)

🔘 **Listen and repeat.** Then practice with a partner.

Lesson objectives
- Introduce questions with *How often?* and *How long?*
- Describe number of times and length of time
- Ask and answer questions about a bus schedule
- Talk about personal transportation habits

Warm-up and review
- Before class. Write today's lesson focus on the board.
Lesson B:
<u>*How often?* and *How long?*</u>
Describe number of times and length of time
Read a bus schedule
- Begin class. Books open. Direct Ss' attention to the big picture on page 58.
- Review the key words from Lesson A. Say each of the phrases and have Ss repeat. Ask Ss to point to the corresponding part of the picture as they say the phrases.
- Tell Ss: *Listen carefully. Where do I need to go?* (Ss respond with the key words.)
I need to ask a question. (an information desk)
I need to buy a ticket. (a ticket booth)
I need to wait for the train. (a waiting area)
I need to know what time the train leaves. (a departure board or information desk)
- Ask several Ss: *How do you get to class?* Elicit: *I take the bus,* etc. List Ss' responses on the board.

Presentation
- Point to the phrase *How often?* written on the board. Say the phrase and ask Ss to repeat.
- Ask Ss: *How often do we have English class?* If no one responds, rephrase the question: *How many times do we have English class each week?* Write the correct answer on the board, for example: *twice a week.*
- Point to the phrase *How long?* written on the board. Say the phrase and ask Ss to repeat.
- Ask Ss: *How long is this English class?* If necessary, rephrase the question: *What time does class begin? What time does class end? How much time are we in class?* Write the correct answer on the board.
- Books open. Direct Ss' attention to the grammar chart in Exercise **1**. Read aloud the questions and answers with *How often* and ask Ss to repeat. Read aloud the first set of time phrases and have Ss repeat.
- Do the same for the questions, answers, and time phrases with *How long.*

> ▼ **Teaching tip**
> Point out the difference between frequency (number of times) and duration (length of time) in the following way: On the board, write the corresponding question and answer that is tailored to your class: *How often do we have class? Three times a week.* Then, write on the board: *How long is this class? One hour and twenty minutes.*

- Ss in pairs. Have Ss practice reading the top part of the grammar chart (Questions and Answers) to each other. Ask Ss to use all the time phrases at least once in their answers.
- Repeat the procedure with the bottom part of the grammar chart.

Practice
- Direct Ss' attention to Exercise **2A** and read the instructions aloud. Ask two Ss to read the example question aloud. Ask the class: *What is the correct answer? Thirty minutes or twice a month?* Ss should respond with: *Twice a month.*
- Ss complete the task individually. Remind them to use the grammar chart to help them choose the correct answer. Walk around and help as needed.
- [Class Audio CD1 track 35] Read the second part of the instructions for Exercise **2A**. Play or read the audio program (see audio script, page T-156). Have students check their answers as they listen and repeat. Correct pronunciation as needed.
- Ss practice the questions and answers in pairs.
- Ask several pairs to say the questions and answers for the rest of the class.

Comprehension check
- Ask several Ss questions about their lives, for example: *Cecilia, how often do you go to Venezuela? Houa, how long does it take you to eat lunch?*
- If a S uses the grammar incorrectly, ask that S to try again. If he or she still doesn't use correct grammar, say: *Listen.* Then, ask another S the same question, and after that S answers correctly, give the first S another chance to answer the question.

Lesson B   T-60

Lesson B How often? How long?

Presentation

- Direct Ss' attention to the bus schedule in Exercise **2B**. Ask Ss: *What is this?* (a bus schedule)
- Read the instructions for Exercise **2B** and ask Ss the question, *Where does the bus go?* (New York City, Boston, Capital Airport, and Washington, D.C.) Ask Ss: *Where do the bus trips begin?* (Springfield)
- Write on the board: *Departs / Arrives / Duration*. Point to each word and say it aloud. Ask Ss to repeat the words. Say each word again, and for each word, ask the class: *What does this mean?* Write appropriate synonyms that Ss suggest under each word, for example: *leaves / gets to a place / how long it takes*. If Ss don't know what a word means, suggest a synonym yourself.
- Point out the letters *h* and *m* on the schedule and ask Ss what the letters mean (hour, minute).
- Use the synonyms written on the board to go over a part of the schedule. For example, direct Ss' attention to the first line of the Springfield to New York City schedule. Say: *OK, so the bus leaves Springfield at 6:30 a.m. and it gets to New York at 9:00 a.m. It takes 2 hours and 30 minutes to get from Springfield to New York.*
- Ask for a volunteer to do the same with the next trip on the schedule.

> **Useful language**
> Read aloud the first two time expressions in the tip box. Tell Ss that the first two expressions have the same meaning. Explain that any time expression with "30 minutes" can be expressed in this way, for example: five and a half hours = five hours and 30 minutes. Read aloud the remaining expressions. Tell Ss that there are three different ways to say "30 minutes."

Practice

- Direct Ss' attention to Exercise **2C** and read aloud the instructions. Ask two Ss to read aloud the example conversation.
- Tell Ss that they may use the time expressions from the grammar chart on page 60 in their conversations. Make sure Ss understand the exercise.
- Ss complete the exercise in pairs. Walk around and help as needed.
- Ask several pairs to perform the conversations for the class.

Application

- Read aloud the instructions for Exercise **3**. Ask two Ss to read the example conversations aloud, with one S reading role *A* and the other role *B*. Point out the answers that have been written in the chart.
- Model the exercise. Point to the second line of the chart. Ask a S: *How often do you take the bus to work?* (S responds.) Hold up your Student's Book and write the S's response in the first column of the chart. Then, ask the same S: *How long does it take?* (S responds.) Write the S's answer in the second column.
- Ss complete the exercise in pairs. Help as needed.
- Tell Ss to cross out *every day* and *half an hour* in the chart before they write their partner's answers.
- Ask several pairs to perform one of the conversations for the rest of the class.

Community building *(student pairs)*

- Bring to class local bus schedules. If you live in a city without bus service, perhaps you can bring the schedule for a coach line that operates between your community and other communities.
- Have Ss work in pairs to answer questions you've created using *How often?* and *How long?* You can write the questions on the board or create a handout.
- Call on several pairs to report their answers to the class.

Evaluation

- Direct Ss' attention to the lesson focus written on the board. Ask Ss questions with *How often?* and *How long?* Elicit answers that describe the number of times things happen in a given time period and the length of time things take.
- Write this departure board on the board:

Departures		
Departs	Arrives	Duration
Boston 11:00 a.m.	Miami 2:30 p.m.	3h 30m
Boston 1:00 p.m.	Miami 4:30 p.m.	3h 30m
Boston 3:00 p.m.	Miami 6:30 p.m.	3h 30m

Ask Ss: *How often do planes fly from Boston to Miami?* (three times a day / every two hours) Ask: *How long does it take to get there?* (three hours and 30 minutes / three and a half hours)

- Check off each part of the lesson focus as Ss demonstrate an understanding of what they have learned in the lesson.

> **More Ventures** *(whole group, pairs, individual)*
> Assign appropriate exercises from the *Teacher's Toolkit Audio CD / CD-ROM, Add Ventures*, or the *Workbook*.

B Read the bus schedule. Where does the bus go?

US Bus Schedule

Springfield to New York City			Springfield to Capital Airport		
Departs	Arrives	Duration	Departs	Arrives	Duration
6:30 a.m.	9:00 a.m.	2h 30m	5:30 a.m.	6:50 a.m.	1h 20m
11:00 a.m.	1:30 p.m.	2h 30m	9:00 a.m.	10:20 a.m.	1h 20m
2:00 p.m.	4:30 p.m.	2h 30m	3:00 p.m.	4:20 p.m.	1h 20m
6:30 p.m.	9:00 p.m.	2h 30m	5:00 p.m.	6:20 p.m.	1h 20m
			6:00 p.m.	7:20 p.m.	1h 20m

Springfield to Boston			Springfield to Washington, D.C.		
Departs	Arrives	Duration	Departs	Arrives	Duration
8:00 a.m.	4:15 p.m.	8h 15m	7:45 a.m.	11:15 a.m.	3h 30m
9:30 a.m.	5:45 p.m.	8h 15m	9:45 a.m.	1:15 p.m.	3h 30m
11:00 a.m.	7:15 p.m.	8h 15m	11:00 a.m.	2:30 p.m.	3h 30m
			1:00 p.m.	4:30 p.m.	3h 30m

h = hour   m = minute

C Talk with a partner. Change the **bold** words and make conversations.

> A Excuse me. How often do buses go to **New York City**?
> B They go **four** times a day.
> A How long does it take to get there?
> B It takes about **two and a half hours**.

Useful language
two and a half hours = two hours and 30 minutes
a half hour = half an hour = 30 minutes

1. New York City   2. Boston   3. Washington, D.C.   4. the airport

3 Communicate

Talk with a partner. Ask questions. Complete the chart.

> A How often do you walk to school?
> B I walk to school every day. OR
>   I don't walk to school. I take a bus.

> A How long does it take?
> B It takes about half an hour.

	How often?	How long?
walk to school	*every day*	*half an hour*
take the bus to work	*(Answers will vary.)*	
drive to the store		
fly to another country		

Around town

Lesson C She often walks to school.

1 Grammar focus: adverbs of frequency

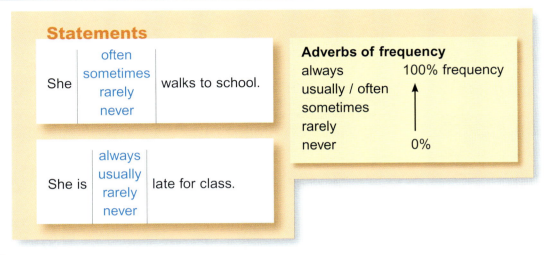

| She | often / sometimes / rarely / never | walks to school. |

| She is | always / usually / rarely / never | late for class. |

Adverbs of frequency
always — 100% frequency
usually / often
sometimes
rarely
never — 0%

2 Practice

A Write. Use adverbs of frequency and make new sentences.

1. Teresa drives to work in the morning.
   Teresa always drives to work in the morning.
   (always)
2. She is late.
   She is rarely late.
   (rarely)
3. Her husband walks to work.
   Her husband usually walks to work.
   (usually)
4. He takes a taxi.
   He sometimes takes a taxi.
   (sometimes)
5. He drives.
   He never drives.
   (never)
6. Their daughter rides her bike to school.
   Their daughter always rides her bike to school.
   (always)
7. She is tired in the morning.
   She is often tired in the morning.
   (often)

🔘 **Listen and repeat.** Check your answers.

Lesson objectives
- Introduce adverbs of frequency
- Talk about personal habits

Warm-up and review

- Before class. Write today's lesson focus on the board.
  Lesson C:
  Adverbs of frequency
  Personal habits
- Begin class. Books closed. Write on the board: *How often?* Ask Ss questions such as: *How often do you walk to work? How often do you cook dinner? How often do I give you homework?* Write Ss' responses on the board. Say sentences using Ss' responses, for example: *Mike walks to work every day.*
- Point to the phrase *Adverbs of frequency* written on the board. Tell Ss: *Adverbs of frequency are words that tell us how often something happens.*

Presentation

- Books open. Direct Ss' attention to the adverbs of frequency scale in the grammar chart in Exercise **1**. Read aloud each adverb of frequency and ask Ss to repeat.
- Point out the 0 percent to 100 percent scale to the right of the adverbs. Explain that 0 percent means that something *never* happens, 100 percent means that something *always* happens, and the other adverbs are somewhere in between. The adverbs that are closer to 100 percent show that something happens more frequently. The adverbs that are closer to 0 percent show that something happens less frequently.

▼ **Teaching tip**
Although it is true that 0 percent corresponds with "never" and 100 percent with "always," the other adverbs are harder to quantify and correspond better with "more often" and "less often" than with a specific percentage.

- Read aloud each statement in the grammar chart in Exercise **1**. Have Ss repeat.
- Have pairs practice saying the statements in the grammar chart.

▼ **Teaching tip**
Ss will probably wonder about the two different sentence patterns in the grammar chart. Tell Ss that adverbs of frequency go before the main verb in a sentence unless the verb is a form of *be*. In sentences with *be*, the adverb of frequency goes after the verb.

Practice

- Direct Ss' attention to Exercise **2A** and read the instructions aloud. Ask a S to read number 1 to the class. Ask a different S to read the example answer aloud. Make sure Ss understand the exercise.
- Ss complete the exercise individually. Walk around and help as needed.

Comprehension check

- Direct Ss' attention to the picture in Exercise **2A**. Ask Ss: *Who is the woman?* Elicit: *Teresa.* Ask about the other people in the picture: *Who is the man?* (Teresa's husband) *Who is the girl?* (their daughter)
- Read aloud the second part of the instructions in Exercise **2A**.
- [Class Audio CD1 track 36] Play or read the audio program (see audio script, page T-156). Ss listen and repeat as they check their answers. Repeat the audio program as needed.
- Write the numbers *2–7* on the board. Ask a few Ss to come to the board and write their complete sentences next to the numbers. Read each sentence aloud and ask the class: *Is this correct?* If there are any errors with adverb placement, go over the rule: *The adverb goes before the verb or after the verb "be."* Make necessary corrections on the board.

Expansion activity (student pairs)

- Write the following on the board:

Teresa	always
Teresa's husband	usually / often
Their daughter	sometimes
	rarely
	never

- Ask pairs to write at least two sentences about each person in the family pictured in Exercise **2A**. For example, Ss might write: *Teresa rarely eats breakfast in the morning.* Encourage Ss to use all the adverbs of frequency if they can.

Lesson C She often walks to school.

Presentation

- Books closed. Point to the phrase *Personal habits* written in the lesson focus on the board. Tell Ss: *Your personal habits are things you do frequently or often.* Ask Ss a few questions to illustrate the meaning of personal habits, for example: *Luke, do you usually get up early in the morning? Kim, do you often ride your bicycle to work?* Tell Ss: *These are your personal habits.*
- Books open. Direct Ss attention to the charts in Exercise **2B**. Point to the first chart and tell Ss: *This is John.* Read aloud each item as a sentence, for example: *John walks to school.*
- Do the same with the second chart. Tell Ss: *This is Sunita.* Read aloud each item as a sentence, for example: *Sunita walks to school.*
- Point to the adverbs of frequency at the top of each chart. Say each adverb and have Ss repeat.
- Ask Ss a few questions about the chart using *How often?* For example, ask: *How often does John walk to school?* (never) *How often does Sunita walk to school?* (often) Make sure Ss understand that the check marks in the chart indicate the frequency of the actions in the sentences.
- Ask two Ss to read aloud the example conversation in Exercise **2B**.

> **Useful language**
> Read aloud the expressions in the Useful language box. Ask Ss to repeat. Point to the sample conversation and read aloud the second line: *How about Sunita?* Explain that instead of asking the long question, *How often does Sunita walk to school?*, Speaker A can ask the shorter questions *How about Sunita?* or *What about Sunita?*

Practice

- Read aloud the instructions for Exercise **2B**. Make sure Ss understand the exercise.
- Ss have conversations in pairs. Walk around and help as needed.
- Call on several pairs to perform one of the conversations for the class.

Expansion activity *(student pairs)*

- Ask Ss to make check marks in one of the charts in Exercise **2B** to show their own personal habits.
- Have Ss say the conversations in Exercise **2B**. Model the activity. Say to a S: *I rarely walk to school. What about you?* Elicit an appropriate response, for example: *I sometimes walk to school.*

- Ss discuss their personal habits in pairs. When Ss are finished, ask the class follow-up questions, for example: *Is there anyone in the class who never walks to school?*

Application

- Direct Ss' attention to Exercise **3A** and read the instructions aloud. Ask a volunteer to read the example sentence.
- Model the exercise. Read aloud the partial sentence in number 2. Ask Ss: *What kind of word do you need in number 2? Do you need a verb, like "eat," or an adjective, like "hungry"?* (an adjective)
- Generate a list of adjectives for Ss to use in number 2. Ask Ss: *How do you feel on Saturday?* Elicit and write on the board as many adjectives as Ss can think of, for example: *happy; relaxed; tired; bored.* Ask a volunteer to say an example sentence for number 2. Ss complete the exercise individually.

Comprehension check

- Write the numbers *2–8* on the board. Ask a few Ss to come to the board and write their sentences from Exercise **3A** next to each number. Read each sentence aloud and ask the class: *Is this correct?* If there are any errors, ask other Ss to suggest a correction. Make corrections on the board.
- Read aloud the instructions for Exercise **3B**. Ask two Ss to read aloud the example conversation. Ask the class: *What does this mean: "What about you?"* Elicit an appropriate response about this expression from the Useful language box.
- Ss complete the exercise in pairs. Help with vocabulary and grammar as needed.

Evaluation

- Direct Ss' attention to the lesson focus written on the board. Ask for volunteers to come to the board to write the example sentences with adverbs of frequency. Ask Ss to tell you where adverbs of frequency go in a sentence.
- Call on several Ss and ask about their personal habits. Have them use adverbs of frequency.
- Check off each part of the lesson focus as Ss demonstrate an understanding of what they have learned in the lesson.

> **More Ventures** *(whole group, pairs, individual)*
> Assign appropriate exercises from the *Teacher's Toolkit Audio CD / CD-ROM*, *Add Ventures*, or the *Workbook*.

B **Talk** with a partner. Change the **bold** words and make conversations.

John		Never	Rarely	Usually	Always
	1. walks to school	✓			
	2. drives to school				✓
	3. is tired in the morning		✓		
	4. is hungry around 11:00			✓	

Sunita		Never	Sometimes	Often	Always
	1. walks to school			✓	
	2. drives to school		✓		
	3. is tired in the morning				✓
	4. is hungry around 11:00	✓			

A John **never walks to school**.
How about Sunita?
B She **often walks to school**.

Useful language
How about . . . ?
What about . . . ?

3 Communicate

A **Write.** Complete the sentences about yourself.

1. I usually __eat lunch__ after class.
2. I am often _____(Answers will vary.)_____ on Saturday.
3. I usually _____ during the summer.
4. I am never _____ in the afternoon.
5. I sometimes _____ late at night.
6. I always _____ on the weekend.
7. I rarely _____ in the morning.
8. I never _____ during the week.

B **Talk** with a partner. Use your answers from Exercise A.

I usually eat lunch after class. What about you?

I usually go to work.

Lesson D  Reading

1 Before you read

Look at the picture. Answer the questions.

1. Who do you see in the picture?
2. Where is she?
3. What is she doing?

2 Read

  Read the letter. Listen and read again.

Dear Layla,

   Right now, my mother is visiting me here in Philadelphia. I rarely see her because she comes to Philadelphia only once a year. She usually stays for one month. Here is a photo of my mother at the airport last week. She was happy to see me!
   This year, I want to take my mother to New York City. I want to show her the Statue of Liberty and Central Park. It takes about one and a half hours to get to New York by train. We are excited about our trip. Can you meet us there? Let me know.

   Your friend,
   Binh

Capital letters can show you the names of cities or places.
New **Y**ork **C**ity
Statue of **L**iberty

3 After you read

Write. Correct the sentences.

1. Binh's mother comes to Philadelphia three times a year.
   Binh's mother comes to Philadelphia once a year.
2. Binh often sees his mother.
   Binh rarely sees his mother.
3. Binh wants to take his mother to Los Angeles.
   Binh wants to take his mother to New York City.
4. Binh wants to show his mother the White House.
   Binh wants to show his mother the Statue of Liberty and Central Park.
5. It takes two hours to get from Philadelphia to New York by train.
   It takes about one and a half hours to get from Philadelphia to New York by train.

Lesson objectives
- Introduce and read Binh's letter
- Scan for capital letters to determine names of cities and places
- Practice using new topic-related words

Warm-up and review
- Before class. Write today's lesson focus on the board.
Lesson D:
Read and understand Binh's letter
Look for capital letters in the names of cities and places
Learn vocabulary for travel activities
- Begin class. Books closed. Ask Ss questions about a place they go to using *How often?* and *How long?* For example: *How often do you go to the supermarket? How long does it take to get to the supermarket from your house?*
- Books open. Direct Ss' attention to Exercise **1** and read aloud the instructions. Point to the picture; ask Ss the questions in the exercise and discuss their responses.

Presentation
- Direct Ss' attention to the letter in Exercise **2**. Ask the class: *What is this?* (a letter) *Who wrote the letter?* (Binh) *Who did Binh write the letter to?* (Layla)

> Read aloud the information in the tip box. Write on the board the terms *capital letters* and *lowercase letters*. Then, write on the board the greeting, *Dear Layla,* from Binh's letter. Ask Ss: *What are the capital letters?* (D and L) Circle the capital letters and ask Ss: *What are the lowercase letters?* (all the other letters) Underline the lowercase letters. Have Ss quickly scan the reading to find the places shown in the tip box. Then, ask Ss to scan the reading again and look for other cities or places that begin with a capital letter (Philadelphia and Central Park).

- Read aloud the instructions for Exercise **2**. Ss read the letter silently.
- [Class Audio CD1 track 37] Play or read the audio program (see audio script, page T-156) and ask Ss to read along. Repeat the audio program as needed.

Expansion activity (whole group)
- Discuss the uses of capital letters. Go through the reading, and for each capital letter, ask Ss: *Why did Binh use a capital letter here?* List the uses on the board: *the first word in a sentence, a person's name, names of cities, names of places.*

Learner persistence (individual work)
- [Self-Study Audio CD track 19] Exercise **2** is recorded on the Ss' self-study CD at the back of the Student's Book. Ss can listen to the CD at home for reinforcement and review. They can also listen to the CD for self-directed learning when class attendance is not possible.

Comprehension check
- Direct Ss' attention to Exercise **3** and read the instructions aloud.
- Model the exercise of correcting the sentences. Read the example sentence aloud. Ask Ss: *Is that correct? Does Binh's mother come to Philadelphia three times a year?* (No.) Tell Ss: *You're right. Binh's mother does not come to Philadelphia three times a year.*
- Ask a S to read aloud the corrected sentence in number 1. Point to and read aloud the second sentence in Binh's letter: *I rarely see her because she comes to Philadelphia only once a year.*
- Ss complete the exercise individually. Walk around and help as needed.
- Check answers with the class. Write the numbers *2–5* on the board. Ask a few Ss to come to the board and write the corrected sentences next to the numbers. Read each sentence aloud and ask: *Is this correct?* If there are any errors, ask other Ss to suggest a correction. Make any necessary corrections on the board.

Lesson D Reading

Warm-up and review

- Point to the last item in the lesson focus written on the board. Tell Ss: *Travel activities are things you do when you travel.*
- Direct Ss' attention to the picture dictionary in Exercise 4. Go over each picture and ask Ss questions that recycle grammar and vocabulary from this unit and previous units. Tell Ss: *Look at each picture. Listen and answer my questions.*
  Picture 1: *Where is this?* (a clothing store) *How often do you go shopping for clothes?*
  Picture 2: *What is the man carrying?* (a suitcase)
  Picture 3: *Where is this?* (an airport, a baggage carousel) *How often do you fly?*
  Picture 4: *What is the woman buying?* (a T-shirt / souvenirs)
  Picture 5: *Where is this?* (the beach / the ocean / etc.) *What does the man on the beach have to do?* (watch / save lives / sit in the sun for a long time / etc.)
  Picture 6: *Who are these people? Do you think they're friends or family?* (Answers will vary.)
  Picture 7: *What is the man doing?* (taking pictures / taking photos) *How often do you take pictures?*
  Picture 8: *What is the woman doing?* (writing postcards) *When do you usually write postcards?* (on vacation / on a trip / etc.)
  Picture 9: *Where is this?* (Washington, D.C.) *How do you write the name of a city or place?* (by beginning with a capital letter)

Presentation

- Books open. Direct Ss' attention to the word bank in Exercise 4A. Say each phrase and ask Ss to repeat. Listen to Ss' pronunciation. Correct as needed.
- Say: *Write the vocabulary in the picture dictionary.* Point to the example. Make sure Ss understand the exercise.
- Ss complete the exercise individually. Help as needed.

Comprehension check

- 💿 [Class Audio CD1 track 38] Say: *Listen and repeat.* Play or read the audio program (see audio script, page T-157). Ss listen and repeat as they check their answers. Listen to Ss' pronunciation and make any necessary corrections. Repeat the audio program if necessary.

Learner persistence *(individual work)*

- 💿 [Self-Study Audio CD track 20] Exercise 4A is recorded on the Ss' self-study CD at the back of the Student's Book. Ss can listen to the CD at home for reinforcement and review. They can also listen to the CD for self-directed learning when class attendance is not possible.

Practice

- Read aloud the instructions for Exercise 4B. Ask two different pairs of Ss to read the example conversations. Point to the appropriate phrases in the word bank as Ss say the conversations.
- Ss have conversations in pairs.
- Call on several pairs to perform one of the conversations for the class.

Expansion activity *(student pairs)*

- Ask pairs of Ss to think of at least one travel activity that is not in the picture dictionary.
- Have one S from each pair come to the board and write the activity.
- Go over each activity on the board. Make sure Ss have used correct grammar and collocations, for example: *visit a museum; eat at restaurants; take presents for friends and relatives.*
- Ask each pair if their activity is something they usually do on a trip.

Evaluation

- Direct Ss' attention to the lesson focus written on the board. Ask Ss some questions about Binh's letter, such as: *How often does Binh's mother travel to Philadelphia? Where does Binh want to take his mother? What does Binh want to show his mother in New York City?*
- Call on Ss to come to the board. Tell them names of familiar cities and places to write on the board. Make sure Ss use capital letters.
- Ask Ss questions using vocabulary from the picture dictionary, for example: *Do you usually stay at a hotel or stay with relatives or friends on a trip? Do you always buy souvenirs? How often do you go swimming on a trip?*
- Check off each part of the lesson focus as Ss demonstrate an understanding of what they have learned in the lesson.

> **More Ventures** *(whole group, pairs, individual)*
> Assign appropriate exercises from the *Teacher's Toolkit Audio CD / CD-ROM, Add Ventures,* or the *Workbook.*

T-65 Unit 5

4 Picture dictionary — Travel activities

1. _go shopping_
2. _stay at a hotel_
3. _take a suitcase_

4. _buy souvenirs_
5. _go swimming_
6. _stay with relatives_

7. _take pictures_
8. _write postcards_
9. _go sightseeing_

A Write the words in the picture dictionary. Then listen and repeat.

buy souvenirs	go swimming	take a suitcase
go shopping	stay at a hotel	take pictures
go sightseeing	stay with relatives	write postcards

B Talk with a partner. Change the **bold** words and make conversations.

> **A** Do you **go shopping** on a trip?
> **B** Yes, I do. I always **go shopping**.

> **A** Do you **stay at a hotel** on a trip?
> **B** No, I don't. I never **stay at a hotel**.

Around town 65

Lesson E Writing

1 Before you write

A Talk with a partner. Ask and answer the questions.

1. When was your last trip?
2. Where did you go?
3. What did you do there?

B Read the letter from Alicia.

> Dear Margarita,
> How are you? I just got back from a trip to California. I went to visit my cousin, Isaac. Isaac lives in San Diego. I always go to visit him once a year. It usually takes about six hours to get there from Boston by plane.
> This year we drove to San Francisco for three days. We went sightseeing. I saw the Golden Gate Bridge and Pier 39. We also went shopping, and I bought souvenirs. It was a fun trip!
> Hope you are well. Write soon!
>
> Your friend,
> Alicia

C Write. Answer the questions about Alicia's letter. Write complete sentences.

1. Where did Alicia go? <u>Alicia went to California.</u>
2. Who did she visit? <u>She visited her cousin Isaac.</u>
3. How often does she go there? <u>She goes there once a year.</u>
4. How long does it usually take to get there? <u>It usually takes about six hours to get there from Boston by plane.</u>
5. What did she do there? <u>She drove to San Francisco. She went sightseeing. She saw the Golden Gate Bridge and Pier 39. She also went shopping and bought souvenirs.</u>

Lesson objectives
- Write a personal letter about a trip
- Spell out hours and minutes from one to ten

Warm-up and review
- Before class. Write today's lesson focus on the board.
Lesson E:
Write a personal letter about a trip
Spell out hours and minutes from one to ten
- Begin class. Books closed. Point to the first part of the lesson focus. Say: *Today, you will write a personal letter.* Ask Ss: *Who do you usually write personal letters to?* Elicit: *friends and family.*
- Books open. Direct Ss' attention to the pictures next to Exercise **1B**. Point to the first picture and ask Ss: *What is this?* (the Golden Gate Bridge) Ask Ss: *Where is this?* (San Francisco, California)
- Point to the second picture and ask Ss: *What is this?* (Pier 39 – some Ss may recognize Fisherman's Wharf)

Presentation
- Direct Ss' attention to Exercise **1A** and read the instructions aloud. Read each question to the class. Make sure Ss understand the exercise.
- Ss ask and answer the questions in pairs. Ask several Ss to tell the whole class about their last trip.

Practice
- Direct Ss' attention to the letter in Exercise **1B**. Read the instructions aloud. Ss read the letter silently.
- Call on individual Ss to read aloud one sentence of the letter. Explain any words Ss don't know.

▼ **Culture tip**
Pier 39 at Fisherman's Wharf is one of San Francisco's greatest tourist attractions. Fisherman's Wharf is an area by San Francisco Bay that is popular for its restaurants and shops. The Golden Gate Bridge, one of the longest bridges in the United States, is recognized by people worldwide as a symbol of San Francisco.

Expansion activity *(whole group)*
- Have Ss scan Alicia's letter to find all the capital letters that identify the names of cities and places. Tell Ss: *Quickly read the letter again. Look for capital letters. What names of cities and places can you find?*
- Call on individual Ss to come to the board to write the name of one city or place from the letter. Make sure Ss use capital letters correctly.

▼ **Teaching tip**
Some Ss may feel as if greetings such as "Dear (name)" and closings such as "Love, (name)" often used in English letters are overly familiar or even romantic. Tell Ss that these expressions are very common in letter-writing. In fact, "Dear (name)" is even used to open many business letters. However, you may also want to teach a few options for closing letters, such as "Best regards," "Best wishes," "Sincerely," and the option in the reading: "Your friend."

Comprehension check
- Direct Ss' attention to Exercise **1C** and read the instructions aloud. Ask two Ss to read the example question and answer to the class.
- Check answers. Write the numbers *2–5* on the board. Ask a few Ss to come to the board and write their complete sentences next to the numbers. Point to each sentence and ask: *Is this correct?* Have the Ss come back to the board to correct any errors.

Lesson E Writing

Warm-up and review

- Direct Ss' attention to the letter on page 66 of Lesson E. Tell Ss: *Alicia took a trip to California. How about you? What places have you traveled to?*
- Elicit and list on the board places Ss have been. Ask a few follow-up questions, including: *When did you go to (place name)? Did you fly to (place name)?*

> **▼ Teaching tip**
> If some Ss are quiet during this warm-up activity, it may be because they haven't traveled much or the traveling they have done has been out of necessity rather than for enjoyment. Don't insist that these Ss participate in the warm-up. In the letter-writing exercise, be sure to give Ss the option to write about an imagined trip.

Practice

- Direct Ss' attention to Exercise **1D** and read the instructions aloud. Point to the first item in the lesson focus written on the board and remind Ss that they will write a personal letter about a trip. Tell Ss: *Now, you need to get ideas for your letter.*
- Call on individual Ss to read aloud one of the questions in Exercise **1D**. Focus Ss' attention on the question in number 3 before you introduce the Useful language.

> **Useful language**
> Read the tip box aloud. Explain that the phrases can be used to answer the question in number 3 in Exercise **1D**; for example: *I got to Las Vegas by train.*

- Ss complete Exercise **1D** individually. Help as needed.

Application

- Direct Ss' attention to Exercise **2** and read the instructions aloud. Remind Ss that they can write about a real or an imagined trip. Either way, Ss should use the simple past tense.

- Read the writing tip aloud. Direct Ss' attention to Alicia's letter on page 66 and ask: *Did Alicia write any numbers in her letter?* (She wrote "six" and "three.") Point out that Alicia spelled out those numbers. Ask Ss: *Why did the writer spell out those numbers?* Then, ask Ss to point out other numbers in the unit. Reinforce the writing tip by asking about each example: *Did the writer spell out the number?*

Community building (individual students)

- Use Exercise **2** to establish rapport among Ss.
- Give Ss a small piece of paper and ask them to write their name on it. Have Ss fold the paper and put it in a container such as a bowl or hat.
- Walk around the room and ask each S to take a name from the container.
- Tell Ss that the person whose name they drew is their "class buddy" today. Have Ss write a personal letter to their buddy about a trip. Remind Ss to use Exercises **1B** and **1D** to help them get ideas for their letters.
- When Ss are finished writing, ask them to give the letters to their buddies. Give Ss time to silently read the letters their buddies wrote before doing Exercises **3A** and **3B**.

Comprehension check

- Read aloud the instructions for Exercise **3A**. Ask the "class buddies" to return the letters to the writer and then take turns reading their letters to each other.
- Direct Ss' attention to Exercise **3B** and read the instructions aloud. Ask a S to read the three questions aloud. Ask Ss to take out a piece of paper and write down the three questions.
- Have Ss exchange letters. Say: *Read your partner's letter again. Write answers to the three questions.* When Ss are done, have partners share answers.

Evaluation

- Direct Ss to the lesson focus on the board. Ask Ss if they can write a personal letter about a trip now. Ask Ss to tell you what kind of information is in a personal letter about a trip. Have them tell you at least one way to begin a personal letter (Dear _____,) and at least one way to close a personal letter (Your friend, _____).
- Ask Ss to tell you which numbers are usually spelled out in writing (one through ten).
- Check off each part of the lesson focus as Ss demonstrate an understanding of what they have learned in the lesson.

> **More Ventures** (whole group, pairs, individual)
> Assign appropriate exercises from the *Teacher's Toolkit Audio CD / CD-ROM*, *Add Ventures*, or the *Workbook*.

D Write. Answer the questions about yourself.

1. When was your last trip?
   (Answers will vary.)

2. Where did you go?

3. How did you get there?

4. How often do you go there?

5. How long does it usually take to get there?

6. Who did you go with?

7. What did you do there?

> **Useful language**
> How did you get there?
> By train.   By bus.
> By plane.   By car.

2 Write

Write a letter to a friend about your last trip. Use Exercises 1B and 1D to help you.

> Spell out hours and minutes from one to ten:
> **one** hour and **five** minutes
> Write all other time numbers:
> **11** hours and **30** minutes

3 After you write

A Read your letter to a partner.

B Check your partner's letter.
- Where did your partner go?
- How long does it usually take to get there?
- Did your partner write the hours and minutes correctly?

Around town

Lesson F Another view

1 Life-skills reading

MetroTrack Train Schedule

Train	From	To	Departs	Arrives
763 EXPRESS	PHILADELPHIA	NEW YORK	6:35 A.M.	7:35 A.M.
565	PHILADELPHIA	NEW YORK	6:55 A.M.	8:05 A.M.
567	PHILADELPHIA	NEW YORK	7:25 A.M.	8:44 A.M.
769 EXPRESS	PHILADELPHIA	NEW YORK	7:50 A.M.	8:50 A.M.
573	PHILADELPHIA	NEW YORK	8:22 A.M.	9:40 A.M.
775	PHILADELPHIA	NEW YORK	8:43 A.M.	10:00 A.M.
583	PHILADELPHIA	NEW YORK	10:47 A.M.	12:00 NOON

A Read the questions. Look at the train schedule. Circle the answers.

1. How long does it take to go to New York on Train 763?
   a. one hour ✓
   b. one hour and five minutes
   c. one hour and ten minutes
   d. one hour and 15 minutes

2. How often does the express train go to New York before 11:00 a.m.?
   a. once
   b. twice ✓
   c. three times
   d. eight times

3. How long does it take to go to New York on Train 565?
   a. one hour and five minutes
   b. one hour and ten minutes ✓
   c. an hour and a half
   d. two hours and ten minutes

4. How many trains arrive in New York before 9:00 a.m.?
   a. one train
   b. two trains
   c. three trains
   d. four trains ✓

B Talk with a partner. Ask and answer the questions.

1. How long does it take to go from Philadelphia to New York on Train 769?
2. How many trains go from Philadelphia to New York in the morning?
3. What time does the first train leave Philadelphia to go to New York?
4. What time does the last train leave Philadelphia to go to New York?

Lesson objectives
- Practice reading a train schedule
- Review *How often?* and *How long?*
- Review adverbs of frequency
- Review unit vocabulary
- Introduce the project
- Complete the project and self-assessment

Warm-up and review
- Before class. Write today's lesson focus on the board.
  Lesson F:
  Read a train schedule
  Review How often? and How long?
  Complete the project and the self-assessment
- Begin class. Books open. Direct Ss' attention to the train schedule above Exercise **1A**. Ask the class: *What is this?* (a train schedule) Point to the first item in the lesson focus and ask: *What will we do with the train schedule?* (learn how to read it)

Presentation
- Point to the train schedule above Exercise **1A** and ask Ss: *How often do trains go from Philadelphia to New York?* (seven times a day) Ask Ss: *How often do express trains go from Philadelphia to New York?* (twice a day / two times a day)

> ▼ **Teaching tip**
> Tell Ss that express trains are faster than other trains because they stop at fewer places. Help Ss find this information on the schedule in Exercise **1A** if needed. However, approximate a real test-taking situation by encouraging Ss to try to answer the questions by themselves.

- Read aloud the instructions for Exercise **1A**. This exercise helps prepare Ss for standardized-type tests they may have to take. Make sure Ss understand the exercise. Have Ss individually scan for and circle the answers. Walk around and help as needed.

Comprehension check
- Go over the answers to Exercise **1A** with the class. Make sure that Ss have followed the instructions and circled their answers.

Expansion activity *(student pairs)*
- Have pairs of Ss practice saying to each other the questions and answers in Exercise **1A**.

- Encourage Ss to use complete sentences when they answer the questions.
- Have Ss write and then ask their partners two original questions about the train schedule – one question with *How often?* and the other with *How long?*

Application
- Read aloud the instructions for Exercise **1B**. Give Ss time to find the answers individually.
- Ss complete the exercise in pairs. When Ss are finished, call on several pairs to ask and answer the questions for the class.

Expansion activity *(individual work)*
- Have Ss use the train schedule above Exercise **1A** to write a story about Binh and his mother.
- Direct Ss' attention back to the big picture on page 58. Ask Ss warm-up questions about Binh and his mother, for example: *Where does Binh live?* (in Philadelphia) *Where does Binh want to take his mother?* (to New York) *What does Binh want to show his mother in New York?* (the Statue of Liberty and Central Park)
- Tell Ss: *Binh and his mother are at the train station in Philadelphia.* Point to the train schedule above Exercise **1A** on page 68 and say: *This is the schedule for trains from Philadelphia to New York. Write a story about Binh and his mother's trip to New York by train. Use your imagination. Give details.*
- As a class, generate a list of details Ss could include in their stories, for example:
  What time did their train leave Philadelphia?
  Did they arrive in New York late or on time?
  Did they talk to anyone on the train?
  What was the first thing they did in New York?
- When Ss have finished writing, have volunteers read their stories to the class.

Lesson F   T-68

Lesson F Another view

Warm-up and review

- Review adverbs of frequency. Write on the board the frequency scale from the grammar chart in Lesson C.
- Ask Ss questions with *How often?* Write Ss' responses on the board in order to provide model sentences for adverb placement.
  How often do you take the bus to work? (e.g., *I usually take the bus to work.*)
  How often are you late for work? (e.g., *I'm never late for work.*)
  How often do you eat your lunch at work? (e.g., *I always eat my lunch at work.*)
  How often are you tired after work? (e.g., *I'm sometimes tired after work.*)

Presentation

- Direct Ss' attention to Exercise **2A**. Read aloud each question in the first column, and ask Ss to repeat, for example: *How often do you stay at a hotel?*

Practice

- Read aloud the instructions for Exercise **2A**. Make sure Ss understand the exercise.
- When Ss have finished filling out the chart, read aloud the second part of the instructions for Exercise **2A**. Ask two Ss to read the example conversation to the class.
- Ss complete the exercise in pairs. When Ss have finished, ask individual Ss the questions from the chart. Encourage Ss to add details to their answers.

Practice

- Direct Ss' attention to Exercise **2B** and read the instructions aloud.
- Model the exercise. Point to the chart. Read aloud the first prompt as a complete sentence: *Find someone who usually drives a truck.* Tell Ss: *I need to find someone who usually drives a truck.* Point to the example conversation. Tell one S: *You are Danny.* Read aloud the example question and elicit the example answer from "Danny." Point to where *Danny* has been written in the chart.
- Ss complete the exercise in small groups, or if you have a small class, have Ss walk around the room and talk to their classmates.

Comprehension check

- When Ss have completed the chart in Exercise **2B**, call on individual Ss and ask, for example: *Ya-Ling, who in the class often takes a bus?* (Ya-Ling responds with a classmate's name, for example: *Nadia often takes a bus.*) Ask the classmate a follow-up question, for example: *Nadia, where do you usually go on the bus?*

Learner persistence (whole group)

- Find out if any of your Ss are having trouble getting to class because of transportation problems. If so, suggest ways for them to solve the problems, such as taking a different bus or sharing a ride with a classmate.

> **More Ventures** (whole group, pairs, individual)
> Assign appropriate exercises from the *Teacher's Toolkit Audio CD / CD-ROM, Add Ventures,* or the *Workbook.*

Application

Community building

- **Project** Ask Ss to turn to page 138 in their Student's Book to complete the project for Unit 5.

Evaluation

- Before asking Ss to turn to the self-assessment on page 143, do a quick review of the unit. Have Ss turn to Lesson A. Ask the class to talk about what they remember about this lesson. Prompt Ss, if necessary, with questions. For example: *What are the conversations about on this page? What vocabulary is in the big picture?* Continue in this manner to review each lesson quickly.
- **Self-assessment** Read the instructions for Exercise **3**. Ask Ss to turn to the self-assessment page to complete the unit self-assessment.
- If Ss are ready, administer the unit test on pages T-173–T-174 of this *Teacher's Edition* (or on the *Teacher's Toolkit Audio CD / CD-ROM*). The audio and audio script for the tests are on the *Teacher's Toolkit Audio CD / CD-ROM.*

2 Fun with language

A Write. Complete the chart with your own information. Check (✓) the answers.
(Answers will vary.)

How often do you	Always	Often / Usually	Sometimes	Rarely	Never
stay at a hotel?					
stay with relatives?					
fly on a plane?					
go sightseeing?					
take pictures?					
write postcards?					
go on vacation?					
take a trip?					

Work with a partner. Talk about your charts.

> I often stay with relatives. I stay with relatives five or six times a year.

> I rarely stay with relatives. I stay with relatives only once or twice a year.

B Work in a group. Ask questions. *(Answers will vary.)*

> Danny, how often do you drive a truck?

> Almost every day.

Find someone who:	
usually drives a truck	*Danny*
often takes a bus	
never takes a train	
rarely walks	
sometimes rides a bike	
always drives a car	

3 Wrap up

Complete the **Self-assessment** on page 143.

Around town

Time

Lesson A *Get ready*

1 Talk about the picture

A Look at the picture. What do you see?

B Point to: a class picture • a family picture • a photo album
a baby picture • a graduation picture • a wedding picture

C Look at the people. What are they doing?

UNIT 6

Lesson objectives
- Introduce Ss to the topic
- Find out what Ss know about the topic
- Preview the unit by talking about the picture
- Practice key vocabulary
- Practice listening skills

Warm-up and review

- Before class. Write today's lesson focus on the board.
  Lesson A:
  Use key vocabulary to talk about the big picture
  Talk about life events in the past
- Begin class. Books closed. Ask Ss questions to review the simple past tense.
- Ask a S: *What did you do last night?* Elicit, for example: *I worked last night.*
- Ask a different S: *How about you,* (S's name)? *Did you work last night?* Elicit, for example: *No, I didn't. I watched TV last night.*
- Continue in this manner, asking Ss *Wh-* questions with *What* as well as *Yes / No* questions about their activities last night, last weekend, last Friday, etc.

Presentation

- Books open. Set the scene. Direct Ss' attention to the picture on page 70. Ask: *Where is this?* (a home / a living room) Ask the question from Exercise **1A**: *What do you see?* Elicit and write on the board as much vocabulary about the picture as possible (two women, a sofa, a lamp, pictures, a table, a photo album, etc.).
- Direct Ss' attention to the key words in Exercise **1B**. Read each vocabulary phrase aloud while pointing to the corresponding item in the picture. Ask the class to repeat and point.
- Listen to Ss' pronunciation and repeat the words as needed.

Comprehension check

- Ask Ss *Yes / No* questions about the picture. Say: *Listen to the questions. Answer "Yes" or "No."*
  Point to the two women. Ask: *Are they looking at a photo album?* (Yes.)
  Point to the picture of St. Basil's Cathedral. Ask: *Is this a family picture?* (No.)
  Point to the picture of a baby. Ask: *Is this a baby picture?* (Yes.)
  Point to the wedding picture. Ask: *Did the man and woman get married?* (Yes.)
  Point to the large picture above Olga's head. Ask: *Is this a class picture?* (No.)
  Point to the class picture. Ask: *Is this a class picture?* (Yes.)
  Point to the graduation picture. Ask: *Did he graduate?* (Yes.)

Practice

- Direct Ss' attention to Exercise **1B**. Model the exercise. Hold up the Student's Book. Say to a S: *Point to a class picture.* Have the S point to the appropriate picture.
- Ss in pairs. Say to one S: *Say the words in Exercise 1B.* Say to his or her partner: *Point to the correct picture.*
- Walk around and help as needed. When pairs finish, have them change roles. If time allows, have Ss repeat the exercise with new partners.
- Ask several pairs to perform the exercise for the rest of the class to check Ss' understanding.
- Direct Ss' attention to Exercise **1C** and read the instructions aloud. Tell Ss: *Talk about the picture.* Ss complete the task in pairs.

Expansion activity (student pairs)

- Ask Ss to talk in pairs about all the pictures in the big picture.
- Model the activity. Point to the wedding picture and ask Ss: *What is happening in this picture?* (two people are getting married / having a wedding) Ask: *Who do you think the people are?* (maybe Olga and her husband) *When do you think they got married?* (five years ago, ten years ago, etc.)

Community building (whole group)

- Point to the picture of St. Basil's Cathedral on page 70 and ask Ss: *Where is this?* (Moscow, Russia) Write the name of the cathedral on the board. Say the name aloud and ask Ss to repeat.
- Tell Ss: *For many people in the world, St. Basil's Cathedral is a symbol of Moscow. When people see the cathedral, they think of Moscow.*
- If you have any Russian Ss in your class, ask them to tell the class about the cathedral.
- Ask Ss if they know of any other famous buildings or monuments that are symbols for cities or countries. Invite Ss to come to the board to write the name, and if they'd like, to draw a picture. Ask volunteers to tell the rest of the class about the famous building or monument. Examples might include the Eiffel Tower in Paris, the Leaning Tower of Pisa in Italy, Angkor Wat in Cambodia, or the Taj Mahal in India.

Lesson A   T-70

Lesson A Get ready

Presentation

- Books open. Direct Ss' attention to the pictures in Exercise **2A**. Ask Ss questions about the pictures that recycle the key vocabulary from the unit.
  Do you see a wedding picture? (Yes, picture 3.)
  Do you see a picture of a famous place? (Yes, picture 1.)
  Do you see a baby picture? (No.)
  Do you see a family picture? (Yes, picture 2.)

Practice

- Read aloud the instructions for Exercise **2A**. Tell Ss: *The women from the big picture will talk about these three pictures.*
- [Class Audio CD2 track 2] Play or read the audio program (see audio script, page T-157). Pause the audio program after the first conversation and ask Ss: *Which picture are the women talking about in conversation A?* (Picture 3) Hold up the Student's Book and write the letter *a* next to number 3. Make sure Ss understand the exercise.
- [Class Audio CD2 track 2] Play or read the complete audio program.

> **Teaching tip**
> After doing Exercise **2A**, ask Ss a few comprehension questions to help you assess how much of the audio program your Ss understand after listening only once. For this exercise, you could point to each picture and ask questions such as: *Where is this?* (Moscow) *Who are the people in this picture?* (Olga and her family) *When was this wedding?* (in 1983)

- Check answers. Ask Ss which pictures the women are talking about in the other conversations.
- Direct Ss' attention to Exercise **2B** and read the instructions aloud.
- [Class Audio CD2 track 2] Model the exercise. Say: *Listen to conversation A.* Play or read the first two lines of conversation A. Direct Ss' attention to the example sentence. Read it aloud and point to where the letter *T* (True) is written. Make sure Ss understand the exercise.
- [Class Audio CD2 track 2] Read aloud each group of sentences before listening to the corresponding conversation. Read aloud the sentences for conversation A. Then, play or read conversation A on the audio program (see audio script, page T-157). Do the same for conversations B and C.
- Ss complete the exercise individually. When Ss are finished writing their answers, play or read the complete audio program once more to allow Ss to check the answers they wrote.

Comprehension check

- Check answers. Write the numbers *2–9* on the board. Ask a few Ss to come to the board to write the correct answers to Exercise **2B** next to the numbers. Point to each answer and ask: *Is this correct?* If Ss are not sure about an answer, play or read the appropriate part of the audio program again.

Learner persistence *(individual work)*

- [Self-Study Audio CD track 21] Exercises **2A** and **2B** are recorded on the Ss' self-study CD at the back of the Student's Book. Ss can listen to the CD at home for reinforcement and review. They can also listen for self-directed learning when class attendance is not possible.

Application

- Direct Ss' attention to Exercise **2C** and read the instructions aloud. Read each question aloud or call on Ss to read them. Explain any language Ss don't understand.
- Ss complete the exercise in pairs. Help as needed.
- Go over each question and ask for volunteers to tell the class about their answers.

Evaluation

- Direct Ss' attention to the lesson focus on the board. Say to Ss: *Tell me about Olga's children.* Elicit, for example: *Olga's daughter is Natalya. She is tall and 14 years old. She started high school on Tuesday. Olga's son is Sergey. He is 19 years old. His birthday was three days ago. He started college in September.* Ask questions about any information Ss do not produce themselves, for example: *When did Natalya start high school?*
- Direct Ss' attention to the big picture on page 70. Point to the wedding picture and ask Ss: *Is this a graduation picture?* (No, it's a wedding picture.) Ask: *Who are the man and the woman in the picture?* (Olga and her husband)
- Check off each part of the lesson focus as Ss demonstrate an understanding of what they have learned in the lesson.

> **More Ventures** *(whole group, pairs, individual)*
> Assign appropriate exercises from the *Teacher's Toolkit Audio CD / CD-ROM*, *Add Ventures*, or the *Workbook*.

UNIT 6

2 Listening

 A **Listen.** What is Olga talking about? Write the letter of the conversation.

1. _c_   2. _b_   3. _a_

 B **Listen again.** Write *T* (true) or *F* (false).

Conversation A
1. Olga moved into her apartment two months ago.   _T_
2. Olga got married in 1993.   _F_
3. Victoria got married 30 years ago.   _F_

Conversation B
4. Sergey is 14.   _F_
5. Sergey started college in September.   _T_
6. Natalya started college on Tuesday.   _F_

Conversation C
7. Olga met her husband in Moscow.   _T_
8. Olga moved to Russia about 14 years ago.   _F_
9. Natalya was born in Russia.   _F_

Listen again. Check your answers.

C **Talk** with a partner. Ask and answer the questions.

1. When do children start high school and college in countries you know?
2. At what age do people get married in countries you know?
3. When do people usually start their first jobs?

Time

Lesson B: When did you move here?

1 Grammar focus: *When* questions and simple past

Questions			Answers	
When did	you / she / they	move here?	I / She / They	moved here in July.

For a complete grammar chart, turn to page 148.

Regular verbs
finish → finished
graduate → graduated
start → started
study → studied

Irregular verbs
begin → began   have → had
find → found   leave → left
get → got   meet → met

2 Practice

A Write. Complete the conversations. Use the simple past.

1. **A** When did Min leave Korea?
   B She __left__ Korea in 1974.
   A When did she move to New York?
   B She _____*moved*_____ to New York in 1995.

2. **A** When did Carlos start school?
   B He _____*started*_____ school in September.
   A When did he graduate?
   B He _____*graduated*_____ in June.

3. **A** When did Paul and Amy meet?
   B They _____*met*_____ in 2003.
   A When did they get married?
   B They _____*got*_____ married in 2005.

🎧 **Listen and repeat.** Then practice with a partner.

Lesson objectives
- Introduce *When* questions with the simple past tense
- Ask and answer questions about past events

Warm-up and review
- Before class. Write today's lesson focus on the board. *Lesson B: Ask and answer questions with When and the simple past*
- Before class. Write the following words from Unit 3 on the board:
  play / go / have / watch / eat / call / take / buy / meet / study
- Begin class. Books closed. Review the formation of the simple past tense. Point to and say each of the verbs on the board and ask Ss: *What is the simple past of* (verb)?
- As Ss answer, ask them: *How do you spell* (verb)? Write each verb on the board exactly as Ss spell it. Write the simple past form of each verb under its simple present form on the board.
- If Ss make a spelling mistake, point to the word on the board and ask the class: *Is this correct?* Ask Ss to suggest corrections.
- Draw a simple T-chart on the board with a vertical line down the middle and two columns labeled *Regular verbs* and *Irregular verbs*. Write the word *played* in the *Regular* column and *went* in the *Irregular* column. Ask two volunteers to fill in the chart on the board with the rest of the simple past tense verbs.
- Check that Ss have written all the regular verbs (played, watched, called, studied) and irregular verbs (went, had, ate, took, bought, met) in the correct columns.
- Point to the column with regular verbs. Read aloud the verbs and ask Ss to repeat. Ask Ss: *How do we form the simple past with regular verbs?* (add *-ed*)
- Point to the column with irregular verbs. Read the verbs and have Ss repeat. Ask Ss: *How do we form the simple past with irregular verbs?* (in many different ways)

> **Teaching tip**
> T-charts, which resemble a large capital letter "T," are a quick-and-easy graphic organizer. Use T-charts to list on the board similarities and differences, customs from two different countries, or any other information that can be presented in two columns.

Presentation
- Books open. Direct Ss' attention to the grammar chart in Exercise **1**. Read aloud the questions and answers. Ask Ss to repeat.
- Ss in pairs. Have Ss practice reading the questions and answers to each other while pointing to an appropriate person in the class (I, you, she, they).
- Point to the box with regular verbs. Read aloud the present and past forms of each verb and ask Ss to repeat. Ask Ss a few questions with *When* and the regular verbs, for example: *When did you finish working yesterday? When did you graduate from high school?*
- Point to the box with irregular verbs. Read aloud the present and past forms of each verb and ask Ss to repeat. Ask Ss a few questions with *When* and the irregular verbs, for example: *When did you begin to study English? When did you get married?*

Expansion activity *(whole group)*
- If you want to expand the grammar presentation, turn to the grammar charts on page 148. Practice asking questions and giving affirmative and negative answers with regular and irregular verbs. Add the subject pronouns *he, it, we,* and *you (plural)*.
- Have Ss turn to page 152 in the Student's Book for a reference list of common verbs that are irregular in the simple past.

Practice
- Direct Ss' attention to Exercise **2A**.
- Read aloud the instructions and the example question. Call on a S to read the answer.
- Ss complete the exercise individually. Remind Ss to use the grammar chart to help them.

Comprehension check
- Ask Ss about each picture in Exercise **2A**, for example: *What is the woman doing in the first picture?* (She is moving.)
- [Class Audio CD2 track 3] Read the second part of the instructions for Exercise **2A**. Play or read the audio program (see audio script, page T-157). Ss listen and repeat as they check their answers.
- Ask Ss to come to the board and write the answers with the past tense verbs. Ask different Ss to read the sentences aloud. Make any corrections on the board.
- Ss practice the questions and answers in pairs.

Expansion activity *(student pairs)*
- Write on the board the following verb phrases: *meet your best friend / start going to school / learn to cook / leave your parents' house / get your first job.*
- Pairs of Ss take turns asking and answering questions with *When* and the phrases on the board, for example: *When did you meet your best friend?*
- When Ss are finished, ask each question and ask for volunteers to say their answers to the class.

Lesson B When did you move here?

Presentation

- Books closed. Draw on the board a simple time line of major events in your life or in the life of a historical person. Label each event on the time line with the year in which the event happened.
- Point to the time line on the board and talk about the events, for example: *In 1981, I graduated from high school.* Ask Ss if they have any questions about your life.

Learner persistence *(whole group)*

- Ss usually want to know as much as possible about their teacher. Knowing about your past, your family, and your work experiences helps Ss see you as an approachable person, which means they're more likely to ask for help, talk about problems they might be having, and return to class after absences.
- Write on the board: *time line*. Point to the time line of your life events and tell Ss: *This is a time line. It shows when important things happened in the past.*

Practice

- Books open. Point to Kasem's picture in Exercise **2B**. Ask the class: *What is the man's name?* (Kasem) Point to Kanya's picture and ask: *What is the woman's name?* (Kanya)
- Read aloud the instructions for Exercise **2B**. Say to Ss: *Let's start with Kasem's time line.*
- Read aloud the first three boxes on Kasem's time line and ask Ss to repeat.
- Repeat the process with Kanya's time line. Say: *Now, let's read Kanya's time line.* Read aloud the first four boxes on Kanya's time line and ask Ss to repeat.
- Point to where the two time lines merge and say: *Now, there is only one time line. What happened?* Elicit, for example: *They got married!* Read aloud the last three boxes and ask Ss to repeat.
- Read aloud the second part of the instructions for Exercise **2B**. Ask two Ss to read aloud the example question and answer.
- Model the exercise. Point to and read aloud number 2: *Kanya / begin computer classes.* Ask a S: *When did Kanya begin computer classes?* Elicit: *She began computer classes in 1999.*
- Ss complete the exercise in pairs. Walk around and help as needed.
- Call on several pairs to ask and answer the questions for the class.

Application

- Direct Ss' attention to Exercise **3** and read the instructions aloud.
- Ask two Ss to read aloud the example question and answer. Point to the first item in the chart, "start English classes," and to where Ali's answer has been written. Make sure Ss understand the exercise.

> **Useful language**
> Read aloud the phrase in the tip box. Tell Ss that this is a possible answer to the second question in the chart. Have a S ask you the second question: *When did you move to this country?* Answer using the phrase in the tip box: *I was born here.* Make sure Ss understand the meaning of the phrase. Ss complete Exercise **3** in pairs. Encourage Ss to change partners and have new conversations. Ask several pairs to ask and answer the three questions for the class.

Expansion activity *(individual work)*

- Direct Ss' attention to the big picture on page 70. Ask the class: *What do we know about Olga's life?* List Ss' responses on the board, for example: *She's from Moscow. / She's married. / She has two children. / Victoria is her friend.*
- Ask Ss to make a time line of Olga's life. Tell Ss not to worry about exactly when the events happened; they can invent the years. Have them imagine additional events in Olga's life.
- When Ss are finished, ask them to show their time lines to a partner and talk about Olga's life using the simple past tense.

Evaluation

- Direct Ss' attention to the lesson focus written on the board. Ask Ss questions with *When* and the simple past; for example: *Megan, when did you have your first baby?*
- Point to your time line written on the board. Say to Ss: *Ask me questions with When about important events in my life.* Elicit, for example: *When did you get your first teaching job?*
- Check off each part of the lesson focus as Ss demonstrate an understanding of what they have learned in the lesson.

> **More Ventures** *(whole group, pairs, individual)*
> Assign appropriate exercises from the *Teacher's Toolkit Audio CD / CD-ROM*, *Add Ventures,* or the *Workbook*.

B Read Kasem's and Kanya's time lines.

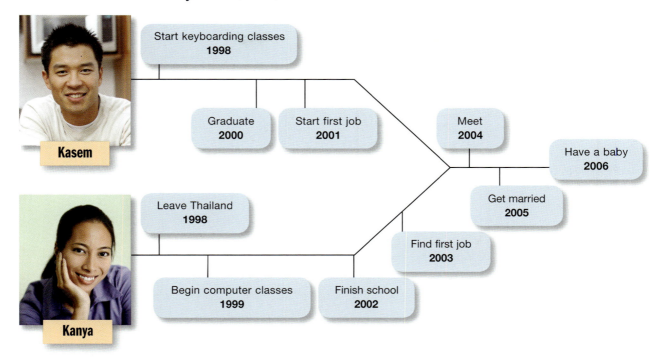

Talk with a partner. Change the **bold** words and make conversations.

> A When did **Kasem start keyboarding classes**?
> B **He started keyboarding classes** in **1998**.

1. Kasem / start keyboarding classes
2. Kanya / begin computer classes
3. Kasem / graduate
4. Kasem and Kanya / meet
5. Kanya / find her first job
6. Kasem and Kanya / have a baby
7. Kanya / finish school
8. Kasem and Kanya / get married
9. Kanya / leave Thailand
10. Kasem / start his first job

3 Communicate

Talk with a partner. Complete the chart.

> A Ali, when did you start English classes?
> B I started English classes in 2006.

Useful language
I was born here.

start English classes	*in 2006*
move to this country	*(Answers will vary.)*
start your first job	

Time 73

Lesson C — He graduated two years ago.

1 Grammar focus: time phrases

Statements

He graduated	two years ago. two weeks ago. in May. in 2004. on Wednesday. on May 4th, 2004.	She got married	at 3:00 p.m. at 12:00 noon. before she came to the U.S. after she came to the U.S. last year. this week.

2 Practice

A Write. Complete the conversations. Use *at, in, on,* or *ago*.

1. **A** When did Lou and Angela buy their new car?
   B They bought their new car __three weeks ago__ .
   (three weeks)

2. **A** When did Lou and Angela get married?
   B They got married __four years ago__ .
   (four years)

3. **A** When did Angela have a baby?
   B She had a baby yesterday __at 8:20 a.m__ .
   (8:20 a.m.)

4. **A** When did Lou begin his new job?
   B He began his new job __on Tuesday__ .
   (Tuesday)

5. **A** When did Lou move to the United States?
   B He moved to the United States __on December 15th__ .
   (December 15th)

6. **A** When did Angela come to the United States?
   B She came to the United States __three years ago__ .
   (three years)

7. **A** When did Angela take the citizenship exam?
   B She took the citizenship exam __in March__ .
   (March)

> **Culture note**
> The citizenship exam is a test you have to take to become an American citizen.

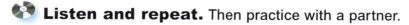 **Listen and repeat.** Then practice with a partner.

74   Unit 6

Lesson objectives
- Introduce time phrases
- Ask and answer questions about major life events in the past

Warm-up and review
- Before class. Write today's lesson focus on the board.
Lesson C:
Use time phrases
Talk about major life events in the past
- Begin class. Books closed. Ask Ss questions with *When,* for example: *When did you move to this country? When did you meet your husband? When did you start this English class?* Try to elicit a variety of time phrases, for example: *in 1998, five years ago,* or *in September.* Write Ss' responses on the board.

▼ Teaching tip
Use the personal information you've learned about your Ss when asking them questions with *When.* This will help you elicit time phrases other than the *in + year* and *in + month* structures Ss practiced in Lesson B. For example, if you know that a S got a job last week, ask the S: *When did you get your new job?* You can also paraphrase Ss' answers in order to model different types of time phrases.

- Point to the lesson focus written on the board. Point to the time phrases on the board and tell Ss: *These are time phrases. They tell us exactly when something happened.*

Presentation
- Books open. Direct Ss' attention to the grammar chart in Exercise **1**. Read each statement aloud and ask Ss to repeat.
- Ss in pairs. Have Ss practice reading the grammar chart to each other while pointing to an appropriate person in the class (he, she).

Comprehension check
- Assess Ss' understanding of time phrases. Say to Ss: *My friend got married two years ago. What year was that?* Elicit the correct year. Ask Ss: *What was the date two weeks ago?* Point to a classroom calendar if you have one and elicit the correct date.
- Draw a time line on the board with two events – *2003: came to the U.S.* and *2006: got married.*
- Point to the right-hand section of the grammar chart. Read aloud the statements on the chart that use *before* and *after.* Ask Ss: *Which statement is true?* (She got married before she came to the U.S.)

Practice
- Direct Ss' attention to Exercise **2A** and read the instructions aloud. Ask two Ss to read aloud the example question and answer.
- Focus Ss' attention on the picture in Exercise **2A**. Ask Ss: *Who are these people?* Elicit: *Lou and Angela.*
- Ss complete the exercise individually. Walk around and help as needed.

Culture note
Read aloud the tip box. The U.S. citizenship exam contains questions about U.S. government and history. If any Ss in the class have taken the citizenship exam, ask them to tell the class about it.

Comprehension check
- Read aloud the second part of the instructions for Exercise **2A**.
- [Class Audio CD2 track 4] Play or read the audio program (see audio script, page T-157). Ss listen and repeat as they check their answers. Repeat the audio program as needed.
- Pairs practice the conversations from Exercise **2A**. Walk around and listen to Ss' use of time phrases. Make any necessary corrections.
- Call on pairs to read the conversations to the class. Answer any questions about the grammar and vocabulary.

Expansion activity (whole group)
- Books closed. Divide the board into four columns with vertical lines. Write across the top of the board: *at, in, on,* and *ago.*
- Ask Ss to tell you three or four time phrases to write in each column. Elicit phrases, such as: *at 6:00 a.m.; in February; in the afternoon; on Monday; on March 12;* and *four months ago.*
- Call on Ss to say sentences using the simple past tense and the time phrases on the board.

Lesson C   T-74

Lesson C   He graduated two years ago.

Presentation
- Direct Ss' attention to the pictures in Exercise **2B**. Tell Ss: *This is Anna, and these are some important events in Anna's life.*
- Point to the top group of pictures. Recycle sequence words as you ask Ss: *What happened first?* (Anna graduated.) *What happened next?* (She got married.) *What happened then?* (She had a baby.)

Practice
- Read aloud the first part of the instructions for Exercise **2B**. Ss complete the sentences individually.
- Check answers as a class. Write on the board the numbers 2–8. Ask Ss about each pictured event using *When*, for example: *When did Anna graduate?* Elicit: *Anna graduated in 1998.*
- Write the correct preposition next to each number on the board.
- Read aloud the second part of the instructions for Exercise **2B**. Ask two Ss to read the sample conversation aloud.
- Point out the events in 1–6. Tell Ss that there may be two correct ways to say some of the events, for example: *Anna got married after she graduated and before she had a baby.* Make sure Ss understand the exercise.
- Pairs ask and answer questions. Walk around and help as needed.

Community building *(small groups)*
- Divide the class into groups with as many Ss of different cultural backgrounds as possible in each group.
- Point to the second picture in Exercise **2B**. Say to Ss: *Anna got married in 2001. This is a picture from Anna's wedding.* Write the word *wedding* on the board. Say the word aloud and ask Ss to repeat.
- Tell Ss: *Tell your classmates about weddings in your country.*
- Model the task by talking about weddings in this country – or in your own country, if it is not the United States. Discuss how people decide to get married, how old they usually are, what happens at a wedding, and who pays for a wedding. If you are married, talk about your own wedding and show the class a wedding picture.
- Walk around and help Ss with vocabulary. When Ss are finished talking in groups, ask them to tell the class what they found out about weddings in other cultures.

Application
- Direct Ss' attention to Exercise **3** and read the instructions aloud. Model the exercise. Hold up the Student's Book. Point to and say the first item: *get married.* If you're married, say: *I got married.* Place a check mark in the first box. If you're not married, keep reading items until you find one you've done.
- Ss complete the exercise individually. Walk around and help as needed.
- Read aloud the second part of the instructions for Exercise **3**. Ask two Ss to read aloud the example question and answer.

Useful language
Read aloud the sentences in the Useful language box. Tell Ss: *You can use answers like these for things you didn't do.*

- Pairs ask and answer questions. Remind Ss to use time phrases in their answers.
- Ask several pairs to perform one of their conversations for the rest of the class.

Expansion activity *(individual work)*
- Have Ss make time lines showing the events from Exercise **3** that they've done. Encourage Ss to add any other life events that are not part of the exercise.
- When Ss are finished, have them talk about events in their lives using the simple past tense and time phrases.

Evaluation
- Direct Ss' attention to the lesson focus written on the board. Write on the board: _____ Thursday / _____ 4:00 p.m. / _____ 1971 / 12 years _____. Say each word from Exercise **2** (at, in, on, ago) and have Ss tell you where to write that word on the board.
- Ask Ss questions about major events in their lives. Elicit answers with time phrases.
- Check off each part of the lesson focus as Ss demonstrate an understanding of what they have learned in the lesson.

> **More Ventures** *(whole group, pairs, individual)*
> Assign appropriate exercises from the *Teacher's Toolkit Audio CD / CD-ROM*, *Add Ventures*, or the *Workbook*.

B Write. Complete the sentences. Use *at*, *in*, or *on*.

1. Anna graduated _in_ 1998.
2. She got married _on_ Saturday, August 16th, 2001.
3. She had a baby _on_ June 21st, 2003, _at_ 2:30 a.m.
4. She and her family moved to the United States _in_ 2005.

5. She bought a house _in_ April.
6. She took the citizenship exam _on_ May 16th.
7. She became a citizen _on_ Tuesday.
8. She started her new job yesterday _at_ 9:00 a.m.

Talk with a partner. Change the **bold** words and make conversations. Use *before* or *after*.

> **A** When did Anna **graduate**?
> **B** She **graduated before** she moved to the United States.

1. graduate
2. buy a house
3. become a citizen
4. get married
5. take the citizenship exam
6. have a baby

3 Communicate

Read. What did you do? Check (✓) the boxes.

- ☐ get married
- ☐ have a baby
- ☐ get a driver's license
- ☐ get a new job
- ☐ register for English class
- ☐ buy a car
- ☐ move here
- ☐ study computers

> **Useful language**
> I'm not married.
> I don't have children.
> I didn't study computers.

Talk with a partner. Ask and answer questions.

> **A** When did you get married?
> **B** I got married three years ago on August 25th.

Lesson D Reading

1 Before you read

Look at the picture. Answer the questions.

1. Who are the people?
2. Where are they?
3. What are they doing?

2 Read

  Read the interview. Listen and read again.

An Interesting Life

Interviewer: What happened after you graduated from high school?

Olga: I went to university in Moscow, and I met my husband there. It was a long time ago! We were in the same class. We fell in love and got married on April 2nd, 1983. We had a small wedding in Moscow.

Interviewer: What happened after you got married?

Olga: I finished university and found a job. I was a teacher. Then, I had a baby. My husband and I were very excited to have a little boy.

Interviewer: When did you move to the United States?

Olga: We immigrated about 14 years ago. We became American citizens ten years ago.

> The interviewer's questions tell you what the interview is about.

3 After you read

A Write. Answer the questions about Olga.

1. When did Olga meet her husband? _A long time ago._
2. When did they get married? _On April 2nd, 1983._
3. When did they become American citizens? _Ten years ago._
4. When did she and her family move to the U.S.? _About 14 years ago._

B Number the sentences in the correct order.

- _6_ Olga had a baby boy.
- _7_ She moved to the U.S.
- _5_ She found a job.
- _3_ Olga got married.
- _2_ She met her husband.
- _8_ She became a U.S. citizen.
- _1_ Olga graduated from high school.
- _4_ Olga finished university.

Lesson objectives
- Introduce and read a magazine interview
- Scan interview questions to determine what an article is about
- Practice using new topic-related words

Warm-up and review

- Before class. Write today's lesson focus on the board.
Lesson D:
Read and understand a magazine interview
Read the interviewer's questions to find out what the interview is about
Learn new vocabulary for life events
- Begin class. Books open. Direct Ss' attention to the big picture on page 70. Ask Ss questions about the picture to review the topic and the simple past tense for talking about life events:
Point to Olga and ask: *Who is the woman in the yellow shirt?* (Olga)
Point to the picture of St. Basil's and ask: *Where is this?* (Moscow) Ask: *Does Olga live in Moscow now?* (No.) *What happened?* Elicit, for example: *She moved to the United States.*
Point to the wedding picture and ask: *What kind of picture is this?* (a wedding picture) *What did Olga and the man in the picture do?* (They got married.)
Point to the family picture and ask: *What happened after they got married?* (They had two children.)
- Direct Ss' attention to Exercise **1** and read aloud the instructions. Point to the picture. Ask Ss the questions in the exercise and discuss their responses: *Who are the people?* (Olga and an interviewer) *Where are they?* (at Olga's house / at a café / etc.) *What are they doing?* (They're talking / They're doing an interview / She's drinking coffee / He's writing in a notebook, etc.)

Presentation

- Direct Ss' attention to the reading in Exercise **2**. Ask the class: *What is this?* (an interview) *Who wrote this?* (the man in the picture)

> Read aloud the information in the tip box. Say to Ss: *What is the interview about? Read the questions first.* Have Ss read the interview questions and tell you what the interview is about. (Olga's life)

- Read aloud the instructions for Exercise **2**. Ss read the complete interview silently.
- [Class Audio CD2 track 5] Play or read the audio program and ask Ss to read along (see audio script, page T-157). Repeat the audio program as needed.

Learner persistence (individual work)
- [Self-Study Audio CD track 22] Exercise **2** is recorded on the Ss' self-study CD at the back of the Student's Book. Ss can listen to the CD at home for reinforcement and review. They can also listen to the CD for self-directed learning when class attendance is not possible.

Comprehension check

- Read aloud the instructions for Exercise **3A**. Read the example question and call on a S to read the answer. Point to Olga's first response to show Ss where the answer is located in the reading.
- Ss complete the exercise individually. Walk around and help as needed.
- Go over answers with the class. Ask Ss to read aloud the questions and their answers.

Expansion activity (student pairs)
- Ask pairs of Ss to choose either the role of Olga or the role of the interviewer and practice saying the interview. When Ss are finished, have them switch roles.
- Ask for a pair of volunteers to come to the front of the classroom and perform the interview for the class. If possible, set up chairs and a desk or table to resemble the scene in the picture in Exercise **1**.

Practice

- Read aloud the instructions for Exercise **3B**.
- Model the exercise. Read aloud all the sentences and ask Ss to repeat. Then, ask Ss: *What happened first?* Point to where the number 1 is written next to *Olga graduated from high school.*
- Ss complete the exercise individually. Walk around and help as needed.
- Go over answers with the class. Write the numbers *1–8* on the board. Write the sentence *Olga graduated from high school* next to number 1.
- Call on Ss to write the number 2 sentence on the board, the number 3 sentence, and so on. Then, ask a different S to read aloud all eight sentences in order.

Lesson D T-76

Lesson D Reading

Warm-up and review
- Books closed. Write *Life events* on the board. Say the words and ask Ss to repeat.
- Ask Ss: *What are life events?* Elicit, for example: *Important things that happen to you in life.*
- Ask Ss: *What events happened in Olga's life?* List Ss' responses on the board, for example: *Olga graduated from high school; She got married; She graduated from university; She found a job; She had a baby boy; She moved to the United States.*

Presentation
- Books open. Direct Ss' attention to the word bank in Exercise **4A**. Say each word or phrase in the word bank aloud and ask Ss to repeat. Listen to Ss' pronunciation. Correct pronunciation as needed.
- Say: *Write the words in the picture dictionary.* Point to the first example, which has been done. Make sure Ss understand the exercise.
- Ss complete the exercise individually. Walk around and help as needed.

Comprehension check
- [Class Audio CD2 track 6] Say: *Listen and repeat.* Play or read the audio program (see audio script, page T-158). Ss listen and repeat as they check their answers. Listen to Ss' pronunciation and make any necessary corrections. Repeat the audio program if necessary.

Learner persistence (individual work)
- [Self-Study Audio CD track 23] Exercise **4A** is recorded on the Ss' self-study CD at the back of the Student's Book. Ss can listen to the CD at home for reinforcement and review. They can also listen for self-directed learning when class attendance is not possible.

Expansion activity (whole group)
- Review life events and *Yes / No* questions in the simple past.
- Direct Ss' attention to the picture dictionary. Ask Ss: *Did these life events happen to Olga?* (Some of them did.) *Did Olga retire?* (No.) *Did Olga open a business?* (No. / We don't know.) *Did Olga have a baby?* (Yes.) Ask about all nine life events in the pictures.
- Ask Ss to talk about events in Olga's life that she might have experienced but that are mentioned in the unit; for example, Olga probably fell in love and got engaged before she got married.

Practice
- Read aloud the instructions in Exercise **4B**. Ask a S to read the example aloud.
- Encourage pairs to tell each other about their lives.

Community building (student pairs)
- After Ss complete Exercise **4B**, ask them to tell the class about their partners. Give them a few minutes to prepare. They may want to double-check their information with their partners and take brief notes before standing up and talking to the class.

> ▼ **Teaching tip**
> Although Ss are usually very interested in knowing more about their classmates, it's important to realize that some life events can be painful experiences. Tell Ss that they don't have to talk about every event in their lives, only events that they want to share with the class.

Evaluation
- Direct Ss' attention to the lesson focus written on the board. Ask Ss questions about the interview with Olga, such as: *Where did Olga meet her husband? What job did Olga have after she got married? When did Olga and her husband immigrate to the United States?*
- Ask Ss: *What can I do to find the main idea of an interview?* Elicit: *Read the interviewer's questions first.*
- Print out the Picture dictionary cards from the *Teacher's Toolkit Audio CD / CD-ROM*. Cover up the vocabulary words and phrases as you hold up each card and ask Ss: *What happened to this person? What happened to these people?*
- Check off each part of the lesson focus as Ss demonstrate an understanding of what they have learned in the lesson.

> **More Ventures** (whole group, pairs, individual)
> Assign appropriate exercises from the *Teacher's Toolkit Audio CD / CD-ROM*, *Add Ventures*, or the *Workbook*.

4 Picture dictionary — Life events

1. retired

2. started a business

3. had a baby

4. fell in love

5. got engaged

6. got married

7. got a divorce

8. immigrated

9. got promoted

A Write the words in the picture dictionary. Then listen and repeat.

fell in love	got married	immigrated
got a divorce	got promoted	retired
got engaged	had a baby	started a business

B Talk with a partner. Which life events happened to you? When did they happen? What happened after that?

> I retired two years ago. After I retired, I started English classes.

Lesson E Writing

1 Before you write

A Talk with a partner. Ask and answer the questions.

1. What three events were important in your life?
2. When was each event?

Write. Make a time line. Use your partner's information.

My partner's time line

1. _(Answers will vary.)_
2. _____
3. _____

B Read about Bo-Hai in his company newsletter.

COMPUTER SYSTEMS INC.

A New Employee: Bo-Hai Cheng

I was born in 1983 in Beijing. I started university in 2001. I studied civil engineering. In 2004, I moved to Miami. After I moved, I bought a car. I also got engaged. Then I studied computers at a vocational school. I graduated on July 3rd. Three weeks ago, I found a computer job. In October, I'm going to get married!

C Write. Complete Bo-Hai's time line.

| bought a car | graduated from vocational school | started university |
| found a job | moved to Miami | was born in 1983 |

Bo-Hai's time line

1. _was born in 1983_
2. _started university_
3. _moved to Miami_
4. _bought a car_
5. _graduated from vocational school_
6. _found a job_

78 Unit 6

Lesson objectives
- Write a narrative paragraph about important life events
- Introduce the use of a comma after a time phrase at the beginning of a sentence

Warm-up and review
- Before class. Write today's lesson focus on the board.
Lesson E:
Write a paragraph about life events
Use a comma after a time phrase at the beginning of a sentence
- Begin class. Books closed. Ask Ss questions about their lives as you recycle vocabulary and grammar from the unit. For example, ask Ss:
When were you born? / Where were you born?
When did you start going to school?
When did you move to this country?
When did you get married?
When did you begin studying English?
- Point to the first part of the lesson focus. Say: *Today, you will write about events in your life.*

Presentation
- Direct Ss' attention to Exercise **1A** and read the first part of the instructions aloud. Call on two Ss to read aloud the two questions.
- Read aloud the second part of the instructions for Exercise **1A**. Make sure Ss understand the exercise.
- Ss talk in pairs and write their partners' time lines.
- Have each pair join another pair. Each S talks to the "newcomers" about his or her partner's time line.

Expansion activity *(individual work)*
- Have Ss write sentences based on their partner's time line from Exercise **1A**.
- To get Ss started, write on the board: *My partner's name is _____. Several events were important in his / her life. First, . . .*
- When pairs are finished writing, ask them to read their sentences to their partners to check for accuracy. Then, ask volunteers to read their sentences to the class. You may also want to collect Ss' sentences and return them with individual feedback.

Practice
- Direct Ss' attention to the paragraph in Exercise **1B**. Read the instructions aloud.
- Ask Ss: *What's the name of Bo-Hai's company?* (Computer Systems Inc.) Ask: *What's the title of the article?* (A New Employee: Bo-Hai Cheng)
- Ss read the paragraph silently. Explain any words Ss don't know.

▼ Culture tip
Civil engineering is a broad field focusing on the design and construction of large-scale projects that benefit a town, region, or country. These projects include building roads, rail systems, power plants, bridges, and dams.

Comprehension check
- Direct Ss' attention to Exercise **1C** and read the instructions aloud. Point to Bo-Hai's time line at the bottom of the page. Ask Ss: *What happened first?* (Bo-Hai was born in 1983.)
- Read aloud each phrase in the word bank and ask Ss to repeat. Make sure Ss understand the exercise.
- Check answers. Reproduce Bo-Hai's time line on the board with blanks where Ss can write the answers. Call on Ss to come to the board to write the answers. Point to each answer and ask: *Is this correct?* Make corrections on the board.

Expansion activity *(student pairs)*
- Have pairs take turns reading the paragraph about Bo-Hai, but since they're not Bo-Hai, ask Ss to change every *I* in the paragraph to *he*.
- Monitor Ss' pronunciation and check to see that Ss are saying *he is* in the last sentence.
- Ask for a volunteer to read the paragraph in this way to the class.

Lesson E T-78

Lesson E Writing

Presentation

- Have Ss turn to page 78 and look for a time phrase at the beginning of a sentence in the paragraph about Bo-Hai.
- Ss should point out the comma after *In 2004* in the fourth sentence of the paragraph.
- Ask Ss to read the rest of the paragraph to find the time phrase at the end of the paragraph that has a comma near the beginning of the sentence. (Three weeks ago)

Read the tip box aloud. Remind Ss to use a comma after a time phrase (such as *In 2004* or *On July 3rd*) at the beginning of a sentence.

Practice

- Direct Ss' attention to Exercise **1D**. Read the instructions aloud and ask two Ss to read aloud the example sentences in number 1. Ask Ss why the second sentence has a comma (it's after a time phrase at the beginning of a sentence). Ss complete the exercise individually.
- Check answers as a class. Write the numbers 2–5 on the board. Ask a few Ss to come to the board and write the correct answers to Exercise **1D** next to each number.
- Direct Ss' attention to Exercise **1E**. Read aloud the instructions and point to the example in the time line. Ask a S: *What will you write here?* Elicit the year in which that S was born.
- As a class, brainstorm and list on the board a few ideas for life events to write in the time line. Ask Ss to use the simple past tense, for example: *began school; learned to read; graduated from high school.*
- Make sure Ss understand that they can choose any life events they want to write on the time line.
- Ss complete the exercise individually. Help as needed.

Application

- Direct Ss' attention to Exercise **2** and read the instructions aloud.
- Tell Ss that their paragraph will be similar to the one in Exercise **1B**. Explain that they can use the time line from Exercise **1E** to get ideas for their writing.
- Ss write their paragraphs individually. Encourage Ss to write time phrases in a variety of ways, as they did in Exercise **1D**.
- Help with vocabulary, grammar, and punctuation.

Comprehension check

- Direct Ss' attention to Exercise **3A** and read the instructions aloud. Partners take turns reading their paragraphs to each other. Help with pronunciation.
- Direct Ss' attention to Exercise **3B** and read the instructions aloud. Have Ss read the three questions aloud. Ask Ss to take out a piece of paper and write down the three questions.
- Have Ss exchange paragraphs. Tell Ss: *Read your partner's paragraph. Write answers to the three questions.* When Ss are finished, have them share their answers and discuss their paragraphs.

▼ **Teaching tip**
It's not always necessary to collect Ss' writings. You can also give Ss feedback during peer reviews. As Ss read each other's paragraphs, walk around and do spot checks. Scan Ss' paragraphs quickly for the correct use of time phrases and verbs in the simple past tense.

Expansion activity

- In Exercise **1D**, Ss did a sentence manipulation exercise in which they reversed the position of time phrases. Have Ss do the same exercise using their own sentences.
- Ask Ss to rewrite their paragraphs and change the position of each time phrase. If the time phrase in the original paragraph was at the beginning of the sentence, the same sentence in the new paragraph will have the time phrase at the end. Remind Ss to use a comma after a time phrase at the beginning of a sentence.

Evaluation

- Direct Ss' attention to the lesson focus written on the board. Ask Ss to tell you how they wrote a paragraph about life events. Ask, for example: *What verb tense did you use? What events did you include? What time phrases did you use?*
- Write on the board a few sentences with time phrases, some at the beginning, others at the end. Don't include commas. Call on Ss to come to the board and place commas where they are needed.
- Check off each part of the lesson focus as Ss demonstrate an understanding of what they have learned in the lesson.

More Ventures (whole group, pairs, individual)
Assign appropriate exercises from the *Teacher's Toolkit Audio CD / CD-ROM*, *Add Ventures*, or the *Workbook*.

D **Write** each sentence a different way.

1. I started college in 2001.
   In 2001, I started college.
2. In 2004, I moved to Miami.
   I moved to Miami in 2004.
3. I graduated on July 3rd.
   On July 3rd, I graduated.
4. Three weeks ago, I found a computer job.
   I found a computer job three weeks ago.
5. In October, I'm going to get married.
   I'm going to get married in October.

> Use a comma (,) after time phrases like *In 2001* or *On July 3rd* at the beginning of a sentence.

E **Write.** Complete the time line about yourself. *(Answers will vary.)*

My time line

1. was born in ____
2.
3.
4.
5.
6.
7.

2 Write

Write a paragraph about yourself. Use Exercises 1B and 1E to help you.

3 After you write

A **Read** your paragraph to a partner.

B **Check** your partner's paragraph.
- What are the important events?
- What time phrases are in the paragraph?
- Are there commas after time phrases at the beginning of sentences?

Lesson F Another view

1 Life-skills reading

APPLICATION FOR A MARRIAGE LICENSE

Groom's Personal Data

1A. Name of Groom (First) Antonio	1B. Middle Marco	1C. Last Velez		2. Birthdate (Mo / Day / Yr) 06/12/83
3A. Residence (Street & Number) 16 Ocean Parkway, Apt. 6A	3B. City San Diego	3C. Zip Code 92124	3D. State CA	4. Place of Birth Mexico City, Mexico
5. Number of Previous Marriages 1	6A. Last Marriage Ended by Divorce			6B. Date (Mo / Day / Yr) 08/13/07

Bride's Personal Data

1A. Name of Bride (First) Maria	1B. Middle Luisa	1C. Last Camacho		2. Birthdate (Mo / Day / Yr) 11/17/87
3A. Residence (Street & Number) 1994 Grant Avenue, Apt. 403	3B. City San Diego	3C. Zip Code 92124	3D. State CA	4. Place of Birth Lima, Peru
5. Number of Previous Marriages None	6A. Last Marriage Ended by			6B. Date (Mo / Day / Yr)

Groom's Driver's License / I.D.#: C0581316429	Bride's Driver's License / I.D.#: C0901516531
Ceremony Date: June 20, 2009	Ceremony Location: City Hall

A Read the questions. Look at the application for a marriage license. Circle the answers.

1. When was the bride born?
   a. in 1985
   (b.) in 1987
   c. in 1994
   d. in 2007

2. When was the groom born?
   (a.) on June 12, 1983
   b. on December 6, 1983
   c. on August 13, 1984
   d. on November 17, 1987

3. When did the groom get divorced?
   a. in 1997
   b. in 2001
   (c.) in 2007
   d. in 2010

4. When is their wedding ceremony?
   a. on 6/2/08
   b. on 2/6/09
   (c.) on 6/20/09
   d. on 6/28/09

B Talk with a partner. Ask and answer the questions.

1. When was the last wedding you attended?
2. Where was the ceremony?
3. Who were the bride and groom? Where did they meet?

Lesson objectives
- Practice reading an application for a marriage license
- Review questions with *When* and the simple past tense
- Introduce the project
- Complete the project and self-assessment

Warm-up and review

- Before class. Write today's lesson focus on the board.
  Lesson F:
  Read an application for a marriage license
  Review questions with When and the simple past tense
  Complete the project and the self-assessment
- Begin class. Books open. Point to and read aloud the first part of the lesson focus. Ask Ss to repeat.
- Direct Ss' attention to the application for a marriage license in Exercise **1**. Ask the class: *What do you see?* (an application for a marriage license) Tell Ss: *You have to fill out an application for a marriage license before you get married.*
- Ask Ss questions about the license to review unit vocabulary and grammar, for example: *Who wants to get married?* (Antonio Marco Velez and Maria Luisa Camacho) *When was Antonio born?* (on June 12th, 1983) *When was Maria born?* (on November 17th, 1987)

Presentation

- Direct Ss' attention to Exercise **1A** and read the instructions aloud. This exercise helps prepare Ss for standardized-type tests they may have to take. Make sure Ss understand the exercise. Have Ss individually scan for and circle the correct answers. Walk around and help as needed.

> ▼ **Teaching tip**
> The application for a marriage license contains some vocabulary that Ss may not know, and it may be fairly difficult for Ss to read. Nevertheless, give Ss a chance to try answering the questions without much help from you. This will approximate real test-taking conditions and Ss will have a chance to practice their compensating skills. Most Ss will be able to figure out enough information to answer the questions.

Comprehension check

- Go over the answers to Exercise **1A** together. Make sure that Ss have followed the instructions and circled their answers.
- Have pairs practice asking and answering the questions in Exercise **1A**.

Expansion activity *(whole group)*

- Go over the application for a marriage license and explain any vocabulary Ss do not know.
- Ask Ss questions using this same vocabulary, for example: *What is the groom's place of birth?* (Mexico City) *Where is the bride's residence?* (1994 Grant Avenue, etc.) *Did the groom ever get divorced?* (Yes.) *Did the groom have two previous marriages?* (No, he had one.) *Did the bride ever get divorced?* (No.)

Application

- Read aloud the instructions for Exercise **1B**. Ss complete the exercise in pairs.
- When Ss are finished, ask volunteers to tell the class about the last wedding ceremony they attended.
- Leave time for the class to ask questions about the wedding ceremony and reception.

Lesson F Another view

Warm-up and review
- Books closed. Review vocabulary for life events related to love and marriage.
- Say to Ss: *Let's talk about love and marriage. Usually, what happens first?* Elicit, for example: *You meet someone.* Write on the board: *meet someone.*
- Continue in this way, asking Ss: *What happens next?* Elicit: *fall in love, get engaged, get married,* etc. Write Ss' responses on the board.

Presentation
- Books open. Direct Ss' attention to the pictures in Exercise **2**.
- Preview the events in the story by pointing to each picture in turn and asking Ss: *What is happening in this picture?* Elicit the phrases written on the board and add other phrases that Ss suggest.

Practice
- Books open. Direct Ss' attention to Exercise **2** and read the instructions aloud.
- Divide the class into small groups and ask each group to choose a secretary.
- Ask Ss to look at each picture and to take turns reading the sentences under each picture; then have Ss discuss the possible meaning of the idiom in bold print. Have the secretary in each group write down that group's best guess or guesses about the meaning of the idiom.
- When the groups are finished, ask the secretaries to report their group's ideas to the class.

▼ **Teaching tip**
Here are some possible ways to explain the idioms in Exercise **2**:
- People who **have stars in their eyes** believe that a romance, or some other life event, can only be successful.
- **To pop the question** means to propose marriage, for example: *Will you marry me?*
- When people **get cold feet**, they worry about doing something important such as getting married. Sometimes they change their mind and don't do the thing.
- **To tie the knot** means to get married.
- When a marriage is **on the rocks**, the couple is having serious problems and may be in danger of getting divorced.
- **Smooth sailing** means that everything is going well in a marriage or in another area of life.

Practice
- Read aloud the second part of the instructions for Exercise **2**.
- Model the exercise. Read aloud the first idiom: *They both had stars in their eyes.* Say: *Well, when you have stars in your eyes, you're dreaming about the future, and how great it will be.*
- Write on the board: *She had stars in her eyes when she started acting school.*
- Ask Ss to write their sentences. Identify Ss' sentences that capture the meaning of the idioms.
- Call on Ss to write their sentences on the board.

▼ **Teaching tip**
Understanding the meaning of idioms requires repeated exposure to correct examples. Instead of going over all the sentences Ss write in Exercise **2**, you may want to collect their papers and circle the sentences in which the idiom is used correctly.

More Ventures (whole group, pairs, individual)
Assign appropriate exercises from the *Teacher's Toolkit Audio CD / CD-ROM*, *Add Ventures*, or the *Workbook*.

Application

Community building
- **Project** Ask Ss to turn to page 138 to complete the project for Unit 6.

Evaluation
- Before asking Ss to turn to the self-assessment on page 143, do a quick review of the unit. Have Ss turn to Lesson A. Ask the class to call out what they remember about this lesson. Prompt Ss, if necessary, with questions, for example: *What are the conversations about on this page? What vocabulary is in the big picture?* Continue in this manner to review each lesson quickly.
- **Self-assessment** Read the instructions for Exercise **3**. Ask Ss to turn to the self-assessment page and complete the unit self-assessment.
- If Ss are ready, administer the unit test on pages T-179–T-180 of this *Teacher's Edition* (or on the *Teacher's Toolkit Audio CD / CD-ROM*). The audio and audio script for the tests are on the *Teacher's Toolkit Audio CD / CD-ROM*.

2 Fun with language

Work in a group. Look at the pictures. Read the idioms. Guess the meanings.

Jack and Kate met in 1994. They both **had stars in their eyes**.

In 1996, Jack **popped the question**. Kate said yes.

Before they got married, Jack **got cold feet**. He was worried.

On June 15, Jack and Kate **tied the knot**. They were very happy.

One year later, their marriage was **on the rocks**. They had many problems.

Jack and Kate talked about their problems. It was **smooth sailing** after that.

Write a new sentence for each idiom. Read your sentences to the class.

3 Wrap up

Complete the **Self-assessment** on page 143.

Review

1 Listening

Read the questions. Then listen and circle the answers.

1. Where are Pablo and Marie?
   a. at a bus station
   (b.) at an airport
2. Why is Marie there?
   (a.) She just came back from Florida.
   b. She is meeting her parents.
3. How often does Marie visit her parents?
   (a.) every three months
   b. three times a year
4. Why is Pablo there?
   a. to meet Marie
   (b.) to meet his brother
5. How often does David visit?
   a. every weekend
   (b.) every vacation
6. How long does David usually stay?
   a. for three days
   (b.) for a week

Talk with a partner. Ask and answer the questions. Use complete sentences.

2 Grammar

A Write. Complete the story.

Christina's Last Vacation

Twice a year, Christina ___takes___ a two-week vacation. Last
                        1. take
year, she ___visited___ her brother in Chicago. It ___took___
          2. visit   3. take
two days to get there by train. She and her brother ___saw___
                                                    4. see
a baseball game at Wrigley Field and ___went___ to a concert in
                                     5. go
Grant Park. It ___was___ a great vacation. Christina always
               6. be
___has___ a good time with her brother.
   7. have

B Write. Look at the answers. Write the questions.

1. **A** How often _does Christina take a vacation_ ?
   B Christina takes a vacation twice a year.
2. **A** When _did she visit her brother_ ?
   B She visited her brother in Chicago last year.
3. **A** How long _did it take to get there_ ?
   B It took two days to get there.
4. **A** Where _did they see a baseball game_ ?
   B They saw a baseball game at Wrigley Field.

Talk with a partner. Ask and answer the questions.

Lesson objectives
- Review vocabulary and grammar from Units 5 and 6
- Introduce intonation in questions

UNITS 5 & 6

Warm-up and review
- Before class. Write today's lesson focus on the board.
  Review unit:
  Review vocabulary and grammar from Units 5 and 6
  Practice question intonation
- Begin class. Point to and read aloud the parts of the lesson focus. Ask the class: *What was the topic of Unit 5?* (transportation / travel)

Presentation
- Books closed. Write on the board: *Pablo / Marie / David.* Tell Ss: *We'll listen to a conversation. Who are Pablo, Marie, and David?*
- [Class Audio CD2 track 7] Play or read the audio program for Exercise **1** (see audio script, page T-158). Ss listen to find out who the people named on the board are.
- Point to each person and ask: *Who is he / she?* Elicit: *Pablo and David are brothers. Pablo is probably Marie's friend.*

Practice
- Books open. Direct Ss' attention to Exercise **1**.
- Call on a S to read aloud the example question. Call on another S to read aloud the example answer choices. Continue until Ss have read aloud all the questions and the answer choices. Say: *Now listen and circle the correct answers.*
- [Class Audio CD2 track 7] Play or read the audio program (see audio script, page T-158). Ss listen and circle the answers to the questions.
- Check answers. Read each question aloud and call on different Ss to answer.
- Read aloud the second part of the instructions for Exercise **1**. Ss complete the exercise in pairs.
- Ask several pairs to ask and answer the questions for the rest of the class, using complete sentences.

Expansion activity *(whole group)*
- Draw on the board two time lines, one with the months of the year as points on the line and the other with the days of the week.
- Go over the meaning of each time phrase in the answer choices in Exercise **1**, numbers 3, 5, and 6. Ask for volunteers to come to the board and mark the meaning of each phrase on the time lines. For example, number 3a, *every three months,* could be shown by writing an *X* on the time line at the following points: *January, April, July,* and *October.*

Practice
- Direct Ss' attention to Exercise **2A** and read the instructions aloud. Ask Ss: *What's the title of this story?* (Christina's Last Vacation)
- Ask a S to read aloud the first sentence of the paragraph. Point to where the word *takes* has been written for number 1.
- Ss complete the exercise individually. Help as needed.
- Check answers as a class. Write the numbers *2–7* on the board. Ask a few Ss to come to the board and write the correct answers to Exercise **2A** next to the numbers. Ask the class: *Are these answers correct?* Make corrections on the board.
- Call on individual Ss to each read aloud one sentence of the story.
- Direct Ss' attention to Exercise **2B** and read the instructions aloud. Ask two Ss to read the example question and answer to the class.
- Ss write the questions individually. Walk around and help as needed.
- Check answers as a class. Write the numbers *2–4* on the board. Ask for a few Ss to come to the board and write their questions next to the numbers.
- Read aloud the second part of the instructions for Exercise **2B**.
- Pairs ask and answer the questions. Help as needed.
- Ask several pairs to ask and answer the questions for the rest of the class.

Expansion activity *(small groups)*
- Before class, make sets of index cards. On each card, write one time phrase from Unit 5 that answers the question *How long?* or *How often?* For example, write: *every hour; two and a half hours; every 30 minutes; five minutes; once a year; a long time; three times a year; two months;* etc.
- Give each group a set of cards face-down. Have Ss take turns turning over the top card and reading aloud the time phrase, then saying either *How often?* or *How long?* If the group agrees that a S has said the correct question, he or she may keep the card. Otherwise, the S returns the card to the bottom of the stack.
- Model the activity. Turn over the top card from one group's stack. Read aloud the time phrase, for example: *every day.* Say to yourself, *Hmmm . . . How often?* or *How long?* Then, say: *How often!* and pretend to keep the card.

Review: Units 5 & 6 T-82

Review

Presentation

- Write on the board: *intonation*. Say the word and ask Ss to repeat. Tell Ss: *Intonation is part of the sound of a language. When you ask questions in English, you use two types of intonation.*
- Draw on the board: one "up arrow," and one "down arrow." (See Exercise **3A** for models of up arrows and down arrows.)
- Point to each arrow and tell Ss: *Listen.* As you point to the up arrow, say the word *up* with a long, rising intonation. Point to the down arrow and say the word *down* with a long, falling intonation.

Practice

- Focus Ss' attention on Exercise **3A**. Read the instructions aloud.
- [Class Audio CD2 track 8] Play or read the audio program (see audio script, page T-158). Ss just listen. Repeat the audio program as needed, making sure Ss can hear the falling or rising / falling intonation in the two question types.

Presentation

- Direct Ss' attention to Exercise **3B**. Point out the two sections: *Wh-* questions and *Or* questions.
- Ask Ss: *What are* Wh- *questions?* Explain that *Wh-* questions ask for information and use question words, such as *who; where; what; when; how often;* and *why.*
- Ask Ss for an example of a *Wh-* question. Elicit, for example: *What time is it?* Write the question on the board with a down arrow, say it with the correct falling intonation, and ask Ss to repeat.
- Ask Ss: *What are* Or *questions?* Explain that *Or* questions ask you to choose between two or more things, for example: *Do you work during the day or at night?* Write the question on the board with intonation arrows. Say the word *day* with a rising intonation and the word *night* with a falling intonation. Ask Ss to repeat the question.

Practice

- [Class Audio CD2 track 9] Play or read the audio program for Exercise **3B** (see audio script, page T-158). Ss listen and repeat. Say the lines along with Ss, emphasizing the intonation.
- Make sure Ss understand that *Wh-* questions have falling intonation and *Or* questions have rising / falling intonation.

- Direct Ss' attention to Exercise **3C** and read the instructions aloud.
- Go over each question and ask Ss to tell you what type of question it is. For *Wh-* questions, have Ss draw a falling intonation arrow over the last part of the question. For *Or* questions, have Ss draw a rising arrow before the word *or* and a falling arrow over the last part of the question.
- Have pairs ask and answer the questions. Listen to pronunciation. Correct pronunciation as needed.
- Call on several Ss to say the questions aloud for the class. Call on different Ss to give their answers.

▼**Teaching tip**
The intonation patterns in this review unit do not include *Yes / No* questions. If Ss ask you about *Yes / No* questions, explain that this type of question uses a rising intonation at the end.

- Direct Ss' attention to Exercise **3D** and read the instructions aloud.
- Model the exercise. Look through Units 5 and 6 in the Student's Book. Write on the board either a *Wh-* question or an *Or* question using topics from the units. Make sure Ss understand that they are to write only *Wh-* questions and *Or* questions.
- When Ss have written five questions, model the second part of the exercise. Point to the sentence you wrote on the board. Read the question aloud and ask Ss to repeat. Ask a volunteer to come to the board and draw the correct intonation arrow or arrows.
- Read aloud the second part of the instructions for Exercise **3D**. Ss ask and answer questions in pairs.
- Walk around and listen to pronunciation.
- Call on several Ss to ask the class one of their questions.

Evaluation

- Direct Ss' attention to the lesson focus written on the board. Ask Ss questions with *How long?* and *How often?*
- Ask Ss: *When did Christina visit her brother in Chicago?* (last year) Ask Ss to tell you about their last trip, vacation, or visit with a relative using a time phrase and the simple past tense.
- Finally, have Ss ask one of their questions from Exercise **3D** using correct intonation.
- Check off each part of the lesson focus as Ss demonstrate an understanding of what they have learned in the lesson.

UNITS 5 & 6

3 Pronunciation: intonation in questions

A 🔊 **Listen** to the intonation in these questions.

> Where is the train station?   Is the train station on Broadway or on Main Street?

B 🔊 **Listen and repeat.**

Wh- questions
A How often do you eat at a restaurant?
B Once a week.

Or questions
A Do you eat at a restaurant once a week or once a month?
B Once a week.

C **Talk** with a partner. Ask and answer the questions.

1. How often do you take a vacation?
2. Do you like to take a vacation in the summer or in the winter?
3. When was your last vacation?
4. Where did you go?
5. Did you go alone or with your family?
6. What did you do there?

D **Write** five questions. Make at least two questions using *or*.

Do you take a bus or a train to school?
1. *(Answers will vary.)*
2.
3.
4.
5.

Talk with a partner. Ask and answer the questions.

> Do you take a bus or a train to school?   I take a bus.

Review: Units 5 & 6   83

Lesson A Get ready

1 Talk about the picture

A Look at the picture. What do you see?
B Point to: a customer • a piano • appliances • a sofa
furniture • a price tag • a salesperson • a stove
C Describe the furniture. How much do the items cost?

UNIT 7

Lesson objectives
- Introduce Ss to the topic
- Find out what Ss know about the topic
- Preview the unit by talking about the picture
- Practice key vocabulary
- Practice listening skills

Warm-up and review

- Before class. Write today's lesson focus on the board. *Lesson A: Shopping*
- Begin class. Books closed. Point to and underline the word *Shopping* on the board. Say the word and ask Ss to repeat.
- Ask the class: *Does anyone in the class like to go shopping? Where do you usually go shopping?* Elicit and list on the board places Ss shop, for example: *the grocery store; the discount store; the mall.*
- Write on the board: *a sofa, a table, four chairs.* Say the words aloud and ask Ss to repeat. Say to Ss: *I need to buy these things. Where can I shop for these things?* Elicit: *a furniture store.*

Presentation

- Books open. Set the scene. Direct Ss' attention to the picture on page 84. Ask: *Where is this?* (downtown, a shopping center, a mall, etc.) Ask the question from Exercise **1A**: *What do you see?* Elicit and write on the board vocabulary about the picture (a furniture store, pianos, customers, refrigerators, sofas, lamps, etc.).
- Direct Ss' attention to the key words in Exercise **1B**. Read each word aloud while pointing to the corresponding item or person in the picture. Ask the class to repeat and point. Listen to Ss' pronunciation.

Comprehension check

- Ask Ss Yes / No questions about the picture. Say: *Listen to the questions. Answer "Yes" or "No."*
  Point to the big picture. Ask: *Is this a clothing store?* (No.)
  Point to the salesperson in the lower part of the picture. Ask: *Is this a salesperson?* (Yes.)
  Point to the man and woman sitting in chairs. Ask: *Are they shopping for furniture?* (Yes.)
  Point to the sign in the lower right-hand corner of the picture. Ask: *Is this a price tag?* (No.)
  Point to the sofa. Ask: *Is this a piano?* (No.)
  Point to the refrigerators and stoves. Ask: *Are these appliances?* (Yes.)
  Point to one of the price tags. Ask: *Is this a price tag?* (Yes.)

Practice

- Direct Ss' attention to Exercise **1B**. Model the exercise. Hold up the Student's Book. Say to a S: *Point to a customer.* The S points to any person in the picture except the salesperson in the foreground or the salesperson near the piano.
- Ss in pairs. Say to one S: *Say the words in Exercise 1B.* Say to his or her partner: *Point to the correct part of the picture.*
- Ss complete the exercise in pairs. Help as needed. When pairs finish, have them change roles. If time allows, have Ss repeat the exercise with new partners.
- Ask several pairs to perform the exercise for the class to check Ss' understanding.
- Direct Ss' attention to Exercise **1C** and read the instruction line and the question aloud.
- Model the exercise. Hold up the Student's Book. Point to the piano on which the salesperson is putting the price tag. Describe the piano by saying: *This is a tall piano. It costs one thousand two hundred dollars.* Point to the green lamp and say: *This is a small green lamp. It costs twenty-two dollars.*
- Ask pairs to talk about the furniture. Help as needed.
- Ask several Ss to describe an item to the class.

Expansion activity (student pairs)

- Direct Ss' attention to Nick and Denise in the lower left-hand corner of the big picture. Write on the board the following questions: *Who are Nick and Denise? / Where are they from? / What do they do in their lives? / What are they thinking right now? / What will they do next?*
- Have pairs discuss possible answers to the questions. When pairs are finished, ask Ss to report their ideas about Nick and Denise to the rest of the class.

Expansion activity (whole group)

- Practice saying numbers by using the price tags in the big picture.
- Ask the class about different items in the big picture. For example, point to the lamp on the table near the wall. Ask Ss: *How much is the lamp?* Write correct responses as words on the board, for example: *one hundred and five dollars.* Ask Ss: *Is there a different way to say this?* Elicit or suggest: *one oh five.* Continue focusing on numbers that can be said in more than one way, for example: *one thousand two hundred dollars* or *twelve hundred dollars.*
- When the prices have been written on the board, have Ss practice saying the numbers. Write on the board: *How much is the _____?* Ask pairs to take turns asking and answering the question.

Lesson A T-84

Lesson A Get ready

Presentation
- Books open. Direct Ss' attention to the pictures in Exercise **2A**. For each picture, ask Ss: *What do you see?* (e.g., a price tag, a piano, a sign for a 20% off sale)

Practice
- Read aloud the instructions for Exercise **2A**. Make sure Ss understand the exercise.
- [Class Audio CD2 track 10] Play or read the audio program (see audio script, page T-158). Ss listen and write the letter of each conversation in the appropriate blank. Repeat the audio program as needed.
- [Class Audio CD2 track 10] Check answers. Play or read the audio program again. After each conversation, pause the audio program and ask Ss which picture shows that conversation.
- Direct Ss' attention to Exercise **2B** and read the instructions aloud.
- [Class Audio CD2 track 10] Model the exercise. Say: *Listen to conversation A*. Play or read the first lines spoken by the salesperson and Denise in conversation A. Direct Ss' attention to the example sentence. Read it aloud and point to where the letter *T* (True) is written. Make sure Ss understand the exercise.
- [Class Audio CD2 track 10] Read aloud each group of sentences before listening to the corresponding conversation. Read aloud the three sentences for conversation A. Then, play or read conversation A of the audio program (see audio script, page T-158). Do the same for conversations B and C.
- Ss complete the exercise individually. When Ss are finished writing their answers, play or read the complete audio program once more to allow Ss to check their answers.

Comprehension check
- Check answers. Write the numbers *2–9* on the board. Ask a few Ss to come to the board and write the correct answers to Exercise **2B** next to the numbers. Point to each answer and ask: *Is this correct?* If Ss are not sure about an answer, play or read the appropriate part of the audio program again.

Learner persistence *(individual work)*
- [Self-Study Audio CD track 24] Exercises **2A** and **2B** are recorded on the Ss' self-study CD at the back of the Student's Book. Ss can listen to the CD at home for reinforcement and review. They can also listen for self-directed learning when class attendance is not possible.

> **Culture note**
> Read aloud the information in the tip box. Ask Ss whether there are any used-furniture stores in your community. If there are, ask Ss to tell the class where the stores are located and whether they have ever shopped there. Discuss other kinds of thrift or secondhand stores in your community. For example, many communities have stores with secondhand clothing and household items. There may also be stores that sell used building materials such as doors and light fixtures that were salvaged from buildings before they were demolished.

Application
- Direct Ss' attention to Exercise **2C** and read the instructions aloud. Ask three Ss to read aloud the example questions.
- Ss complete the exercise in pairs. Walk around and help as needed.
- When pairs have finished, call on Ss to tell the class about good ways to find furniture, and about their own experiences with buying furniture in this country.

Evaluation
- Direct Ss' attention to the word *Shopping* underlined on the board. Go back to the big picture on page 84 and ask Ss: *What kind of store is this?* (a furniture store)
- While pointing to the first picture in Exercise **2A**, say to Ss: *Point to the price tag on the blue sofa on page 84*. Make sure that Ss understand you. Ask Ss: *How much does the blue sofa usually cost?* ($400) Say to Ss: *There is a sale at the furniture store today. How much does the blue sofa cost today?* ($320 after 20% off)
- Check off each part of the lesson focus as Ss demonstrate an understanding of what they have learned in the lesson.

> **More Ventures** *(whole group, pairs, individual)*
> Assign appropriate exercises from the *Teacher's Toolkit Audio CD / CD-ROM*, *Add Ventures*, or the *Workbook*.

UNIT 7

2 Listening

A **Listen.** What are Nick and Denise talking about? Write the letter of the conversation.

1. _b_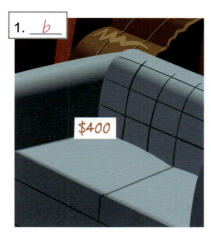
2. _c_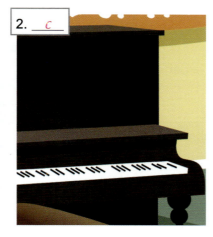
3. _a_

B **Listen again.** Write *T* (true) or *F* (false).

Conversation A

1. Denise and Nick need furniture. _T_
2. Denise and Nick bought a house two days ago. _T_
3. The furniture and appliances are 10 percent off. _F_

Conversation B

4. Denise likes the brown sofa. _F_
5. Nick wants a big sofa. _T_
6. The brown sofa is more expensive than the blue sofa. _T_

Conversation C

7. Denise and Nick need a piano. _F_
8. The upright piano is very old. _T_
9. The smaller piano is more expensive. _F_

Listen again. Check your answers.

C **Talk** with a partner. Ask and answer the questions.

1. What are some good ways to find furniture?
2. Did you ever buy furniture in this country?
3. What did you buy?

> **Culture note**
>
> Many stores in the U.S. sell furniture and appliances that are *not* new. The prices are cheaper. These stores are often called *used-furniture*, *thrift*, or *secondhand* stores.

Shopping

Lesson B — The brown sofa is bigger.

1 Grammar focus: comparatives

Statements

| The brown sofa is | bigger. |
| | more expensive. |

Comparatives

big → bigger
cheap → cheaper
heavy → heavier
small → smaller
comfortable → more comfortable
expensive → more expensive
good → better

For additional comparative adjectives, turn to page 151.

2 Practice

A Write. Complete the conversations. Use comparatives.

1. **A** Which sofa is more comfortable?
   B <u>The green striped sofa is more comfortable.</u>
   (green striped sofa / blue plaid sofa)

2. **A** Which chair is heavier?
   B <u>The orange chair is heavier.</u>
   (orange chair / purple chair)

3. **A** Which refrigerator is more expensive?
   B <u>The silver refrigerator is more expensive.</u>
   (white refrigerator / silver refrigerator)

4. **A** Which table is bigger?
   B <u>The square table is bigger.</u>
   (square table / round table)

5. **A** Which stove is better?
   B <u>The black stove is better.</u>
   (white stove / black stove)

🎧 **Listen and repeat.** Then practice with a partner.

Lesson objectives
- Introduce comparatives
- Compare price and quality using descriptive adjectives
- Ask and answer questions to compare furniture, appliances, and stores

Warm-up and review
- Before class. Write today's lesson focus on the board.
  Lesson B:
  Compare two things
  Ask and answer questions about price and quality
- Before class. Draw a T-chart on the board with a horizontal line across the top and a vertical line separating the chart into two columns. Label one column *Furniture* and the other *Appliances*.
- Before class. List on the board in random order the appliances and furniture items pictured on page 86: *sofa, refrigerator, chair, stove, table*. (You will use the chart and the words in Exercise **2A**.)

Presentation
- Books open. Direct Ss' attention to the grammar chart in Exercise **1**. Read the statement aloud and ask Ss to repeat.
- Point to the two sofas in the grammar chart. Ask Ss: *How many sofas are there?* (two) Tell Ss: *Comparatives tell us about the differences between two things, for example, two sofas.*
- Read aloud the adjectives and their comparative forms. Have Ss repeat.

Expansion activity (whole group)
- Bring to class several pairs of items and arrange them on a desk or table where Ss can see them. For example, bring a hand towel and a bath towel; a small paperback book and a heavy hardcover book; a small juice glass and a large water glass.
- Pick up each item, say what it is, and write the word or phrase on the board for Ss to refer to. For the items above, you might write: *hand towel; bath towel; paperback book; hardcover book; juice glass; water glass.*
- Write on the board one of the adjectives from the grammar chart, for example, *expensive*. Hold up two items, for example, the two towels. Ss form the comparative and say a sentence about the two items similar to the sentences in the grammar chart, for example: *The bath towel is more expensive than the hand towel.* Repeat the process for each pair of items.
- More than one comparison might be possible with some of the items; for example, the hardcover book might be both *heavier* and *bigger* than the paperback book.

▼ **Teaching tip**
In order to assess prior knowledge, ask Ss about the three different ways comparatives are formed. Write on the board: *bigger / more comfortable / better*. Ask Ss to tell you the rules for comparatives. Ss may already know that *-er* is added to most one- or two-syllable adjectives, *more* is added to adjectives with three or more syllables, and irregular forms are used with some words, such as *good* and *bad*.

Presentation
- Introduce new vocabulary. Point to each type of furniture and appliance pictured in Exercise **2A**. Ask Ss: *What is this?* Underline the word you wrote on the board earlier as Ss tell you the word. Then, say: *Repeat after me.* Read aloud each word as you point to the item in the picture.
- Point to the T-chart you drew on the board. In the column labeled *Furniture*, write the word *sofa*. In the column labeled *Appliances*, write the word *refrigerator*.
- Ask for two volunteers to come to the board to write the remaining words in the T-chart.

▼ **Teaching tip**
Although the word *furniture* is an uncountable noun in English, the equivalent word in Ss' other languages may be countable. Listen carefully to Ss' pronunciation of the word, and make corrections if you hear errors such as *furnitures* or *a furniture*.

Practice
- Books open. Direct Ss' attention to Exercise **2A**.
- Model the exercise. Read aloud the example question. Point to the two sofas in the pictures. Say to the class: *The green striped sofa looks very soft. The blue plaid sofa looks harder.* Ask a S to read aloud the example answer: *The green striped sofa is more comfortable.*
- Have Ss work individually to write the sentences.

Comprehension check
- [Class Audio CD2 track 11] Read aloud the second part of the instructions for Exercise **2A**. Play or read the audio program (see audio script, page T-158). Ss check their answers as they listen and repeat.
- Write on the board the numbers *2–5*. Ask volunteers to write their sentences on the board next to the numbers.
- Ss practice the conversations in pairs.

Lesson B

Lesson B The brown sofa is bigger.

Presentation

- Books open. Direct Ss' attention to the pictures in Exercise **2B**. Read aloud the words for each pictured item and ask Ss to repeat.
- Ask questions to clarify the meaning of the new vocabulary. For example, ask the class: *Where do you usually see a dining table?* (e.g., in a dining room) *Where do you usually see a kitchen table?* (e.g., in a kitchen) Discuss the ways Ss use these tables at home. For example, ask Ss: *Do you always eat at the dining table? Do you do your homework at the dining table?* Ask Ss: *What do you do at the kitchen table?* Elicit, for example: *cut vegetables for meals; write letters; eat breakfast,* etc.
- Talk about *desk lamp* and *floor lamp.* If you have an example of either kind of lamp in your classroom, ask Ss: *Is this a desk lamp or a floor lamp?* Otherwise, ask Ss: *Can we put a desk lamp in this classroom?* (Yes.) *Where?* (on a desk / on a table) Do the same for *floor lamp,* for example: *Can we put a floor lamp in this classroom? Where?*

Practice

- Read aloud the instructions for Exercise **2B**. Direct Ss' attention to number 1 and read the two words aloud. Ask two Ss to read aloud the example question and answer.

> **Useful language**
>
> Read aloud the sentences in the Useful language box. Ask Ss to repeat. Encourage Ss to practice the useful language as they ask and answer questions for Exercise **2B**. Tell Ss that they can use both of these sentence patterns in this exercise. Have pairs ask and answer questions in Exercise **2B**. Walk around and help as needed.

Presentation

- Direct Ss' attention to the pictures in Exercise **3**. Point to the store on the left and ask: *What's the name of the store?* (Perry's Thrift Shop) Ask Ss: *What do they sell at Perry's Thrift Shop?* (used furniture)
- Do the same with Greg's Used-Furniture Mart. Then, ask Ss: *Are used furniture and secondhand furniture different?* (No, they mean the same thing.)

Application

- Read aloud the instructions for Exercise **3**. Ask two Ss to read the example conversation aloud.

- Review furniture vocabulary. Ask Ss to tell you what they see in the store windows. List the items on the board: *lamp, desk, chair, table.*
- Tell Ss they can use the adjectives from the grammar chart and Exercise **2B** as they have their conversations. Walk around and help with other vocabulary Ss might need, for example: *new; modern; traditional; beautiful.*
- Ss have conversations in pairs. When they finish, ask Ss to switch partners and have different conversations.

Community building (small groups)

- Have small groups of Ss take turns describing the furniture in their living room and kitchen. Write on the board: *What furniture do you have in your living room? What furniture and appliances do you have in your kitchen?* Point to each question as you read it aloud. Ask Ss to repeat.
- Ask Ss to answer these questions as they talk to their classmates about their homes. Encourage Ss to give details, such as the color of their sofa or the size of their kitchen table. Ss will enjoy hearing about their classmates' lives outside of class.
- Keep in mind that some Ss may live in efficiency apartments, in rooming houses, or in hotel rooms. If Ss don't have a living room, for example, ask them to describe any room they live in now or have lived in before.

Evaluation

- Direct Ss' attention to the first part of the lesson focus written on the board. Ask Ss questions with *Which* and comparative adjectives. Use the art in the Student's Book as well as classroom realia. For example, point to the two refrigerators in the big picture and ask: *Which refrigerator is heavier?* Ask two Ss to stand up and ask a third S: *Which person is taller?*
- Direct Ss' attention to the second part of the lesson focus. Have Ss ask their classmates questions with *Which* and comparative adjectives. If you brought in realia for the Expansion activity, hold up two of the items. Say to a S: *Ask another S in the class a question with* Which. The S will ask a classmate, for example: *Which towel is bigger?* The classmate responds.
- Check off each part of the lesson focus as Ss demonstrate an understanding of what they have learned in the lesson.

> **More Ventures** (whole group, pairs, individual)
> Assign appropriate exercises from the *Teacher's Toolkit Audio CD / CD-ROM, Add Ventures,* or the *Workbook.*

B Talk with a partner. Change the **bold** words and make conversations.

$300 — dining table
$100 — kitchen table
$75 — desk lamp
$40 — floor lamp

A Which **table** is **heavier**?
B The **dining table** is **heavier**.

1. table / heavy
2. table / small
3. table / expensive
4. table / long
5. lamp / short
6. lamp / pretty
7. lamp / cheap
8. lamp / good

Useful language
The dining table is heavier.
The dining table is heavier than the kitchen table.

3 Communicate

Talk with a partner. Compare the furniture in each store window.

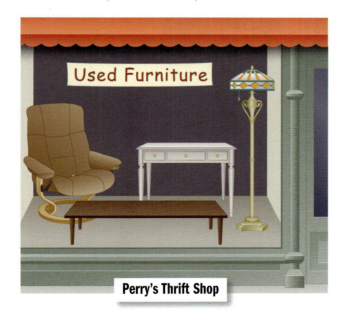

Perry's Thrift Shop

Greg's Used-Furniture Mart

A I like the **lamp** at **Perry's Thrift Shop**.
B Why?
A It's **prettier**.

Shopping

Lesson C The yellow chair is the cheapest.

1 Grammar focus: superlatives

Statements
- The blue chair is cheap.
- The red chair is cheaper.
- The yellow chair is the cheapest.

Superlatives
- big → the biggest
- cheap → the cheapest
- heavy → the heaviest
- old → the oldest
- small → the smallest
- expensive → the most expensive
- good → the best

For additional superlative adjectives, turn to page 151.

2 Practice

A Write. Complete the conversations. Use superlatives.

$1,000 $75 $200

1. **A** Which TV is _the cheapest_ ?
      (cheap)
   B _The brown TV is the cheapest._

2. **A** Which TV is _the heaviest_ ?
      (heavy)
   B _The brown TV is the heaviest._

3. **A** Which TV is _the most expensive_ ?
      (expensive)
   B _The red TV is the most expensive._

4. **A** Which TV is _the oldest_ ?
      (old)
   B _The brown TV is the oldest._

5. **A** Which TV is _the smallest_ ?
      (small)
   B _The white TV is the smallest._

6. **A** Which TV is _the biggest_ ?
      (big)
   B _The red TV is the biggest._

🔊 **Listen and repeat.** Then practice with a partner.

Lesson objectives
- Introduce superlatives
- Ask and answer questions comparing furniture, appliances, and stores

Warm-up and review
- Before class. Write today's lesson focus on the board.
Lesson C:
Compare three or more things
Ask and answer questions comparing furniture, appliances, and stores
- Begin class. Books closed. Review vocabulary and grammar from Lessons A and B as you ask Ss questions about the big picture on page 84. Ask Ss about pairs of items in the picture.
Point to the two pianos and ask: *Which piano is taller?* (the $1,200 piano)
Point to the two refrigerators and ask: *Which refrigerator is cheaper?* (the white refrigerator)
Point to the two chairs and ask: *Which chair is more comfortable?* (the red chair)
- Tell Ss: *Good! Now, you can compare two things.*

Presentation
- Books open. Direct Ss' attention to the grammar chart in Exercise **1**. Read aloud each of the statements and ask Ss to repeat.
- Point to the chairs pictured in the grammar chart. Write across the board: *the yellow chair / the red chair / the blue chair.* Ask Ss how much each chair costs, and write the prices under the words on the board.
- Draw on the board a circle that encloses the price of the blue chair ($79) and the price of the red chair ($59). Point to the two prices and ask Ss: *Which chair is cheaper?* (the red chair) Point to the second statement in the grammar chart. Read it aloud and ask Ss to repeat.
- Erase the circle you drew and draw a new circle that encloses all three prices. Ask Ss: *Which chair is the cheapest?* (the yellow chair) Point to the third statement in the grammar chart. Read it aloud and ask Ss to repeat.
- Tell Ss: *We use superlatives to compare three or more things.*
- Read aloud the adjectives and their superlative forms, and ask Ss to repeat.
- Write on the board:

Comparatives	Superlatives
bigger	the biggest
more expensive	the most expensive
better	the best

- Read each column aloud and ask Ss to repeat. Ask Ss to tell you how to form comparatives and how to form superlatives.

▼ **Teaching tip**
Asking Ss to tell you grammar rules helps you to do a quick assessment of Ss' understanding. It also makes Ss responsible for remembering the rules themselves.

Practice
- Direct Ss' attention to Exercise **2A** and read the instructions aloud. Call on two Ss to read aloud the example question and answer. Point out the adjectives in parentheses under the blanks.
- Direct Ss' attention to the three televisions pictured in Exercise **2A**. Point to the TV in the middle and say: *This is the brown TV.* Point to the TV on the left and ask: *What can we call this TV?* Elicit: *the red TV.* Do the same for the TV on the right. Elicit: *the white TV.*
- Ss complete the exercise individually. Walk around and help as needed.

Comprehension check
- Read aloud the second part of the instructions for Exercise **2A**.
- [Class Audio CD2 track 12] Play or read the audio program (see audio script, page T-159). Ss listen and repeat as they check their answers. Repeat the audio program as needed.
- Have pairs practice the questions and answers. Help with pronunciation as needed.

Learner persistence (whole group)
- Ask the Ss who watch TV in English to suggest shows that help them improve their English. List Ss' responses on the board, and make your own suggestions, for example: children's shows that teach reading skills or dramas with continuing story lines that keep Ss motivated to watch again and again.
- Discuss the advantages of using closed captioning while watching TV. Some language learners say that using it helps them develop reading speed. However, the closed captioning doesn't always match what the actors are saying and might prevent learners from improving their listening comprehension.

Lesson C The yellow chair is the cheapest.

Presentation
- Direct Ss' attention to the picture in Exercise **2B**. Ask Ss: *What do you see?* Elicit and write on the board as much vocabulary about the picture as possible (a mall, a shopping center, clothes stores, people with shopping bags, signs, etc.).
- Point to the man and woman in the foreground in the picture. Ask Ss: *What are they doing?* (They're shopping.) *What will they do next?* (They will go to a store. / They will buy something.)

Practice
- Read aloud the instructions for Exercise **2B**. Call on a S to read the example to the class. Direct Ss' attention to the word *new* under the blank, and the superlative form *the newest* written in the blank.
- Ss complete Exercise **2B** individually. Walk around and help as needed.

> **Useful language**
> Read aloud the two sentences from the Useful language box. Tell Ss: *You can use this language to talk about stores that are not expensive.* Ask a S to read aloud sentence number 4 in Exercise **2B**: *It usually has the lowest prices.* Ask the class: *Is there a different way to say this?* Elicit: *It usually has the cheapest prices.*

Comprehension check
- [Class Audio CD2 track 13] Read aloud the second part of the instructions for Exercise **2B**. Play or read the audio program (see audio script, page T-159). Have students check their answers as they listen and repeat.
- Write the numbers *2–10* on the board. Ask a few Ss to come to the board and write their answers next to each number. Ask the same Ss to read each sentence aloud using the superlative form they wrote on the board. After each sentence is read, point to the answer on the board and ask the class: *Is this correct?* Make corrections on the board, and be sure that number 10 is spelled correctly: *friendliest*.
- Ss practice the conversation in pairs. Listen for any words that are difficult for Ss to pronounce. When pairs are finished, write any difficult words on the board and practice pronouncing them as a class.

Expansion activity (whole group)
- Give Ss another look at the language from Exercise **2B**, and help them visually to arrange the information about the stores using a simple graphic organizer.

- Draw on the board three columns with the names of the three stores from Exercise **2B** at the top: *Mega Store / Cleo's Boutique / Madison's*. Point to each name and say, for example: *Tell me about Mega Store*. Elicit and list under each name some of the descriptive phrases from the exercise. For example, under *Mega Store,* you might write: *It's the biggest store; It usually has the lowest prices; It's the most crowded store.*

Application
- Direct Ss' attention to Exercise **3** and read the instructions aloud. Call on individual Ss to read one of the questions aloud. Remind Ss that we use superlatives to compare three or more things.
- Ss complete the exercise in small groups. Walk around and help as needed.
- Draw four columns on the board and label the columns: *the biggest clothing store / the clothing store with the lowest prices / the cheapest supermarket / the best restaurant*.
- Discuss each category. List the groups' ideas on the board.

Evaluation
- Direct Ss' attention to the first part of the lesson focus written on the board. Write on the board a large letter *A,* a small letter *B,* and a medium-sized letter *C*. Ask Ss: *Which letter is the smallest?* (B) Write three "price tags" under the letters with three different prices. Ask: *Which letter is the cheapest? Which letter is the most expensive?*
- Direct Ss' attention to the second part of the lesson focus. Have Ss turn to the big picture on page 84 and ask their classmates questions with *Which* and superlative adjectives. Write on the board items in the picture that Ss can choose from: *four appliances / three chairs / three lamps / three signs*.
- Write on the board at least three stores in the same category that Ss thought of in Exercise **3**. Ask Ss questions similar to those in Exercise **3**, for example: *Which store has the lowest prices? Which store is the biggest? Which store is the best place to buy _____?*
- Check off each part of the lesson focus as Ss demonstrate an understanding of what they have learned in the lesson.

> **More Ventures** (whole group, pairs, individual)
> Assign appropriate exercises from the *Teacher's Toolkit Audio CD / CD-ROM, Add Ventures,* or the *Workbook*.

B Write. Complete the conversation. Use superlatives.

Useful language
It has low prices.
It has cheap prices.

A This is ___the newest___ shopping mall in the city. It's great.
               1. new

B Where's ___the best___ place to buy clothes?
            2. good

A Well, there are three clothing stores. Mega Store is ___the biggest___
                                             3. big

   one. It usually has ___the lowest___ prices, but it's ___the most crowded___ .
                         4. low   5. crowded

   I never go there.

B What about Cleo's Boutique?

A Cleo's Boutique is ___the most beautiful___ store. It's nice, but it's ___the most expensive___ .
                            6. beautiful   7. expensive

B What about Madison's?

A Well, it's ___the smallest___ , but it's my favorite. It has ___the nicest___
               8. small   9. nice

   clothes and ___the friendliest___ salespeople.
                   10. friendly

B Look! Madison's is having a big sale. Let's go!

🔘 **Listen** and check your answers. Then practice with a partner.

3 Communicate

Talk in a group. Ask and answer the questions about places in your community.

1. Which clothing store is the biggest?
2. Which clothing store has the lowest prices?
3. Which supermarket is the cheapest?
4. Which restaurant is the best?

Shopping

Lesson D Reading

1 Before you read

Look at the picture. Answer the questions.

1. Who is the woman?
2. What did she buy?

2 Read

  Read the newspaper article. Listen and read again.

Today's Question
What's the best thing you ever bought?

The best thing I ever bought was an old piano. I bought it in a used-furniture store last month. It was the most beautiful piano in the store, but it wasn't very expensive. It has a beautiful sound. Now my two children are taking piano lessons. I love to hear music in the house.

Denise Robinson
Charleston, SC

I bought a used van five years ago. I used my van to help people move and to deliver stoves and refrigerators from a secondhand appliance store. I made a lot of money with that van. Now I have my own business. That van is the best thing I ever bought.

Sammy Chin
Myrtle Beach, SC

> Guess the meaning of new words from other words nearby.
> appliances = stoves, refrigerators

3 After you read

Write. Answer the questions about the article.

1. What did Denise buy? _She bought an old piano._
2. What did Sammy buy? _He bought a used van._
3. Who is taking piano lessons? _Denise's two children are taking piano lessons._
4. Who has a business? _Sammy has a business._
5. Which was probably more expensive – the piano or the van? _The van was probably more expensive._

Lesson objectives
- Introduce and read a short newspaper article
- Guess the meaning of new words from other words nearby
- Practice using new topic-related words

Warm-up and review
- Before class. Write today's lesson focus on the board.
  Lesson D:
  Read and understand a newspaper article
  Guess the meaning of new words
  Learn vocabulary for furniture
- Begin class. Books closed. Review superlatives by asking Ss about furniture and other items in your classroom. Ask, for example: *Which desk is the biggest? Which window is the tallest? Which computer is the newest? Which table is the heaviest?* Ask questions that recycle vocabulary from the unit and that apply to your classroom.
- Review the language from the Culture note in Lesson A. Write on the board: *used-furniture store, thrift store, secondhand store.* Point to the first phrase and ask Ss: *What is this?* (a store with used furniture) Point to the second two phrases and ask: *Can you buy used furniture here?* (Yes. / Probably.) *What other things can you buy at these stores?* (lamps, clothes, musical instruments, dishes, etc.) *Do they have low prices at these stores?* (Yes.)

Presentation
- Books open. Direct Ss' attention to Exercise **1** and read the instructions aloud. Ask Ss the two questions about the picture, and remind Ss that Denise was shopping with Nick in Lesson A. Elicit appropriate answers from Ss.

Practice
- Direct Ss' attention to Exercise **2** and read the instructions aloud. Ask Ss: *What's the title of the article?* (Today's Question) Ask Ss: *What's today's question?* (What's the best thing you ever bought?)
- Point out the names and cities under the two parts of the article. Explain that people wrote letters to the newspaper to answer the question. Ss read the newspaper article individually.

> Read the tip box aloud. Explain that if a person reading the newspaper article didn't know the meaning of *appliance store*, the nearby words *stoves* and *refrigerators* would help explain it. These words are context clues.

- [Class Audio CD2 track 14] Play or read the audio program and ask Ss to read along (see audio script, page T-159). Repeat the audio program as needed. Answer any questions Ss have about the reading.

Expansion activity *(student pairs)*
- Ask Ss in pairs to practice reading aloud the newspaper article. Have Ss ask each other the question, *What's the best thing you ever bought?* Then read aloud the answers to the question that Denise and Sammy wrote.
- When pairs are finished, have them switch roles and repeat the activity.

Learner persistence *(individual work)*
- [Self-Study Audio CD track 25] Exercise **2** is recorded on the Ss' self-study CD at the back of the Student's Book. Ss can listen to the CD at home for reinforcement and review. They can also listen to the CD for self-directed learning when class attendance is not possible.

Comprehension check
- Direct Ss' attention to Exercise **3** and read the instructions aloud. Ask two Ss to read the example question and answer to the class. Ask Ss to write complete sentences.
- Ss complete the exercise individually. Walk around and help as needed.
- Check answers with the class. Write the numbers *2–5* on the board and ask a few Ss to come to the board and write their sentences next to the numbers. Have different Ss read the sentences aloud.
- Ss may have different ideas about number 5. Discuss the question as a class. Ss might remember how much the piano cost, or they can look at the big picture on page 84 to remind them ($1,200). Some Ss might think that Sammy found a van for less than $1,200. Discuss the kind of van someone might buy for $1,200 and whether or not it would be reliable enough for a business.

Community building *(whole group)*
- Ask Ss whether anyone in the class has a piano or another musical instrument. Find out whether Ss or their children play musical instruments or are taking music lessons.
- Ask Ss whether anyone in the class has his or her own business. Encourage Ss to tell about any business they have now or have had in the past. Ask Ss to tell the class about any plans they might have to start their own business in the future.

Lesson D   T-90

Lesson D Reading

Warm-up and review
- Books closed. Write the word *Furniture* on the board. Elicit and write on the board as many examples of furniture as possible. If Ss don't mention all of the furniture from Lessons A and B, have them look at page 86 for ideas. Help Ss with vocabulary for other types of furniture they might know.

Presentation
- Books open. Direct Ss' attention to the picture dictionary in Exercise **4**. Ask: *What do you see?* (a room, an apartment, pictures, a sofa bed, plants, etc.) Ask: *Who might live here?* (e.g., a single woman, a couple with no children, etc.)
- Recycle vocabulary from the unit. Ask Ss questions about things in the picture they didn't already mention, for example: *Do you see a lamp?* (Yes.) *Is it a desk lamp or a floor lamp?* (It's a desk lamp.) *Do you see a table?* (Yes.) *Do you see a piano?* (No.)
- Direct Ss' attention to the word bank. Say each word in the word bank and ask Ss to repeat. Listen to Ss' pronunciation. Correct pronunciation as needed.
- Read aloud the instructions in Exercise **4A**. Point to number 1, which has been done. Make sure Ss understand the exercise.
- Ss complete the exercise individually. Walk around and help as needed.

Comprehension check
- [Class Audio CD2 track 15] Say: *Listen and repeat.* Play or read the audio program (see audio script, page T-159). Ss check their answers and repeat the words. Repeat the audio program as needed.

Learner persistence (individual work)
- [Self-Study Audio CD track 26] Exercise **4A** is recorded on the Ss' self-study CD at the back of the Student's Book. Ss can listen to the CD at home for reinforcement and review. They can also listen to the CD for self-directed learning when class attendance is not possible.

Practice
- Read aloud the instructions for Exercise **4B**. Ask two Ss to read aloud the example conversations.
- Generate a list of adjectives from the unit. Have Ss turn to each page of Lessons A and B and find descriptive adjectives. List the base form of the adjectives on the board, for example: *big; expensive; heavy.*

- Make sure Ss understand that they are to use the words in the picture dictionary as well as comparatives. Ss complete the exercise in pairs. Walk around and help as needed.
- Ask several pairs of Ss to perform one of their conversations for the class.

▼ **Teaching tip**
Since the second example conversation in Exercise **4B** doesn't include a negative answer, you could suggest some polite ways to give one. Write on the board: *No, not really.* and *It's OK, but . . .* Explain that both of these expressions are followed by a reason, for example:
A: *Do you like the bookcase?*
B: *It's OK, but it's bigger than it should be. The apartment is quite small.*

Expansion activity *(whole group)*
- As a class, recycle vocabulary for furniture by organizing it according to rooms in a house.
- Make five columns on the board labeled: *bedroom / living room / kitchen / dining room / bathroom*
- Point to each column and ask Ss: *What furniture do you usually find in the _____?* Encourage Ss to add and explain any words not covered in the unit.

Evaluation
- Direct Ss' attention to the lesson focus written on the board. Ask Ss some questions about the newspaper article, such as: *What does Denise like about her piano?* (the sound / It wasn't expensive.) *Who plays Denise's piano?* (her children) *What did Sammy do with his van?* (He helped people move. / He used it to deliver appliances.) *Did Sammy make much money with his van?* (Yes, he did.)
- Ask the class to tell you one way to guess the meaning of new words when they are reading.
- Point to pieces of furniture in the picture on page 91, and ask Ss to tell you what the pieces are.
- Check off each part of the lesson focus as Ss demonstrate an understanding of what they have learned in the lesson.

More Ventures *(whole group, pairs, individual)*
Assign appropriate exercises from the *Teacher's Toolkit Audio CD / CD-ROM, Add Ventures,* or the *Workbook.*

4 Picture dictionary — Furniture

1. end table
2. bookcase
3. dresser
4. entertainment center
5. sofa bed
6. mirror
7. china cabinet
8. coffee table
9. recliner

 A Write the words in the picture dictionary. Then listen and repeat.

bookcase	dresser	mirror
china cabinet	end table	recliner
coffee table	entertainment center	sofa bed

B Talk with a partner. Change the **bold** words and make conversations.

> A Which is **bigger**, the **coffee table** or the **end table**?
> B The **coffee table** is **bigger**.

> A Do you like the **bookcase**?
> B **Yes**, I **do**. It's **nicer** than my **bookcase**.

Shopping

Lesson E Writing

1 Before you write

A Talk with a partner. These blankets are gifts. Which gift is the best? Tell why.

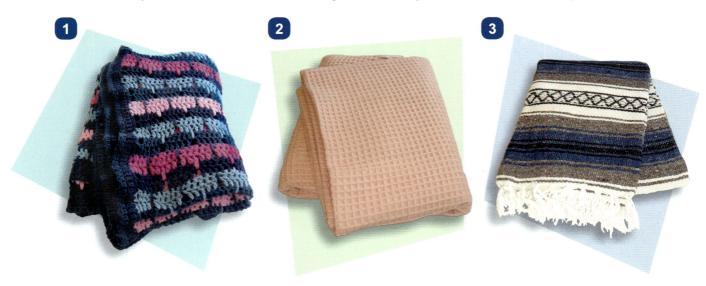

1   2   3

B Talk with three classmates. Ask questions and complete the chart.

1. What's the best gift you ever received?
2. Who gave it to you?
3. When did you receive this gift?
4. Why was it the best gift?

Name	Paolo	(Answers will vary.)		
Best gift	a trip to Brazil			
From	his wife			
When	last summer			
Why	because he saw his parents again			

Talk. Share your information with the class.

> Paolo's best gift was a trip to Brazil last summer. His wife gave it to him. It was the best gift because he saw his parents again.

92   Unit 7

Lesson objectives
- Write a descriptive paragraph about a gift
- Use *because* to answer *Why* and to give a reason

Warm-up and review

- Before class. Write today's lesson focus on the board.
  Lesson E:
  Write a paragraph about a gift
  Use because to give a reason
- Begin class. Books closed. Point to the first part of the lesson focus. Say to Ss: *Today, you will write a paragraph about a gift.* Ask Ss: *What is a gift?* (something a person gives to you) Ask Ss: *When do people usually give gifts?* (birthdays, holidays, anniversaries, retirement parties, etc.) Ask Ss: *Do you know another word for "gift"?* (Ss may know the word *present*.)
- Write on the board: *good*. Ask Ss: *What is the comparative form of "good"?* (better) *What is the superlative form of "good"?* (the best) Tell Ss: *We're going to talk and write about the best gifts.*

Presentation

- Direct Ss' attention to the pictures in Exercise **1A** and read the instructions aloud.
- Model the exercise with a S. Say, for example: *I think all of these blankets are nice gifts. Which blanket do you like?* If the S gives a short answer, such as *I like the pink blanket*, ask the S: *Why do you like the pink blanket?*
- Work with Ss to generate and write on the board a list of useful language. First, ask Ss: *What can we call the first blanket?* Decide on good ways to refer to the blankets. Next, suggest vocabulary for discussing the qualities of the blankets, for example: *made by hand; machine-made; colorful; warm; decorative;* etc.
- Ask pairs of Ss to discuss which blanket is the best gift.
- When Ss are finished, call on several Ss to tell the rest of the class why they think one of the blankets is the best gift. Encourage Ss to give detailed reasons for their choice.

Practice

- Direct Ss' attention to Exercise **1B** and read the instructions to the class. Call on Ss to read the four questions aloud.
- Model the exercise. Say to a S: *I am Paolo. Please ask me the four questions.* Have the S ask you the questions. Answer the questions as Paolo, changing the language in the chart to first person; for example: *My wife gave it to me.* Make sure Ss understand the exercise.
- Ask Ss to stand up, walk around the room, talk to three classmates, and fill in their charts.

Comprehension check

- Read aloud the second part of the instructions for Exercise **1B**. Call on a S to read the example to the class.
- Ask the class: *Who can tell me about the best gift (S' name) ever received?* Ask about each S in the class. Make sure that every S talks about the information in his or her chart at least once.

Expansion activity (small groups)

- Divide the class into small groups of three or four Ss. Ask Ss to work together to write a story about Paolo, the man in the example in Exercise **1B**.
- Ask a few questions to get Ss started, and elicit various answers to each question. For example, ask: *Where was Paolo born? Where does he live now? What is his wife's name? When and where did he meet his wife? What do Paolo and his wife do for a living? Do they have any children? When Paolo arrived in Brazil, what was the first thing he did?*
- Have each group choose a secretary to write down the group's story, and give Ss a time limit.
- When Ss are finished, ask a volunteer from each group to stand up and read its story to the class.

Lesson E T-92

Lesson E Writing

Presentation

- Direct Ss' attention to Exercise **1C** and read the instructions aloud.
- Ask Ss: *What is the title of the story?* (The Best Gift) Ask: *What do you see in the picture?* (a necklace / a heart / jewelry) Ask: *What do you think the story is about?* (e.g., the best gift the writer ever got: a necklace)
- Read aloud the words in the word bank and ask Ss to repeat. Explain any words Ss don't know. Ask a S to read aloud the first sentence of the story and point to where *necklace* has been written above number 1.
- Ss complete the story individually using the words in the word bank.
- Check answers. Call on individual Ss to read aloud one sentence of the story. If there are any errors, ask the class: *Does anyone have a different answer?* Ask a S with a different answer to suggest a correction.

Practice

- Direct Ss' attention to Exercise **1D** and read the instructions aloud. Tell Ss that this exercise will help them get ideas for the paragraphs they'll write in Exercise **2**. Make sure Ss write complete sentences.

Expansion activity (student pairs)

- Have pairs share their sentences from Exercise **1D**. Ask Ss to take turns asking and answering the questions.
- When Ss have finished, ask pairs to read aloud the questions and their answers for the rest of the class.

Application

- Tell Ss that they will write a paragraph about the best gift they have ever received.
- Direct Ss' attention to Exercise **2** and read the instructions aloud. Point to Exercises **1C** and **1D** to show Ss where to look for help.

> Read the tip box aloud. Ask Ss to find the word *because* in the paragraph in Exercise **1C**. (It's in the last sentence.) Ask Ss: *Why was the necklace the best gift the writer ever received?* (It was the best gift because it was from the writer's mother.)

- Ss take out a piece of paper and write their paragraphs individually. Walk around and help as needed.

▼ **Teaching tip**
Remind Ss to indent the first sentence of their paragraph and to capitalize people's names, the names of cities and places, and the first word of each sentence.

Comprehension check

- Direct Ss' attention to Exercise **3A** and read the instructions aloud. Partners take turns reading their paragraphs to each other. Walk around and help with pronunciation as needed.
- Direct Ss' attention to Exercise **3B** and read the instructions aloud. Ask Ss to read the three questions aloud. Have Ss take out a piece of paper and write down the three questions.
- Have Ss exchange paragraphs. Tell Ss: *Read your partner's paragraph. Write answers to the three questions.* When Ss are finished, have them share their answers and discuss their paragraphs.

Evaluation

- Direct Ss' attention to the lesson focus written on the board.
- Ask Ss to tell you some of the things they wrote in their paragraphs. Ask several Ss to come to the board and to each write a sentence with *because*.
- Check off each part of the lesson focus as Ss demonstrate an understanding of what they have learned in the lesson.

> **More Ventures** (whole group, pairs, individual)
> Assign appropriate exercises from the *Teacher's Toolkit Audio CD / CD-ROM*, *Add Ventures*, or the *Workbook*.

C Read the story. Complete the sentences.

ago	heart	necklace
birthday	mother	store

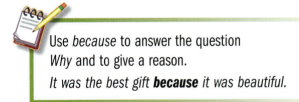

The Best Gift

The best gift I ever received was a ____necklace____ . My
                                           1
____mother____ bought it in a jewelry ____store____ .
        2   3
The necklace was in the shape of a ____heart____ . She gave
                                          4
it to me for my ____birthday____ a long time ____ago____ .
                        5   6
My mother said it was her heart. It was the best gift because it

was from her.

D Write. Answer the questions about yourself.

1. What is the best gift you ever received? ____(Answers will vary.)____
2. Who gave it to you? _____
3. Why did you receive it? _____
4. Did the gift come from a store? _____
5. When did you receive this gift? _____
6. Why was it the best gift? _____

2 Write

Write a paragraph about the best gift you ever received.
Use Exercises 1C and 1D to help you.

> Use *because* to answer the question *Why* and to give a reason.
> It was the best gift **because** it was beautiful.

3 After you write

A Read your paragraph to a partner.

B Check your partner's paragraph.
- What was the gift?
- Why was it the best gift?
- Did your partner use *because* to say why?

Shopping 93

Lesson F Another view

1 Life-skills reading

Al's Discount Furniture
2100 Willow Boulevard
Charleston, SC 29401
(843) 555-0936

SALES RECEIPT
Sold to:
Nick Robinson
2718 Central Avenue
Charleston, SC 29412

Item #	Description	Price
1.	Blue sofa	$699.00
2.	Coffee table	$295.00
3.	Table lamp	$39.95
4.	Bookcase	$149.00
	Subtotal	$1,182.95
	Sales tax 7.5%	$88.72
	TOTAL	**$1,271.67**
	VISTA/MASTERCHARGE	$1,271.67

No refunds or exchanges after 30 days.

A Read the questions. Look at the sales receipt. Circle the answers.

1. Which is the cheapest item?
   a. the blue sofa
   b. the bookcase
   c. the coffee table
   (d.) the table lamp

2. Which is the most expensive item?
   (a.) the blue sofa
   b. the bookcase
   c. the coffee table
   d. the table lamp

3. When can a customer *not* exchange an item?
   a. after 7 days
   b. after 15 days
   c. before 30 days
   (d.) after 30 days

4. What is the total of the receipt?
   a. $88.72
   b. $699.00
   c. $1,182.95
   (d.) $1,271.67

B Talk with a partner. Ask and answer the questions.

1. What percent is the sales tax on the receipt for Al's Discount Furniture?
2. What percent is the sales tax in your town or city?
3. Did you buy any furniture this year? What did you buy?

94 Unit 7

Lesson objectives
- Practice reading a sales receipt
- Review unit vocabulary
- Introduce the project
- Complete the project and self-assessment

Warm-up and review

- Before class. Write today's lesson focus on the board.
*Lesson F:
Read a sales receipt
Review topic vocabulary
Complete the project and the self-assessment*
- Begin class. Books open. Have Ss turn to the picture in the picture dictionary on page 91. Ask questions to review furniture vocabulary including the words Ss will see in Exercise **1A** (sofa, coffee table, bookcase). Ask, for example: *Do you see a bookcase?* (Yes.) Say: *Please point to a bookcase.* (Ss point.) Ask: *Do you see a desk?* (No.) Ask: *Do you see a coffee table?* (Yes.)
- Review superlatives. Write on the board: *cheap / expensive / good*. Point to each word and ask Ss: *What's the superlative form?* Write the superlative form under each of the words on the board.
- Point to the first part of the lesson focus. Tell the class: *Today, we will practice reading a sales receipt.*

Presentation

- Books open. Direct Ss' attention to the sales receipt above Exercise **1A**. Say: *This is a sales receipt.* Write on the board: *receipt*. Say the word and ask Ss to repeat. Listen to Ss' pronunciation and make sure they are not pronouncing the silent "p."
- Ask Ss: *When do you get a sales receipt?* Elicit: *You get a sales receipt when you buy something.* Ask Ss: *What is a sales receipt?* Elicit: *It shows the things you bought and the prices you paid.* Point to the sales receipt and ask: *What did this person buy?* (a blue sofa, a coffee table, a table lamp, a bookcase)

Practice

- Read aloud the instructions for Exercise **1A**. This exercise helps prepare Ss for standardized-type tests they may have to take. Make sure Ss understand the exercise. Have Ss individually scan for and circle the answers. Walk around and help as needed.

Comprehension check

- Go over the answers to Exercise **1A** together. Make sure that Ss have followed the instructions and circled their answers.

Expansion activity (whole group)

- Go over and discuss each part of the sales receipt. For example, ask Ss: *What's the name of the store? What's the address of the store?* Ask Ss: *Who bought this furniture? Where does he live?*
- Continue in this manner and explain any vocabulary Ss do not know.

Community building (whole group)

- Ask Ss if they think the furniture listed on the sales receipt is expensive or inexpensive. Have a class discussion about how much new and used furniture usually costs.

Application

- Direct Ss' attention to Exercise **1B** and read the instructions aloud.
- Have pairs ask and answer the questions in Exercise **1B**. If Ss are not sure about the answer to question number 2, tell them how much sales tax is in your town or city.
- When pairs are finished, ask Ss to tell the class about any furniture they bought this year.

▼ **Culture tip**

Besides the secondhand stores mentioned in the unit, garage sales, yard sales, or flea markets are also popular ways to buy and sell used furniture, clothing, books, toys, and many other items. Write the phrases on the board and ask Ss if they have ever bought secondhand goods at these sales. Explain that garage sales or yard sales refer to people displaying and selling their secondhand items at their homes, while flea markets have a large number of sellers and are held regularly in public places, often on the weekend. If some of your Ss are experienced bargain hunters, invite them to share any useful information about such sales with the rest of the class.

Lesson F Another view

Warm-up and review

- Ask Ss several questions about the items Ss have in class. Use superlatives. For example, ask: *Who has the smallest pencil in the class?* Ask Ss who have wooden pencils to hold them up for everyone to see. Look for pencils that have been sharpened many times. When you see some pencils that look small, say, for example: *Paul, your pencil is small, but Lucia, is your pencil smaller than Paul's pencil?* Let Ss determine who has the smallest pencil in the class.
- Continue in this manner asking about other items; for example: *Who has the biggest purse in the class? / Who has the oldest notebook in the class? / Who has the most colorful clothes in the class?*

Practice

- Direct Ss' attention to Exercise **2A** and read the instructions aloud. Ask a S to read the example question aloud. Point to where the name has been written in the chart.
- Divide the class into small groups of five or six Ss. Walk around and help as needed.
- Read aloud the second part of the instructions for Exercise **2A**. Have all the Ss in each small group share the task of reporting their information to the class.

Expansion activity *(small groups)*

- In the same small groups, have each S use a superlative to write one question similar to the ones in the chart in Exercise **2A**.
- Have groups repeat the process of answering the questions and reporting to the class.

Practice

- Direct Ss' attention to Exercise **2B** and read the instructions aloud. Point to where *sofa* has been written on a piece of paper.
- Ask Ss to think about a piece of furniture in their homes and write the word. Have them cover up or put away the paper.
- Read aloud the second part of the instructions in Exercise **2B**. Ask two Ss to read the example conversation aloud.
- Ss complete the exercise in pairs. When Ss are finished, ask for volunteers to let the class ask them questions about the piece of furniture they wrote on the paper.

Expansion activity *(student pairs)*

- Repeat Exercise **2B** using appliances instead of furniture. Start by asking Ss to look through the unit for appliances. List those appliances on the board. Then, brainstorm the names of appliances that have not been covered in the unit, including small appliances such as: *microwave oven; blender; coffeemaker; toaster;* etc.
- Ss write the name of an appliance on a piece of paper and then complete the activity in pairs. Walk around and help as needed.
- When Ss are finished, ask for volunteers to let the class ask them questions about the appliance they wrote.

> **More Ventures** *(whole group, pairs, individual)*
> Assign appropriate exercises from the *Teacher's Toolkit Audio CD / CD-ROM, Add Ventures*, or the *Workbook*.

Application

Community building

- **Project** Ask Ss to turn to page 139 to complete the project for Unit 7.

Evaluation

- Before asking Ss to turn to the self-assessment on page 144, do a quick review of the unit. Have Ss turn to Lesson A. Ask the class to talk about what they remember about this lesson. Prompt Ss, if necessary, with questions. For example: *What are the conversations about on this page? What vocabulary is in the big picture?* Continue in this manner to review each lesson quickly.
- **Self-assessment** Read the instructions in Exercise **3**. Ask Ss to turn to the self-assessment page and complete the unit self-assessment.
- If Ss are ready, administer the unit test on pages T-181–T-182 of this *Teacher's Edition* (or on the *Teacher's Toolkit Audio CD / CD-ROM*). The audio and audio script for the tests are on the *Teacher's Toolkit Audio CD / CD-ROM*.

2 Fun with language

A Work in a group. Complete the chart with names of people in your group.

1. Who has the oldest child?	Teresa
2. Who has the shortest first name?	(Answers will vary.)
3. Who has the longest last name?	
4. Who has the most brothers and sisters?	
5. Who is the tallest?	
6. Who is the youngest?	
7. Who has the longest hair?	
8. Who has the smallest shoe size?	
9. Who is wearing the biggest ring?	
10. Who has the oldest pet?	

Talk. Share your information with the class.

> Teresa has the oldest child. Her son is 24 years old.

B Write. Think of a piece of furniture in your home. Write it on the paper.

> sofa
> (Answers will vary.)

Work with a partner. Ask and answer questions to guess the pieces of furniture. You can only answer *Yes* or *No*.

> **A** Is it in your bedroom?
> **B** No.
> **A** Is it in your living room?
> **B** Yes.
> **A** Do you sit on it?
> **B** Yes.
> **A** Is it a sofa?
> **B** Yes.

3 Wrap up

Complete the **Self-assessment** on page 144.

Shopping

Lesson A Get ready

1 Talk about the picture

A Look at the picture. What do you see?

B Point to: a lab • linens • a patient • a walker
supplies • co-workers • an orderly • a wheelchair

C Look at these people. What are they doing?

Work

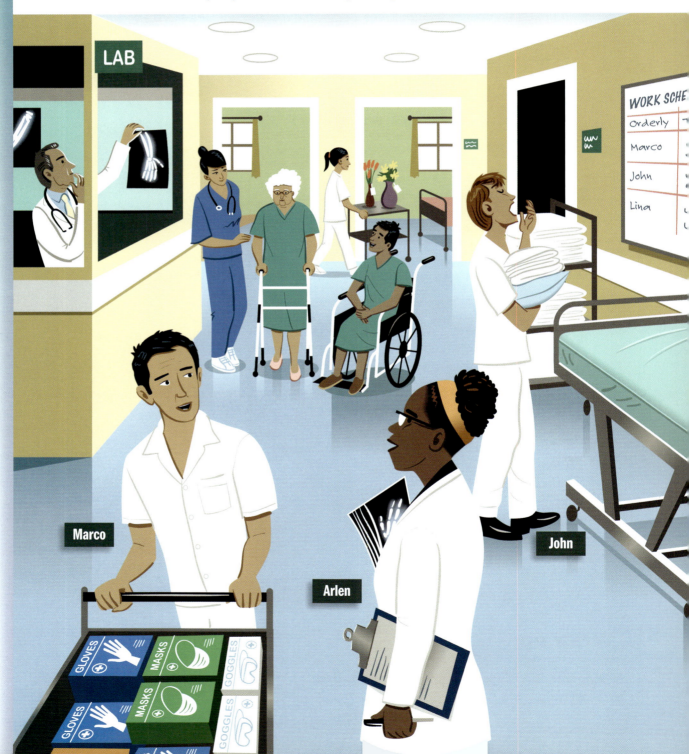

Lesson objectives
- Introduce Ss to the topic
- Find out what Ss know about the topic
- Preview the unit by talking about the picture
- Practice key vocabulary
- Practice listening skills

Warm-up and review

- Before class. Write today's lesson focus on the board. *Lesson A: Work history and job skills*
- Begin class. Books closed. Point to the words *Work history* on the board. Say the words and ask Ss to repeat. Tell Ss: *Work history is the same as job experience.*
- Tell Ss about your current job as well as one or two jobs you have had in the past. Use the simple past tense. Say, for example: *I'm an English teacher. Before I became an English teacher, I was a salesperson for an insurance company.* Check Ss' comprehension of your work history. Ask a S: *What do I do now?* Ask a different S: *What did I do before?*
- Point to the words *job skills* on the board. Say the words and ask Ss to repeat. Tell Ss: *Job skills are things you know how to do at work.*
- Tell Ss about some of the job skills that are required to be an English teacher and that were required at your previous job. Say, for example: *As an English teacher, I have to understand and explain English very well. When I was a salesperson, I contacted many people by mail, e-mail, and telephone. I had to know a lot about the company's insurance plans.*
- Check Ss' comprehension of your job skills. Ask a S: *What job skills does an English teacher need?* Ask a different S: *What job skills does an insurance salesperson need?*

Presentation

- Books open. Set the scene. Direct Ss' attention to the picture on page 96. Ask: *Where is this?* (a hospital / a clinic) Ask the question from Exercise **1A**: *What do you see?* Elicit and write on the board as much vocabulary about the picture as possible (X-rays, a wheelchair, a walker, a bed, an elderly woman, etc.).
- Direct Ss' attention to the key words in Exercise **1B**. Read each word aloud while pointing to the appropriate part of the picture. Ask the class to repeat and point.
- Listen to Ss' pronunciation and repeat the words as needed.

Comprehension check

- Ask Ss *Yes / No* questions about the picture. Say: *Listen to the questions. Answer "Yes" or "No."*
Point to the big picture. Ask: *Are people working here?* (Yes.)
Point to Marco in the lower left part of the picture. Ask: *Is Marco a nurse?* (No.)
Point to Marco and Arlen. Ask: *Are Marco and Arlen co-workers?* (Yes.)
Point to the wheelchair. Ask: *Is this a wheelchair?* (Yes.)
Point to the woman with the walker. Ask: *Is the woman using a walker?* (Yes.)
Point to John, the yawning man. Ask: *Is the man with the linens tired?* (Yes.)
Point to the man in the lab. Ask: *Is the man in the lab a patient?* (No.)

Practice

- Direct Ss' attention to Exercise **1B**. Model the exercise. Hold up the Student's Book. Say to a S: *Point to a lab.* The S points to the appropriate part of the picture.
- Ss in pairs. Say to one S: *Say the words in Exercise* **1B**. Say to his or her partner: *Point to the correct part of the picture.*
- Walk around and help as needed. When pairs finish, have them change roles. If time allows, have Ss repeat the exercise with new partners.
- Ask several pairs to perform the exercise for the rest of the class to check Ss' understanding.

Practice

- Direct Ss' attention to Exercise **1C** and read aloud the instructions and the question.
- Model the exercise. Hold up the Student's Book. Say to a S: *Point to a person in the picture.* Describe what the person the S indicates is doing. For example, if the S points to Arlen, you could say: *She is working at the hospital. She is talking to Marco. She is carrying an X-ray.*
- Ss in pairs. Say to one S: *Point to a person in the picture.* Say to his or her partner: *Say what the person is doing.*
- Walk around and help as needed. Make sure every S has a chance to describe people in the picture.
- Ask several pairs to perform the exercise for the rest of the class.

Lesson A   T-96

Lesson A Get ready

Presentation

- Books open. Direct Ss' attention to the pictures in Exercise **2A**. Point to picture 1 and ask: *Is this during the day or at night?* (at night) Point to picture 2 and ask: *Is this a Human Resources office?* (Yes.) Point to picture 3. Ask: *Does the person who wrote this list need to deliver flowers?* (No, he or she has already delivered flowers.)

▼ **Teaching tip**
Explain to Ss that people in Human Resources, or HR, for short, hire and train employees, evaluate employees' job performance, and manage employee pay and benefits.

Practice

- Read aloud the instructions for Exercise **2A**.
- [Class Audio CD2 track 16] Play or read the audio program (see audio script, page T-159). Pause the audio program after the first conversation and ask Ss: *Which picture shows conversation A?* (Picture 3) Hold up the Student's Book and write the letter *a* next to number 3. Make sure Ss understand the exercise.
- [Class Audio CD2 track 16] Play or read the complete audio program and repeat as needed.
- Check answers. Ask Ss which picture shows each conversation.
- Direct Ss' attention to Exercise **2B** and read the instructions aloud.
- [Class Audio CD2 track 16] Model the exercise. Say: *Listen to conversation A*. Play or read conversation A. Direct Ss' attention to the example sentence. Read it aloud, and point to where the letter *T* (True) is written. Make sure Ss understand the exercise.
- [Class Audio CD2 track 16] Read aloud each group of sentences before listening to the corresponding conversation. Read aloud the three sentences for conversation A. Then, play or read conversation A of the audio program (see audio script, page T-159). Do the same for conversations B and C.
- Ss complete the exercise individually. When Ss are finished writing their answers, play or read the complete audio program once more to allow Ss to check the answers they wrote.

Comprehension check

- Check answers. Write the numbers *2–9* on the board. Ask a few Ss to come to the board to write the correct answers to Exercise **2B** next to each number. Point to each answer and ask: *Is this correct?* If Ss are not sure about an answer, play or read the appropriate part of the audio program again.

Learner persistence *(individual work)*

- [Self-Study Audio CD track 27] Exercises **2A** and **2B** are recorded on the Ss' self-study CD at the back of the Student's Book. Ss can listen to the CD at home for reinforcement and review. They can also listen for self-directed learning when class attendance is not possible.

Culture note
Read aloud the Culture note. Ask Ss whether anyone in the class works the night shift or has worked the night shift in the past. You could discuss why a hospital needs people to work the night shift and why working the night shift has advantages and disadvantages.

Expansion activity *(whole group)*

- In Exercise **2B**, Ss learn that although Marco likes his job, he doesn't want to be an orderly forever. He wants to go back to school and become a nurse. Bring in information about different types of nurses and the nursing programs that are available in your community.

Application

- Direct Ss' attention to Exercise **2C** and read the instructions aloud. Ask three Ss to read the questions to the class.
- Pairs ask and answer the questions. Help as needed.
- When Ss are finished, call on several Ss to report their answers to the rest of the class.

Evaluation

- Direct Ss' attention to the lesson focus written on the board. Talk about Marco's work history and job skills. First, ask Ss what Marco's job is now. Then, ask Ss what Marco does as a hospital orderly.
- Hold up the big picture in the Student's Book or print out the vocabulary cards from the *Teacher's Toolkit Audio CD / CD-ROM*. Ask about the key words, for example: *Who is this person?* (a patient) *What is this?* (a lab)
- Check off each part of the lesson focus as Ss demonstrate an understanding of what they have learned in the lesson.

More Ventures *(whole group, pairs, individual)*
Assign appropriate exercises from the *Teacher's Toolkit Audio CD / CD-ROM, Add Ventures,* or the *Workbook.*

UNIT 8

2 Listening

A **Listen.** What is Marco talking about? Write the letter of the conversation.

1. _b_   2. _c_   3. _a_

B **Listen again.** Write *T* (true) or *F* (false).

Conversation A
1. Marco picked up X-rays this morning.   _T_
2. Marco delivered linens to the third floor.   _T_
3. Marco needs to prepare rooms on the second floor.   _F_

Conversation B
4. John is tired.   _T_
5. Marco worked the night shift.   _F_
6. Marco wants to go back to school.   _T_

Conversation C
7. Suzanne works in Human Resources.   _T_
8. Marco wants to be a nurse.   _T_
9. Marco wants to work full-time.   _F_

> **Culture note**
> People who work at night work the *night shift*.

Listen again. Check your answers.

C **Talk** with a partner. Ask and answer the questions.

1. Do you have a job? What do you do?
2. Did you have a job before? What did you do?
3. What job do you want in the future?

Lesson B Where did you go last night?

1 Grammar focus: *What* and *Where* questions and simple past

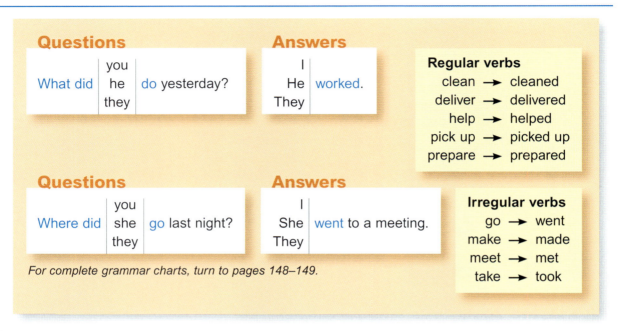

For complete grammar charts, turn to pages 148–149.

2 Practice

A Write. Complete the conversations. Use *What* or *Where* and the simple past.

1. **A** __What__ did Linda do after breakfast?
   B She __made__ the beds.
   (make)
2. **A** __What__ did Brenda and Leo do this morning?
   B They __picked up__ patients in the reception area.
   (pick up)
3. **A** __What__ did Trevor do this morning?
   B He __delivered__ X-rays.
   (deliver)
4. **A** __Where__ did Jill and Brad take the linens?
   B They __took__ the linens to the second floor.
   (take)
5. **A** __What__ did Felix do yesterday?
   B He __helped__ patients with their walkers
   (help)
   and wheelchairs.
6. **A** __Where__ did Juan and Ivana go after work?
   B They __went__ to the coffee shop across the street.
   (go)

Listen and repeat. Then practice with a partner.

98 Unit 8

Lesson objectives
- Introduce *What* and *Where* questions and the simple past
- Ask and answer questions about completed actions

Warm-up and review
- Before class. Write today's lesson focus on the board.
Lesson B:
<u>What</u> and <u>Where</u> questions and the simple past
Ask and answer questions about completed actions
- Begin class. Books closed. Review the simple past with regular and irregular verbs. Write on the board: *What did you do last night?* Ask Ss the question. Write the name of each S who answers, and next to the name, write what that S did, for example:
  Celia   worked at Wong's Restaurant
  Howard   watched a movie at home
  Nahomi   met with her son's teacher
- Ask other Ss in the class what each of these Ss did last night, for example: *What did Celia do last night?* Elicit: *She worked at Wong's Restaurant.*
- Ask Ss *Yes / No* questions about what each of these Ss did last night, for example: *Did Howard work last night?* (No, he didn't.)

Presentation
- Books open. Direct Ss' attention to the grammar chart in Exercise **1**. Read the questions and the answers aloud. Ask Ss to repeat. Tell Ss that we use *Where* to ask questions about places.
- Go over the regular verbs. Say each verb and its past tense form. Have Ss repeat the words. Ask the class: *How do you form regular past tense verbs?* (You add *-ed*.)
- Go over the irregular verbs. Say each verb and its past tense form. Have Ss repeat the words. Ask the class: *How do you form irregular past tense verbs?* (in many ways)

Expansion activity (whole group)
- If you want to expand the grammar presentation, turn to the grammar charts on page 148. Practice asking questions and giving affirmative and negative answers with regular and irregular verbs. Add the subject pronouns *it, we,* and *you (plural)* to the presentation.
- Turn to page 152 for a reference list of common verbs that are irregular in the simple past.

Practice
- Books open. Direct Ss' attention to Exercise **2A** and read the instructions aloud. Read the example aloud and make sure students understand the exercise.
- Point to the picture in Exercise **2A**. Ask Ss: *Who is the woman?* (Linda) Ask: *What did Linda do after breakfast?* (She made the beds.)
- Have Ss complete the sentences individually. Walk around and help as needed.

Comprehension check
- [Class Audio CD2 track 17] Read aloud the second part of the instructions for Exercise **2A**. Play or read the audio program (see audio script, page T-160). Have students check their answers as they listen and repeat.
- Ss practice the questions and answers in pairs. Walk around and listen to Ss' pronunciation. Correct pronunciation as needed.
- Call on different pairs to read one of the conversations to the class.

Expansion activity (whole group)
- Give Ss extra practice asking and answering questions with *What* and *Where* and the simple past.
- Say to Ss: *Let's talk about Marco. Do you remember Marco?* (Marco is the orderly from Lesson A.)
- Direct Ss' attention to the grammar chart in Exercise **1**. Ask Ss questions with *What* using the regular verbs in the box. For example, ask: *What did Marco clean yesterday?* Accept reasonable answers (e.g., He cleaned the floor; He cleaned the rooms). Ask Ss: *What did Marco deliver yesterday?* (e.g., He delivered flowers; He delivered linens). Make sure Ss answer using the simple past tense.
- Using *Where*, ask Ss: *Where did Marco go yesterday?* (e.g., He went to a patient's room; He went to the lab). You might think of additional verb phrases to enable you to make suitable questions.

Lesson B Where did you go last night?

Presentation

- Books open. Write on the board: *Day planner*. Direct Ss' attention to the day planner pictured in Exercise **2B**. Tell Ss: *This is Rosa's day planner. Rosa writes the things she needs to do in her day planner.*
- Ask the class: *Does Rosa still need to do these things?* (Point to the check marks next to each activity.) Elicit, for example: *No, she doesn't. She did these things already.*
- Read each time and activity aloud, and ask Ss to repeat. Explain any language Ss don't understand.

Practice

- Read aloud the instructions for Exercise **2B**. Ask two Ss to read the example conversation aloud.
- Model the exercise. Point to the second activity on the day planner. Ask a S: *Where did Rosa go at 9:30?* (She went to the fourth floor.) Ask the same S: *What did she do there?* (She prepared rooms.)
- Ss complete the exercise in pairs. Walk around and help as needed.
- Ask several pairs to perform one of the conversations for the class.

▼ **Culture tip**
There are different ways of referring to the floors in buildings. In the United States, the first floor is usually the floor at ground level, but in some places, that's called the *ground floor*, and the first floor is the one above it. In Exercise **2B**, when Rosa goes to the fourth floor, ask a S to come to the board to draw a building with four floors. Ask Ss if they all agree with the S. Talk about the different ways floors can be numbered.

Expansion activity *(individual work / student pairs)*

- Have Ss take out a piece of paper and create their own day planner page to show what they did yesterday. Ask Ss to use Rosa's day planner as a model, and to write times and actions in the simple present.
- Ask pairs to show each other their day planners and talk about what they did yesterday. Remind Ss to use the simple past tense to talk about their day. Encourage Ss who are listening to ask their partners questions about the activities in the day planner.

Application

- Direct Ss' attention to Exercise **3** and read the instructions aloud. Ask two Ss to read aloud the example conversation. Point to where Rachel's answers have been written in the chart.
- Model the exercise. Point to the second line of the chart. Read aloud: *last Monday*. Ask a S, for example: *Ya-Yun, where did you go last Monday?* (S answers. Pretend to write S's answer in the chart.) Ask the same S: *What did you do?* and any other appropriate follow-up questions.
- Have Ss cross out the example written in the chart so that they can write their partner's answers there.
- Pairs complete the exercise, taking turns asking and answering. When Ss finish, have volunteers ask and answer questions in front of the class.

Evaluation

- Direct Ss' attention to the lesson focus written on the board. Write two questions on the board:
What did you do this morning?
Where did you go after breakfast?
- Point to the first question and ask Ss: *Is this question asking about a place or a completed action?* (a completed action) Ask Ss: *What is a completed action?* (e.g., something you did in the past that's finished)
- Point to the second question and ask Ss: *Is this question asking about a place or a completed action?* (It's asking about a place.)
- Write on the board: *yesterday*. Have Ss ask each other questions similar to the ones in Exercise **3**. Tell Ss: *Ask a classmate two questions about yesterday. Use* Where *and* What. As an example, ask a S: *Where did you go yesterday? What did you do?*
- Check off each part of the lesson focus as Ss demonstrate an understanding of what they have learned in the lesson.

> **More Ventures** *(whole group, pairs, individual)*
> Assign appropriate exercises from the *Teacher's Toolkit Audio CD / CD-ROM, Add Ventures,* or the *Workbook.*

B Talk with a partner. Change the **bold** words and make conversations.

> **A** Where did Rosa go at **8:00**?
> **B** She went to the **coffee shop**.
> **A** What did she do there?
> **B** She **ate breakfast**.

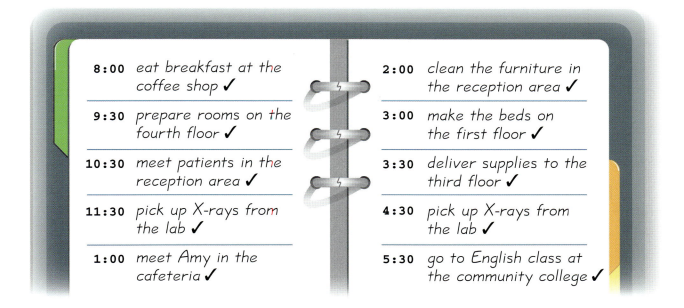

8:00	eat breakfast at the coffee shop ✓
9:30	prepare rooms on the fourth floor ✓
10:30	meet patients in the reception area ✓
11:30	pick up X-rays from the lab ✓
1:00	meet Amy in the cafeteria ✓
2:00	clean the furniture in the reception area ✓
3:00	make the beds on the first floor ✓
3:30	deliver supplies to the third floor ✓
4:30	pick up X-rays from the lab ✓
5:30	go to English class at the community college ✓

3 Communicate

Talk with a partner. Ask questions. Write your partner's answers in the chart.

> **A** Rachel, where did you go last weekend?
> **B** I went to the mall.
> **A** What did you do?
> **B** I ate lunch and went shopping.
> **A** Did you have fun?
> **B** Yes, I did.

	Where?	What?
last weekend	the mall *(Answers will vary.)*	ate lunch and went shopping
last Monday		
this morning		
last summer		
last night		

Work 99

Lesson C *I work on Saturdays and Sundays.*

1 Grammar focus: conjunctions *and, or, but*

Statements

I work on Saturdays. I also work on Sundays.	I work on Saturdays **and** Sundays.
Sometimes he works on Saturdays. Sometimes he works on Sundays.	He works on Saturdays **or** Sundays.
She works on Saturdays. She doesn't work on Sundays.	She works on Saturdays, **but** she doesn't work on Sundays.

2 Practice

A Write. Combine the sentences. Use *and*, *or*, or *but*.

1. Sometimes Irene eats Chinese food for lunch. Sometimes she eats Mexican food for lunch.
   Irene eats Chinese food or Mexican food for lunch.

2. Tito works the day shift. Tito also works the night shift.
   Tito works the day shift and the night shift.

3. Marco had an interview. He didn't get the job.
   Marco had an interview, but he didn't get the job.

4. Brian likes his co-workers. He doesn't like his schedule.
   Brian likes his co-workers, but he doesn't like his schedule.

5. Erica takes care of her children. She also takes care of her grandmother.
   Erica takes care of her children and her grandmother.

6. Carl cleaned the carpets. He didn't make the beds.
   Carl cleaned the carpets, but he didn't make the beds.

7. Sometimes Kate works in New York. Sometimes she works in San Diego.
   Kate works in New York or in San Diego.

8. Ilya speaks Russian at home. He also speaks Russian at work.
   Ilya speaks Russian at home and at work.

Listen and repeat. Check your answers.

Lesson objective
- Introduce the conjunctions *and, or, but*

Warm-up and review
- Before class. Write today's lesson focus on the board. *Lesson C: Connect ideas with conjunctions: <u>and</u>, <u>or</u>, <u>but</u>*
- Before class. Write the following schedule on the board:

Weekend Work Schedule	
Saturday	**Sunday**
Jill / Becky	Jill / Paul
Jill / Becky / Paul	Jill
Jill / Becky	Jill / Paul
Jill / Becky / Paul	Jill

- Begin class. Books closed. Direct Ss' attention to the lesson focus written on the board. Tell Ss: *Today, we'll make sentences with the words* and, or, *and* but. *Before we do that, let's look at this work schedule.*
- Point to the schedule on the board and ask Ss: *Does Jill work on Saturday?* (Yes.) Ask: *Does Jill work on Sunday?* (Yes.) Point to where Jill's name is on the schedule to show that she works each Saturday and every Sunday.
- Ask Ss about the other two workers: *Does Becky work on Saturday?* (Yes.) Ask: *Does Becky work on Sunday?* (No.) Ask: *Does Paul work on Saturday?* (Yes / Sometimes / Twice a month) Ask: *Does Paul work on Sunday?* (Yes / Sometimes / Twice a month)

Presentation
- Books open. Direct Ss' attention to the grammar chart in Exercise **1**. For each section of the chart, read aloud the two statements on the left and then the statement on the right. Ask Ss to repeat. Make sure Ss understand that the one statement on the right side of the chart has the same meaning as that of the two statements on the left side.
- As you read the grammar chart, point to the names on the schedule on the board – first to Jill, then to Paul, then to Becky.
- Have pairs read the statements aloud. Ask Ss to take turns reading the two sides of the chart.

Practice
- Direct Ss' attention to Exercise **2A** and read the instructions aloud. Ask a S to read the example aloud.
- Model the exercise. Ask a S to read aloud the sentences in number 2. Write on the board: *and / or / but*. Ask the class: *Which conjunction can we use?* Elicit: *and*. Write *Tito works the day shift* on the board. Then, ask for a volunteer to come to the board to finish the sentence: *and the night shift*. To check comprehension, ask the class: *When does Tito sleep?* Answering this will require a bit of thinking.
- Ss complete the exercise individually. Remind Ss to refer to the statements in the grammar chart as they do the exercise. Walk around and help as needed.

Comprehension check
- Read aloud the second part of the instructions in Exercise **2A**.
- [Class Audio CD2 track 18] Play or read the audio program (see audio script, page T-160). Ss listen and repeat as they check their answers. Repeat the program as needed.
- Write the numbers *2–8* on the board. Ask Ss to come to the board to write their complete sentences next to each number.
- In some cases, there may be more than one correct answer. In number 5, for example, a S could write: *Erica takes care of her children, and she also takes care of her grandmother.* This sentence is perfectly correct, but it is long and repetitive. If you see this as you go over each sentence with the class, tell Ss that it is correct. Then, ask the class: *Is there a shorter way to say this?* (Erica takes care of her children and grandmother.) Move your hands together or in some other way to show Ss that you'd like them to reduce the length of the sentence.
- Read aloud each sentence on the board and ask Ss: *Is this correct?*

Expansion activity *(student pairs)*
- Have each S take out a piece of paper and write two short sentences similar to the ones in Exercise **2A**. It should be possible to combine the sentences into one sentence using a conjunction – *and, or, but*.
- When Ss have finished, ask them to exchange papers with a partner and write one new sentence using a conjunction. Ask volunteers to write their sentences on the board for the entire class to combine.

Lesson C T-100

Lesson C *I work on Saturdays and Sundays.*

Presentation

- Books open. Direct Ss' attention to the pictures in Exercise **2B**. Point to the picture of Jill in number 1. Say to Ss: *This is Jill. Is Jill at work?* (Yes.) Ask Ss: *Does Jill feel well?* (No.)
- Point to the phrases under the first picture. Read the phrases aloud and ask Ss to repeat.
- Ask two Ss to read the example conversation aloud. Ask the class: *What verb tense will you use?* (the simple past)

Practice

- Have pairs of Ss make conversations using *but* and the language under the first three pictures in Exercise **2B**.
- Call on pairs to perform the conversations in numbers 2 and 3 for the rest of the class.
- Repeat the process for numbers 4 to 6 and numbers 7 to 9. Point out that the conversations in 4 to 6 are about Al and the conversations in 7 to 9 are about "you." Call on Ss to model the example conversations, and point out that Ss will use the simple past tense for 4 to 6 and the simple present tense in the last set of dialogs.
- Ss complete the exercise in the same pairs using *and* for numbers 4 to 6 and *or* for 7 to 9.
- Call on pairs to perform the conversations for the rest of the class.

> ▼ **Teaching tip**
> You might want to explain to Ss that *and* is like a plus sign in math – it lets you add something. The conjunction *or* indicates an option or a choice; in other words, two (or more) things are possible. Explaining *but* may be the most difficult. It indicates a contrast, often between what we expect to happen and what actually does happen. Use a clear context, such as the situations in Exercise **2B**, to help convey these meanings.

Expansion activity *(whole group)*

- Expand the presentation of *or* with the question *Would you rather . . . ?*
- After Ss have completed Exercise **2B**, write on the board: *Would you rather eat lunch _____ or _____ ?*
- Point to the pictures in numbers 7 to 9. For each picture, ask Ss about their personal preference between the two choices. For example, for number 7, ask several Ss: *Would you rather eat lunch in a restaurant or at your desk?* If Ss don't seem to understand the question, paraphrase by saying: *For you, which is better?* Encourage Ss to give reasons for their choices.
- Don't insist that Ss use complete sentences during this activity, but if Ss want to know how to do that, write on the board: *I would rather _____ because _____ .* Give Ss an example, such as, *I would rather eat lunch at my desk because it's cheaper.*

Application

- Direct Ss' attention to Exercise **3** and read the instructions aloud. Call on two Ss to read the example conversation aloud.
- Point to the first speech bubble and ask Ss: *What conjunction is in the first part of the example?* (and) Ask Ss: *What conjunction is in the second part of the example?* (but) Say to Ss: *Can you think of an example with "or"?* Elicit and write an example on the board, or if Ss have trouble thinking of an example, suggest: *I usually go jogging or ride my bicycle in the morning. How about you?*
- Ss complete the exercise in pairs. Walk around and help as needed.

Evaluation

- Direct Ss' attention to the lesson focus written on the board. Keep Ss in the same pairs they were in for Exercise **3**. Tell Ss that they will perform a conversation in front of the class and that they will need to use each conjunction at least once. They can use their conversations from Exercise **3** if they wish.
- Give Ss time to prepare, and if they wish, to write down the conversation they plan to perform.
- Ask each pair to perform its conversation for the class. Listen carefully to the use of conjunctions.
- **Option** Write on the board *and / or / but*. As you listen to the conversations, make a check mark next to each conjunction when you hear it.
- Check off each part of the lesson focus as Ss demonstrate an understanding of what they have learned in the lesson.

> **More Ventures** *(whole group, pairs, individual)*
> Assign appropriate exercises from the *Teacher's Toolkit Audio CD / CD-ROM*, *Add Ventures*, or the *Workbook*.

B **Talk** with a partner. Change the **bold** words and make conversations.

go to work / feel well

go to a meeting / take notes

write a letter / finish it

A What did Jill do yesterday?
B She **went to work**, but she didn't **feel well**.

write reports / check e-mail

make copies / deliver mail

answer calls / take messages

A What did Al do this morning?
B He **wrote reports** and **checked e-mail**.

in a restaurant / at my desk

in the cafeteria / outside

at home / in my car

A Where do you eat lunch?
B I eat lunch **in a restaurant** or **at my desk**.

3 Communicate

Talk with a partner. Make statements with *and*, *or*, or *but*.

Last night, I watched TV and did my homework. What about you?

I did my homework, but I didn't watch TV.

Work 101

Lesson D Reading

1 Before you read

Look at the picture. Answer the questions.

1. Who are these people?
2. What are they doing?

2 Read

 Read the letter of recommendation. Listen and read again.

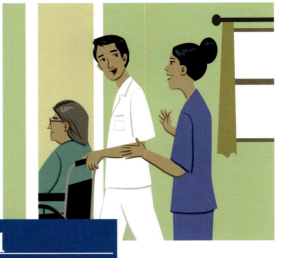

Valley Hospital

Dear Mr. O'Hara:

I am happy to write this letter of recommendation for Marco Alba. Marco started working at Valley Hospital as an orderly in 2003. He takes patients from their rooms to the lab, delivers X-rays, and takes flowers and mail to patients. He also delivers linens and supplies. He is an excellent worker, and his co-workers like him very much.

We are sorry to lose Marco. He wants to go to school and needs to work part-time, but we don't have a part-time job for him right now. I recommend Marco very highly. Please contact me for more information.

Sincerely,

Suzanne Briggs
Suzanne Briggs
Human Resources Assistant

Look through the text quickly for specific information, like names and dates.
Marco Alba   2003

Culture note
Teachers and employers often write letters of recommendation to help you get a job or get into a school.

3 After you read

Write. Answer the questions about Marco.

1. When did Marco start his job at Valley Hospital? <u>He started his job in 2003.</u>
2. What does he do there? <u>He is an orderly.</u>
3. Why is Marco leaving? <u>He wants to go to school and needs to work part-time.</u>
4. Who wrote the letter? <u>Suzanne Briggs wrote the letter.</u>

Lesson objectives
- Introduce and read a letter of recommendation
- Scan text for names and dates

Warm-up and review
- Before class. Write today's lesson focus on the board.
  Lesson D:
  Read and understand a letter of recommendation
  Scan text for names and dates
  Learn new vocabulary for job duties
- Begin class. Books open. Direct Ss' attention to the big picture on page 96. Point to Marco and ask Ss: *Do you remember Marco? What is Marco's job?* (He's an orderly at a hospital.) Ask Ss: *What does an orderly at a hospital do?* List Ss' responses on the board. Elicit language from the unit, for example: *delivers flowers; picks up X-rays; makes beds; prepares rooms; delivers supplies,* etc.
- Ask Ss: *Does Marco like his job as an orderly?* Elicit: *Yes, he does, but he doesn't like the pay.* Ask Ss: *What does Marco want to do?* Elicit: *He wants to go back to school and become a nurse.*

Presentation
- Direct Ss' attention to Exercise **1** and read the instructions aloud. Ask Ss the first question: *Who are these people?* Ss should recognize Marco, and they should know that the woman in a wheelchair is a patient.
- Ask Ss the second question: *What are they doing?* Elicit and list appropriate responses, for example:
  Marco is pushing the patient's wheelchair.
  Marco and the woman are talking.

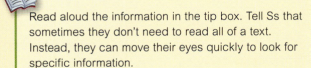
Read aloud the information in the tip box. Tell Ss that sometimes they don't need to read all of a text. Instead, they can move their eyes quickly to look for specific information.

- Ask Ss to look quickly for the name and year in the tip box. Ss who locate the information hold up their book and point to the name and year. Then, ask Ss: *What's the name of the hospital where Marco works?* (Valley Hospital) Ask Ss: *Who wrote this letter?* (Suzanne Briggs)

Practice
- Direct Ss' attention to Exercise **2** and read the instructions aloud. Ss read the letter silently.
- [Class Audio CD2 track 19] Play or read the audio program and ask Ss to read along (see audio script, page T-160). Repeat the audio program as needed.

Learner persistence (individual work)
- [Self-Study Audio CD track 28] Exercise **2** is recorded on the Ss' self-study CD at the back of the Student's Book. Ss can listen to the CD at home for reinforcement and review. They can also listen to the CD for self-directed learning when class attendance is not possible.

Culture note
Read aloud the information in the Culture note. Explain that letters of recommendation are sometimes required when you apply for a job.

Practice
- Ask Ss whether anyone in the class has ever needed a letter of recommendation. If so, ask those Ss to tell the class who wrote the letter and how they asked for the letter. If no one in the class has asked for a letter of recommendation, have Ss imagine what they would do in that situation.

Comprehension check
- Read aloud the instructions in Exercise **3**. Ask two Ss to read aloud the example question and answer. Ask Ss to write complete sentences.
- Ss complete the exercise individually. Walk around and help as needed.
- Check answers with the class. Ask Ss to write their answers on the board. Then ask different Ss to read the answers aloud.

Expansion activity (student pairs)
- Give pairs time to practice reading the letter in Exercise **2**.
- Ask Ss which words in the reading were difficult to say. Write the words on the board and practice the pronunciation of each one.

Expansion activity (whole group)
- In the unit, we learn that Marco wants to become a nurse because the pay is more than what he makes as an orderly. As a class, brainstorm other good-paying jobs that Marco might be interested in, and list them on the board. Ask Ss how much they think people are paid for the positions and how long they think Marco would have to be in school to learn the necessary job skills.

Lesson D   T-102

Lesson D Reading

Warm-up and review
- Books closed. Draw yourself or another person on the board and write the words *English teacher* under the picture. Next to the picture, write the words *job duties*. Say *job duties* aloud and ask Ss to repeat. Say to Ss: *Job duties are things you have to do for your job. What are some job duties of an English teacher?* Keep the mood light as you list on the board Ss' ideas about your job duties. If Ss need some examples, you could tell them how you prepare for class, teach class, grade quizzes, and read journals and books to find out what's new in the field.

Presentation
- Books open. Direct Ss' attention to the picture dictionary in Exercise **4**. Ask a few questions to encourage Ss to preview the pictures, for example: *Which picture shows a hospital?* (Picture 5) *Which picture shows a dentist's office?* (Picture 9) *Which picture shows a restaurant kitchen?* (Picture 4) *Which picture shows a family at home?* (Picture 6)
- Direct Ss' attention to the word bank. Say each phrase in the word bank and ask Ss to repeat. Listen to Ss' pronunciation. Correct pronunciation as needed.
- Read aloud the instructions in Exercise **4A**. Point to the first example, which has been done. Make sure Ss understand the exercise.
- Ss complete the exercise individually. Walk around and help as needed.

Comprehension check
- 🔊 [Class Audio CD2 track 20] Say: *Listen and repeat.* Play or read the audio program (see audio script, page T-160). Ss should check their answers and repeat the words after they hear them. Repeat the audio program if necessary.

Learner persistence (individual work)
- 💿 [Self-Study Audio CD track 29] Exercise **4A** is recorded on the Ss' self-study CD at the back of the Student's Book. Ss can listen to the CD at home for reinforcement and review. They can also listen for self-directed learning when class attendance is not possible.

Practice
- Direct Ss' attention to the word bank in Exercise **4B**. Say each phrase and ask Ss to repeat.
- Read aloud the instructions in Exercise **4B**. Ask two Ss to read aloud the example conversation.
- Make sure Ss understand the exercise. Ss complete the exercise in pairs. Walk around and help as needed.
- Call on pairs of Ss to perform the conversation for one of the jobs.

Community building (small groups)
- Divide the class into groups of five to seven Ss and ask Ss to talk about people they know who work in the places shown in the picture dictionary.
- Model the activity. Point to the picture dictionary and say to Ss, for example: *Do you know any people who work in these places? I do. My brother is a cook at Lombardi's Restaurant.*
- **Option** If your class is small enough, you can do this activity as a whole-group discussion.

Evaluation
- Direct Ss' attention to the lesson focus written on the board.
- Ask Ss some questions about Marco's letter of recommendation, for example: *When did Marco start his job at Valley Hospital?* (2003) *Do Marco's co-workers like him?* (Yes, they like him very much.) *Is Suzanne Briggs happy that Marco is leaving the hospital?* (No, she is sorry to lose him.)
- Ask Ss how to find information such as names and dates in a reading.
- Hold up the Student's Book and point to the picture dictionary. Ask Ss questions about the pictures, for example: *What is his job? What is one of his job duties?*
- Check off each part of the lesson focus as Ss demonstrate an understanding of what they have learned in the lesson.

> **More Ventures** (whole group, pairs, individual)
> Assign appropriate exercises from the *Teacher's Toolkit Audio CD / CD-ROM*, *Add Ventures*, or the *Workbook*.

4 Picture dictionary   Job duties

1. _repair cars_

2. _operate large machines_

3. _clear tables_

4. _prepare food_

5. _help the nurses_

6. _take care of a family_

7. _handle money_

8. _pump gas_

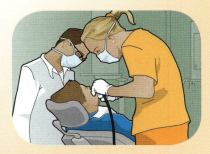
9. _assist the dentist_

A **Write** the words in the picture dictionary. Then listen and repeat.

assist the dentist	help the nurses	pump gas
clear tables	operate large machines	repair cars
handle money	prepare food	take care of a family

B Talk with a partner. Match the pictures with the jobs.

an auto mechanic	a construction worker	a gas station attendant
a busboy	a cook	a housewife
a cashier	a dental assistant	an orderly

He repairs cars.   He's an auto mechanic.

Work 103

Lesson E Writing

1 Before you write

A Talk with a partner. Ask and answer the questions.

1. What are some of your duties at home?
2. What are some of your duties at your job?
3. What were some of your duties at your last job?

B Read Marco's employment history. Complete the sentences. Use the correct form of the verb.

Capitalize the names of businesses.
Valley **H**ospital

Employment History: Marco Alba

Marco Alba is an orderly. He __works__ at Valley Hospital. He
                                1. work
started in 2003. He __has__ many duties. He __takes__
                      2. have   3. take
patients from their rooms to the lab. He __delivers__ X-rays, linens,
                                           4. deliver
and supplies. He also __takes__ flowers and mail to patients.
                        5. take
  From 2001 to 2003, Marco __worked__ at Sam's Soup and
                              6. work
Sandwich Shop. He __was__ a busboy. He __cleaned__ the
                     7. be   8. clean
floor and __picked up__ dirty dishes. From 2000 to 2001, he
           9. pick up
__worked__ at Fratelli's Construction Company. He __was__ a
 10. work   11. be
construction worker. He __made__ repairs on houses and
                          12. make
__operated__ large machines.
 13. operate

C Write Marco's job duties now and in the past.

Now	Before
1. He takes patients from their rooms to the lab.	1. He cleaned the floor.
2. He delivers X-rays, linens, and supplies.	2. He picked up dirty dishes.
3. He takes flowers and mail to patients.	3. He made repairs on houses.
	4. He operated large machines.

Lesson objectives
- Write a summary paragraph about employment history
- Capitalize the names of businesses

Warm-up and review

- Before class. Write today's lesson focus on the board.
  Lesson E:
  Write a paragraph about your work history
  Capitalize the names of businesses
- Begin class. Books closed. Point to the first part of the lesson focus. Ask Ss: *What is your work history?* Elicit, for example: *Your work history is your job experience; the jobs you do now and did before.*
- Tell Ss: *Today, you will write a paragraph about your work history, or employment history.*
- Write on the board: *job duties*. Ask Ss: *What are job duties?* Elicit, for example: *Job duties are things you need to do at your job.*
- Ask Ss who have jobs to tell the class some of the job duties they perform at work.

Presentation

- Books open. Direct Ss' attention to Exercise **1A** and read the instructions aloud. Call on Ss to read the three questions to the class.
- Discuss the idea of "duties at home." Ask Ss to give you some examples of things they need to do at home, for example: *prepare food; get the children dressed in the morning; pay bills.*
- Have pairs ask and answer the questions. When Ss are finished, ask them to change partners.

> **Teaching tip**
> Don't hesitate to have Ss say something more than once. In Exercise **1A**, talking to more than one classmate about home and job duties can help Ss develop fluency and self-correction skills. As Ss repeat, they gain confidence and can make language improvements as they go along.

Read the tip box aloud. Ask Ss to scan Marco's employment history for the names of businesses. List on the board: *Valley Hospital, Sam's Soup and Sandwich Shop,* and *Fratelli's Construction Company.*

Practice

- Direct Ss' attention to the paragraph in Exercise **1B**. Read the instructions aloud. Ask a S to read aloud the first two sentences. Make sure Ss understand the exercise.
- Ss fill in the blanks individually. Walk around and help as needed.
- Check answers as a class. Write the numbers *2–13* on the board. Call on Ss to come to the board to write their answers next to the numbers.
- Read each sentence of the employment history aloud using the answers Ss wrote on the board. Ask the class whether each answer is correct. Since the exercise requires the use of two verb tenses, ask Ss what time expressions in the employment history told them which verb tense to use.
- Direct Ss' attention to Exercise **1C** and read the instructions aloud. Ask a S to read the example aloud. Say to Ss: *Now, Marco has job duties at Valley Hospital. Where did he have job duties in the past?* Elicit: *Sam's Soup and Sandwich Shop* and *Fratelli's Construction Company.*
- Point to the left side of the chart in Exercise **1C**. Say: *Write Marco's job duties at the hospital.* Point to the right side of the chart. Say: *Write Marco's job duties at the restaurant and the construction company.*
- Check to see that Ss are using the simple present tense for Marco's present job duties and the simple past tense for his duties in the past.

Comprehension check

- Ask pairs to compare their sentences in Exercise **1C**. Call on Ss to read the sentences aloud.

Expansion activity (whole group)

- Use the information in Exercises **1B** and **1C** to conduct an interview with Marco about his employment history. Ask a volunteer to sit with you at the front of the room. Ask the S to answer the following questions as Marco:
  Hello. What's your name?
  Where do you work now? What are your job duties at the hospital?
  Where did you work before? What were your job duties there?
- Elicit answers that describe Marco's current and past job duties. Repeat the activity with at least one more S, or write the questions on the board and have pairs interview each other.

Lesson E T-104

Lesson E Writing

Presentation

- Books open. Direct Ss' attention to the worksheet in Exercise **1D** and read the instructions aloud. Point to and ask the class the question on the left side of the chart: *Do you have a job?* Tell Ss: *Please raise your hand if you have a job. OK, you will write answers to these questions.* (Point to the questions on the left.)
- Point to and ask the class the question on the right side of the chart: Tell Ss: *Please raise your hand if you do NOT have a job. OK, you will write answers to these questions.* (Point to the questions on the right.)

Practice

- Ss write their answers individually. Walk around and help as needed. Check to see that Ss are writing complete sentences and using the appropriate verb tense for each sentence.

> ▼ **Teaching tip**
> Since space in the Student's Book is limited in Exercise **1D**, have Ss take out a full-size piece of paper for this prewriting exercise. Encourage Ss to write about their work history and job duties in detail since the more ideas they can get on paper now, the better their paragraphs (employment history) will be.

Application

- Tell Ss that they will use the sentences they wrote in Exercise **1D** to write an employment history similar to the one on page 104.
- Direct Ss' attention to Exercise **2** and read the instructions aloud. Point to Exercises **1B** (on page 104) and **1D** (on page 105) to show Ss where to look for help.
- Ss write their employment history individually. Walk around and help as needed.

Comprehension check

- Direct Ss' attention to Exercise **3A** and read the instructions aloud. Partners take turns reading their employment history to each other. Walk around and help with pronunciation as needed.

- Direct Ss' attention to Exercise **3B** and read the instructions aloud. Ask Ss to read aloud the three questions. Have Ss take out a piece of paper to write down the three questions.
- Have Ss exchange employment histories. Tell Ss: *Read your partner's employment history. Write answers to the three questions.* When Ss are finished, have them share their answers.

Expansion activity (whole group)

- Conduct interviews with Ss at the front of the room, using Ss' own information from the employment history they wrote in Exercise **2**.
- **Option** Write interview questions on the board that pairs can use to interview each other.

Evaluation

- Direct Ss' attention to the lesson focus written on the board.
- Ask Ss to tell you what is included in an employment history. Elicit, for example: *The job you have now and the jobs you had before; the names of businesses; employment dates; job duties.* Call on Ss to give you examples of these things from the employment history they wrote.
- Ask volunteers to come to the board and write the names of businesses they have worked for.
- Check off each part of the lesson focus as Ss demonstrate an understanding of what they have learned in the lesson.

> *More Ventures* (whole group, pairs, individual)
> Assign appropriate exercises from the *Teacher's Toolkit Audio CD / CD-ROM, Add Ventures,* or the *Workbook.*

D Write. Answer the questions about yourself. *(Answers will vary.)*

Do you have a job? Yes?
Answer these questions.

1. What is your job?
   _____
   _____

2. Where do you work?
   _____
   _____

3. What are your duties?
   _____
   _____

4. Did you have a job before?
   What jobs did you have?
   _____
   _____

5. Where did you work?
   _____
   _____

6. What were your duties?
   _____
   _____

Do you have a job? No?
Answer these questions.

1. Where do you study?
   _____
   _____

2. What do you study at school?
   _____
   _____

3. Did you have a job before?
   What jobs did you have?
   _____
   _____

4. Where did you work?
   _____
   _____

5. What were your duties?
   _____
   _____

2 Write

Write your employment history. Use Exercises 1B, 1C, and 1D to help you.

3 After you write

A Read your employment history to a partner.

B Check your partner's employment history.
- What are the jobs?
- What are the duties?
- Do the names of businesses start with capital letters?

Work

Lesson F Another view

1 Life-skills reading

LARRY'S DISCOUNT STORE – WEEKLY TIME SHEET

Employee: *Iara da Silva*   Social Security Number: *000-99-0531*
Rate: *$9.00/hour*

DAY	DATE	TIME IN	TIME OUT	TIME IN	TIME OUT	HOURS
MONDAY	8/7	9:00 A.M.	12:00 NOON	1:00 P.M.	4:00 P.M.	6
TUESDAY	8/8	8:30 A.M.	12:30 P.M.	1:30 P.M.	5:30 P.M.	8
WEDNESDAY	8/9	9:00 A.M.	2:00 P.M.	3:00 P.M.	7:00 P.M.	9
THURSDAY	8/10	7:30 A.M.	12:30 P.M.	1:30 P.M.	3:30 P.M.	7
FRIDAY	8/11	9:00 A.M.	12:00 NOON	1:00 P.M.	5:00 P.M.	7
TOTAL HOURS						37

I have worked these hours. I understand that false information will result in my termination with the company.

Employee's signature *Iara da Silva*   Date: *8/25*
Supervisor's signature *Helen Wilson*   Date: *8/25*

A Read the questions. Look at the time sheet. Circle the answers.

1. What is Iara's hourly rate?
   a. 9:00–5:00
   b. 8 hours
   c. $9
   d. $37

2. When did Iara start work on Tuesday?
   a. 7:30 a.m.
   b. 8:30 a.m.
   c. 9:00 a.m.
   d. 9:30 a.m.

3. When did Iara leave work on Friday?
   a. 3:30 p.m.
   b. 4:30 p.m.
   c. 5:00 p.m.
   d. 5:30 p.m.

4. What day did Iara start work at 7:30?
   a. Monday
   b. Tuesday
   c. Wednesday
   d. Thursday

B Talk with a partner. Ask and answer the questions.

1. When do you start school or work?
2. What days do you study or work?
3. How many hours do you study or work each day?
4. Do you like your schedule? Why or why not?

Lesson objectives
- Practice reading a time sheet
- Review unit vocabulary
- Introduce the project
- Complete the project and self-assessment

Warm-up and review

- Before class. Write today's lesson focus on the board.
  Lesson F:
  Read a time sheet
  Review topic vocabulary
  Complete the project and the self-assessment
- Begin class. Books closed. Ask several Ss who have jobs: *How many hours do you work each week?* Write Ss' responses on the board. Ask the same Ss: *How does your employer know how many hours you work?* Ss may have different responses, for example: *I punch a time clock; I pass my ID card through a machine; I fill out a time sheet.*
- Direct Ss' attention to the first part of the lesson focus. Tell Ss: *Today, we'll practice reading a time sheet.*

Presentation

- Books open. Direct Ss' attention to the time sheet above Exercise **1A**. Go over the different sections of the time sheet as a class. Ask Ss: *What's the name of the business?* (Larry's Discount Store) Ask: *What's the employee's name?* (Iara da Silva) Ask: *How much money does Iara make an hour?* ($9.00)
- Read aloud each word on the first line of the time sheet grid (Day; Date; Time in; etc.) and ask Ss to repeat. Direct Ss' attention to Monday's line. Ask Ss: *What was the date on Monday?* (August 7th) *What time did Iara start work on Monday?* (9:00 a.m.) *Why are there two "time ins" and two "time outs" every day?* (Iara is not paid for her lunch break.) *How many hours did Iara work this week?* (37)

Practice

- Read aloud the instructions for Exercise **1A**. This exercise helps prepare Ss for standardized-type tests they may have to take. Make sure Ss understand the exercise. Have Ss individually scan for and circle the answers. Walk around and help as needed.

Comprehension check

- Go over the answers to Exercise **1A**. Make sure that Ss followed the instructions and circled their answers.

Expansion activity *(whole group)*

- Go over the time sheet and explain any vocabulary Ss do not know.

Practice

- Ss in pairs. Say: *Ask and answer the questions in Exercise 1B.*
- Walk around and listen to Ss' pronunciation. Write difficult words on the board. When Ss are finished, say the words aloud and ask Ss to repeat.
- Call on several Ss to tell the class their answers to the questions.

Expansion activity *(individual work)*

- Bring to class real time sheets or time cards from your school or a friendly local business. Go over the time sheets as a class so that Ss understand the meaning of any new vocabulary as well as the proper way to fill in the necessary information.
- When Ss are finished, have them talk about their time sheets in pairs. Ask Ss to tell their partners which days and how many hours they worked, and whether they had any overtime hours, sick leave, or other factors that would affect their pay.
- **Option** You might be able to find time sheet templates to use with a spreadsheet program online. Enter the words "time sheet" in a search engine and look for a template you can use to create a customized time sheet for your Ss.

Lesson F Another view

Warm-up and review

- Books closed. Review *want to, need to,* and *can.* Write three sentence starters on the board:
  I want to _____. / I need to _____. / I can _____.
- Ask Ss to say complete sentences. Write several responses on the board.
- Review *and, or,* and *but.* Write the following on the board:
  cats + dogs   good job / low pay
  work as a housewife / work outside the home
- Point to the first set of words and say to Ss: *I like cats. I also like dogs. Should I use* and, or, *or* but? (and) Ask Ss: *Can you give me a sentence?* Elicit and write on the board: *I like cats and dogs.*
- Point to the second set of words. Draw a smiling face under *good job* and a frowning face under *low pay.* Say to Ss: *Marco likes his job. He doesn't like the pay. Should I use* and, or, *or* but? (but) Ask Ss: *Can you give me a sentence?* Elicit and write on the board: *Marco likes his job, but he doesn't like the pay.*
- Point to the last set of words and read them aloud. Say to Ss: *My friend has a new baby. She can't take care of the baby and work outside the home at the same time. What can she do?* Elicit the conjunction *or* and write on the board: *She can work as a housewife or work outside the home.*

Practice

- Books open. Direct Ss' attention to Exercise **2A** and read the instructions aloud.
- Ss complete the activity in pairs. Walk around and help as needed.
- Go around the room. Ask each pair to say one of their sentences with *and.* Repeat the process with the *or* and *but* sentences.

Presentation

- Direct Ss' attention to the pictures in Exercise **2B**.
- Point to each picture in turn and ask Ss questions, such as: *Where is this?* or *What is the woman doing?* Elicit appropriate responses.

Practice

- Read aloud the instructions for Exercise **2B**.
- Divide the class into small groups and ask each group to choose a secretary.
- Ask Ss to look at each picture and to take turns reading aloud the sentence that goes with the picture. Have Ss discuss the possible meaning of the expression or idiom in bold print. Have the secretary in each group write down that group's best guess or guesses about the meaning of the idiom.
- When groups have finished, ask the secretaries to report their group's ideas to the class. Give Ss feedback on their guesses and explain the meaning of any expressions that Ss don't understand.

▼ **Teaching tip**
Here are some possible ways to explain the idioms in Exercise **2B**:
- When people can't **make up their mind**, it is difficult for them to decide.
- **To give someone a hand** means to help with something, often with a physical task such as carrying, cleaning, cooking, or repairing something.
- **Junk mail** is mail that people don't want to receive such as catalogs, offers for credit cards, or ads.
- If something is **a piece of cake**, it is easy to do.

More Ventures (whole group, pairs, individual)
Assign appropriate exercises from the *Teacher's Toolkit Audio CD / CD-ROM, Add Ventures,* or the *Workbook.*

Application

Community building

- **Project** Ask Ss to turn to page 139 in their Student's Book to complete the project for Unit 8.

Evaluation

- Before asking Ss to turn to the self-assessment on page 144, do a quick review of the unit. Have Ss turn to Lesson A. Ask the class to talk about what they remember about this lesson. Prompt Ss, if necessary, with questions. For example: *What are the conversations about on this page? What vocabulary is in the big picture?* Continue in this manner to review each lesson quickly.
- **Self-assessment** Read the instructions for Exercise **3**. Ask Ss to turn to the self-assessment page to complete the unit self-assessment.
- If Ss are ready, administer the unit test on pages T-183–T-184 of this *Teacher's Edition* (or on the *Teacher's Toolkit Audio CD / CD-ROM*). The audio and audio script for the tests are on the *Teacher's Toolkit Audio CD / CD-ROM.*

2 Fun with language

A Work with a partner. Complete the sentences. Share them with the class.

Use *and*:
1. I want to buy some new shoes and (Answers will vary.)   .
2. I need to clean my house and _____ .
3. I can speak English and _____ .

Use *or*:
4. I want to work in an office or _____ .
5. I need to save money for a car or _____ .
6. I can work on Saturday or _____ .

Use *but*:
7. I want to work on the weekends, but _____ .
8. I want to buy a new car, but _____ .
9. I can speak English, but _____ .

B Work in a group. Look at these expressions. What do they mean? Talk about them in your group.

1. I can't **make up my mind**.
2. Can you **give me a hand**?
3. There's a lot of **junk mail**.
4. That test was a **piece of cake**.

3 Wrap up

Complete the **Self-assessment** on page 144.

Work 107

Review

1 Listening

Read the questions. Then listen and circle the answers.

1. What does Yuri do?
   a. He's a salesperson. ✓
   b. He's a manager.

2. Why did the Chans want a new sofa?
   a. Their sofa wasn't clean.
   b. Their sofa wasn't comfortable. ✓

3. Which sofa was cheaper?
   a. the first sofa ✓
   b. the second sofa

4. Why did they like the second sofa?
   a. It was bigger and more comfortable. ✓
   b. It was nicer and more expensive.

5. What did Mr. and Mrs. Chan buy?
   a. a sofa and two lamps ✓
   b. a sofa and an entertainment center

6. Where did Yuri go after work?
   a. to a supermarket
   b. to a restaurant ✓

Talk with a partner. Ask and answer the questions. Use complete sentences.

2 Grammar

A Write. Complete the story.

Vanessa's Last Job

Last year, Vanessa __worked__ (1. work) the day shift at the Hometown Hotel. First, she __went__ (2. go) to the supply room at 8:00 a.m. Next, she __took__ (3. take) her cart to the third floor. Then, she __made__ (4. make) the beds. After that, she __cleaned__ (5. clean) the rooms and __picked up__ (6. pick up) dirty linens. Vanessa's job __was not__ (7. not / be) easy, but she liked it because she __met__ (8. meet) a lot of nice people.

B Write. Look at the answers. Write the questions.

1. A Where _did Vanessa work last year_?
   B Vanessa worked at the Hometown Hotel last year.
2. A What shift _did she work_?
   B She worked the day shift.
3. A When _did she go to the supply room_?
   B She went to the supply room at 8:00 a.m.
4. A Where _did she take her cart_?
   B She took her cart to the third floor.

Talk with a partner. Ask and answer the questions.

UNITS 7 & 8

Lesson objectives
- Review vocabulary and grammar from Units 7 and 8
- Introduce pronunciation of the -s ending

Warm-up and review

- Before class. Write today's lesson focus on the board.
  Review unit:
  Review vocabulary from Units 7 and 8
  Review comparatives
  Review What and Where questions and the simple past
  Practice pronunciation of the -s ending
- Begin class. Books closed. Review comparatives. Write several descriptive adjectives on the board:
  big, old, small, pretty, comfortable, expensive, good, etc.
- Ask Ss to come to the board to write the comparative form under each adjective. Call on Ss to say example sentences using the comparatives, for example: *Your desk is bigger than my desk.*
- Review *What* and *Where* questions and the simple past. Ask several Ss: *What did you do yesterday?* List Ss' responses on the board using the simple past tense.
- Ask several Ss: *Where did you go last Saturday?* List Ss' responses on the board using the simple past tense.
- Write on the board the verbs from Unit 8 that are irregular in the simple past: *go, make, meet, take.* Ask Ss to come to the board to write the simple past tense form under each verb. Call on Ss to say example sentences using the verbs, for example: *I made spaghetti for dinner last night.*

Practice

- Books open. Direct Ss' attention to Exercise **1** and read the instructions aloud.
- Call on a S to read the example question aloud. Call on another S to read aloud the example answer choices. Point to where the answer *a* has been circled in number 1. Continue until Ss have read aloud all the questions and the answer choices. Say: *Now listen and circle the correct answers.*
- [Class Audio CD2 track 21] Play or read the audio program (see audio script, page T-160). Ss listen and circle the answers to the questions. Repeat the audio program as needed.
- Check answers. Read each question aloud and call on different Ss to answer.
- Read aloud the second part of the instructions for Exercise **1**. Emphasize that answers need to be in complete sentences.
- Ss complete the exercise in pairs. Help as needed.
- Ask several pairs to ask and answer the questions for the rest of the class.

- Direct Ss' attention to Exercise **2A** and read the instructions aloud. Ask Ss: *What's the title of the story?* (Vanessa's Last Job)
- Ask a S to read aloud the first sentence of the paragraph. Point to and read the time phrase *Last year*. Point to where the word *worked* (in the simple past) has been written for number 1.
- Ss complete the exercise individually. Help as needed.
- Check answers as a class. Write the numbers *2–8* on the board. Ask a few Ss to come to the board and write their answers next to the numbers. Ask the class: *Are these answers correct?* Make corrections on the board.
- Ask individual Ss to read aloud one sentence of the story.
- Direct Ss' attention to Exercise **2B** and read the instructions aloud. Ask two Ss to read the example question and answer.
- Ss write the questions individually. Help as needed.
- Check answers as a class. Write the numbers *2–4* on the board. Ask for volunteers to come to the board to write the questions next to the numbers. Ask the class: *Are these questions correct?*
- Read aloud the second part of the instructions for Exercise **2B**.
- Have pairs practice asking and answering the questions. Walk around and help as needed.
- Ask several pairs to ask and answer the questions for the rest of the class.

Community building (small groups)

- Divide the class into small groups that have Ss from as many different cultures as possible. Ask Ss to discuss employment in their home countries. Ask Ss: *What jobs do people have? What jobs are available to people who are looking for work?*
- When Ss have finished talking about their home countries, ask them to compare employment in those places with employment in the United States. Ask Ss: *Do people you know in the United States have the same jobs as people you know in your country? Are job duties, pay, and benefits similar or different?*
- Ask groups to report to the class what they have discussed.

Review

Presentation
- Books closed. Write on the board:
  /s/   /z/   /ɪz/
- Say to Ss: *These are three sounds. Repeat the sounds after me.* Point to the first symbol and say a sustained *sssssssssss* sound. Then, make a buzzing *zzzzzzzzzz* sound and a sustained *iiizzzzzzzz* sound with a vowel.
- Check Ss' understanding by pointing to the symbols in random order and having Ss say the sound.

Presentation
- Books open. Direct Ss' attention to Exercise **3A**. Read the instructions aloud.
- [Class Audio CD2 track 22] Play or read the audio program (see audio script, page T-160). Ss just listen. Repeat the audio program as needed, making sure Ss can hear the three different pronunciations of the *-s* ending.
- Direct Ss' attention to Exercise **3B**. Read the instructions aloud.
- [Class Audio CD2 track 23] Play or read the audio program (see audio script, page T-161). Ss listen and repeat each word. Say the words along with Ss, emphasizing the *-s* ending.

Practice
- Direct Ss' attention to Exercise **3C** and read the instructions aloud.
- [Class Audio CD2 track 24] Model the exercise. Play or read the first word on the audio program (see audio script, page T-161). Have Ss listen and repeat the word *drives*. Ask: *Which sound did you hear: /s/, /z/, or /ɪz/?* (/z/) Point to the middle box in the first line and tell Ss: *Make a check mark here for /z/.*
- [Class Audio CD2 track 24] Play or read the complete audio program (see audio script, page T-161). Have Ss listen and repeat each word before checking one of the boxes. Repeat the audio program as needed.
- Check answers as a class. Call on Ss to say one of the words. Ask: *How do you pronounce the -s ending?* As Ss answer, point to the correct symbol on the board.

▼ **Teaching tip**
Ss may want to know why there are three different ways to pronounce the same letter. The explanation is complicated, but the important pronunciation issue for Ss to understand is that the /ɪz/ pronunciation of the *-s* ending adds an extra syllable to words. People are not likely to misunderstand someone who says an /s/ sound instead of a /z/, but the sentences "I fix cars" and "She fixes cars" sound very different to English speakers because of the number of syllables.

Comprehension check
- Direct Ss' attention to the chart in Exercise **3D** and read the instructions aloud.
- Model the exercise. Look through Units 7 and 8 in the Student's Book. Write on the board a verb from one of the units, for example: *delivers*. Ask the class: *Which box should I check?* (/z/)
- After Ss have written their six verbs, read aloud the second part of the instructions for Exercise **3D**. Have pairs read their verbs aloud. Correct pronunciation.
- Call on several Ss to tell the class one of their verbs and to say how the *-s* ending is pronounced.
- If possible, check each S's verb chart before class ends.

Expansion activity *(student pairs)*
- Expand the presentation of the *-s* ending in English by including plural nouns. Make three columns on the board and label them with the three symbols.
- List in each column some common nouns. The /s/ column should contain nouns that end in voiceless sounds, such as *lamp*; the /z/ column should have nouns that end in voiced sounds, such as *sofa*; the /ɪz/ column should have nouns that end in sibilants, such as *bus*.
- Have Ss practice saying the nouns with the correct plural ending sound.

Evaluation
- Direct Ss' attention to the lesson focus written on the board. Ask Ss to turn to the big picture on page 84 in Unit 7 and make sentences using comparatives. Say, for example: *Please compare the refrigerators.*
- Ask Ss *What* and *Where* questions in the simple past, for example: *What did you take to work yesterday? Where did you eat lunch yesterday?*
- Have each S read aloud one of his or her verbs from the chart in Exercise **3D**, using correct pronunciation.
- Check off each part of the lesson focus as Ss demonstrate an understanding of what they have learned in the lesson.

UNITS
7&8

3 Pronunciation: the -s ending in the simple present

A **Listen** to the *-s* ending in these simple present verbs.

/s/	/z/	/ɪz/
talks	is	watches
makes	has	fixes

B **Listen and repeat.**

/s/	/z/	/ɪz/
looks	buys	relaxes
shops	delivers	teaches
speaks	plays	fixes

C **Listen** and check (✓) the correct column.

	/s/	/z/	/ɪz/		/s/	/z/	/ɪz/
1. drives	☐	✓	☐	5. takes	✓	☐	☐
2. gets	✓	☐	☐	6. pushes	☐	☐	✓
3. goes	☐	✓	☐	7. sleeps	✓	☐	☐
4. uses	☐	☐	✓	8. needs	☐	✓	☐

D **Write** six verbs from Units 7 and 8 in the present tense. Check (✓) the correct column for the *-s* ending.

	/s/	/z/	/ɪz/		/s/	/z/	/ɪz/
1. *(Answers will vary.)*	☐	☐	☐	4.	☐	☐	☐
2.	☐	☐	☐	5.	☐	☐	☐
3.	☐	☐	☐	6.	☐	☐	☐

Talk with a partner. Read the words.

Lesson A Get ready

1 Talk about the picture

A Look at the picture. What do you see?
B Point to: a dishwasher • a leak • a lightbulb • a lock
a dryer • garbage • a sink • a washing machine
C Look at the woman. What's she doing?

Daily living

UNIT 9

Lesson objectives
- Introduce Ss to the topic
- Find out what Ss know about the topic
- Preview the unit by talking about the picture
- Practice key vocabulary
- Practice listening skills

Warm-up and review

- Before class. Write today's lesson focus on the board. *Lesson A: Solving common problems*
- Begin class. Books closed. Ask Ss: *Have you ever had a problem at your house or apartment? For example, did you ever have a broken refrigerator or a light that didn't work?* If Ss say "yes," ask them what kind of problem they have had.
- Say to Ss: *If you are at home and something breaks, what can you do?* Elicit and list on the board any reasonable responses, for example: *try to fix it; call a repair person; ask a neighbor to help.*

Presentation

- Books open. Set the scene. Direct Ss' attention to the picture on page 110. Ask: *Where is this?* (a kitchen, a home) Ask the question from Exercise **1A**: *What do you see?* Elicit and write on the board as much vocabulary about the picture as possible (a family, a kitchen table, dirty dishes, a purse, a clock, etc.)
- Direct Ss' attention to the key words in Exercise **1B**. Read aloud each word or phrase while pointing to the corresponding part of the picture. Ask the class to repeat and point. Listen to Ss' pronunciation and correct as needed.

Comprehension check

- Ask Ss *Yes / No* questions about the picture. Say: *Listen to the questions. Answer "Yes" or "No."*
Point to the big picture. Ask: *Is there water on the floor?* (Yes.)
Point to the dishwasher. Ask: *Is water coming out of the dishwasher?* (Yes.)
Point to the garbage. Ask: *Is water coming out of the garbage?* (No.)
Point to the washing machine. Ask: *Is there a problem with the washing machine?* (Yes.)
Point to the sink. Ask: *Are there any dishes in the sink?* (No.)
Point to the dryer. Ask: *Is the dryer open?* (No.)
Point to the ceiling light fixture. Ask: *Do they need a new lightbulb?* (No.)

Practice

- Direct Ss' attention to Exercise **1B**. Model the exercise. Hold up the Student's Book. Say to a S: *Point to a dishwasher.* The S points to the appropriate part of the picture.
- Ss in pairs. Say to one S: *Say the words in Exercise **1B**.* Say to his or her partner: *Point to the correct part of the picture.*
- Ss complete the exercise in pairs. Walk around and help as needed. When pairs finish, have them switch roles. Then, ask Ss to repeat the exercise with new partners.
- Ask several pairs to perform the exercise for the rest of the class to check understanding.
- Direct Ss' attention to Exercise **1C** and read the instruction and question aloud. Ask the class: *What is the woman doing?* Write Ss' responses on the board. (talking on the telephone / calling for help)

Expansion activity (whole group)

- After Ss talk about what the woman in the big picture is doing, talk about what the children in the picture are doing. Point to each child and ask: *What's he / she doing?* Help Ss with new vocabulary and write appropriate phrases on the board, for example: *carrying the plates to the sink; taking out the garbage; playing with the soap bubbles from the washing machine.*

Expansion activity (student pairs)

- Ask Ss to imagine who the woman in the picture is calling on the phone.
- Have Ss work in pairs to write the woman's telephone conversation. Give Ss a time limit of five minutes for writing to keep the pace of the class lively and to keep the conversations short and focused.
- When Ss are finished writing, ask each pair to tell the class who the woman is talking to and then role-play the conversation for the class.

Lesson A T-110

Lesson A *Get ready*

Presentation
- Books open. Direct Ss' attention to the pictures in Exercise **2A**. Tell Ss: *These are the people Stella is talking to on her telephone.* Ask Ss to guess who the people in the pictures might be.

Practice
- Read aloud the instructions for Exercise **2A**.
- [Class Audio CD2 track 25] Play or read the audio program (see audio script, page T-161). Pause the audio program after the first conversation and ask Ss: *Who is Stella talking to in conversation A?* (the building manager; Picture 2) Hold up the Student's Book and write the letter *a* next to number 2.
- [Class Audio CD2 track 25] Play or read the complete audio program and repeat as needed.
- Check answers. Ask Ss which picture shows the person Stella is talking to in the other conversations.
- Direct Ss' attention to Exercise **2B** and read the instructions aloud.
- [Class Audio CD2 track 25] Read aloud each group of sentences before listening to the corresponding conversation. Read aloud the three sentences for conversation A. Then, play or read conversation A of the audio program (see audio script, page T-161). Do the same for conversations B and C.
- Ss complete the exercise individually. When Ss are finished writing their answers, play or read the complete audio program once more to allow Ss to check their answers.

Comprehension check
- Write the numbers 2–9 on the board. Ask a few Ss to come to the board and write the correct answers to Exercise **2B** next to the numbers.
- [Class Audio CD2 track 25] Play or read the audio program again. Pause the audio program after each conversation. Point to each answer on the board. Ask: *Is this correct?* Make any corrections on the board. Be sure Ss understand which information in the audio program answers the questions.

Learner persistence (individual work)
- [Self-Study Audio CD track 30] Exercises **2A** and **2B** are recorded on the Ss' self-study CD at the back of the Student's Book. Ss can listen to the CD at home for reinforcement and review. They can also listen to the CD for self-directed learning when class attendance is not possible.

Expansion activity (student pairs)
- Have partners practice the telephone conversations from Exercise **2B**. Ask Ss to turn to the self-study audio script on page 161 in the Student's Book.
- Ask Ss to choose the role of Stella or the people Stella calls and read aloud the conversations. Then, have Ss switch roles and say the conversations again. Walk around and help as needed.
- [Class Audio CD2 track 25] After Ss have practiced the conversations, ask them to close their books, relax, and listen to the audio program one more time. Ss will be pleased with how much of the audio program they can understand at this point.

Application
- Direct Ss' attention to Exercise **2C** and read the instructions aloud. Ss complete the activity in pairs. Walk around and help as needed.
- Call on pairs to tell the class about their experiences with plumbers or other repair people.

Evaluation
- Direct Ss' attention to the lesson focus written on the board. Ask Ss to tell you about the problems at Stella's apartment and what Stella did to solve the problems.
- Check off each part of the lesson focus as Ss demonstrate an understanding of what they have learned in the lesson.

> **More Ventures** (whole group, pairs, individual)
> Assign appropriate exercises from the *Teacher's Toolkit Audio CD / CD-ROM*, *Add Ventures*, or the *Workbook*.

UNIT 9

2 Listening

A **Listen.** Who is Stella talking to? Write the letter of the conversation.

1. _c_

2. _a_

3. _b_

B **Listen again.** Write *T* (true) or *F* (false).

Conversation A

1. Stella lives in Apartment 4B. _T_
2. Stella is talking to a plumber. _F_
3. Don Brown is a neighbor. _F_

Conversation B

4. Stella wants to speak to her husband. _F_
5. Don Brown will come in one hour. _T_
6. Stella will unlock the door for the plumber. _F_

Conversation C

7. Russell wants Stella to call a neighbor. _F_
8. Stella already called the plumber. _T_
9. Stella is going to school. _F_

Listen again. Check your answers.

C **Talk** with a partner. Ask and answer the questions.

1. Who fixes things in your home?
2. Did you ever need to call a plumber or other repair person?
3. Who did you call?
4. What happened?

Daily living 111

Lesson B Which one do you recommend?

1 Grammar focus: Which questions and simple present

Questions

| Which | plumber
electrician
one | do
does
do | you
he
they | recommend? |

Answers

| I
He
They | recommend
recommends
recommend | Home Repair. |

For a complete grammar chart, turn to page 147.

2 Practice

A Write. Complete the conversations. Use *Which* and the simple present.

1. **A** Which plumber do you recommend ?
   B I recommend Brown's Plumbing Service. It's cheaper.
2. **A** Which plumber does he recommend ?
   B He recommends Harrison's Plumbing Service. It's clean.
3. **A** Which plumber do they recommend ?
   B They recommend Brown's Plumbing Service. It's licensed.
4. **A** Which plumber does she recommend ?
   B She recommends Brown's Plumbing Service. It's insured.
5. **A** Which plumber do they recommend ?
   B They recommend Harrison's Plumbing Service. It's more experienced.
6. **A** Which plumber does he recommend ?
   B He recommends Harrison's Plumbing Service. It's open 24 hours a day.

Listen and repeat. Then practice with a partner.

Culture note
Plumbers and electricians are usually licensed. You can ask to see their license.

Lesson objectives
- Introduce *Which* questions and the simple present
- Practice asking for and making recommendations
- Introduce descriptive adjectives

Warm-up and review
- Before class. Write today's lesson focus on the board.
  Lesson B:
  Which questions and the simple present
  Ask for and make recommendations
  Use descriptive adjectives
- Begin class. Books open. Recycle superlatives and vocabulary from Lesson A as you assess Ss' prior knowledge of *Which* questions and the simple present. Direct Ss' attention to the big picture on page 110. Ask the class: *Do you remember Stella? What are some of the problems at Stella's apartment?* (e.g., the dishwasher is leaking; the washing machine isn't working right) Ask: *Which problem is the worst problem?* (e.g., the washing machine has the most water coming out) *Which child looks the happiest?* (the child who is playing in the soap bubbles)

Presentation
- Books open. Direct Ss' attention to the grammar chart in Exercise **1** on page 112. Read aloud each question and answer. Ask Ss to repeat the questions and answers.
- Ss in pairs. Have Ss practice reading the grammar chart to each other while pointing to an appropriate person or persons in the class (I, you, he, they).

> ▼ **Teaching tip**
> Remind Ss that *does* is used in simple present questions with *he* and *she*. In simple present statements with *he* and *she*, the verb ends in *-s*, for example, *recommends*.

Expansion activity (whole group)
- Expand the grammar presentation by turning to the grammar charts on page 147. Practice asking and answering questions in the simple present with *Which* and the pronouns *we, she, it,* and *you (plural)*.

Comprehension check
- Call on individual Ss to answer the first question from the grammar chart. First, point to the two plumbing advertisements in Exercise **2A**. Read aloud the names of the two businesses and have Ss repeat. Then, ask the question: *Which plumber do you recommend?* Elicit from several Ss: *I recommend (Harrison's Plumbing Service / Brown's Plumbing Service).*

Expansion activity (whole group)
- To clarify the words *plumber* and *electrician* from the grammar chart, draw a T-chart on the board. Label one column: *Things a plumber can fix.* Label the other column: *Things an electrician can fix.*
- As a class, brainstorm items to write in each column. For example, a plumber can fix *a sink,* while an electrician can fix *a lamp.* Some appliances may fit into both columns, for example: Stella's dishwasher and washing machine seem to be having trouble holding water right now, but they may also have electrical problems in the future since they are both electrical appliances.

Practice
- Direct Ss' attention to the advertisements in Exercise **2A**. Ask Ss to scan the ads for specific information: *Which company has more experience?* (Harrison's) *Which company costs more?* (Harrison's) *Which company is licensed and insured?* (Brown's) *Which company is always open?* (Harrison's)

> **Culture note**
> Read aloud the information in the tip box. Plumbers and electricians go through an examination process in order to get a license, so the license is one way to know that you're hiring a knowledgeable professional.

- Read aloud the instructions in Exercise **2A**. Ask two Ss to read aloud the question and answer.
- Ss complete the sentences individually. Walk around and help as needed.

Comprehension check
- Read aloud the second part of the instructions in Exercise **2A**.
- [Class Audio CD2 track 26] Check answers as a class. Play or read the audio program (see audio script, page T-161). Ss listen and repeat as they check their answers.
- Have pairs practice saying the questions and answers in Exercise **2A**. Help with pronunciation as needed.

Lesson B T-112

Lesson B Which one do you recommend?

Presentation

- Books open. Direct Ss' attention to the two advertisements in Exercise **2B**.
- Point to the six numbered items in Exercise **2B** and use them to ask Ss questions about the ads: *Which company is open 24 hours a day?* (XYZ Electric) *Which company is fully licensed?* (Midway Electric) *Which company is owner-operated?* (XYZ Electric) *Which company is on Main Street?* (Midway Electric) *Which company is fully insured?* (XYZ Electric) *Which company is cheaper?* (Midway Electric)
- Explain the meaning of any words Ss don't know.

> **Culture note**
> Read the tip box aloud. Ask Ss if they know of any businesses where the owner works for and manages the company. Ask whether these owner-operated businesses are small and friendly.

Practice

- Read aloud the instructions for Exercise **2B**. Ask two Ss to read the sample dialog. Make sure Ss understand the exercise.
- Ss complete the exercise in pairs. Walk around and help as needed.
- Ask several pairs to perform the conversations for the rest of the class.

Application

- Direct Ss' attention to Exercise **3** and read the instructions aloud.
- Model the exercise. Ask a S to read the first question aloud. Answer the question, for example: *I like Wellman's Supermarket.* Say: *Write complete sentences and remember to capitalize names of businesses.*
- Ss complete the task individually. Walk around and help as needed.

> **Useful language**
> Read aloud each expression in the Useful language box and ask Ss to repeat. Tell Ss that they can use the expressions to begin their sentences in Exercise **3**; for example: *I recommend Hungry Joe's restaurant.*

Community building

- Read aloud the second part of the instructions for Exercise **3**.

- Divide the class into small groups. Ask Ss to talk about which places in the community they recommend and why. Encourage Ss to use descriptive adjectives to give reasons, for example: *It's small and friendly; It's cheap; It's close to my apartment.* Ss can find a list of adjectives on page 151.
- When Ss are finished, consolidate Ss' ideas on the board. Write on the board each type of business in Exercise **3**, and have volunteers from the small groups report their answers. Be sure to ask Ss to give reasons for their choices. Put a check mark next to businesses that many Ss in the class recommend.

Expansion activity (student pairs)

- Give each pair of Ss two unlined pieces of paper and at least two markers.
- Have each pair design and draw two advertisements, either for two different plumbing companies or two different electric companies. (When they finish, each pair will have two different ads for the same type of company.)
- When the pairs are finished designing their two advertisements, ask them to join another pair of Ss. Have pairs exchange ads. Then, ask each pair to talk about and compare their two companies with those of the other pair. Ask Ss to use descriptive adjectives and questions with *Which*, for example:
  A: *Which plumber do you suggest?*
  B: *Barney's is cheaper, but they're not insured. I recommend A-to-Z because they're fully insured.*

Evaluation

- Direct Ss' attention to the lesson focus written on the board. With their books closed, have Ss ask you questions with *Which* and the simple present about places in the community. Answer with recommendations.
- Ask Ss about places in the community that they recommend, for example: *Which shopping mall do you like? Which furniture store do you recommend?* Ask Ss to use descriptive adjectives to support the reasons for their recommendations.
- Check off each part of the lesson focus as Ss demonstrate an understanding of what they have learned in the lesson.

> **More Ventures** (whole group, pairs, individual)
> Assign appropriate exercises from the *Teacher's Toolkit Audio CD / CD-ROM*, *Add Ventures*, or the *Workbook*.

B Talk with a partner. Change the **bold** words and make conversations.

A Which electrician do you recommend?
B I recommend **XYZ Electric**. It's **open 24 hours a day**.

1. open 24 hours a day
2. fully licensed
3. owner-operated
4. on Main Street
5. fully insured
6. cheaper

Culture note
An owner-operated business is usually small and friendly.

3 Communicate

Write. Answer the questions about your community.

1. Which supermarket do you like? *(Answers will vary.)*
2. Which restaurant do you recommend? _____
3. Which drugstore do you recommend? _____
4. Which gas station do you suggest? _____
5. Which bank do you like? _____
6. Which department store do you suggest? _____
7. Which dentist do you like? _____
8. Which hospital do you recommend? _____

Talk with your classmates. Ask and answer questions about your community.

> Which supermarket do you like?

> I like SaveMore Supermarket on Broadway. It's clean.

> I like Acme Supermarket. It's cheap.

Useful language
I recommend . . .
I suggest . . .
I like . . .

Daily living

Lesson C Can you call a plumber, please?

1 Grammar focus: requests with *Can, Could, Will, Would*

Questions

| Can / Could / Will / Would | you | call a plumber, please? |

2 Practice

A Write. Complete the conversations. Make requests with *can*, *could*, *will*, or *would*.

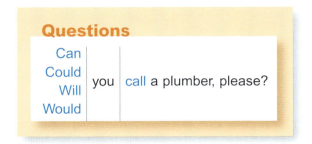

1. fix the dryer
2. unclog the sink
3. clean the bathroom

4. fix the lock
5. change the lightbulb
6. repair the dishwasher

1. **A** Could _you fix the dryer, please_ ?
   B Yes, of course.
2. **A** Can _you unclog the sink, please_ ?
   B No, not now. Maybe later.
3. **A** Would _you clean the bathroom, please_ ?
   B Sorry, I can't right now.
4. **A** Will _you fix the lock, please_ ?
   B Sure. I'd be happy to.
5. **A** Could _you change the lightbulb, please_ ?
   B Yes, of course.
6. **A** Would _you repair the dishwasher, please_ ?
   B Sure. I'd be happy to.

Listen and repeat. Then practice with a partner.

Lesson objectives
- Introduce requests with *can, could, will, would*
- Practice agreeing to and refusing requests politely

Warm-up and review
- Before class. Write today's lesson focus on the board.
  Lesson C:
  Make polite requests with <u>can</u>, <u>could</u>, <u>will</u>, and <u>would</u>
  Agree to and refuse requests politely
- Begin class. Books closed. Make simple requests using *can, could, will,* and *would*. Pretend that you want to write something but your pen isn't working. Walk up to a S and say: *Could you lend me your pen?* Take the pen, write something, and return it. Tell the S: *Thanks!*
- Ask different Ss to do simple things in the classroom: *Can you close the window shade, please? Would you turn on the computer? Will you please move to the front of the room?*
- Point to the first part of the lesson focus. Tell Ss: *Today, we will make polite requests. That means we will ask people to do things in a nice way.* Underline *requests* on the board. Say: *Did you notice that I asked Ss in the class to do things? I* requested *those things.*

Presentation
- Books open. Direct Ss' attention to the grammar chart in Exercise **1**. Read each question aloud. Ask Ss to repeat.
- Have pairs practice asking each other the questions in the grammar chart.

> ▼ **Teaching tip**
> Some of your Ss have probably heard that there is a difference in the degree of politeness between *can* and *will* for making requests and *could* and *would*. Tell Ss that it's true that *can* and *will* are a little more direct than *could* and *would*. However, in ordinary conversation, all four expressions are used for making polite requests. If Ss are concerned about this issue, they need only add the word *please* to their requests to make them sound more polite.

Comprehension check
- Have Ss ask questions similar to the questions in the grammar chart. Say to a S: *You have a broken dishwasher and no telephone. What can you ask your neighbor?* (*Can you call a plumber, please?*) Say to a different S: *You have a broken lamp and no telephone. What can you ask your neighbor?* (*Could you call an electrician, please?*)

- Continue in this way, telling Ss that they have a broken washing machine, a broken dryer, a clogged sink, and other items that require a plumber or an electrician.

Practice
- Direct Ss' attention to Exercise **2A**. Read aloud the verb phrase under each picture. Explain any words that Ss don't know.
- Read aloud the instructions for Exercise **2A**. Ask two Ss to read the example question and answer aloud. Point to the second part of the lesson focus written on the board. Tell Ss: *Speaker B in number 1 agreed to the request. The speaker said "yes."*
- Model the exercise. Point to picture number 2. Ask a S: *Can you unclog the sink?* The S reads the answer: *No, not now. Maybe later.* Point to the second part of the lesson focus again. Tell Ss: *(S's name)* refused the request. *(S's name)* said "no."
- Ss complete the questions and answers individually. Walk around and help as needed.

Comprehension check
- Read aloud the second part of the instructions for Exercise **2A**.
- 💿 [Class Audio CD2 track 27] Check answers with the class. Play or read the audio program (see audio script, page T-161). Ss listen and repeat as they check their answers.
- Have pairs practice saying the questions and answers in Exercise **2A**. Walk around and help as needed.
- Ask several pairs to say the questions and answers for the rest of the class.

> ▼ **Teaching tip**
> Point out to Ss that the word *please* at the end of polite requests is separated from the rest of the question by a comma. You could also tell Ss that *please* is often used without a comma immediately before the verb; for example: *Will you please clean the bathroom?*

Lesson C T-114

Lesson C Can you call a plumber, please?

Presentation

- Direct Ss' attention to the picture in Exercise **2B**. Ask Ss: *Are there any problems in this apartment?*
- Elicit and list on the board problems that Ss point out, for example, the water flowing from the toilet and the sink, the broken window, and the crooked ceiling light.
- Read aloud each verb phrase in items 1–8 in Exercise **2B**. Explain any words that Ss don't know.

Practice

- Read aloud the instructions for Exercise **2B**. Ask two Ss to read aloud the sample conversation at the left. Ask Ss: *Did Speaker B agree to the request or refuse the request?* (Speaker B agreed to it.)
- Ask two Ss to read aloud the example conversation at the right. Ask Ss: *Did Speaker B agree to the request or refuse the request?* (Speaker B refused the request.)
- Point to items 1–4 under the example conversation at the left. Tell Ss: *In 1 through 4, Speaker B agrees to the request*. Point to items 5–8 under the example conversation at the right. Tell Ss: *In 5 through 8, Speaker B refuses the request*. Make sure Ss understand the exercise.
- Ss complete the exercise in pairs. When Ss are finished, call on several pairs to perform the conversations for the class.

Application

- Direct Ss' attention to Exercise **3** and read the instructions aloud. Have a volunteer read the example.
- Model the exercise. Ask the class: *Does anyone in the class have requests for a landlord?* Call on a volunteer to tell you about problems at his or her apartment. Make a short list of verb phrases on the board, such as: *fix the toilet; repair the radiators; change the light bulb in the hall*.
- Ss complete the lists individually.

> **Useful language**
> Read aloud the expressions in the Useful language box and ask Ss to repeat. Encourage Ss to use the useful language as they make conversations in the second part of Exercise **3**.

- Read aloud the second part of the instructions in Exercise **3**. Call on two Ss to read the example conversation aloud.

- Remind Ss that the landlord can agree to the request or can politely refuse the request. To model a refusal, have a S ask you the question in the example. Say: *Sorry, I can't right now. Maybe tomorrow.*

> **Culture note**
> Read aloud the definitions of *tenant* and *landlord*. Find out how many Ss in the class are tenants. Ask if there are any landlords in the class.

- Ss make conversations in pairs.
- When Ss are finished, ask each pair to perform one conversation for the class.

Expansion activity *(small groups)*

- Before class, make sets of index cards with a simple or perhaps silly action on each card. For example, actions might include: *hand me your textbook; sit in a different chair; raise your right hand; stand up; put your pen or pencil under your chair; close your eyes; sing a song.*
- Write on the board the useful language expressions from the tip box.
- Give each small group a set of cards face-down. Ask Ss to take turns turning over a card and making a request to one of their classmates using the action on the card. The classmate can either agree to the request or politely refuse it.

Evaluation

- Direct Ss' attention to the lesson focus written on the board. Ask Ss to pretend you are the landlord and make polite requests of you.
- Write on the board: *agree to the request / refuse the request*. Ask Ss to do various things. Point to one of the expressions on the board to indicate that the Ss you call on should either agree to or refuse your request. Ss respond to your request accordingly.
- Check off each part of the lesson focus as Ss demonstrate an understanding of what they have learned in the lesson.

> **More Ventures** *(whole group, pairs, individual)*
> Assign appropriate exercises from the *Teacher's Toolkit Audio CD / CD-ROM*, *Add Ventures*, or the *Workbook*.

B Talk with a partner. Change the **bold** words and make conversations.

A Can you **fix the window**, please?
B Yes, of course.

A Would you **fix the stove**, please?
B Sorry, I can't right now.

1. fix the window
2. repair the refrigerator
3. unclog the sink
4. fix the toilet

5. fix the stove
6. fix the light
7. call an electrician
8. repair the lock

3 Communicate

Write. What are some problems in your home or in a friend's home? Make a list of requests for the landlord.

Requests for the landlord

1. fix the window
(Answers will vary.)

Culture note
A tenant rents an apartment or house from the landlord. The landlord is the owner.

Talk. Role-play with a partner. One person is the tenant. The other is the landlord.

Tenant Could you fix the window, please?
Landlord Yes, of course. I'll be there tomorrow.

Useful language
Yes, of course.
Sure. I'd be happy to.
No, not now. Maybe later.
Sorry, I can't right now.

Lesson D Reading

1 Before you read

Look at the picture. Answer the questions.

1. Who is the woman?
2. What's the problem?

2 Read

 Read Stella's notice. Listen and read again.

Attention, tenants:

Do you have problems in your apartment? Is anyone fixing them?

- Many tenants have broken windows.
- Tenants on the third floor have no lights in the hall.
- A tenant on the second floor has a leaking ceiling.
- Tenants on the first floor smell garbage every day.

I'm really upset! We need to get together and write a letter of complaint to the manager of the building.

Come to a meeting Friday night at 7:00 p.m. in Apartment 4B.

Stella Taylor, Tenant 4B

> Sometimes it is not necessary to know the exact meaning of a word. It is enough to know if the meaning is positive (good) or negative (not good).
>
> *upset, complaint* = negative

3 After you read

Write. Answer the questions about Stella's notice.

1. Which tenant has a leaking ceiling? <u>A tenant on the second floor.</u>
2. Which tenants have no lights in the hall? <u>Tenants on the third floor.</u>
3. Which tenants smell garbage? <u>Tenants on the first floor.</u>
4. What does Stella want to write? <u>A letter of complaint.</u>
5. Where is the meeting? <u>In Apartment 4B.</u>

Lesson objectives
- Introduce and read a notice on a notice board
- Determine if new words are positive or negative in meaning
- Practice using new topic-related words

Warm-up and review

- Before class. Write today's lesson focus on the board.
  Lesson D:
  Read and understand a notice on a notice board
  Know if new words are positive or negative in meaning
  Learn new vocabulary for home problems
- Begin class. Books closed. Review the meaning of *tenant* and *landlord*. Write the words on the board. Say the words and ask Ss to repeat. Ask Ss: *Who is the owner of a house or an apartment building?* (landlord) *Who lives in the house or building and pays rent to the landlord?* (tenant)
- Books open. Direct Ss' attention to the big picture on page 110. Say to Ss: *Sometimes there are problems at home. What are some problems Stella has at her home?* Elicit and list on the board vocabulary from the unit (e.g., a clogged sink, a leaking dishwasher, an overflowing washing machine).
- Say to Ss: *Stella is a tenant. What should she do if she has problems?* (call the landlord, call the building manager) *What can Stella say to the landlord or building manager?* (e.g., Can you please fix the sink? Would you repair the washing machine, please?)
- Say to Ss: *Imagine that you are Stella. You called the building manager, but he didn't fix the problems. You're not very happy, right?*

Presentation

- Direct Ss' attention to the picture in Exercise **1** and read the instructions aloud. Ask and elicit answers to the two questions. Discuss Ss' ideas about why Stella looks unhappy in the picture.
- If you have a notice board in your classroom, tell Ss that the messages people put on the board can be called *notices*. Direct Ss' attention to the notice in Exercise **2**.
- Ask the class: *Who wrote this notice?* (Stella Taylor) Ask a S to read aloud the first line of the notice. Ask: *Who does Stella want to read this notice?* (the tenants in her building)
- Ask a S to read the two questions at the top of the notice. Ask the class: *Why did Stella write this notice?* (e.g., There are problems in the apartments, but no one is fixing them.)

Practice

- Read aloud the instructions for Exercise **2**. Ask Ss to read the notice silently.

- [Class Audio CD2 track 28] Play or read the audio program and ask Ss to read along (see audio script, page T-162). Repeat the audio program as needed. Answer any questions Ss have about the reading.

Read aloud the information in the tip box. Explain that when people are reading, they don't always want to stop and look up new words in a dictionary, especially if they can make a good guess about the meaning of the new word.
  Discuss how the reader knows that *upset* and *complaint* have negative meanings. For example, since Stella lists four problems, she can't feel happy, so the word *upset* must have a negative meaning. Similarly, if Stella is upset and wants to write a *complaint* letter, then the word *complaint* probably has a negative meaning, too.

Learner persistence (individual work)

- [Self-Study Audio CD track 31] Exercise **2** is recorded on the Ss' self-study CD at the back of the Student's Book. Ss can listen to the CD at home for reinforcement and review. They can also listen to the CD for self-directed learning when class attendance is not possible.

Comprehension check

- Read aloud the instructions in Exercise **3**. Ask two Ss to read the example question and answer aloud. Ask Ss to write complete sentences.
- Ss complete the exercise individually. Walk around and help as needed.
- Go over answers with the class. Ask Ss to write their answers on the board. Have different Ss read the answers aloud. Ask: *Are the sentences correct?* Make any necessary corrections on the board.

Expansion activity (whole group)

- Draw on the board four "bullets" to correspond to the four items in the bulleted list in Stella's notice. Call on a S to read aloud each bullet point from the notice. For each point, ask Ss: *What does the building manager need to do?* Elicit and write on the board Ss' ideas, such as: *He needs to repair the windows. He needs to change the light bulbs. He needs to call an electrician to repair the lights. He needs to call a plumber to fix the leaking ceiling. He needs to take out the garbage every day.*

Lesson D Reading

Presentation

- Books open. Direct Ss' attention to the picture dictionary in Exercise **4**. Point to the words *Home problems*. Read the words aloud and ask Ss to repeat.
- Point to the pictures in the picture dictionary and tell Ss: *These are problems people might have at home.* Ask the class: *Do you know the words for things in the pictures?* Elicit any vocabulary about the pictures that Ss already know, for example: *broken window, chair, light, mirror.*
- Direct Ss' attention to the word bank. Say each word in the word bank and ask Ss to repeat. Listen to Ss' pronunciation. Correct pronunciation as needed.

Practice

- Tell Ss: *Write the words in the picture dictionary.* Point to the first example, which has been done. Make sure Ss understand the exercise.
- Ss complete the exercise individually. Walk around and help as needed.

Comprehension check

- [Class Audio CD2 track 29] Say: *Listen and repeat.* Play or read the audio program (see audio script, page T-162). Ss should check their answers and repeat the words after they hear them. Repeat the audio program if necessary.

Expansion activity *(student pairs)*

- Have pairs of Ss count the syllables in the words and the phrase in the word bank.
- Draw on the board a T-chart. Label the first column: *one syllable*. Label the second column: *two syllables*. Call on pairs to tell you in which column to write the words.
- When each of the words is in the correct column on the board, practice pronouncing the words as a class as you clap the syllables.

Learner persistence *(individual work)*

- [Self-Study Audio CD track 32] Exercise **4A** is recorded on the Ss' self-study CD at the back of the Student's Book. Ss can listen to the CD at home for reinforcement and review. They can also listen for self-directed learning when class attendance is not possible.

Practice

- Direct Ss to Exercise **4B** and read the instructions aloud. Ask two Ss to read the example conversation. Make sure Ss understand that they should use the home problems in the picture dictionary.
- Ss make conversations in pairs. Walk around and help as needed.
- Ask several pairs of Ss to perform one of their conversations for the rest of the class.

Evaluation

- Direct Ss' attention to the lesson focus written on the board.
- Ask Ss some questions about the notice Stella wrote, for example: *What are some problems at Stella's apartment building?* (e.g., broken windows; no lights in the hall; a leaking ceiling; smelly garbage) *How does Stella feel about the problems?* (She's upset.) *What is she doing about the problems?* (e.g., she wrote a notice; she'll have a meeting at her apartment; the tenants will write a letter of complaint)
- Ask Ss if they always need to know the exact meaning of a new word. Then, have them explain why it's not always necessary to know the exact meaning.
- Hold up the Student's Book and point to the picture dictionary. Ask Ss about the problems in the pictures, for example: *What's the problem in picture 1?* (a broken window) *What's the problem in picture 2?* (a dripping faucet) *What's the problem in picture 3?* (a torn chair)
- Check off each part of the lesson focus as Ss demonstrate an understanding of what they have learned in the lesson.

> **More Ventures** *(whole group, pairs, individual)*
> Assign appropriate exercises from the *Teacher's Toolkit Audio CD / CD-ROM*, *Add Ventures*, or the *Workbook*.

4 Picture dictionary — Home problems

1. broken

2. dripping

3. torn

4. scratched

5. bent

6. burned out

7. cracked

8. stained

9. jammed

A Write the words in the picture dictionary. Then listen and repeat.

bent	cracked	scratched
broken	dripping	stained
burned out	jammed	torn

B Talk with a partner. Change the **bold** words and make conversations.

A What's the problem?
B My **window** is **broken**. Could you fix it, please?
A Sure. I'll try.

Daily living 117

Lesson E Writing

1 Before you write

A Talk in a group. Ask and answer the questions.

1. Did you ever write a letter of complaint?
2. Who did you write to?
3. What did you write about?
4. What happened?

B Read the letter of complaint.

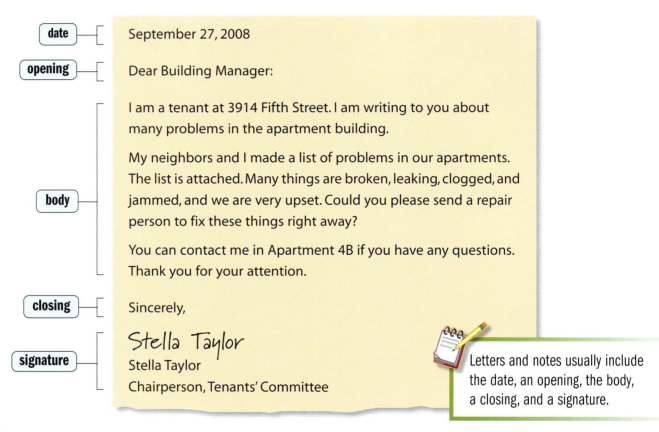

Letters and notes usually include the date, an opening, the body, a closing, and a signature.

C Write. Answer the questions about Stella's letter.

1. What is the date of this letter? _September 27, 2008._
2. Who is the letter to? _The Building Manager._
3. Who is the letter from? _Stella Taylor._
4. How many paragraphs are in the body of the letter? _Three._
5. What is the closing? _Sincerely._

Lesson objectives
- Write a letter of complaint
- Identify the parts of a letter

Warm-up and review
- Before class. Write today's lesson focus on the board.
  Lesson E:
  Write a letter of complaint
  Learn the five parts of a letter
- Begin class. Books open. Point to the first part of the lesson focus. Say: *Today, you will write a letter of complaint.*
- Direct Ss' attention to page 116 in Lesson D. Point to Exercise **2** on that page and ask Ss: *Who had to write a letter of complaint?* Elicit: *The tenants in Stella's building.*
- Review vocabulary from the unit. Direct Ss' attention to the big picture on page 110. Ask Ss: *What problems does Stella have?* (e.g., a leaking dishwasher; an overflowing washing machine). List Ss' responses on the board.
- Direct Ss' attention back to Exercise **2** on page 116. Ask Ss: *What are some other problems in Stella's building?* (e.g., broken windows; no lights in the hall; a leaking ceiling; smelly garbage). List Ss' responses on the board.

Presentation
- Direct Ss' attention to Exercise **1A** and read the instructions aloud. Ss ask and answer the questions in small groups.
- When Ss are finished, ask each group to tell the rest of the class about any experiences they've had with writing a letter of complaint.
- Direct Ss' attention to the letter of complaint in Exercise **1B**.

> Read aloud the information in the tip box. Call on Ss to locate and read aloud the date, opening, closing, and signature in the letter. Ask the class to point to the body of the letter.

- Read the instructions in Exercise **1B** to the class. Ss read the letter silently.
- Answer any questions Ss have about the letter.

Comprehension check
- Direct Ss' attention to Exercise **1C**. Read the instructions aloud and ask a S to read the example question aloud. Ask the class: *What is the date of this letter?* (September 27, 2008) Point to where the date has been written in the example.
- Ss complete the exercise individually. When Ss are finished, ask pairs to compare their answers. Then, ask individual Ss to read one of the answers aloud.

Expansion activity (student pairs)
- Have pairs practice reading the letter of complaint to each other.

Community building (small groups)
- Divide the class into groups of Ss with diverse cultural backgrounds.
- Ask Ss to talk about the differences between renting a house or an apartment in the United States and renting a house or an apartment in other countries. Ask Ss whether it is easy or difficult to find and rent places in other countries and whether landlords or tenants own the furniture and appliances. Ss might also want to talk about how long people usually live in rented houses or apartments, and whether it's common for people to buy their own house or condo after living in rented housing.
- Ss will enjoy hearing about their classmates' experiences as they practice using some of the language from the unit.

Lesson E   T-118

Lesson E Writing

Presentation
- Direct Ss' attention to Exercise **1D** and read the instructions aloud. Read the words in the word bank and ask Ss to repeat. Listen to Ss' pronunciation and make any necessary corrections.
- Point to Exercise **1D** and tell Ss: *This is a list of problems at Stella's apartment building.* Ask a S to read aloud the heading: *Problems at 3914 Fifth Street.*
- Model the exercise. Point to number 1 and say: *The carpet is . . .* Point to the words in the word bank. Elicit: *stained.* Hold up your Student's Book and write *stained* for number 1.

Practice
- Ss complete the exercise individually.
- Check answers as a class. Ask individual Ss to read aloud each of the sentences. If there are any errors, ask the class: *Does anyone have a different answer?* Ss suggest corrections.
- Read aloud the instructions in Exercise **1E**. Tell Ss that if they don't have problems in their own apartment or house, they can write sentences about the home of a friend or a family member.
- Ss write sentences individually. Walk around and help as needed.

Application
- Direct Ss' attention to Exercise **2** and read the instructions aloud. Point to Exercises **1B**, **1D**, and **1E** so that Ss know where to look for help.
- Ss write a letter of complaint individually. Remind Ss to include the five parts of a letter. Walk around and help with vocabulary, grammar, and punctuation.

> ### ▼ Teaching tip
> As Ss are writing their letters of complaint, spot-check the letters for any impolite or extreme language. Explain to Ss that although letters of complaint are often written by angry or upset people, they are formal letters and should not be overly emotional. A letter that sounds reasonable is more likely to get a good result than a letter that insults the person who is reading it.

Comprehension check
- Ss in pairs. Direct Ss' attention to Exercise **3A** and read the instructions aloud.
- Have pairs take turns reading their letters to each other. Help with pronunciation.
- Direct Ss' attention to Exercise **3B** and read the instructions aloud. Ask a S to read the three questions to the class.
- Ask Ss to take out a piece of paper and write the three questions from Exercise **3B**.
- Have Ss exchange letters. Tell Ss: *Read your partner's letter. Write answers to the three questions.*
- When Ss are finished, have the pairs share their answers and discuss their letters.

Expansion activity (individual students)
- As a class, brainstorm and list on the board times when people might write a letter of complaint. For example, people might need to write to a landlord to complain about a neighbor. They might write to a delivery company about receiving something they ordered late or in poor condition. At times, workers might need to complain about treatment on the job. Many people might find it necessary to disagree with a bill or credit card statement.

Evaluation
- Direct Ss' attention to the lesson focus written on the board. Ask Ss to tell the class some of the problems they wrote about in their letters of complaint.
- Draw on the board a large rectangle to resemble a piece of paper. To the left of the rectangle, write the five parts of a letter. The drawing should resemble Exercise **1B** on page 118 but without any writing.
- Call on Ss to come to the board and write the date, an opening, a closing, and a signature. Fill in the body portion of the letter with squiggly lines to indicate writing.
- Check off each part of the lesson focus as Ss demonstrate an understanding of what they have learned in the lesson.

> **More Ventures** (whole group, pairs, individual)
> Assign appropriate exercises from the *Teacher's Toolkit Audio CD / CD-ROM, Add Ventures,* or the *Workbook.*

D **Write.** Read the list of problems. Complete the sentences.

| broken | clogged | cracked | jammed | leaking | stained |

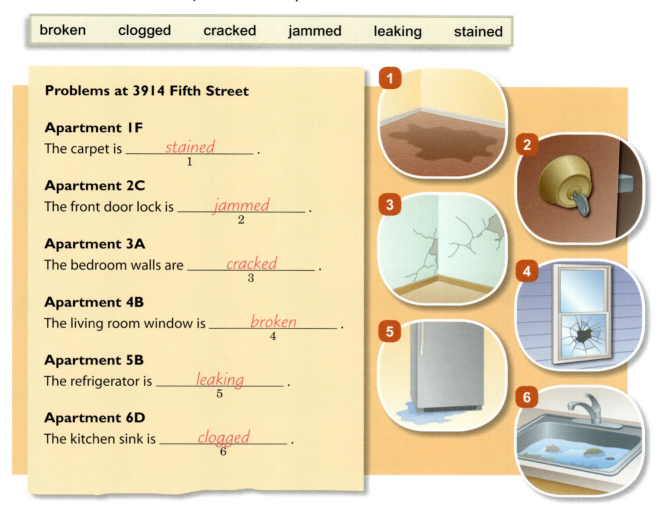

Problems at 3914 Fifth Street

Apartment 1F
The carpet is ____*stained*____ .
                          1

Apartment 2C
The front door lock is ____*jammed*____ .
                                      2

Apartment 3A
The bedroom walls are ____*cracked*____ .
                                     3

Apartment 4B
The living room window is ____*broken*____ .
                                         4

Apartment 5B
The refrigerator is ____*leaking*____ .
                                5

Apartment 6D
The kitchen sink is ____*clogged*____ .
                                6

E **Write** three sentences about problems in your apartment or house.

2 Write

Write a letter of complaint to your building manager or landlord. Use Exercises 1B, 1D, and 1E to help you.

3 After you write

A **Read** your letter to a partner.

B **Check** your partner's letter.
- What are the problems?
- Who is the letter to?
- Does the letter have an opening and a closing?

Daily living   119

Lesson F Another view

1 Life-skills reading

A+ PLUMBING REPAIRS
Montague, New Jersey 07827

Free Estimates
We charge less and don't leave a mess!
(973) 555-2399   30-day guarantee on all repairs

CUSTOMER INVOICE 102051

CUSTOMER NAME: Victor Waters
CUSTOMER ADDRESS: 1872 Valley Street, Newton, New Jersey 07860
SERVICE TECHNICIAN: Russ

DESCRIPTION OF PROBLEM	ACTUAL COST
SINK CLOGGED	$30.00
BATHROOM SHOWER LEAKING	$35.00
DISHWASHER OVERFLOWED	$40.00
TOTAL	$105.00

A Read the questions. Look at the invoice. Circle the answers.

1. How much is the total?
   a. $20.00
   b. $35.00
   c. $50.00
   d. $105.00 *(circled)*

2. How much did it cost to fix the dishwasher?
   a. $30.00
   b. $35.00
   c. $40.00 *(circled)*
   d. $105.00

3. What was leaking?
   a. the bathroom shower *(circled)*
   b. the dishwasher
   c. the sink
   d. the washing machine

4. Which repair was the most expensive?
   a. the bathroom shower
   b. the dishwasher *(circled)*
   c. the dryer
   d. the sink

B Talk with a partner. Ask and answer the questions.

1. What repair problems do you sometimes have?
2. Can you repair things in your home?
3. Do you have a friend or family member who can repair things?
4. What does that person help you with?

Unit 9

Lesson objectives
- Practice reading a customer invoice for service and repairs
- Review unit vocabulary and grammar
- Introduce the project
- Complete the project and self-assessment

Warm-up and review
- Before class. Write today's lesson focus on the board.
Lesson F:
Read a service invoice
Review vocabulary from the unit
Review requests with can, could, will, *and* would
Complete the project and the self-assessment
- Begin class. Books closed. Point to the first part of the lesson focus and tell Ss: *Today, we will practice reading a service invoice. What's an invoice?* Elicit, for example: *It's like a bill. It shows how much money you have to pay.* Explain to Ss that you get a service invoice when someone repairs something such as your dishwasher or your car.

Presentation
- Books open. Direct Ss' attention to the service invoice above Exercise **1A**. Tell Ss: *This is a service invoice.* Ask Ss: *What's the name of the plumbing company?* (A+ Plumbing Repairs) Ask: *What's the customer's name?* (Victor Waters) Ask: *What problems did Victor Waters have?* Elicit: *The sink was clogged; The bathroom shower was leaking; The dishwasher overflowed.*

Practice
- Read aloud the instructions for Exercise **1A**. This exercise helps prepare Ss for standardized-type tests they may have to take. Make sure Ss understand the exercise. Have Ss individually scan for the answers and circle the correct letters.

Comprehension check
- Go over the answers to Exercise **1A**. Make sure that Ss followed the instructions and circled their answers.
- Ss in pairs. Have Ss ask and answer the questions in Exercise **1A**. Encourage Ss to answer in complete sentences.

Expansion activity *(whole group)*
- Go over the service invoice in detail and discuss any words Ss don't know, for example: *estimates; leave a mess; guarantee; service technician;* etc.

▼ **Culture tip**
Emphasize to Ss the importance of reading a service invoice carefully before they pay for any service. Customers should also keep service invoices in their records in case the invoices are needed later.

Application
- Read aloud the instructions for Exercise **1B**. Pairs ask and answer the questions.
- Go over each question and ask for volunteers to tell the class their answers.

Expansion activity *(individual work)*
- Bring to class copies of a real service invoice, and prepare questions about the invoice for Ss to answer.
- Write the questions on the board and have Ss scan the invoice for the answers.
- Check answers as a class and answer any questions Ss might have about reading an invoice.

Lesson F Another view

Warm-up and review
- Books closed. Write on the board: *can / could / will / would*.
- Books open. Direct Ss' attention to the picture dictionary on page 117 or print out the picture dictionary flash cards from the *Teacher's Toolkit Audio CD / CD-ROM*. Point to or hold up each picture and ask Ss: *What's the problem?* Elicit, for example: *The window is broken*. As Ss answer, ask them: *How can you request help with this problem? What can you say?* Point to the words on the board and elicit polite requests, for example: *Could you please fix my window?*

Practice
- Direct Ss' attention to Exercise **2A** and read the instructions aloud. Read aloud the list of problems and ask Ss to repeat. Do the same with the list of repair people. Make sure Ss understand the exercise.
- Ss complete the exercise in pairs.

▼ **Teaching tip**
Some of the vocabulary for repair people in Exercise **2A** is likely to be new to Ss. Give Ss a chance to exercise their passive vocabulary recognition and their coping skills as they attempt to do the exercise by themselves. Allowing Ss to use dictionaries is also an option. Then, as you go over the answers, make sure Ss understand the meaning of the words.

- Check answers as a class. Write the numbers *1–5* on the board and ask a few Ss to come to the board and write their answers next to each number. Point to each answer and ask the class: *Is this correct?*
- Review the vocabulary words for repair people. For each one, ask Ss, for example: *What can a carpenter repair?* Elicit the correct answer from Exercise **2A**, and ask Ss if they know of any other things that a carpenter can repair. Explain, for example, that since carpenters work with wood, they can repair doors, furniture, stairs, etc.

Application
- Direct Ss' attention to Exercise **2B** and read the instructions aloud. Ask a S to read the example to the class.
- Ss work in small groups to think of as many questions as possible. Encourage Ss to use all four words for making requests.

- When the groups are finished, call on one group to read aloud all the requests they thought of for a carpenter. Ask the other groups if they have any additional requests.
- Repeat the process for the other professions, calling on different groups to read aloud all their requests for that person and asking the other groups to supply any additional requests.

Expansion activity (whole group)
- Bring in information to share with the class about the professions from Exercise **2**. Use the Internet to find out what percentage of people in each profession are male and what percentage are female; what the average hourly wage or yearly salary is for each profession; and what kind of training is involved in learning to do these jobs. (*The Occupational Outlook Handbook* that the U.S. Department of Labor posts on its Web site might be a good source of information.)

> **More Ventures** (whole group, pairs, individual)
> Assign appropriate exercises from the *Teacher's Toolkit Audio CD / CD-ROM*, *Add Ventures*, or the *Workbook*.

Application

Community building
- **Project** Ask Ss to turn to page 140 in their Student's Book to complete the project for Unit 9.

Evaluation
- Before asking Ss to turn to the self-assessment on page 145, do a quick review of the unit. Have Ss turn to Lesson A. Ask the class to talk about what they remember about this lesson. Prompt Ss, if necessary, with questions. For example: *What are the conversations about on this page? What vocabulary is in the big picture?* Continue in this manner to review each lesson quickly.
- **Self-assessment** Read the instructions for Exercise **3**. Ask Ss to turn to the self-assessment page to complete the unit self-assessment.
- If Ss are ready, administer the unit test on pages T-185–T-186 of this *Teacher's Edition* (or on the *Teacher's Toolkit Audio CD / CD-ROM*). The audio and audioscript for the tests are on the *Teacher's Toolkit Audio CD / CD-ROM*.

2 Fun with language

A Work with a partner. Match the home problems with the correct repair person.

1. a broken key __c__
2. a burned-out light __b__
3. a jammed window __a__
4. an overflowing toilet __e__
5. a stained wall __d__

a. a carpenter
b. an electrician
c. a locksmith
d. a painter
e. a plumber

B Work in a group. Make a list. How many questions can you think of? Use *Can*, *Could*, *Will*, or *Would*.

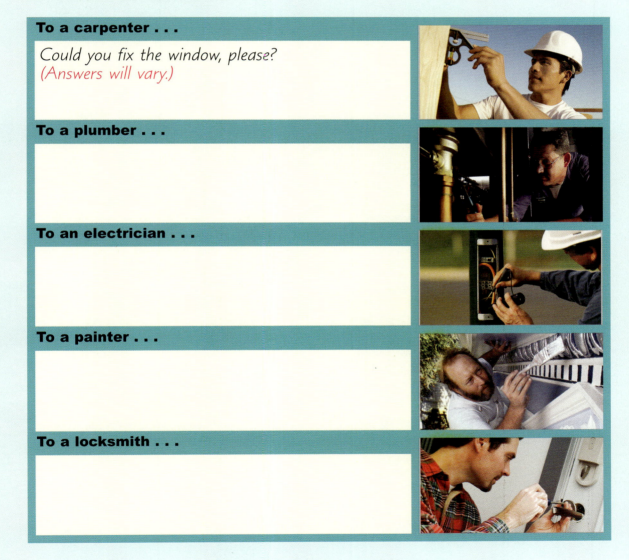

To a carpenter . . .
Could you fix the window, please?
(Answers will vary.)

To a plumber . . .

To an electrician . . .

To a painter . . .

To a locksmith . . .

3 Wrap up

Complete the **Self-assessment** on page 145.

Lesson A Get ready

1 Talk about the picture

A Look at the picture. What do you see?

B Point to: a card • a graduation cake • flowers • a guest
perfume • a piece of cake • balloons • a present

C Look at the people. What are they doing?

Leisure

Celia

UNIT 10

Lesson objectives
- Introduce Ss to the topic
- Find out what Ss know about the topic
- Preview the unit by talking about the picture
- Practice key vocabulary
- Practice listening skills

Warm-up and review

- Before class. Write today's lesson focus on the board. *Lesson A: Special occasions*
- Begin class. Books closed. Point to the lesson focus and tell Ss: *Special occasions are times when we celebrate something, perhaps with a party.* Ask Ss: *Can you think of some special occasions?* Elicit examples and list Ss' responses on the board (e.g., a birthday party; a wedding or an anniversary; a graduation party; a retirement party; a religious ceremony; etc.).

Presentation

- Books open. Set the scene. Direct Ss' attention to the picture on page 122. Ask: *What kind of party is this?* (a graduation party) Ask: *Is this party indoors or outdoors?* (outdoors) Ask the question from Exercise **1A**: *What do you see?* Elicit and write on the board as much vocabulary about the picture as possible (children, balloons, a table with food, flowers, a tree, a woman named Celia, etc.).
- Direct Ss' attention to the key words in Exercise **1B**. Read aloud each word or phrase while pointing to the corresponding part of the picture. Ask the class to repeat and point. Listen to Ss' pronunciation and correct as needed.

Comprehension check

- Ask Ss *Yes / No* questions about the picture. Say: *Listen to the questions. Answer "Yes" or "No."*
  Point to the big picture. Ask: *Is this a birthday party?* (No.)
  Point to the woman greeting Celia. Ask: *Did this woman bring flowers?* (Yes.)
  Point to the cake. Ask: *Is this a chocolate cake?* (Yes.)
  Point to the woman behind the table holding a card. Ask: *Does she have a piece of cake?* (No.)
  Point to the young girl. Ask: *Does she have a piece of cake?* (Yes.)
  Point to the gifts on the table. Ask: *Did people bring presents?* (Yes.)
  Point to the bottle of perfume. Ask: *Is this a balloon?* (No.)

Practice

- Direct Ss' attention to Exercise **1B**. Model the exercise. Hold up the Student's Book. Say to a S: *Point to a graduation cake.* The S points to the appropriate part of the picture.
- Ss in pairs. Say to one S: *Say the words or phrases in Exercise* **1B**. Say to his or her partner: *Point to the correct part of the picture.*
- Ss complete the exercise in pairs. Walk around and help as needed. When Ss finish, have them switch roles. Then, ask Ss to repeat the exercise with new partners.
- Ask several pairs to perform the exercise for the class to check understanding.
- Direct Ss' attention to Exercise **1C** and read the instructions and the question aloud.
- Model the exercise. Hold up the Student's Book. Point to the woman in blue at the table in the background. Say: *The woman is eating. She is smiling, so the food is probably good!*
- Ask pairs to talk about the people. Walk around and help as needed.
- Ask several Ss to tell the class what the people in the picture are doing.

Expansion activity (whole group)

- As a class, brainstorm and list on the board things that the two women in the foreground might be saying to each other.
- Discuss Ss' ideas and make suggestions. For example, the women are probably not saying, "It's nice to meet you." They probably already know each other, so perhaps they're saying, "It's nice to see you." Other possibilities include:
  Hi, Celia. Thanks for inviting me!
  Congratulations!
  Thank you for coming!
  It's a beautiful day for a party!

Expansion activity (student pairs)

- Have Ss make a list of all the food and drinks in the big picture.
- Compile a class list on the board. A few of the items should be recognizable to everyone, for example: *cake, salad,* and *soda.* Ss can make guesses about the other items. If some of the foods are not familiar to anyone in the class, ask Ss to guess the cultures those foods might come from.

Lesson A

Lesson A Get ready

Presentation

- Books open. Direct Ss' attention to the pictures in Exercise **2A**. For each picture, ask Ss: *What is this?* (a card, flowers, perfume)
- Direct Ss' attention back to the big picture on page 122. Ask about each gift item, for example: *Who brought the card?* (the tall woman behind the table) *Who brought the flowers?* (the woman greeting Celia) *Who brought the perfume?* (Ss won't know who brought the perfume, but thinking about it will help them with the listening exercise.)

Practice

- Read aloud the instructions for Exercise **2A**.
- [Class Audio CD2 track 30] Play or read the audio program (see audio script, page T-162). Pause the audio program after the first conversation and ask Ss: *Who is Celia talking to in conversation A?* (Aunt Ana, the woman who brought the flowers; Picture 2) Hold up the Student's Book and write the letter *a* next to number 2.
- [Class Audio CD2 track 30] Play or read the complete audio program and repeat as needed.
- Check answers. Ask Ss which picture represents the person Celia is talking to in the other conversations.
- Direct Ss' attention to exercise **2B** and read the instructions aloud.
- [Class Audio CD2 track 30] Model the exercise. Say: *Listen to conversation A.* Play or read the first lines spoken by Aunt Ana and Celia in conversation A. Direct Ss' attention to the example sentence. Read it aloud and point to where the letter *F* (False) is written. Make sure Ss understand the exercise.
- [Class Audio CD2 track 30] Read aloud each group of sentences before listening to the corresponding conversation. Read aloud the three sentences for conversation A. Then, play or read conversation A on the audio program (see audio script, page T-162). Do the same for conversations B and C.
- Ss complete the exercise individually. When Ss are finished writing their answers, play or read the complete audio program once more to allow Ss to check the answers they wrote.

Comprehension check

- Check answers. Write the numbers 2–9 on the board and ask a few Ss to come to the board and write the correct answers to Exercise **2B** next to each number.

- [Class Audio CD2 track 30] Play or read the audio program again. Pause the audio program after each conversation. Point to each answer on the board. Ask: *Is this correct?*

Learner persistence (individual work)

- [Self-Study Audio CD track 33] Exercises **2A** and **2B** are recorded on the Ss' self-study CD at the back of the Student's Book. Ss can listen to the CD at home for reinforcement and review. They can also listen to the CD for self-directed learning when class attendance is not possible.

Expansion activity (whole group)

- Ask Ss to explain which gift from Exercise **2A** is the best gift. List Ss' ideas on the board.

> **Culture note**
> Read aloud the information in the Culture note. Ask Ss: *Is Celia celebrating her graduation party with family and friends?* (Yes.)

Application

- Read aloud the instructions for Exercise **2C** and call on Ss to read the questions.
- Ss complete the task in pairs. Walk around and help as needed.
- Call on pairs to tell the class about their families' celebration customs.

Evaluation

- Direct Ss' attention to the lesson focus written on the board. Ask questions about the big picture. Use the key vocabulary:
  Point to Aunt Ana (greeting Celia) and ask: *Is the woman a guest?* (Yes.)
  Point to the gifts on the table and ask: *Which present did Celia open?* (the perfume)
  Point to the piece of cake next to the gifts and ask: *What's on the plate near the presents?* (a piece of cake)
- Check off each part of the lesson focus as Ss demonstrate an understanding of what they have learned in the lesson.

> ***More Ventures*** (whole group, pairs, individual)
> Assign appropriate exercises from the *Teacher's Toolkit Audio CD / CD-ROM, Add Ventures,* or the *Workbook.*

UNIT 10

2 Listening

A **Listen.** Which gift is Celia talking about? Write the letter of the conversation.

1. _b_
2. _a_
3. _c_

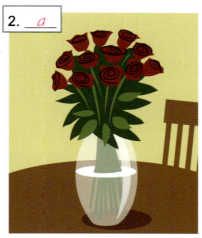
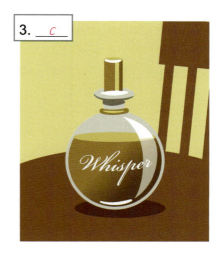

B **Listen again.** Write *T* (true) or *F* (false).

Conversation A

1. Celia is having a birthday party. _F_
2. Celia's mother made a cake. _T_
3. Ana gave Celia some flowers. _T_

Conversation B

4. Mrs. Campbell is a student. _F_
5. Celia started English class three years ago. _T_
6. Mrs. Campbell brought Celia a card. _T_

Conversation C

7. Sue brought her children to the party. _F_
8. Sue would like some water. _T_
9. Sue gave Celia some balloons. _F_

Listen again. Check your answers.

C Talk with a partner. Ask and answer the questions.

1. Does your family celebrate graduations?
2. How does your family celebrate?
3. What other special days does your family celebrate?

Culture note
People often celebrate someone's graduation with a party for family and friends.

Leisure 123

Lesson B Would you like some cake?

1 Grammar focus: *Would you like . . . ?*

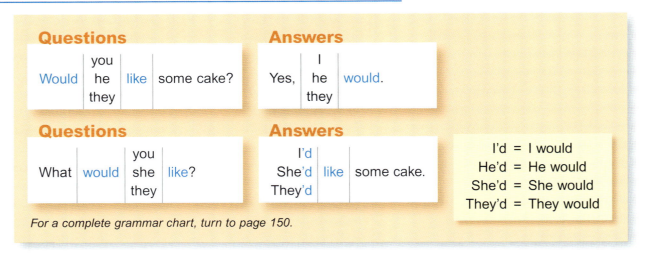

Questions	Answers
Would you / he / they like some cake?	Yes, I / he / they would.

Questions	Answers
What would you / she / they like?	I'd / She'd / They'd like some cake.

I'd = I would
He'd = He would
She'd = She would
They'd = They would

For a complete grammar chart, turn to page 150.

2 Practice

A Write. Complete the conversations.

1. A ___Would you like___ a cup of coffee?
   (you)
   B Yes, ___I would___ .

2. A ___Would he like___ a balloon?
   (he)
   B Yes, ___he would___ .

3. A ___Would she like___ some ice cream?
   (she)
   B Yes, ___she would___ .

4. A ___Would you like___ a sandwich?
   (you)
   B Yes, ___I would___ .

5. A ___Would they like___ some salad?
   (they)
   B Yes, ___they would___ .

6. A ___Would you like___ a hot dog?
   (you)
   B Yes, ___I would___ .

Listen and repeat. Then practice with a partner.

Lesson objectives
- Introduce *Would you like . . . ?*
- Practice making and responding to offers politely

Warm-up and review
- Before class. Write today's lesson focus on the board.
Lesson B:
<u>Would you like . . . ?</u>
Make offers politely
Respond to offers politely
- Before class. On several index cards write the words *a piece of cake*. You could also draw a rectangular piece of cake on each card that resembles the pieces of cake in the big picture.
- Begin class. Books open. Direct Ss' attention to the big picture on page 122. Ask the class: *What's the special occasion?* (It's Celia's graduation party.) Ask: *What presents did Celia get from the guests?* (a card, flowers, perfume) Ask: *What other things do you see in the picture?* (Elicit key vocabulary, such as: *a graduation cake, balloons, soda, salad.*)
- Point to the graduation cake in the big picture. Ask the class: *Would you like a piece of cake?* Walk up to Ss who say "yes" and repeat the question to them. As Ss answer "yes," give them one of the cards as if you're serving cake at a party.

Presentation
- Books open. Direct Ss' attention to the grammar chart in Exercise **1**. Read aloud the questions and answers in the top half of the grammar chart. Do the same with the bottom half of the chart. Ask Ss to repeat the questions and answers.
- Ss in pairs. Have students practice reading the grammar chart to each other while pointing to an appropriate person or persons in the class (I, you, he, they).

> **Contractions**
> Point to the box of contractions in the grammar chart. Read aloud each contraction and then the two words it contracts. Ask Ss to repeat. Practice the pronunciation of the contractions.

Expansion activity *(whole group)*
- If you want to expand the grammar presentation, turn to the grammar charts on page 150. Practice making and responding to offers with *Yes / No* and *Wh-* questions. Include the pronouns *we* and *you (plural)*.

Practice
- Direct Ss' attention to the picture in Exercise **2A**. Ask Ss: *What do you see on the table?* Elicit the vocabulary Ss will see in the exercise.
- Read aloud the instructions in Exercise **2A**. Ask two Ss to read aloud the example question and answer. Point to the top half of the grammar chart to show Ss where to look for help.
- Ss complete the sentences individually. Walk around and help as needed.

Comprehension check
- Read aloud the second part of the instructions in Exercise **2A**.
- [Class Audio CD2 track 31] Check answers with the class. Play or read the audio program (see audio script, page T-162). Ss listen and repeat as they check their answers.
- Have pairs practice saying the questions and answers in Exercise **2A**.
- Call on several pairs to say the questions and answers for the class.

Expansion activity *(small groups)*
- Ask the class: *What foods do you and your family usually serve on special occasions?* List responses on the board from several Ss. Ask Ss to describe any food that may not be familiar to everyone in the class. Say to the class: *Talk to your classmates about the best foods to serve at parties.*
- Ask each group to choose a secretary to write down Ss' suggestions for the best food to serve at parties. Walk around and ask Ss to tell you some of the reasons for their choices, for example: *Everyone likes ice cream. Sandwiches don't have to be hot when you eat them.*
- When Ss are finished, have each group report its list to the class.

Lesson B Would you like some cake?

Presentation
- Books open. Direct Ss' attention to Exercise **2B**. Point to each picture. Read aloud the noun phrase under each picture and ask Ss to repeat.
- Read aloud the instructions for Exercise **2B**. Ask two Ss to read aloud the example question and answer. Point to the bottom half of the grammar chart on page 124 to show Ss where to look for help.

Practice
- Ss complete the exercise in pairs. Walk around and help as needed.
- Ask several pairs to perform the conversations for the rest of the class.

Expansion activity (whole group)
- List on the board several party foods that Ss suggested in the Expansion activity for the exercise at the bottom of page 124. Make sure that singular countable nouns have an indefinite article (*a* or *an*) in front of them and plural or uncountable nouns have the word *some* in front of them.
- Go around the room and ask Ss: *What would you like?* Elicit from each S: *I'd like _____, please.*

▼ **Teaching tip**
Give Ss plenty of controlled practice with new structures, such as the determiners *a* and *some*, so that they can use the grammar successfully and build their confidence levels.

Useful language
Read aloud the information in the Useful language box. Ask Ss to read the dialog in Exercise **3** silently and look for these useful language expressions.

Application
- Read aloud the instructions for Exercise **3**. Ask two Ss to read the dialog to the class.
- Model the exercise. Ask a S to read the dialog with you. S speaks first. After each offer, point to the food and drink choices pictured in Exercise **2B**. Say, for example: *I'd like a cup of tea, please.* Then, to model an affirmative answer to the third question, say, for example: *Yes, please. I'd like some fruit.*
- Ss complete the exercise in pairs. Walk around and help as needed. Make sure Ss are practicing both roles in the dialog.
- Have each pair perform one of its dialogs for the class.

Community building (whole group)
- Ask Ss to think of special occasions in their cultures that might be different from the special occasions you've talked about in class. Have volunteers come to the board and write the name of the special occasion. Invite Ss to tell the class how people in their cultures celebrate the occasion. Encourage the class to ask questions.

Community building (whole group)
- Have a potluck party in which Ss bring in their favorite party foods. Ask Ss to prepare an index card to place next to each dish with the name and ingredients of the food. Ss should also be prepared to tell classmates about the food, for example, whether the dish is served only at celebrations or is something to eat every day.

Evaluation
- Direct Ss' attention to the lesson focus written on the board. Write on the board the nine food and drink choices from Exercise **2B**. With books closed, call on Ss to offer a classmate something to eat or drink using *Would you like something to eat / drink?* And *What would you like?* Ask classmates to give polite responses to the offers.
- Evaluate *Yes / No* questions and short answers by reviewing what the Ss said to each other. Ask a S, for example: *Would Pierre like some cheese?* (No, he wouldn't.)
- Check off each part of the lesson focus as Ss demonstrate an understanding of what they have learned in the lesson.

> **More Ventures** (whole group, pairs, individual)
> Assign appropriate exercises from the *Teacher's Toolkit Audio CD / CD-ROM*, *Add Ventures*, or the *Workbook*.

B Talk with a partner. Change the **bold** words and make conversations.

> **A** What would you like?
> **B** I'd like **some cake**, please.

1. some cake
2. some fruit
3. a piece of pie
4. some cheese
5. a bottle of water
6. some cookies
7. some soda
8. some dessert
9. a cup of tea

3 Communicate

Talk with a partner. Make conversations.

> **A** Would you like something to drink?
> **B** Yes, please.
> **A** What would you like?
> **B** I'd like some soda, please.
> **A** Would you like something to eat?
> **B** No, thank you. I'm full.

Useful language

Would you like something to drink?
Would you like something to eat?

Yes, please. / No, thank you. I'm full.

Lesson C   Tim gave Mary a present.

1 Grammar focus: direct and indirect objects

Statements

| Tim | gave / bought | a present | to / for | Mary. / her. |

| Tim | gave / bought | Mary / her | a present. |

Irregular verbs
bring → brought
buy → bought
give → gave
send → sent
write → wrote

For a complete grammar chart, turn to page 150.

2 Practice

A Write. Look at Joe's "to do" list. What did he do yesterday? Write sentences.

To do
- ✓ bring flowers to Sylvia
- ✓ buy a card for Nick
- ✓ write a letter to Pam
- ✓ buy a cake for Mary and Judy
- ✓ give roses to Eva
- ✓ send an invitation to Paul

1. Joe brought flowers to Sylvia.
2. Joe bought a card for Nick.
3. Joe wrote a letter to Pam.
4. Joe bought a cake for Mary and Judy.
5. Joe gave roses to Eva.
6. Joe sent an invitation to Paul.

Write. Complete the conversations.

1. **A** What did Joe bring Sylvia?
   B Joe brought Sylvia flowers.

2. **A** What did Joe buy Nick?
   B Joe bought Nick a card.

3. **A** What did Joe write Pam?
   B Joe wrote Pam a letter.

4. **A** What did Joe buy Mary and Judy?
   B Joe bought Mary and Judy a cake.

5. **A** What did Joe give Eva?
   B Joe gave Eva roses.

6. **A** What did Joe send Paul?
   B Joe sent Paul an invitation.

Listen and repeat. Then practice with a partner.

Lesson objectives
- Introduce direct and indirect objects
- Practice asking and answering questions with direct and indirect objects

Warm-up and review
- Before class. Write today's lesson focus on the board.
Lesson C:
Direct and indirect objects
Ask and answer questions with direct and indirect objects
- Begin class. Books open. Direct Ss' attention to the pictures on page 123 of Lesson A. Ask Ss: *What presents did people bring to Celia's graduation party?* (a card, flowers, perfume)
- Write on the board: *One person gave _____ to Celia. / One person gave Celia _____.* Read the sentences aloud using the presents Celia received, for example: *One person gave a card to Celia. / One person gave Celia a card.* Ask Ss to repeat. Repeat the process with *flowers* and *perfume*.
- Tell Ss: *At the graduation party, Celia received some presents.* Point to the first part of the lesson focus and underline the word *objects*. Tell Ss: *In grammar, objects receive something. Today, we'll learn about direct and indirect objects.*

Presentation
- Books open. Direct Ss' attention to the grammar chart in Exercise **1**. Read each statement aloud. Ask Ss to repeat.
- Point to the grammar chart and ask Ss: *In these statements, what did Tim give?* (a present) *What did Tim buy?* (a present) Tell Ss: *In these statements, "present" is the direct object. It "receives" the action of the verbs. It tells us what Tim gave or what Tim bought.*
- Point to the grammar chart and ask Ss: *In these statements, who received the present?* (Mary) Tell Ss: *In these statements, "Mary" is the indirect object. She receives the direct object – the present.*
- Point to the box with irregular verbs. Read the present and past forms of the irregular verbs aloud and ask Ss to repeat.

Expansion activity *(student pairs)*
- Point to the list of irregular verbs in the grammar chart. Say the first verb in the list: *bring*. Ask the class: *What is something you can bring to a person?* Elicit, for example: *a cup of coffee*. Write on the board: *Tim brought a cup of coffee to Mary. / Tim brought Mary a cup of coffee.* Say the two statements aloud and ask Ss to repeat.
- Continue in this manner, asking Ss to think of something you can buy, give, send, and write. List each verb followed by Ss' ideas on the board.
- Have Ss practice the statements in the grammar chart using the ideas on the board. One S in each pair says an irregular verb from the chart; the other S says two statements using the verb. Have Ss take turns choosing a verb and making statements.

Practice
- Direct Ss' attention to Exercise **2A** and read the instructions aloud. Ask Ss: *What was the date yesterday?* Have Ss write yesterday's date on Joe's "to do" list.
- Point to Joe's "to do" list and read each item aloud. Ask Ss to repeat. Point to and read aloud the first item on the "to do" list: *bring flowers to Sylvia*. Point to and read aloud the example sentence: *Joe brought flowers to Sylvia*.
- Ss write sentences individually. Walk around and help as needed.
- Check answers as a class. Call on individual Ss to read aloud one sentence each.
- Read aloud the second part of the instructions in Exercise **2A**. Ask two Ss to read aloud the example question and answer.
- Model the exercise. Call on a S to read aloud the question in number 2. Write on the board: *Joe bought Nick _____.* Wait for Ss to say: *a card*. Finish the sentence on the board.
- Ss write sentences individually. Walk around and help as needed.

Comprehension check
- Read aloud the third part of the instructions for Exercise **2A**.
- [Class Audio CD2 track 32] Check answers with the class. Play or read the audio program (see audio script, page T-162). Ss listen and repeat as they check their answers.
- Have pairs practice saying the questions and answers. Walk around and help as needed.
- Call on several pairs to say the questions and answers for the rest of the class.

Lesson C   T-126

Lesson C Tim gave Mary a present.

Presentation
- Books open. Direct Ss' attention to the pictures in Exercise **2B**. Ask Ss: *What are all these things?* (presents)
- Read aloud the noun phrase under each picture in Exercise **2B** and ask Ss to repeat.

Practice
- Read aloud the instructions for Exercise **2B**. Ask two Ss to read the example conversation. Point to the gift card that says *To Daniel* in the picture in number 1. Make sure Ss understand the exercise.

> **Useful language**
> Read aloud the pronouns in the Useful language box and ask Ss to repeat. Point to *Daniel* in the example conversation. Tell Ss: *Daniel is a name for a boy or man, in other words, for a "he."* Point to the Useful language box. Tell Ss: *When it is an indirect object, "he" becomes "him."*

- Ask Ss to tell what word they should use to talk about picture 2. (Marina is a name for a girl or woman, so they should use *her* in the conversation.)
- Ss complete the exercise in pairs. Walk around and help as needed. When Ss are finished, call on several pairs to perform the conversations for the class.

Expansion activity (student pairs)
- Ask Ss to take out a piece of paper and re-create the six pictures in Exercise **2B** without the names on the gift cards. (You might want to show Ss an example that you've done. Divide a piece of paper into six squares. Then, write the noun phrases and draw simple pictures in the squares.)
- Have Ss write new names on all the gift cards. Each gift card could have a woman's name, a man's name, or the names of more than one person.
- Ask Ss to make conversations similar to the ones in Exercise **2B** using the names on their new gift cards. (Ss will have 12 short conversations in all.) Walk around and help as needed.

Application
- Direct Ss' attention to Exercise **3** and read the instructions aloud. Ask a S to read the example aloud.
- Model the exercise. On the board re-create the chart from Exercise **3**. Give three items from your desk to three different Ss. Fill in the chart on the board with the names of the items and of the students.
- Tell Ss: *Now it's your turn. Give three things to three different classmates.* Ss complete the exercise individually.
- Read aloud the second part of the instructions for Exercise **3**. Call on two Ss to read the example conversation aloud. Model the exercise by pointing to the chart on the board and telling the class who you gave your items to.
- Ss exchange information in pairs, telling their partner who they gave things to.
- Read aloud the third part of the instructions for Exercise **3**. Call on two Ss to read the example conversation aloud. Ss ask their classmates to give back their items.
- When Ss are finished, ask them if they have all their items back.

Community building (whole group)
- Conduct a class discussion about gift giving. Start by brainstorming gift-giving occasions as a class. Then, ask Ss about occasions they haven't mentioned, for example, an invitation to somebody's house for dinner. Tell Ss about the occasions on which people in the United States usually give gifts, and ask Ss if customs are different in their native cultures. Finally, ask Ss if they know any special meanings for gifts. For example, some people think that red roses are romantic, while yellow roses are a sign of friendship.

Evaluation
- Direct Ss' attention to the lesson focus written on the board. Use Exercise **3** to evaluate Ss' use of direct and indirect objects. Ask Ss, for example: *Kristi, what did you give Berta?* (e.g., I gave Berta my notebook.) Ask: *Berta, what did you give Tomoko?* (e.g., I gave my pencil case to Tomoko.)
- Ask Ss to tell the class about a present they received in the last year. Model the task. Tell Ss, for example: *My brother gave me a book for my birthday.* Ask Ss: *What present did somebody give you?*
- Check off each part of the lesson focus as Ss demonstrate an understanding of what they have learned in the lesson.

> **More Ventures** (whole group, pairs, individual)
> Assign appropriate exercises from the *Teacher's Toolkit Audio CD / CD-ROM*, *Add Ventures*, or the *Workbook*.

B Talk with a partner. Change the **bold** words and make conversations.

1. some balloons
2. a card
3. some flowers
4. some cookies
5. some perfume
6. some books

A What did you give **Daniel**?
B I gave **him some balloons**.
A That's nice.

Useful language
he → him
she → her
they → them

3 Communicate

Write. Choose three classmates. Choose three items from your desk. Give one thing to each classmate. Then complete the chart.

Classmates	Items
Anika	my Ventures book
1. (Answers will vary.)	
2.	
3.	

Talk with a partner. Share your information.

I gave Anika my Ventures book.

I gave Rudy my pen.

Ask for your things back.

Anika, please give me my Ventures book.

Rudy, please give me my pen.

Leisure 127

Lesson D Reading

1 Before you read

Look at the picture. Answer the questions.

1. Who is the woman?
2. What is she doing?

2 Read

  Read the paragraph. Listen and read again.

Thank you

Celia had a graduation party last Friday. Her husband sent invitations to Celia's teacher and to their relatives and friends. They all came to the party! Some guests brought gifts for Celia. Her teacher Mrs. Campbell gave her a card. Her Aunt Ana brought her flowers. Her friend Sue gave her some perfume. Her classmate Ruth brought her some cookies. After the party, Celia wrote them thank-you notes. Tomorrow, she is going to mail the thank-you notes at the post office.

> Look for examples of the main idea when you read. This paragraph is about gifts. Look for examples of all the gifts.

> **Culture note**
> People often write thank-you notes. It is polite to thank someone for a gift.

3 After you read

Write. Answer the questions about Celia's graduation party.

1. When was Celia's graduation party? _Last Friday._
2. Who came to the party? _Celia's teacher, relatives, and friends._
3. What did Mrs. Campbell give Celia? _A card._
4. What did Sue give Celia? _Some perfume._
5. What did Ruth bring Celia? _Some cookies._
6. What is Celia going to do tomorrow? _Mail the thank-you notes at the post office._

Lesson objectives
- Introduce and read a narrative paragraph about a party
- Look for examples of the main idea while reading
- Practice using new topic-related words

Warm-up and review
- Before class. Write today's lesson focus on the board.
Lesson D:
Read and understand a paragraph about a party
Look for examples of the main idea while you read
Learn new vocabulary for celebrations
- Begin class. Books open. Direct Ss' attention to the big picture on page 122. Show Ss the big picture and ask: *What's the special occasion?* (It's Celia's graduation party.)
- Review questions and answers with direct and indirect objects. Point to the woman with flowers in the foreground. Ask Ss: *What did Aunt Ana give Celia at the graduation party?* (Aunt Ana gave Celia flowers.) Point to the bottle of perfume on the table. Ask Ss: *What did Celia's friend Sue give Celia?* (She gave Celia perfume.) Point to the woman behind the table with the card. Ask Ss: *What did Mrs. Campbell give Celia?* (She gave Celia a card.)

Presentation
- Direct Ss' attention to the picture in Exercise **1** and read the instructions aloud. Ask and elicit answers to the two questions. Discuss Ss' ideas about what Celia is doing in the picture.
- Direct Ss' attention to the paragraph in Exercise **2**. Ask the class: *What's the title of the paragraph?* (Thank you) Ask the class: *What do you think the paragraph will be about?* Elicit Ss' ideas.

> Read aloud the information in the tip box. Explain that when Ss are reading, they can find the main idea by looking for details or specific information that supports what they think the main idea is. Ask Ss to look for examples of gifts as they read the paragraph in Exercise **2**.

Practice
- Read aloud the instructions for Exercise **2**. Ask Ss to read the paragraph silently.
- [Class Audio CD2 track 33] Play or read the audio program and ask Ss to read along (see audio script, page T-162). Repeat the audio program as needed.
- Ask Ss: *What examples of gifts did you find in the reading?* (a card, flowers, some perfume, some cookies)
- Call on individual Ss to read aloud one sentence of the paragraph.

▼ Teaching tip
Make sure Ss understand that the paragraph in Exercise **2** is not a thank-you note. It's a paragraph that narrates, or tells, the story of Celia's party. Ask Ss to think about who wrote the paragraph. Perhaps Celia's friend wrote it for a school assignment.

Learner persistence (individual work)
- [Self-Study Audio CD track 34] Exercise **2** is recorded on the Ss' self-study CD at the back of the Student's Book. Ss can listen to the CD at home for reinforcement and review. They can also listen to the CD for self-directed learning when class attendance is not possible.

Culture note
Read the Culture note aloud. Ask Ss if they sometimes write thank-you notes. Guide Ss to tell if they sometimes make phone calls or send e-mail messages instead of writing thank-you notes. Ask Ss how they like to express their thanks to relatives and friends.

Expansion activity (individual work)
- Have Ss reread the paragraph and look for examples of "relatives and friends."
- Ask Ss: *What examples of relatives and friends did you find in the paragraph?* (Celia's teacher Mrs. Campbell, Celia's Aunt Ana, Celia's friend Sue, Celia's classmate Ruth)

Comprehension check
- Read aloud the instructions for Exercise **3**. Ask two Ss to read the example question and answer aloud. Ask Ss to write complete sentences.
- Ss complete the exercise individually. Walk around and help as needed.
- Go over answers with the class. Ask Ss to write their answers on the board. Then ask different Ss to read the answers aloud. Ask: *Are the sentences correct?* Make necessary corrections on the board.

Lesson D T-128

Lesson D Reading

Presentation

- Direct Ss' attention to the picture dictionary in Exercise 4. Point to the word *Celebrations*. Read the word aloud and ask Ss to repeat. Point to the pictures in the picture dictionary and tell Ss: *These are special occasions that people celebrate in the United States.*
- Point to the pictures in the picture dictionary. Ask questions to preview each picture.
  Point to Picture 1 and ask: *Is this a big dinner or a small dinner?* (a big dinner)
  Point to Picture 2 and ask: *Where is the Statue of Liberty?* (in New York City)
  Point to Picture 3 and ask: *What are they doing?* (They're getting married.)
  Point to Picture 4 and ask: *What's in the box?* (plates / dishes)
  Point to Picture 5 and ask: *What time is it?* (almost 12:00 / 11:59)
  Point to Picture 6 and ask: *What is the boy holding?* (flowers)
  Point to Picture 7 and ask: *What's the girl wearing?* (a cat costume)
  Point to Picture 8 and ask: *Which woman is going to have a baby soon?* (Ss point.)
  Point to Picture 9 and ask: *What present did the woman get?* (chocolates / candy)
- Direct Ss' attention to the word bank. Say each word or phrase in the word bank and ask Ss to repeat. Listen to Ss' pronunciation. Correct pronunciation as needed.

Practice

- Tell Ss: *Write the words in the picture dictionary.* Point to the first example, which has been done. Make sure Ss understand the exercise.
- Ss complete the exercise individually. Walk around and help as needed.

Comprehension check

- [Class Audio CD2 track 34] Say: *Listen and repeat.* Play or read the audio program (see audio script, page T-163). Ss should check their answers and repeat the words after they hear them. Repeat the audio program if necessary.

Community building (whole group)

- Ask Ss if they have questions about any of the celebrations in the picture dictionary that are not universal, for example: Thanksgiving, Independence Day, Halloween. Tell Ss about American customs for those celebrations.

Expansion activity (student pairs)

- Ask pairs of Ss to use the dictionary and their own knowledge to list additional vocabulary about the pictures in the picture dictionary.
- Model the activity. Point to Picture 1 and ask Ss: *What do Americans eat on Thanksgiving?* Elicit and list on the board vocabulary, such as: *turkey and mashed potatoes.*
- When Ss are finished, write the numbers 2–9 across the board. Call on different pairs to come to the board and write their vocabulary words for one of the pictures. Go over each list in turn, and have the Ss who wrote the words say them for the class. Ask the class if they have any other words to add to the lists.

Learner persistence (individual work)

- [Self-Study Audio CD track 35] Exercise **4A** is recorded on the Ss' self-study CD at the back of the Student's Book. Ss can listen to the CD at home for reinforcement and review. They can also listen to the CD for self-directed learning when class attendance is not possible.

Practice

- Direct Ss to Exercise **4B** and read the instructions aloud. Ask two Ss to read the example conversation aloud. Make sure Ss understand that they should talk about the celebrations in the picture dictionary first, but they may also talk about other celebrations.
- Ss make conversations in pairs. Walk around and help as needed.
- Ask several pairs to perform one of their conversations for the class.

Evaluation

- Direct Ss' attention to the lesson focus written on the board. Ask Ss some questions about the paragraph, for example: *Who sent the party invitations?* (Celia's husband) *Who is Mrs. Campbell?* (Celia's teacher) *When will Celia mail the thank-you notes?* (tomorrow)
- Ask Ss to tell you the main idea of the paragraph and some examples of it.
- Point to each picture in the dictionary and ask Ss to name the celebration.
- Check off each part of the lesson focus as Ss demonstrate an understanding of what they have learned in the lesson.

> **More Ventures** (whole group, pairs, individual)
> Assign appropriate exercises from the *Teacher's Toolkit Audio CD / CD-ROM*, *Add Ventures*, or the *Workbook*.

4 Picture dictionary — Celebrations

1. Thanksgiving

2. Independence Day

3. a wedding

4. a housewarming

5. New Year's Eve

6. Mother's Day

7. Halloween

8. a baby shower

9. Valentine's Day

A **Write** the words in the picture dictionary. Then listen and repeat.

a baby shower	Independence Day	Thanksgiving
Halloween	Mother's Day	Valentine's Day
a housewarming	New Year's Eve	a wedding

B **Talk** with a partner. What special days do you celebrate? How do you celebrate them?

Do you celebrate Thanksgiving?

Yes, we do. We always go to my mother-in-law's house for a big turkey dinner.

Lesson E Writing

1 Before you write

A Talk with a partner. Ask and answer the questions.

1. Did you ever receive a thank-you note?
2. Did you ever send someone a thank-you note?
3. In other countries, when do people write thank-you notes?

B Read the thank-you note.

> Indent the paragraphs in an informal note. Don't indent the date or *Dear* _____ .

June 30, 2008
Dear Aunt Ana,

   Thank you for the lovely flowers you gave me for my graduation. They are beautiful! I really like the color of the roses. Red is my favorite color!

   Thank you so much for coming to my graduation party. I hope you had a good time.

                              Love,
                              Celia

Culture note
Use *Love* or *Best wishes* in a personal note.
Use *Sincerely* in a formal letter.

C Write. Answer the questions about Celia's note. Write complete sentences.

1. When did Celia write the note?
   Celia wrote the note on June 30, 2008.
2. Who did Celia write the note to?
   She wrote the note to Aunt Ana.
3. What did Aunt Ana give Celia?
   Aunt Ana gave Celia flowers.
4. Why did Celia like the gift?
   Celia liked the gift because red is her favorite color.

Lesson objectives
- Write a thank-you note for a gift
- Indent paragraphs in an informal note

Warm-up and review
- Before class. Write today's lesson focus on the board.
  Lesson E:
  Write a thank-you note
  Indent paragraphs
- Begin class. Books open. Point to the first part of the lesson focus. Say: *Today, you will write a thank-you note.*
- Direct Ss' attention back to page 128 in Lesson D. Point to the picture in Exercise **1** on that page and ask Ss: *Who is the woman?* (Celia) Ask: *What is Celia writing?* (thank-you notes) Ask: *Why is Celia writing thank-you notes?* (She wants to say "thank you" to the people who gave her presents at her graduation party.)

Presentation
- Direct Ss' attention to Exercise **1A** and read the instructions aloud. Call on Ss to read the three questions. Ss ask and answer the questions in pairs.
- When Ss are finished, ask for volunteers to tell the class about their experiences with thank-you notes.
- Direct Ss' attention to the note in Exercise **1B**.

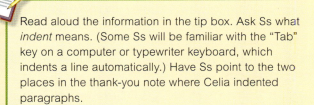

Read aloud the information in the tip box. Ask Ss what *indent* means. (Some Ss will be familiar with the "Tab" key on a computer or typewriter keyboard, which indents a line automatically.) Have Ss point to the two places in the thank-you note where Celia indented paragraphs.

Practice
- Read aloud the instructions for Exercise **1B**. Ss read the thank-you note silently.
- Answer any questions Ss have about the note.

Culture note
Read aloud the information in the Culture note. Point to "Love, Celia" in the thank-you note and ask Ss what part of a letter it is (the closing).

- To show Ss another way Celia could have closed her note, write on the board:
  Best wishes,
  Celia
- Direct Ss' attention to page 118 of Unit 9. Ask Ss to tell you how Stella closed her formal letter of complaint. (Sincerely)

Expansion activity (whole group)
- After reading Celia's thank-you note, ask the class: *Does Celia have a favorite color?* (Yes, red.) Ask Ss: *Do you have a favorite color?* Ask Ss who have a favorite color to explain why they like the color, how it makes them feel, and whether they buy clothes or other items in their favorite color.

Comprehension check
- Direct Ss' attention to Exercise **1C**. Read the instructions aloud and ask a S to read the example question. Ask the class: *What is the date on this note?* (June 30, 2008) Point to and read aloud the example answer.
- Ss complete the exercise individually. When Ss are finished, ask pairs to compare their answers. Then, ask individual Ss to read each of the answers aloud.

Learner persistence (whole group)
- If you and your Ss are nearing the end of your English course, have a class discussion about Ss' plans to continue to improve their English after the course is over.
- If your school offers a higher-level English course, give Ss information about when the course begins, how to register, and other details.
- Remind Ss that they have opportunities every day to use and improve their English. For example, reading a newspaper in English, having conversations with co-workers in English, and going to English-language movies can all be helpful.

Lesson E Writing

Presentation

- Books open. Direct Ss' attention to Exercise **1D** and read the instructions aloud. Read the words in the word bank and ask Ss to repeat. Listen to Ss' pronunciation and make any necessary corrections.
- Ask Ss: *Do you see a special occasion in the word bank?* (birthday) Ask Ss: *Do you see a present in the word bank?* (shirt)
- Model the exercise. Point to the line for today's date. Ask Ss: *What is the date today?* Hold up your Student's Book and write today's date on the line. Point to number 1 and ask: *What can we write before the name?* Point to the words in the word bank. Elicit: *Dear.* Hold up your Student's Book and write *Dear* for number 1.

Practice

- Ss complete the exercise individually.
- Check answers as a class. Ask individual Ss to read aloud each sentence of the thank-you note. If there are any errors, ask the class: *Does anyone have a different answer?* Have Ss suggest a correction.
- Read aloud the instructions for Exercise **1E**. Tell Ss that this exercise will help them get ideas for writing their own thank-you notes in Exercise **2**.
- Ss write sentences individually. Walk around and help as needed.

Application

- Direct Ss' attention to Exercise **2** and read the instructions aloud. Point to Exercises **1B**, **1D**, and **1E** so that Ss know where to look for help.
- Ss write a thank-you note individually. Remind Ss to include all the parts of an informal letter and to indent their paragraphs. Walk around and help with vocabulary, grammar, and punctuation.

▼ **Teaching tip**
While they are writing their thank-you notes, Ss may need help thinking of adjectives to describe their gifts; for example, Paula said the shirt was "beautiful" and "the right size." She also said that she liked the color of the shirt. As you walk around and look at Ss' notes, be prepared to offer advice about the use of appropriate descriptive language.

Comprehension check

- Ss in pairs. Direct Ss' attention to Exercise **3A** and read the instructions aloud.
- Have pairs take turns reading their letters to each other. Help with pronunciation.
- Direct Ss' attention to Exercise **3B** and read the instructions aloud. Ask a S to read the three questions to the class.
- Ask Ss to take out a piece of paper and write the three questions from Exercise **3B**.
- Have Ss exchange letters. Tell Ss: *Read your partner's letter. Write answers to the three questions.*
- When Ss are finished, have pairs share their answers and discuss their letters.

Expansion activity *(individual work)*

- On page 130, Ss read a thank-you note from Celia to her Aunt Ana. Have Ss use it as a model to write a thank-you note from Celia to one of the other guests who brought a present to the graduation party: Mrs. Campbell, Sue, or Ruth.
- Ask Ss to reread the paragraph on page 128 for information about the guests and the presents.
- When Ss are finished, ask for volunteers to read their thank-you notes to the class.

Evaluation

- Direct Ss' attention to the lesson focus written on the board. Ask several Ss to tell the class what they wrote about in their thank-you notes.
- Ask several Ss which word or words they used to close their notes.
- Ask several Ss how many paragraphs they wrote in their notes and if they indented the first word of each paragraph.
- Check off each part of the lesson focus as Ss demonstrate an understanding of what they have learned in the lesson.

More Ventures *(whole group, pairs, individual)*
Assign appropriate exercises from the *Teacher's Toolkit Audio CD / CD-ROM, Add Ventures,* or the *Workbook.*

D Write. Complete the thank-you note.

> Best wishes   birthday   color   Dear   fun   party   shirt   size

_____,
(today's date)

__**Dear**__ John,
     1

Thank you for the beautiful __**shirt**__ you gave me for
                                   2
my __**birthday**__. It is just the right __**size**__.
        3   4
I also really like the __**color**__.
                            5
Thank you so much for coming to my __**party**__. I hope
                                          6
you had __**fun**__.
             7

__**Best wishes**__,
        8
Paula

E Write. Answer the questions.

1. When did a friend give you a present? __**(Answers will vary.)**__
2. What is your friend's name? _____
3. What was the present? _____
4. Why did you like the present? _____
5. What was the celebration? _____

2 Write

Write a thank-you note to a friend for a gift. Use Exercises 1B, 1D, and 1E to help you.

3 After you write

A Read your note to a partner.

B Check your partner's note.
- What was the present?
- What was the celebration?
- Did your partner indent each paragraph?

Lesson F Another view

1 Life-skills reading

It's a party! Please join us!

Dear Will and Katya,

For: A New Year's Eve Party
Date: Wednesday, December 31
Time: 8:00 p.m. until 1:00 a.m.
Place: Tom and Luisa's
76 North Street, Apt. 6A
RSVP: (813) 555-1234 by December 15

Please bring something to drink.
No children, please!
Hope you can come!

A Read the questions. Look at the invitation. Circle the answers.

1. Who is giving the party?
   a. Luisa
   b. Tom and Luisa ✓
   c. Will and Katya
   d. Will and Luisa

2. When do people need to say *yes* or *no* to the invitation?
   a. before December 15 ✓
   b. after December 15
   c. on December 31
   d. after December 31

3. What time will the party begin?
   a. 8:00 a.m.
   b. 1:00 p.m.
   c. 8:00 p.m. ✓
   d. 1:00 a.m.

4. What should people bring to the party?
   a. something to drink ✓
   b. something to eat
   c. their children
   d. nothing

B Talk in a group. Ask and answer the questions.

1. Do you like to go to parties? Do you like to give parties?
2. Do you usually bring something to a party? What?
3. Tell about the last party you went to.

Lesson objectives
- Practice reading a formal invitation to a party
- Review unit vocabulary
- Introduce the project
- Complete the project and self-assessment

Warm-up and review
- Before class. Write today's lesson focus on the board.
Lesson F:
Read an invitation to a party
Review topic vocabulary
Complete the project and the self-assessment
- Begin class. Books closed. Ask Ss: *Did anyone in the class go to a party last weekend?* If not, ask about last month, the month before last, or another time in the recent past until a S answers "Yes." Ask the S or Ss who have been to a party recently: *How did you know about the party? Did the host or hostess invite you?* Write Ss' responses on the board.
- Point to the first part of the lesson focus and tell Ss: *Today, we will practice reading an invitation to a party. What's an invitation?* Elicit, for example: *It's a note that a person sends you to ask you to come to a party.*

Presentation
- Books open. Direct Ss' attention to the invitation above Exercise **1A**. Tell Ss: *This is an invitation to a party.* Ask Ss: *Who received the invitation?* (Will and Katya) Ask: *Where will the party be?* (Tom and Luisa's apartment)
- Point to *RSVP* on the invitation and write the letters on the board. Ask Ss: *What does this mean?* If Ss don't know the meaning of *RSVP,* explain that the person who wrote the invitation wants to know if Will and Katya will come to the party or not. Point out the phone number and the date and explain that Will and Katya should call Tom and Luisa on or before December 15.

> **Culture tip**
> *RSVP* comes from a French phrase that means, "Please respond." Tell Ss that if they receive an invitation that says *RSVP* they should contact the host or hosts to say if they plan to attend the party.

- As a class, brainstorm a few reasons hosts might want to know how many guests will come to their party, for example: *They want to know if they should buy a large cake or a small cake; They want to know how much food to buy; They want to know how many tables and chairs they'll need;* etc.

Practice
- Read aloud the instructions for Exercise **1A**. This exercise helps prepare Ss for standardized-type tests they may have to take. Make sure Ss understand the exercise. Have Ss individually scan for the answers and circle the correct letters.

Comprehension check
- Go over the answers to Exercise **1A** together. Make sure Ss have followed the instructions and circled their answers.
- Ss in pairs. Tell Ss: *Ask and answer the questions in Exercise* **1A**. Encourage Ss to answer using complete sentences.

> **Culture tip**
> Point out the phrase, "No children, please" near the bottom of the invitation. Ask Ss: *Why does the invitation say this?* Elicit, for example: *The party isn't over until after midnight; New Year's Eve celebrations often involve champagne and other alcoholic drinks;* etc.

- Tell Ss that other party invitations might say, "Children welcome." If it's not clear whether the hosts want children to attend the party, the people who are invited can always ask when they RSVP.
- You could also tell Ss about a growing number of cities in the United States that sponsor family-oriented events such as musical performances and fireworks on New Year's Eve. These events typically end well before midnight and do not involve alcohol.

Application
- Read aloud the instructions for Exercise **1B**. Call on Ss to read the questions aloud.
- Ss complete the task in small groups. Walk around and help as needed.
- When Ss have finished, go over each question and ask for a volunteer from each group to tell the class about the group's answer.

Lesson F Another view

Warm-up and review
- Books open. Direct Ss' attention to the picture dictionary on page 129 or print out the picture dictionary flash cards from the *Teacher's Toolkit Audio CD /CD-ROM*. Point to or hold up each picture and ask Ss: *What's the celebration?* Elicit and write on the board the words and phrases from the word bank.

Practice
- Direct Ss' attention to Exercise **2A** and read the instructions aloud.
- Model the exercise. Point to number 1 and say: *It's Independence Day, or July 4th. What's the celebration?* Point to the word bank and to the example answer. Make sure Ss understand the exercise.
- Have pairs fill in the blanks.

> ▼ **Teaching tip**
> If Ss don't understand some of the clues in Exercise **2A**, encourage them to come back to those items later. They can use the process of elimination, along with the number of words and letters, to choose the correct celebration.

- Check answers as a class. Write the numbers 2–9 on the board and ask a few Ss to write their answers on the board next to each number. Point to each answer and ask the class: *Is this correct?* Make corrections on the board.
- Direct Ss' attention to Exercise **2B** and read the instructions aloud. Point to the circled letter in number 1 in Exercise **2A**. Point to where the letter *c* has been written as an example.
- Ss complete the task individually. Walk around and help as needed.
- Read aloud the second part of the instructions in Exercise **2B**. Ss unscramble the letters to form the word *celebration*.

Expansion activity *(student pairs)*
- Write on the board:
  What is your favorite celebration?
  Why do you like it?
- Have Ss interview each other in pairs using these questions. Encourage Ss to talk about any celebration; they're not limited to the celebrations covered in the unit.

- When Ss are finished, ask for volunteers to tell the rest of the class about their partner's favorite celebration. Listen carefully and make sure Ss use the *-s* ending for verbs in the simple present, for example: *She likes the Korean holiday Chuseok because she sees her whole family then.*

> *More Ventures* (whole group, pairs, individual)
> Assign appropriate exercises from the *Teacher's Toolkit Audio CD / CD-ROM, Add Ventures,* or the *Workbook*.

Application

Community building
- **Project** Ask Ss to turn to page 140 in their Student's Book to complete the project for Unit 10.

Evaluation
- Before asking Ss to turn to the self-assessment on page 145, do a quick review of the unit. Have Ss turn to Lesson A. Ask the class to talk about what they remember about this lesson. Prompt Ss, if necessary, with questions, for example: *What are the conversations about on this page? What vocabulary is in the big picture?* Continue in this manner to review each lesson quickly.
- **Self-assessment** Read the instructions for Exercise **3**. Ask Ss to turn to the self-assessment page to complete the unit self-assessment.
- If Ss are ready, administer the unit test on pages T-187–T-188 of this *Teacher's Edition* (or on the *Teacher's Toolkit Audio CD / CD-ROM*). The audio and audio script for the tests are on the *Teacher's Toolkit Audio CD / CD-ROM*.

2 Fun with language

A Work with a partner. Read the clues. Fill in the blanks.

baby shower	Halloween	New Year's Eve
birthday	housewarming	Valentine's Day
graduation party	Independence Day	wedding

1. July 4:
   I n d e p e n d e(n)c e D a y

2. Your child finishes high school:
   g(r)a d u a t i(o)n p a r t y

3. Children wear costumes:
   H a(l)l o w e e n

4. A woman wears a beautiful white dress:
   w(e)d d i n g

5. People bring gifts for a new baby:
   (b)a b y s h o w(e)r

6. December 31:
   (N)e w Y e a r's E v e

7. Your friend is one year older:
   b(i)r t h d a y

8. February 14:
   V a l e n(t)i n e's D a y

9. Your sister has a party in her new apartment:
   h o u s e w(a)r m i n g

B Write the circled letters from Exercise A.
   c r o l e b e n i t a

Write. Unscramble the letters to answer the question.

What's another word for a party?
   c e l e b r a t i o n

3 Wrap up

Complete the **Self-assessment** on page 145.

Leisure | 133

Review

1 Listening

Read the questions. Then listen and circle the answers.

1. Why is Ramona going to have a party?
   a. to celebrate her birthday
   (b.) to celebrate her new apartment
2. When is Ramona's party?
   (a.) next month
   b. next week
3. What does Ramona need?
   (a.) a painter
   b. a plumber
4. How many good painters does Fabio know?
   a. one
   (b.) two
5. Which painter does Fabio recommend?
   a. the first one
   (b.) the second one
6. What is the name of the second painter?
   (a.) Fabio
   b. Walter

Talk with a partner. Ask and answer the questions. Use complete sentences.

2 Grammar

A Write. Complete the conversation.

> **Rita** Saba, could you ___*help*___ me with something? My teacher is going to
> 1. help / helping
> retire tomorrow, and I want to buy a gift ___*for*___ her. What should I get?
> 2. to / for
>
> **Saba** Let's see. Would she ___*like*___ some flowers?
> 3. like / likes
>
> **Rita** Yes, she ___*would*___. She loves flowers. Where can I buy them?
> 4. will / would
>
> **Saba** There's a small flower shop downtown, and a bigger one near the school.
>
> **Rita** ___*Which*___ shop do you recommend?
> 5. Which / Where
>
> **Saba** I ___*like*___ the one near the school. It's cheaper.
> 6. like / likes

B Write. Look at the answers. Write the questions.

1. **A** What _does Rita want to buy her teacher_?
   B Rita wants to buy her teacher a gift.
2. **A** What _would her teacher do_?
   B Her teacher would like some flowers.
3. **A** Which _flower shop does Saba recommend_?
   B Saba recommends the flower shop near the school.
4. **A** Which _flower shop is cheaper_?
   B The flower shop near the school is cheaper.

Talk with a partner. Ask and answer the questions.

UNITS 9 & 10

Lesson objectives
- Review vocabulary and grammar from Units 9 and 10
- Introduce pronunciation of reduced forms

Warm-up and review

- Before class. Write today's lesson focus on the board.
  Review unit:
  Review vocabulary from units 9 and 10
  Review Which questions and the simple present
  Review requests with can, could, will, would
  Review Would you like . . . ?
  Review questions and answers with direct and indirect objects
  Pronounce reduced forms

- Begin class. Books closed. Write on the board several pairs of items, for example:
  vanilla ice cream / chocolate ice cream
  baseball / soccer
  e-mail message / thank-you note
  a bottle of water / a bottle of soda

- Ask Ss questions to review *Which* questions and the simple present, for example: *I'm going to buy ice cream at the supermarket. Which ice cream do you recommend?* Elicit, for example: *I recommend vanilla ice cream.* Ask Ss to give reasons for their answers, for example: *Vanilla ice cream tastes good with every kind of fruit topping.*

Practice

- Books open. Direct Ss' attention to Exercise **1** and read the instructions aloud.

- Ask a S to read aloud the example question. Ask another S to read aloud the example answer choices. Continue until Ss have read all the questions and the answer choices. Say: *Now listen and circle the correct answers.*

- [Class Audio CD2 track 35] Play or read the audio program (see audio script, page T-163). Ss listen and circle the answers to the questions. Repeat the audio program as needed.

- Check answers. Read each question aloud and call on different Ss to answer.

- Read aloud the second part of the instructions for Exercise **1**. Emphasize that answers need to be in complete sentences.

- Ss complete the exercise in pairs. Walk around and help as needed.

- Ask several pairs to ask and answer the questions for the rest of the class.

Expansion activity *(whole group)*

- Discuss Fabio's offer to paint Ramona's apartment. Do Ss agree that Fabio is a good friend? Do Ss have skills that they offer to their friends for free, for example, cooking dinner, fixing cars, or babysitting?

Practice

- Direct Ss' attention to Exercise **2A** and read the instructions aloud.

- Ask a S to read aloud the first sentence of the conversation. Point to where the word *help* has been written for number 1.

- Ss complete the exercise individually. Walk around and help as needed.

- Write the numbers 2–6 on the board. Ask a few Ss to come to the board to write their answers next to each number.

- Ask individual Ss to read aloud each sentence of the conversation.

- Have pairs practice the conversation.

> **Teaching tip**
> If Ss don't understand an item in Exercise **2A**, have them review the following pages in the Student's Book:
> Item number 1: Review pages 114–115
> Item number 2: Review page 126
> Item numbers 3–4: Review pages 124–125
> Item numbers 5–6: Review pages 112–113

- Direct Ss' attention to Exercise **2B** and read the instructions aloud. Ask two Ss to read aloud the example question and answer.

- Ss write the questions individually. Walk around and help as needed.

- Write the numbers 2–4 on the board. Ask for volunteers to come to the board to write the questions next to each number. Ask other Ss to make corrections on the board.

- Read aloud the second part of the instructions for Exercise **2B**.

- Pairs practice asking and answering the questions. Walk around and help as needed.

- Ask several pairs to ask and answer the questions for the rest of the class.

Review: Units 9 & 10 T-134

Presentation

- Write on the board: *Reduced forms*. Read the words aloud and ask Ss to repeat. Ask the class: *What does "reduced" mean?* Elicit, for example: *made smaller*.
- Write on the board: *How are you doing?* Say the question, pronouncing each word clearly and carefully. Ask Ss to repeat. Then, ask: *Is that what English speakers usually say?* Write on the board: *How ya doin'?* Say the question and ask Ss to repeat. Tell Ss that in informal situations, English speakers sometimes reduce words and sounds, especially in common expressions. In this case, *are* has been eliminated, *you* has become *ya*, and *doing* has become *doin*. These changes make the sentence faster to say.
- Repeat the two versions of the question again so that Ss can hear the difference.
- Direct Ss' attention to Exercise **3A**. Read the instructions aloud. Read aloud the full forms of the questions and ask Ss to repeat. Then, say to Ss: *Now, listen to the reduced forms.*
- [Class Audio CD2 track 36] Play or read the audio program (see audio script, page T-163). Ss just listen. Repeat the audio program as needed, making sure Ss can hear the pronunciation of *Could you* and *Would you* in their reduced forms. Ask Ss: *What did you hear?*

Practice

- Direct Ss' attention to Exercise **3B**. Read the instructions aloud.
- [Class Audio CD2 track 37] Play or read the audio program (see audio script, page T-163). Ss listen and repeat each question. Say the questions along with Ss, emphasizing the reduced forms.
- Direct Ss' attention to Exercise **3C** and read the instructions aloud. Explain that Ss will hear questions with either *Could you* or *Would you*. Ss should check the column for the question they hear.
- [Class Audio CD2 track 38] Model the exercise. Play or read the first question on the audio program (see audio script, page T-163). Ask Ss: *What did you hear, Could you or Would you?* (Could you) Hold up your Student's Book and check the first box in the *Could you* column.
- [Class Audio CD2 track 38] Play or read the audio program again (see audio script, page T-163). Have Ss listen and check the appropriate boxes. Repeat the audio program as needed.
- Check answers as a class. Ask Ss to tell you which questions they heard.

▼ **Teaching tip**
Explain to Ss that it's not necessary to use reduced forms when they're speaking. In fact, Ss may be better understood if they use full forms. Yet, Ss need to understand English speakers who do use reduced forms.

Comprehension check

- Direct Ss' attention to Exercise **3D** and read the instructions aloud.
- Model the exercise. Look through Units 9 and 10 in the Student's Book. Write on the board a question with *Would you* or *Could you* from one of the units.
- When Ss have written their four questions, read aloud the second part of the instructions for Exercise **3D**. Pairs read their questions aloud. Encourage Ss to practice saying both the full forms and the reduced forms of *Would you* and *Could you*.
- Walk around and listen to pronunciation. Make corrections as needed.
- Call on several Ss to say one of their questions using the reduced form.

Evaluation

- Direct Ss' attention to the lesson focus written on the board. Write on the board the names of two popular movies that are currently playing. Tell Ss that you are taking your nephew to see a movie soon. Ask Ss: *Which movie do you recommend?* Elicit: *I recommend _____*.
- Make some requests with *can, could, will,* and *would;* for example: *Simon, could you give me your pencil, please?* Elicit a polite response, for example: *Yes, of course.*
- Ask Ss: *What would you like to get for your next birthday?* Call on Ss and ask if they'd like various presents, for example: *Gina, would you like to get a card for your birthday?* (Yes, I would. / No, I wouldn't.)
- Ask Ss to tell you about a present they gave to someone. As an example, say: *Last month, I gave my friend a book.* Elicit sentences with direct and indirect objects.
- Finally, have Ss say one of their questions from the chart in Exercise **3D** using the reduced form.
- Check off each part of the lesson focus as Ss demonstrate an understanding of what they have learned in the lesson.

UNITS 9 & 10

3 Pronunciation: reduced forms

A **Listen** to the reduced forms of *Could you* and *Would you* in these sentences.

Could you
Could you help me?
Could you paint the wall, please?

Would you
Would you like some water?
Would you repair the refrigerator, please?

B **Listen and repeat.**

Could you
Could you send someone to help?
Could you recommend a painter?
Could you please fix this?

Would you
Would you turn on the light, please?
Would you unclog the sink?
Would you like a piece of cake?

C **Listen** to the sentences. Check (✓) the correct column.

	Could you	Would you
1.	✓	
2.		✓
3.		✓
4.		✓
5.	✓	
6.		✓

D **Write** four questions from Units 9 and 10. Find questions that begin with *Would you* or *Could you*.

1. *(Answers will vary.)*
2.
3.
4.

Talk with a partner. Read the questions.

Review: Units 9 & 10 135

Overview

The projects on pages 136–140 in the *Ventures* Student's Book are optional material to be used at the completion of a unit. There is one project per unit, and most of the projects can be completed in one class period.

Projects are valuable activities because they extend students' learning into a real-world context. They work within the unit topic, but they also go beyond the Student's Book.

These projects are designed to be fun and practical, with the goal of helping students become more independent while learning to live in a new culture and speak a new language.

Project set-up and materials

Projects may be done in class as a group activity or outside of class, individually.

There is a reference at the end of each unit in this Teacher's Edition to remind teachers about the projects. Some projects will need the teacher to gather simple materials to be used in class. For example, some require large poster paper, index cards, or authentic materials such as supermarket ads and copies of the local telephone directory. In order to complete other projects, students will need access to a computer that is linked to the Internet.

Skills learned through the projects

Students learn different skills through these projects. For example, half the projects involve use of the Internet. Students search for information using key words. This is an essential skill that most students will need to use in English. In addition, the projects encourage students to practice other essential life skills, such as working collaboratively to make a poster or a book, looking up information on community resources, and learning to manage their time better by making a time-management calendar.

Community building and learner persistence

Ventures projects help build community inside and outside the classroom as students work together, using materials such as local newspapers and telephone directories to find information. Building community, in turn, helps to promote learner persistence. As students apply essential life skills, they will become more confident in their English skills and will be more motivated to come to class to learn additional skills that will help them in daily life.

UNIT 1

Online clothing store

A Use the Internet.
Find an online clothing store.

Keywords: women's clothes | men's clothes | children's clothes

B Make a chart.
Write the names of three people.
Find a gift of clothing for each person.
Write the item and the price.
Print a picture of each item.

Person	Gift	Price
my neighbor Ana	women's gray V-neck sweater	$39.95
my brother Paul	men's striped shirt	$44.50
my daughter Rachel	children's green and yellow dress	$29.99

C Share your information.
Show the pictures.
Talk about the gifts.
Talk about the online clothing stores.
What are the class's favorite store and gift?

UNIT 2

Jobs and education

A Make a list.
What job do you want to have in five years?
Write three ideas.

1. hotel manager
2. nurse
3. receptionist

B Talk to people in your school.
Ask about the jobs on your list.
What education or training do you need?
Make a chart with the information.

C Share your information.
Make a class wall chart.
Talk about the jobs and training.

Job	Education or Training
hotel manager	associate's or bachelor's degree from a college or a degree from a hotel-management school
nurse	associate's or bachelor's degree in nursing
receptionist	high school diploma or GED

Projects 136

Projects

UNIT 3

Weekend activities

A Use the Internet.

Find information about weekend activities in your city.
Find an activity for children, for parents, and for your friends.
If possible, print pictures of the activities.

Keywords (your city), weekend activities

B Take notes. Answer these questions.

1. Who is it for?
2. What kind of place is it?
3. What is the activity?
4. How much does it cost?

For	Place	Activity	Cost
children	pool	go swimming	$5
parents	beach	take a walk	$0
friends	park	play soccer	$0

C Share your information.

Tell your classmates about the places and activities.
Show the pictures.
Make a class wall chart of weekend activities.

UNIT 4

Your medicine cabinet

A Choose a medicine.

What's in your medicine cabinet? Find a medicine.

B Answer these questions.

1. What is the name of the medicine?
2. Is this medicine for adults, for children, or for both?
3. Why should you take this medicine?
4. How much should an adult take at one time?
5. How often should you take this medicine?

1. What is the name of the medicine?
No More Pain.
2. Is this medicine for adults, for children, or for both?
For both.

C Share your information.

Draw a picture of this medicine, or cut out a picture of it from a magazine.
Paste the picture on a piece of paper.
Write the information about it.
Make a class booklet.

UNIT 5

Take a trip

A Choose a city to visit.

Write the name of the city.

B Use the Internet.

Look for train and bus companies near you.

Keywords Train schedule (your city)   Bus schedule (your city)

Read the schedules.
How often do the trains leave and return?
How often do the buses leave and return?

C Make a chart.

Write the information about your trip.

D Share your information.

Show your chart to your classmates.
Talk about the different schedules.

	Date and departure times	Date and return times
Chicago to Detroit by train	May 29 8:30 a.m. 2:30 p.m. 4:00 p.m.	June 1 9:30 a.m. 3:30 p.m. 5:00 p.m.
Chicago to Detroit by bus	May 29 8:00 a.m. 12:30 p.m.	June 1 10:00 a.m. 2:30 p.m.

UNIT 6

Life events

A Think about important life events.

Write questions.

When were you born?

Where were you born?

B Interview a friend or relative.

Use the questions you wrote.
Write down the answers.

C Make a time line.

Include the important events.

1976	1994	1998	2000	2003
born in Mexico	first job	got married	came to the U.S.	first child

D Share your information.

Show your time line to
your classmates. Talk about the person you interviewed.

Projects 138

Projects

UNIT 7

Furniture in a house

A Choose a room in a house.

Make a list of furniture for that room.

B Look in magazines, catalogs, and online.

Find pictures of furniture.
Cut out or print the pictures.

C Make a picture of the room.

Draw the room. Put the furniture pictures in the room.

D Share your information.

Show your room to your classmates.
Select your favorite rooms.
Put them together to make a house.

living room
sofa
recliner
coffee table
bookcase

UNIT 8

Job application

A Check (✓) a job that you would like.

- ☐ auto mechanic
- ☐ busboy
- ☐ cashier
- ☐ construction worker
- ☐ cook
- ☐ dental assistant
- ☐ gas station attendant
- ☐ nurse
- ☐ orderly

B Use the Internet.

Find a sample job application.

Keywords | sample job applications | job application samples |

Print out an application.
Fill it out.
Use the job you checked.

C Share your information.

Share your job application with your classmates.

UNIT 9

Home repairs

A Make a chart.

What are some problems in your home?
What kind of repair person do you need?

B Talk to your neighbors, relatives, and friends.

Write the names and phone numbers of repair people they recommend.

C Share your information.

Talk about the repair people.
Make a class directory.

Problem	Repair person
cracked paint	painter
broken door	carpenter
leaking toilet	plumber

Manuel Maldonado / Painter
310-555-1234

UNIT 10

Holidays and celebrations

A Make groups.

Form 12 groups – one group for each month of the year.

B Use the Internet.

Find the dates of holidays and celebrations for your group.

Keywords: U.S. holidays
U.S. celebrations

international holidays
international celebrations

C Make a chart for your month.

D Share your information.

Show your chart to your classmates.
Make a poster of the holidays, celebrations, and dates for this year.

Month: January		
U.S. holidays and celebrations		
January 1	New Year's Day	
third Monday	Martin Luther King Jr. Day	
January	National Tea Month	
International holidays and celebrations		
January 1–3	Japanese New Year	Japan
January 6	Three Kings Day	Latin America
second Saturday	Children's Day	Thailand

Projects   140

Self-assessments

Overview

Each unit of *Ventures 2* Student's Book ends with a self-assessment. Self-assessments allow students to reflect on what they have learned and to decide whether they need more review of the material.

How self-assessments help students

- It is not possible for English language teachers to teach students all the English they need to know. Therefore, it is important that teachers help students develop strategies for learning and for measuring their learning. One important strategy is self-assessment. With self-assessment, students become aware of their own learning and focus on their own performance. Being able to self-assess is important for developing learner autonomy. It is that autonomy that will equip students for lifelong learning.

- Self-assessment allows students to participate in the assessment process. Responsibility for learning shifts from the teacher to the students as self-assessment makes the students more aware of their role in learning and monitoring their own performance.

- Self-assessment can also contribute to learner persistence. Learners will continue to attend classes when they have verification that learning has taken place. They can measure this learning when they complete the self-assessment checklists.

How self-assessments help teachers

- Teachers can use the results of the self-assessments to identify areas that need further instruction or review. Teachers can use the results of this assessment to meet with students and discuss items that have been mastered as well as those that need further study.

- The information on the self-assessment forms can also be used at the beginning of the unit to identify and discuss the learning objectives of the unit. In this way, students will have a clear understanding of the learning goals. If they know what the learning objectives are, they can better focus on their learning. This results in greater learner gains, which is gratifying to both students and teachers.

Self-assessment in *Ventures*

- Each self-assessment asks students to check the words they have learned and the skills and functions they feel they have mastered. Students then decide if they are ready to take the unit test to confirm this acquisition of unit language. The self-assessments are in checklist form, making it easier for lower-level students to check off how they feel they are progressing.

- If students feel they need additional study for a particular unit, the *Ventures* series provides additional practice in the Workbook and *Add Ventures*.

- The *Teacher's Toolkit Audio CD/CD-ROM* contains the same self-assessments that are found in the Student's Book. However, on the CD-ROM, each unit's self-assessment is on its own page and can be printed, distributed to and completed by the student after each unit, and placed in his or her learner portfolio. It can also be given to students to keep as a personal record of their progress.

Self-assessments

Unit 1 Personal information

A Vocabulary Check (✓) the words you know.

☐ checked	☐ long	☐ shirt	☐ small
☐ curly	☐ pants	☐ short	☐ striped
☐ dress	☐ plaid	☐ skirt	☐ uniform

B Skills and functions Read the sentences. Check (✓) what you know.

I can use adjectives in the correct order: She's wearing a **black striped** shirt.	I can look for key words to answer reading questions.	
I can ask and answer questions using the present continuous: What **are** you **doing** right now? **I'm reading**.	I can write a paragraph describing a person.	
I can ask and answer questions using the simple present: What **does** he **do** every Saturday? He always **watches** TV.	I can understand an order form.	

C What's next? Choose one.

☐ I am ready for the unit test.   ☐ I need more practice with _____ .

Unit 2 At school

A Vocabulary Check (✓) the words you know.

☐ accounting	☐ culinary arts	☐ keyboard	☐ nursing
☐ automotive repair	☐ goal	☐ lab instructor	☐ open a business
☐ computer lab	☐ hotel management	☐ landscape design	☐ vocational course

B Skills and functions Read the sentences. Check (✓) what you know.

I can ask and answer questions using **want** and **need**: What **do** they **want** to do? What **do** you **need** to do?	I can read quickly to get the main idea.	
I can give advice about how to reach goals.	I can write about my goals.	
I can talk about the future using *will*: What **will** she **do** on Tuesday? She**'ll go** to work.	I can understand a course catalog.	

C What's next? Choose one.

☐ I am ready for the unit test.   ☐ I need more practice with _____ .

Self-assessments 141

Unit 3 Friends and family

A Vocabulary Check (✓) the words you know.

☐ broke down	☐ do the laundry	☐ get up	☐ make the bed
☐ buy groceries	☐ fix the engine	☐ have a cell phone	☐ take a bath
☐ do the dishes	☐ get dressed	☐ make lunch	☐ take a nap

B Skills and functions Read the sentences. Check (✓) what you know.

I can ask and answer questions using the simple past with regular and irregular verbs: What **did** they **do** last night? They **went** to the movies and **listened** to music.		I can ask and answer questions about daily activities.	
I can decide when to use the simple present and when to use the simple past: We usually **eat** dinner at 8:00. Yesterday, we **ate** dinner at 6:30.		When I read, I can look for words that tell the order things happened.	
I can write a journal entry about my day.		I can understand cell phone calling plans.	

C What's next? Choose one.

☐ I am ready for the unit test.   ☐ I need more practice with _____ .

Unit 4 Health

A Vocabulary Check (✓) the words you know.

☐ accident	☐ crutches	☐ prescription	☐ take medicine
☐ allergies	☐ hurt	☐ stiff neck	☐ warning label
☐ chills	☐ injury	☐ swollen knee	☐ X-ray

B Skills and functions Read the sentences. Check (✓) what you know.

I can ask and answer questions using **have to**: What **does** she **have to** do? She **has to** take her medicine.		I can read a warning label.	
I can ask and answer questions using **should**: What **should** they do? They **should** stay in the shade.		I can complete an accident report form.	
I can talk about health problems.		I can understand a medicine label.	

C What's next? Choose one.

☐ I am ready for the unit test.   ☐ I need more practice with _____ .

Unit 5 Around town

A Vocabulary Check (✓) the words you know.

☐ buy souvenirs	☐ never	☐ stay with relatives	☐ ticket booth
☐ go sightseeing	☐ rarely	☐ suitcase	☐ waiting room
☐ information desk	☐ sometimes	☐ take pictures	☐ write postcards

B Skills and functions Read the sentences. Check (✓) what you know.

I can ask and answer questions using **How often** and **How long**: **How often** does the train leave? Every 30 minutes. **How long** does it take? About three hours.		I can use adverbs of frequency: He **rarely** rides his bike. She **always** takes a taxi.	
I can read a bus schedule.		I can write a letter to a friend about a trip.	
I can talk about travel activities.		I can understand a train schedule.	

C What's next? Choose one.

☐ I am ready for the unit test.   ☐ I need more practice with _____ .

Unit 6 Time

A Vocabulary Check (✓) the words you know.

☐ become a citizen	☐ find a job	☐ graduate	☐ move
☐ citizenship exam	☐ get married	☐ have a baby	☐ photo album
☐ fall in love	☐ get promoted	☐ immigrate	☐ retired

B Skills and functions Read the sentences. Check (✓) what you know.

I can ask and answer **When** questions to talk about the simple past: **When did** you **get married**? I **got married** in 1980.		I can write a paragraph about important events in my life.	
I can use time phrases: *three weeks ago, on Sunday, at 4:00 p.m., last year.*		I can understand an application for a marriage license.	
I can talk about life events.		I can make a time line.	

C What's next? Choose one.

☐ I am ready for the unit test.   ☐ I need more practice with _____ .

Unit 7 Shopping

A Vocabulary Check (✓) the words you know.

☐ appliances	☐ customer	☐ gift	☐ piano
☐ cheap	☐ expensive	☐ heavy	☐ price tag
☐ comfortable	☐ furniture	☐ lamp	☐ sofa

B Skills and functions Read the sentences. Check (✓) what you know.

I can use comparatives: *bigger, cheaper, heavier, more expensive*.		I can read a newspaper article.	
I can use superlatives: *the biggest, the cheapest, the heaviest, the most expensive*.		I can write about the best gift I ever received.	
I can talk about furniture.		I can understand a sales receipt.	

C What's next? Choose one.

☐ I am ready for the unit test.   ☐ I need more practice with _____.

Unit 8 Work

A Vocabulary Check (✓) the words you know.

☐ clear tables	☐ handle money	☐ linens	☐ pick up
☐ co-worker	☐ job duties	☐ orderly	☐ prepare
☐ deliver	☐ lab	☐ patient	☐ supplies

B Skills and functions Read the sentences. Check (✓) what you know.

I can ask and answer **Where** and **What** questions in the simple past: **What did** he do? **Where did** you go?		I can read and understand a letter of recommendation.	
I can use the conjunctions **and**, **or**, and **but**: She went to work **and** took notes.		I can scan a text for specific information (names, dates).	
I can write about my employment history.		I can understand a weekly time sheet.	

C What's next? Choose one.

☐ I am ready for the unit test.   ☐ I need more practice with _____.

Unit 9 Daily living

A Vocabulary Check (✓) the words you know.

- ☐ clogged
- ☐ electrician
- ☐ fix
- ☐ garbage
- ☐ jammed
- ☐ a leak
- ☐ lightbulb
- ☐ plumber
- ☐ repair
- ☐ a sink
- ☐ tenant
- ☐ unclog

B Skills and functions Read the sentences. Check (✓) what you know.

I can ask **Which** questions using the simple present: **Which** electrician do you recommend?	I can talk about problems in a home or an apartment.
I can make requests using **Can**, **Could**, **Will**, and **Would**: **Could** you clean the bathroom, please?	I can write a letter of complaint to a building manager or landlord.
I can read a notice to tenants.	I can understand an invoice.

C What's next? Choose one.

☐ I am ready for the unit test.   ☐ I need more practice with _____ .

Unit 10 Leisure

A Vocabulary Check (✓) the words you know.

- ☐ balloons
- ☐ cake
- ☐ card
- ☐ celebrate
- ☐ flowers
- ☐ a gift
- ☐ graduation party
- ☐ housewarming
- ☐ invitation
- ☐ a present
- ☐ thank-you note
- ☐ wedding

B Skills and functions Read the sentences. Check (✓) what you know.

I can ask and answer questions with **Would you like . . . ?**: **Would you like** a cup of coffee? Yes, **I would**.	I can look for examples of the main idea in a paragraph.
I can make statements with direct and indirect objects: I gave **her some books**.	I can read and write a thank-you note.
I can talk about celebrations.	I can understand an invitation to a party.

C What's next? Choose one.

☐ I am ready for the unit test.   ☐ I need more practice with _____ .

Self-assessments

Reference

Present continuous

Wh- questions

What	am	I	doing now?
What	is is is	he she it	doing now?
What	are are are	we you they	doing now?

Affirmative statements

I'm	working.
He's She's It's	working.
We're You're They're	working.

I'm = I am	We're = We are
He's = He is	You're = You are
She's = She is	They're = They are
It's = It is	

Simple present

Wh- questions: What

What	do	I you we they	do every day?
What	does	he she it	do every day?

Affirmative statements

I You We They	usually	work.
He She It	usually	works.

Wh- questions: When

When	do	I you we they	usually work?
When	does	he she it	usually work?

Affirmative statements

I You We They	usually	work	on Friday.
He She It	usually	works	on Friday.

Simple present of *need* and *want*

Wh- questions: What

What	do	I / you / we / they	want to do? / need to do?
What	does	he / she / it	want to do? / need to do?

Affirmative statements

I / You / We / They	want / need	to go.
He / She / It	wants / needs	to go.

Simple present of *have to* + verb

Wh- questions: What

What	do	I / you / we / they	have to do?
What	does	he / she / it	have to do?

Affirmative statements

I / You / We / They	have to	go.
He / She / It	has to	go.

Simple present with *Which* questions

Wh- questions: Which

Which one	do	I / you / we / they	recommend?
Which one	does	he / she / it	recommend?

Affirmative statements

I / You / We / They	recommend	Joe's Repair Shop.
He / She / It	recommends	Joe's Repair Shop.

Simple past with regular and irregular verbs

Wh- questions: What

What	did	I / you / he / she / it / we / you / they	do?

Affirmative statements

I / You / He / She / It / We / You / They	stayed. / ate.

Negative statements

I / You / He / She / It / We / You / They	didn't	stay. / eat.

didn't = did not

Yes / No questions

Did	I / you / he / she / it / we / you / they	stay? / eat?

Short answers

Yes,	I / you / he / she / it / we / you / they	did.

No,	I / you / he / she / it / we / you / they	didn't.

Wh- questions: When

When	did	I / you / he / she / it / we / you / they	move? / leave?

Affirmative statements

I / You / He / She / It / We / You / They	moved / left	in July. / last week.

Wh- questions: Where

Where	did	I / you / he / she / it / we / you / they	go?

Affirmative statements

I / You / He / She / It / We / You / They	stayed / went	home.

Future with *will*

Wh- questions: What

| What | will | I / you / he / she / it / we / you / they | do | tomorrow? |

Affirmative statements

| I'll / You'll / He'll / She'll / It'll / We'll / You'll / They'll | probably | work. |

'll = will

Negative statements

| I / You / He / She / It / We / You / They | won't | work. |

won't = will not

Should

Wh- questions: What

| What | should | I / you / he / she / it / we / you / they | do? |

Affirmative statements

| I / You / He / She / It / We / You / They | should | work. |

Negative statements

| I / You / He / She / It / We / You / They | shouldn't | work. |

shouldn't = should not

Would you like . . . ?

Yes / No questions

| Would | you
he
she
we
you
they | like | some cake? |

Short answers

| Yes, | I
he
she
you
we
they | would. |

Wh- questions: What

| What | would | you
he
she
we
you
they | like? |

Affirmative statements

| I'd
He'd
She'd
You'd
We'd
They'd | like | some cake. |

'd = would

Direct and indirect objects

| Tim gave a present to | Mary.
me.
you.
him.
her.
it.
us.
you.
them. |

| Tim gave | Mary
me
you
him
her
it
us
you
them | a present. |

Class audio script

Welcome

Page 3, Exercise 2A – CD 1, Track 2

1. A What's your name?
   B Ben Navarro.
2. A How do you spell your last name?
   B N-A-V-A-R-R-O.
3. A Do you have a middle initial?
   B Yes. It's *J*.
4. A What's your address?
   B 1737 Van Dam Street, Brooklyn, New York.
5. A What's your zip code?
   B It's 11222.
6. A Do you have an apartment number?
   B Yes. It's 3A.
7. A What's your home phone number?
   B 718-555-5983.
8. A What's your date of birth?
   B January 18th, 1982.

Page 4, Exercise 3A – CD 1, Track 3

1. Armin and Stefan do their homework and study in the library every day.
2. Yesterday they wrote paragraphs about their families.
3. Right now they're studying for a vocabulary test.
4. Tomorrow they're not going to study in the library.
5. Stefan is going to go to work tomorrow afternoon, and Armin is going to take his grandmother to the doctor.

Page 4, Exercise 3B – CD 1, Track 4

Right now it's 11:30 p.m., but Stefan isn't sleeping. He's studying for an English test.

Stefan goes to school every morning from 9 o'clock to 12 o'clock. After class, he usually meets Armin in the library, and they study together.

Yesterday was different. Stefan didn't go to the library. He went to work. He worked from 2 p.m. until 10 p.m. Then he came home and started studying. He studied until 2 o'clock in the morning.

Tomorrow Stefan is going to be very tired!

Page 5, Exercise 4A – CD 1, Track 5

A Hi. I'm looking for a job.
B What can you do?
A I can use a computer very well. I can speak English and Korean. I can help students with their homework, and I can read to children.
B Can you write in English?
A Yes, I can.
B Can you speak Spanish?
A No, I can't. But I'm going to learn.

Unit 1: Personal information

Lesson A: Get ready

Page 7, Exercises 2A and 2B – CD 1, Track 6

Conversation A
A Shoko, who's this?
B This is a picture of my daughter, Victoria.
A What's she wearing?
B Her soccer uniform. She plays every day. She's very athletic.
A Wow! She's really tall.
B Yes, she is. She looks like her father.
A She's a pretty girl. Her long black hair is beautiful.

Conversation B
A Shoko, is that your son?
B Yes. This is my teenage son, Eddie.
A What's he doing?
B He's playing computer games. He always plays computer games!
A Does he have a lot of friends?
B No, not many. He's a very quiet boy.

Conversation C
A This is a picture of my husband, Mark.
B Oh, Shoko, he *is* tall!
A Yes, he is. He wears very large shirts and pants. I buy his clothes at a special store.
B What does he do?
A He's an engineer. He's very smart. He studies English, too.
B You have a really nice family.
A Thanks.

Lesson B: She's wearing a short plaid skirt.

Page 8, Exercise 2A – CD 1, Track 7

1. A What's Amy wearing?
   B She's wearing a long black dress.
2. A What's she wearing?
   B She's wearing black and white checked pants.
3. A What does he take to school?
   B He takes a large red backpack.
4. A What do you usually wear to work?
   B I wear a blue and white striped uniform.
5. A What's he wearing today?
   B He's wearing a red and yellow plaid sweater.
6. A What are they wearing?
   B They're wearing short green skirts.

Lesson C: What are you doing right now?

Page 10, Exercise 2A – CD 1, Track 8

1. *A* What does Ed do every night?
   B He relaxes.
   A What's Ed doing right now?
   B He's watching TV.
2. *A* What's Mary doing right now?
   B She's teaching.
   A What does Mary do every Tuesday?
   B She teaches.
3. *A* What's Isaac doing right now?
   B He's studying.
   A What does Isaac do every day?
   B He goes to class.

Lesson D: Reading

Page 12, Exercise 2 – CD 1, Track 9

Hi Karin,
   How are you doing? Guess what! Today is my daughter's birthday. The last time you saw Victoria, she was three years old. Now she's 17! She's tall and very athletic. She likes sports. She plays soccer every afternoon. Here is her photo. She's wearing her red and white striped soccer uniform. She usually wears jeans and a T-shirt. Victoria is also a very good student. She has lots of friends and goes with them to the mall every weekend. How are your daughters? Please send a photo!
Let's stay in touch.
Shoko

Page 13, Exercise 4A – CD 1, Track 10

1. a hat
2. a tie
3. a watch
4. a scarf
5. gloves
6. a purse
7. earrings
8. a necklace
9. a bracelet
10. a ring

Unit 2: At school

Lesson A: Get ready

Page 19, Exercises 2A and 2B – CD 1, Track 11

Conversation A

A Oh, what's wrong with this computer!
B Um, Joseph, do you need help?
A Oh, thanks, Eva. I'm having trouble with this keyboard. I need to take a computer class.
B Ask the teacher about keyboarding classes. She helped me find a citizenship class.
A That's a great idea. I'll talk to Mrs. Lee after class. Thanks!
B You're welcome, Joseph. Good luck!

Conversation B

A Oh, hi, Joseph. Do you need something?
B Yes, Mrs. Lee. I want to learn keyboarding skills. What do I need to do?
A Hmm . . . keyboarding skills. Do you need to use a computer at work?
B No, not right now. But someday I want to open my own business. I'm pretty sure I'll need to use a computer then.
A Well, you can study keyboarding in the computer lab across the hall. You could talk with Mr. Stephens. He's the lab instructor.
B Thanks, Mrs. Lee. I'll talk to Mr. Stephens right now.

Conversation C

A Hello, Mr. Stephens. My name is Joseph. Mrs. Lee told me to come here. I want to learn keyboarding.
B That's great. You can join my keyboarding class. First, you need to register with Mrs. Smith in the Registration Office.
A Great. I'll go register now.
B But there's one problem.
A One problem?
B Yes. The Registration Office is closed today. You can register next week.
A OK. Thanks.

Page 20, Exercise 2A – CD 1, Track 12

1. *A* What do you want to do now?
   B I want to get my GED.
2. *A* What do you need to do?
   B I need to take a GED class.
3. *A* What does Sandra want to do this year?
   B She wants to learn about computers.
4. *A* What does Ali want to do this year?
   B He wants to make more money.
5. *A* What does Celia need to do tonight?
   B She needs to do her homework.
6. *A* What do Sergio and Elena want to do next year?
   B They want to become citizens.

Lesson C: What will you do?

Page 22, Exercise 2A – CD 1, Track 13

1. Sue has a test tomorrow. She'll study tonight. She won't go to the party.
2. She'll volunteer in Tom's class on Wednesday. She won't volunteer on Tuesday.

3. She won't work on Wednesday afternoon. She'll work on Thursday.
4. She won't talk to a counselor on Thursday. She'll talk to a counselor on Friday.

Lesson D: Reading

Page 24, Exercise 2 – CD 1, Track 14

What are your future goals? What steps do you need to take?

I want to open my own electronics store. I need to take three steps to reach my goal. First, I need to learn keyboarding. Second, I need to take business classes. Third, I need to work in an electronics store. I will probably open my store in a couple of years.

Page 25, Exercise 4A – CD 1, Track 15

1. automotive repair
2. computer technology
3. accounting
4. nursing
5. counseling
6. hotel management
7. culinary arts
8. home health care
9. landscape design

Review: Units 1 and 2

Page 30, Exercise 1 – CD 1, Track 16

Fernando Reyes is thirty-five years old. He's from Colombia. He's tall and has curly brown hair and green eyes.

Fernando has a very busy schedule. He goes to school in the morning. After school, he works at Green's Grocery Store from 1 to 9. He's a cashier there. He usually plays soccer with his friends on Saturday.

Fernando wants to study computer technology. He needs to take classes at the community college. Next month, he'll begin computer classes.

Page 31, Exercise 3A – CD 1, Track 17

paper
restaurant
computer

Page 31, Exercise 3B – CD 1, Track 18

necklace
nursing
bracelet
sweater
jacket
cashier
career
repair
achieve
medium
counselor
uniform
manager
citizen
mechanic
accounting
tomorrow
computer
eraser
television
citizenship
usually

Page 31, Exercise 3C – CD 1, Track 19

1. instructor
2. uniform
3. sweatshirt
4. dictionary
5. business
6. enroll
7. management
8. landscape
9. design

Unit 3: Friends and family

Lesson A: Get ready

Page 33, Exercises 2A and 2B – CD 1, Track 20

Conversation A

A Rigatoni Restaurant. Daniel speaking.
B Hi, Daniel? It's me.
A Rosa? Hi. Is everything OK?
B Not really. I went to the supermarket with the children, and the car broke down.
A The car broke down! What's wrong?
B I don't know. I think it's the engine.
A Did you open the hood?
B Yes, I did. There's a lot of smoke!
A Where are you?
B I'm at the side of the road near the supermarket.
A Stay there. I'm going to leave work right now. I'll be there in ten minutes.
B OK. I have a lot of groceries in the trunk. Please hurry.

Conversation B

A Mike's Auto Repair.
B Hi, Mike, it's Rosa – Daniel's wife?
A Oh, hi, Rosa. How are you?
B Well, not so good.
A Why? What's wrong?
B Well, this morning I went to the store to buy groceries for a picnic, but then our car broke down. My husband came and picked us up.
A Oh, I'm sorry, Rosa.
B Could you pick up the car for us? It's on the side of the road near the supermarket.
A Of course. I'll pick it up and take it to my shop this afternoon.
B Thanks, Mike.

Conversation C

A Hello, Swift Dry Cleaner's.
B Hi, Ling. It's Rosa. How are you?
A I'm good. I'm almost done with work. Will I see you tonight?
B I'm not sure. We had car trouble today. I need a ride to school tonight. Can you pick me up?
A Sure. What time?

B I usually leave my house at 7 o'clock.
A OK. I'll pick you up at 7.
B That's great. You're a good friend, Ling. Thank you.
A No problem. See you tonight.

Lesson B: What did you do last weekend?

Page 34, Exercise 2A – CD 1, Track 21

1. A What did Dahlia and her friends do on Sunday?
   B They barbecued hamburgers.
2. A What did the children do on Thursday?
   B They took a walk in the park.
3. A What did your family do last weekend?
   B We drove to the beach.
4. A What did Sarah do Monday night?
   B She went to the movies.
5. A What did Nikos do Saturday morning?
   B He fixed the car.
6. A What did Carlos do Wednesday morning?
   B He bought groceries.

Lesson C: When do you usually play soccer?

Page 36, Exercise 2A – CD 1, Track 22

1. A When does Sharon usually meet her friends?
   B She usually meets her friends after work.
   A When did Sharon meet her friends yesterday?
   B Yesterday, she met them at noon for lunch.
2. A What time do Roberto and Selma usually eat dinner?
   B They usually eat dinner at seven o'clock.
   A When did they eat dinner last night?
   B They ate dinner at eight o'clock.
3. A When do Irma and Ron usually study?
   B They usually study on Saturday.
   A When did they study last weekend?
   B They studied on Friday night.
4. A When do you usually watch movies?
   B I usually watch movies after dinner.
   A What time did you watch a movie last night?
   B I watched a movie at six o'clock.

Lesson D: Reading

Page 38, Exercise 2 – CD 1, Track 23

Thursday, June 20th
   Today was a bad day! On Thursday, my children and I usually go to the park for a picnic, but today we had a problem. We drove to the store to buy groceries, and then the car broke down. I checked the engine, and there was a lot of smoke. Luckily, I had my cell phone! First, I called my husband at work. He left early, picked us up, and took us home. Next, I called the mechanic. Finally, I called Ling and asked for a ride to school tonight. In the end, we didn't go to the park because it was too late. Instead, we had a picnic in our backyard. Then, Ling drove me to school.

Page 39, Exercise 4A – CD 1, Track 24

1. make lunch
2. take a bath
3. do the dishes
4. do the laundry
5. get up
6. do homework
7. take a nap
8. make the bed
9. get dressed

Unit 4: Health

Lesson A: Get ready

Page 45, Exercises 2A and 2B – CD 1, Track 25

Conversation A
A Hello?
B Lily, it's me. I had a little accident.
A Are you OK, Hamid? What happened?
B I fell off a ladder at work. I hurt my leg.
A Hamid, you should go to the hospital!
B I'm at the hospital now. But listen, you have to pick up the children at school. I have to wait for the doctor.
A OK, I'll pick up the children. I'll see you back at home.
B OK, thanks, Lily. Bye.

Conversation B
A Hello?
B Chris, it's Hamid.
A Hey, how's it going?
B Not so good. I had a little accident at work. I fell off a ladder.
A Oh, no. Are you OK?
B Well, I hurt my leg. I'm at the hospital now, and I had to get an X-ray. Could you come to the hospital and drive me home?
A Of course. What's the address?
B It's 3560 East 54th Street. You should take the highway.
A OK, I'm leaving right now.
B Thanks, Chris. Bye.

Conversation C
A Ace Construction.
B Hi, Angie. It's Hamid. I need to talk to Mr. Jackson, please.
A Hi, Hamid. Just a second.
C Hi, Hamid. Jackson here. How's it going? Did you finish

painting the house on Main Street?
B Well, no. I had a little accident. I slipped and fell off the ladder. I'm at the hospital now.
C Oh, no! Are you badly hurt?
B I don't know. I had to get an X-ray of my leg. The doctor is looking at the X-ray now.
C Hamid, you have to fill out an accident report. Call me after you see the doctor.
B OK. What about the paint job?
C Don't worry. Felipe will finish it. Stay home tomorrow. You should rest.
B OK. Thanks, Mr. Jackson. Bye.

Lesson B: What do I have to do?

Page 46, Exercise 2A – CD 1, Track 26

1. A Elian hurt his leg. What does he have to do?
   B He has to get an X-ray.
2. A Kathy and Tom have asthma. What do they have to do?
   B They have to take their medicine.
3. A My son broke his arm. What do I have to do?
   B You have to take him to the hospital.
4. A Marcia has a sprained ankle. What does she have to do?
   B She has to get a pair of crutches.
5. A Nick and Tony had an accident at work. What do they have to do?
   B They have to fill out an accident report.
6. A Pam hurt her back. What does she have to do?
   B She has to go home early.

Lesson C: You should go to the hospital.

Page 48, Exercise 2A – CD 1, Track 27

1. A Ken's eyes hurt. What should he do?
   B He should rest. He shouldn't read right now.
2. A They have stomachaches. What should they do?
   B They shouldn't eat. They should take some medicine.
3. A My tooth hurts. What should I do?
   B You should see a dentist.
4. A Mia has a headache. What should she do?
   B She should take some aspirin.
5. A I hurt my leg. What should I do?
   B You should get an X-ray. You shouldn't walk.
6. A I have a bottle of medicine. What should I do?
   B You should keep it in the refrigerator. You shouldn't freeze it.

Lesson D: Reading

Page 50, Exercise 2 – CD 1, Track 28

WARNING: PREVENT ACCIDENTS.
READ BEFORE USING!
• Face the ladder when climbing up and down.
• Don't carry a lot of equipment while climbing a ladder – wear a tool belt.
• Never stand on the shelf of the ladder – stand on the steps.
• Never stand on the top step of a ladder.
• Be safe! Always read and follow the safety stickers.

Page 51, Exercise 4A – CD 1, Track 29

1. chills
2. a sprained wrist
3. chest pains
4. high blood pressure
5. allergies
6. a swollen knee
7. a bad cut
8. a rash
9. a stiff neck

Review: Units 3 and 4

Page 56, Exercise 1 – CD 1, Track 30

Trinh is a nurse. She works Monday to Friday at City Children's Hospital. On the weekend, she and her family usually stay home. But this was a special weekend for Trinh.
  On Friday morning, she and her husband became citizens. In the afternoon, they went to a restaurant. On Saturday, they took their son and daughter to the beach. The children played all day. Trinh and her husband read and took pictures of the children. In the evening, they had a barbecue with some friends. Then they went home and watched a movie. Trinh is happy to be a citizen and happy that her family had a good time.

Page 57, Exercise 3A – CD 1, Track 31

Tina's car broke down.
Oscar has to take his medicine.

Page 57, Exercise 3B – CD 1, Track 32

1. His wife had to do it.
2. Van has a headache.
3. I played soccer last night.
4. They went to the library yesterday.
5. Eliza works in the afternoon.
6. Sam made breakfast.

Class audio script T-155

Page 57, Exercise 3C – CD 1, Track 33

1. Ali cut his arm.
2. He went to the hospital.
3. His sister took him.
4. He saw the doctor.
5. He has to take some medicine.
6. He shouldn't carry heavy items.

Unit 5: Around town

Lesson A: Get ready

Page 59, Exercises 2A and 2B – CD 1, Track 34

Conversation A

A Attention, please. This is an announcement.
B What's that, Binh?
C That's just an announcement, Mom. The announcer is giving train information. We should listen.
A Trains to Washington, D.C., leave every hour. The next train to Washington, D.C., will leave at 7:20 from Track 1. I repeat. The next train to Washington, D.C., will leave at 7:20 from Track 1.
B That was about trains to Washington. We need information about trains to New York.
C Wait. Here's another announcement.
A Trains to New York City leave every . . . The next train to New York will leave at . . . I repeat. The next train to New York will leave at . . . from Track 2.
B Oh, no! We didn't hear the information about New York!

Conversation B

A There's an information desk over there. You can ask about trains from Philadelphia to New York.
B Oh, good. Excuse me. I need some train information.
C How can I help you?
B I'm taking my mother to New York City today. How often do trains go to New York?
C Trains leave for New York every 30 minutes.
B When does the next train leave for New York?
C The 7:05 train just left. The next train leaves at 7:35 from Track 3.
B Thanks.
C Do you have tickets? You can get them at the ticket booth over there.
B No, we don't have tickets. Thank you very much.

Conversation C

A I got our tickets, Mom. Our train leaves in 25 minutes.
B Good. We don't have to wait long.
A Do you want to sit down? We can sit in the waiting area.
B That's a good idea. My suitcase is heavy. This train station is beautiful.
A Yeah, it really is. I always travel by train. It's a lot easier than driving.
B How long does it take to drive to New York?
A It usually takes about 2 hours to drive. It takes less than one and a half hours by train.
C Attention, please. The train to New York is now boarding on Track 3.
A That's our train, Mom. Let's go!

Lesson B: How often? How long?

Page 60, Exercise 2A – CD 1, Track 35

1. A How often does Binh go to New York?
   B Twice a month.
2. A How long does it take to fly to Mexico?
   B A long time.
3. A How often do you study?
   B Twice a week.
4. A How long does it take to drive to Toronto?
   B Seven hours.
5. A How long does it take to walk to school?
   B 20 minutes.
6. A How often does Sandra cook dinner?
   B Three times a week.
7. A How often does the bus go to Springfield?
   B Once a day.
8. A How often do they go on vacation?
   B Once a year.
9. A How long does it take to drive to the airport?
   B One hour.
10. A How long does it take to walk to the library?
    B 25 minutes.

Lesson C: She often walks to school.

Page 62, Exercise 2A – CD 1, Track 36

1. Teresa always drives to work in the morning.
2. She is rarely late.
3. Her husband usually walks to work.
4. He sometimes takes a taxi.
5. He never drives.
6. Their daughter always rides her bike to school.
7. She is often tired in the morning.

Lesson D: Reading

Page 64, Exercise 2 – CD 1, Track 37

Dear Layla,
   Right now, my mother is visiting me here in Philadelphia. I rarely see her because she comes to Philadelphia only once

a year. She usually stays for one month. Here is a photo of my mother at the airport last week. She was happy to see me!

This year, I want to take my mother to New York City. I want to show her the Statue of Liberty and Central Park. It takes about one and a half hours to get to New York by train. We are excited about our trip. Can you meet us there? Let me know.
Your friend,
Binh

Page 65, Exercise 4A – CD 1, Track 38

1. go shopping
2. stay at a hotel
3. take a suitcase
4. buy souvenirs
5. go swimming
6. stay with relatives
7. take pictures
8. write postcards
9. go sightseeing

Unit 6: Time

Lesson A: Get ready

Page 71, Exercises 2A and 2B – CD 2, Track 2

Conversation A
A Olga, I love your new apartment.
B Thanks, Victoria. We moved in two months ago. You're our first visitor.
A Is that your wedding picture?
B Yes, it is. That's my husband and me a long time ago.
A What a good-looking bride and groom! When did you get married?
B Let's see. We got married in 1983.
A You were young! My husband and I had our third wedding anniversary last month. Do you have more pictures?

B Sure. They're in our photo album. Do you want to see them?
A I'd love to.

Conversation B
A Your pictures are wonderful. You have a lovely family.
B Thanks!
A How old are your children?
B My son, Sergey, is 19 now. His birthday was three days ago. He started college in September.
A When did your daughter start college?
B Start college! Natalya's only 14!
A Wow! She's tall for her age.
B Yes, she is. She started high school on Tuesday.

Conversation C
A Is that a picture of Russia?
B Yes. That's in Moscow.
A Did you live in Moscow?
B Yes. We met in Moscow. We went to school there before we got married.
A It looks like an interesting city.
B Oh, it is!
A When did you move to the United States?
B We moved here about 14 years ago.
A Were your children born here?
B Natalya was. Sergey was born in Russia, like us.

Lesson B: When did you move here?

Page 72, Exercise 2A – CD 2, Track 3

1. A When did Min leave Korea?
   B She left Korea in 1974.
   A When did she move to New York?
   B She moved to New York in 1995.

2. A When did Carlos start school?
   B He started school in September.
   A When did he graduate?
   B He graduated in June.
3. A When did Paul and Amy meet?
   B They met in 2003.
   A When did they get married?
   B They got married in 2005.

Lesson C: He graduated two years ago.

Page 74, Exercise 2A – CD 2, Track 4

1. A When did Lou and Angela buy their new car?
   B They bought their new car three weeks ago.
2. A When did Lou and Angela get married?
   B They got married four years ago.
3. A When did Angela have a baby?
   B She had a baby yesterday at 8:20 a.m.
4. A When did Lou begin his new job?
   B He began his new job on Tuesday.
5. A When did Lou move to the United States?
   B He moved to the United States on December 15th.
6. A When did Angela come to the United States?
   B She came to the United States three years ago.
7. A When did Angela take the citizenship exam?
   B She took the citizenship exam in March.

Lesson D: Reading

Page 76, Exercise 2 – CD 2, Track 5

An Interesting Life
A What happened after you graduated from high school?

B I went to university in Moscow, and I met my husband there. It was a long time ago! We were in the same class. We fell in love and got married on April 2nd, 1983. We had a small wedding in Moscow.
A What happened after you got married?
B I finished university and found a job. I was a teacher. Then, I had a baby. My husband and I were very excited to have a little boy.
A When did you move to the United States?
B We immigrated about 14 years ago. We became American citizens ten years ago.

Page 77, Exercise 4A – CD 2, Track 6

1. retired
2. started a business
3. had a baby
4. fell in love
5. got engaged
6. got married
7. got a divorce
8. immigrated
9. got promoted

Review: Units 5 and 6

Page 82, Exercise 1 – CD 2, Track 7

A Marie! What are you doing here?
B I just came back from Florida. My parents live there now.
A How nice. How often do you see them?
B I go there every three months. So, what are you doing here?
A I'm meeting my brother, David. He always comes here for his vacation. He stays for about a week. Then he goes to Texas to visit our sister.
C Flight 783 from Atlanta is now arriving at Gate 32.

A Well, that's David's flight. I need to go. Good to see you.
B You, too. Have fun with your brother.

Page 83, Exercise 3A – CD 2, Track 8

Where is the train station?
Is the train station on Broadway or on Main Street?

Page 83, Exercise 3B – CD 2, Track 9

Wh- questions
A How often do you eat at a restaurant?
B Once a week.

Or questions
A Do you eat at a restaurant once a week or once a month?
B Once a week.

Unit 7: Shopping

Lesson A: Get ready

Page 85, Exercises 2A and 2B – CD 2, Track 10

Conversation A
A Good afternoon, folks. I'm Mike. How can I help you?
B Hi, I'm Denise. This is my husband, Nick. We need some furniture.
C A *lot* of furniture!
B We bought a house two days ago.
A Congratulations! This is the right place for furniture *and* appliances. We're having our biggest sale of the year. All our furniture is marked down 20 percent.
B Wow! 20 percent.
A We have chairs, lamps, sofas. . . . Look around. We have the best prices in town.
B Are the appliances 20 percent off, too?
A Yes! Refrigerators, stoves – everything in the store is 20 percent off.
C Thanks.

Conversation B
A Nick, look at that sofa. It's very pretty!
B Which one? The brown one?
A No, not the brown one, the blue one. It looks nice and comfortable. I like it.
B Hmm. But the brown sofa is bigger. I want a *big* sofa.
A Well, it *is* bigger, but look at the price, Nick. It's much more expensive than the blue sofa.
B Whoa! A thousand dollars? That's crazy!
A Look, there are some more sofas over there. Maybe they're cheaper.
B I sure hope so.

Conversation C
A Oh, look, Nick. They have pianos for sale.
B Pianos? But we aren't looking for a piano. We're looking for a sofa.
A I *love* this piano. Excuse me, miss? Do you work here?
C Yes. My name is Tara. How can I help you?
A Could you tell me about this piano?
C Oh, the upright piano? It's very old, but it's the most beautiful piano in the store. It also has a beautiful sound. Listen.
A Wow! Is it expensive?
C Well, it's $1,200. This small piano is cheaper, but the sound isn't the same.
A The upright piano is better. Let's buy it, Nick!
B Hey, not so fast! We came here to buy a sofa, not a piano!

Lesson B: The brown sofa is bigger.

Page 86, Exercise 2A – CD 2, Track 11

1. A Which sofa is more comfortable?

B The green striped sofa is more comfortable.
2. A Which chair is heavier?
B The orange chair is heavier.
3. A Which refrigerator is more expensive?
B The silver refrigerator is more expensive.
4. A Which table is bigger?
B The square table is bigger.
5. A Which stove is better?
B The black stove is better.

Lesson C: The yellow chair is the cheapest.
Page 88, Exercise 2A – CD 2, Track 12

1. A Which TV is the cheapest?
B The brown TV is the cheapest.
2. A Which TV is the heaviest?
B The brown TV is the heaviest.
3. A Which TV is the most expensive?
B The red TV is the most expensive.
4. A Which TV is the oldest?
B The brown TV is the oldest.
5. A Which TV is the smallest?
B The white TV is the smallest.
6. A Which TV is the biggest?
B The red TV is the biggest.

Page 89, Exercise 2B – CD 2, Track 13

A This is the newest shopping mall in the city. It's great.
B Where's the best place to buy clothes?
A Well, there are three clothing stores. Mega Store is the biggest one. It usually has the lowest prices, but it's the most crowded. I never go there.
B What about Cleo's Boutique?
A Cleo's Boutique is the most beautiful store. It's nice, but it's the most expensive.
B What about Madison's?

A Well, it's the smallest, but it's my favorite. It has the nicest clothes and the friendliest salespeople.
B Look! Madison's is having a big sale! Let's go!

Lesson D: Reading
Page 90, Exercise 2 – CD 2, Track 14

Today's Question
What's the best thing you ever bought?
   The best thing I ever bought was an old piano. I bought it in a used-furniture store last month. It was the most beautiful piano in the store, but it wasn't very expensive. It has a beautiful sound. Now my two children are taking piano lessons. I love to hear music in the house.
Denise Robinson – Charleston, South Carolina

   I bought a used van five years ago. I used my van to help people move and to deliver stoves and refrigerators from a secondhand appliance store. I made a lot of money with that van. Now I have my own business. That van is the best thing I ever bought.
Sammy Chin – Myrtle Beach, South Carolina

Page 91, Exercise 4A – CD 2, Track 15

1. end table
2. bookcase
3. dresser
4. entertainment center
5. sofa bed
6. mirror
7. china cabinet
8. coffee table
9. recliner

Unit 8: Work
Lesson A: Get ready
Page 97, Exercises 2A and 2B – CD 2, Track 16
Conversation A
A Hey, Marco. How are you?
B Oh, hi, Arlen. I'm fine. I had a busy day today.
A What did you do?
B Hmm . . . let's see. This morning, I delivered flowers to patients and picked up X-rays from the lab. I also delivered clean linens to the third floor. This afternoon, I made the beds on the second floor and prepared the rooms. And now I'm delivering supplies.
A Wow! You did have a busy day!

Conversation B
A Hi, John. How's it going?
B Hi, Marco. I'm tired. I worked the night shift last night.
A Oh, no.
B I like this job, but I don't like the night shift.
A I like this job, too, but I don't like the pay. I'm thinking about going back to school.
B Really? School is expensive.
A I know. Maybe I can find a part-time job and go to school full-time.
B Maybe you can work here part-time. You should ask about it.

Conversation C
A Is this the HR Office? Human Resources?
B Yes, come on in. I'm Suzanne Briggs. I'm the HR Assistant.
A Hi, Suzanne. I'm Marco Alba. I'm an orderly here.
B Hi, Marco. Have a seat. How can I help you?
A I like my job here, but I don't want to be an orderly forever. I want to go to nursing school and become a nurse.

B A nurse? That's great, Marco!
A I want to go to nursing school full-time and work part-time.
B That's a great idea! A lot of employees do that.
A Can I work part-time here at Valley Hospital?
B I don't know. Can you come back tomorrow? I'll find out about part-time jobs for you.
A Sure. Thanks, Suzanne. See you tomorrow.

Lesson B: Where did you go last night?
Page 98, Exercise 2A – CD 2, Track 17

1. *A* What did Linda do after breakfast?
   B She made the beds.
2. *A* What did Brenda and Leo do this morning?
   B They picked up patients in the reception area.
3. *A* What did Trevor do this morning?
   B He delivered X-rays.
4. *A* Where did Jill and Brad take the linens?
   B They took the linens to the second floor.
5. *A* What did Felix do yesterday?
   B He helped patients with their walkers and wheelchairs.
6. *A* Where did Juan and Ivana go after work?
   B They went to the coffee shop across the street.

Lesson C: I work on Saturdays and Sundays.
Page 100, Exercise 2A – CD 2, Track 18

1. Sometimes Irene eats Chinese food for lunch. Sometimes she eats Mexican food for lunch. Irene eats Chinese food or Mexican food for lunch.
2. Tito works the day shift. Tito also works the night shift. Tito works the day shift and the night shift.
3. Marco had an interview. He didn't get the job. Marco had an interview, but he didn't get the job.
4. Brian likes his co-workers. He doesn't like his schedule. Brian likes his co-workers, but he doesn't like his schedule.
5. Erica takes care of her children. She also takes care of her grandmother. Erica takes care of her children and her grandmother.
6. Carl cleaned the carpets. He didn't make the beds. Carl cleaned the carpets, but he didn't make the beds.
7. Sometimes Kate works in New York. Sometimes she works in San Diego. Kate works in New York or in San Diego.
8. Ilya speaks Russian at home. He also speaks Russian at work. Ilya speaks Russian at home and at work.

Lesson D: Reading
Page 102, Exercise 2 – CD 2, Track 19

Dear Mr. O'Hara:
   I am happy to write this letter of recommendation for Marco Alba. Marco started working at Valley Hospital as an orderly in 2003. He takes patients from their rooms to the lab, delivers X-rays, and takes flowers and mail to patients. He also delivers linens and supplies. He is an excellent worker, and his co-workers like him very much.
   We are sorry to lose Marco. He wants to go to school and needs to work part-time, but we don't have a part-time job for him right now. I recommend Marco very highly. Please contact me for more information.
Sincerely,
Suzanne Briggs
Human Resources Assistant

Page 103, Exercise 4A – CD 2, Track 20

1. repair cars
2. operate large machines
3. clear tables
4. prepare food
5. help the nurses
6. take care of a family
7. handle money
8. pump gas
9. assist the dentist

Review: Units 7 and 8

Page 108, Exercise 1 – CD 2, Track 21

Yuri works part-time at Furniture Mart. He's a salesperson. He talks to customers and helps them find good furniture at low prices. He likes his job.
   Yesterday, Yuri met Mr. and Mrs. Chan at the store. They wanted a new sofa and an entertainment center. Their old sofa wasn't comfortable. They looked at two sofas. The first sofa was $599. It was nice, but it wasn't very big. The second sofa was more expensive. It was $749. It was more comfortable, and it was bigger, too. The Chans bought the second sofa and two lamps, but they didn't buy the entertainment center.
   After work, Yuri ate dinner at China House Restaurant. Mr. Chan is the manager there.

Page 109, Exercise 3A – CD 2, Track 22

talks
makes

is
has
watches
fixes

Page 109, Exercise 3B – CD 2, Track 23

looks
shops
speaks
buys
delivers
plays
relaxes
teaches
fixes

Page 109, Exercise 3C – CD 2, Track 24

1. drives
2. gets
3. goes
4. uses
5. takes
6. pushes
7. sleeps
8. needs

Unit 9: Daily Living

Lesson A: Get ready

Page 111, Exercises 2A and 2B – CD 2, Track 25

Conversation A
A Hello, Building Manager.
B Hi, this is Stella Taylor in Apartment 4B. I've got a problem. The washing machine overflowed. And the dishwasher's leaking, too. And the sink is clogged. Could you please recommend a plumber?
A Well, I usually use two different plumbers.
B Which one do you recommend?
A Let's see. His name is Don Brown. He has a company on Main Street. Here's the phone number: 555-4564. He's really good.
B Thanks. I'll call him right away.

Conversation B
A Brown's Plumbing Service, Martha speaking. May I help you?
B I hope so. My washing machine overflowed, and my dishwasher is leaking all over the floor, *and* my sink is clogged. May I speak to Don Brown, please?
A Oh, Don's out right now on a job. But he'll be finished in an hour. He can come then. Can you wait an hour?
B One hour? Hmm. I need to go to work soon. Maybe my neighbor can unlock the door for him. My address is 3914 Fifth Street, Apartment 4B.
A OK. He'll be there in an hour.
B Thank you.

Conversation C
A Russell Taylor speaking.
B Hi, Russell. It's me. I have bad news. The washing machine overflowed, and the dishwasher is leaking on the floor, *and* the sink is clogged!
A Oh, no. Look, I'm really busy at work right now. Could you please call a plumber?
B I already did.
A You did? Which plumber did you call?
B Brown's Plumbing Service. The plumber will be here in an hour.
A But you're going to work.
B It's OK. I asked Mrs. Lee to let him in.
A All right, Stella. I'll see you tonight.

Lesson B: Which one do you recommend?

Page 112, Exercise 2A – CD 2, Track 26

1. *A* Which plumber do you recommend?
   B I recommend Brown's Plumbing Service. It's cheaper.
2. *A* Which plumber does he recommend?
   B He recommends Harrison's Plumbing Service. It's clean.
3. *A* Which plumber do they recommend?
   B They recommend Brown's Plumbing Service. It's licensed.
4. *A* Which plumber does she recommend?
   B She recommends Brown's Plumbing Service. It's insured.
5. *A* Which plumber do they recommend?
   B They recommend Harrison's Plumbing Service. It's more experienced.
6. *A* Which plumber does he recommend?
   B He recommends Harrison's Plumbing Service. It's open 24 hours a day.

Lesson C: Can you call a plumber, please?

Page 114, Exercise 2A – CD 2, Track 27

1. *A* Could you fix the dryer, please?
   B Yes of course.
2. *A* Can you unclog the sink, please?
   B No, not now. Maybe later.
3. *A* Would you clean the bathroom, please?
   B Sorry, I can't right now.
4. *A* Will you fix the lock, please?
   B Sure. I'd be happy to.
5. *A* Could you change the lightbulb, please?
   B Yes, of course.
6. *A* Would you repair the dishwasher, please?
   B Sure. I'd be happy to.

Lesson D: Reading

Page 116, Exercise 2 – CD 2, Track 28

Attention, tenants:
Do you have problems in your apartment? Is anyone fixing them?
- Many tenants have broken windows.
- Tenants on the third floor have no lights in the hall.
- A tenant on the second floor has a leaking ceiling.
- Tenants on the first floor smell garbage every day.

I'm really upset! We need to get together and write a letter of complaint to the manager of the building.
Come to a meeting Friday night at 7 p.m. in Apartment 4B.
Stella Taylor, Tenant 4B

Page 117, Exercise 4A – CD 2, Track 29

1. broken
2. dripping
3. torn
4. scratched
5. bent
6. burned out
7. cracked
8. stained
9. jammed

Unit 10: Leisure

Lesson A: Get ready

Page 123, Exercises 2A and 2B – CD 2, Track 30

Conversation A
A Aunt Ana! Hello!
B Hi, Celia. Congratulations on your graduation! This is a wonderful party!
A Thank you for coming. Would you like some cake? My mother made it.
B I'd love some. I'm starving.
A Would you like something to drink?
B No, thanks. Here. I brought you some flowers. They're from my garden.
A Red roses! They're beautiful! Thank you.

Conversation B
A Hello, Mrs. Campbell. Thank you for coming to my party.
B Celia, I'm so proud of you. You were my best student. You started English class three years ago, and now you have your GED! You worked very hard.
A Thank you, Mrs. Campbell. You helped me a lot.
B Here. I brought you a card.
A Oh, thank you! Oh, that's so nice. Thank you, Mrs. Campbell.
B You're welcome.
A Come and join the party. Would you like a piece of cake?
B Yes, please. I'd love some.

Conversation C
A Hi, Sue. Thanks for coming. Where are your children?
B They're with my mother, so I can't stay long. I just wanted to congratulate you.
A Thank you. Would you like a piece of cake?
B No, thanks. I'm not hungry.
A Would you like something to drink?
B I'd love some water.
A OK. I'll get you some.
B Wait. I brought you a little present.
A Oh, thank you! Oh, Sue! My favorite perfume! Thank you!
B You're welcome. It's from our family.
A That's so nice. Please take some balloons home for your children.
B Thanks. They love balloons.

Lesson B: Would you like some cake?

Page 124, Exercise 2A – CD 2, Track 31

1. A Would you like a cup of coffee?
   B Yes, I would.
2. A Would he like a balloon?
   B Yes, he would.
3. A Would she like some ice cream?
   B Yes, she would.
4. A Would you like a sandwich?
   B Yes, I would.
5. A Would they like some salad?
   B Yes, they would.
6. A Would you like a hot dog?
   B Yes, I would.

Lesson C: Tim gave Mary a present.

Page 126, Exercise 2A – CD 2, Track 32

1. A What did Joe bring Sylvia?
   B Joe brought Sylvia flowers.
2. A What did Joe buy Nick?
   B Joe bought Nick a card.
3. A What did Joe write Pam?
   B Joe wrote Pam a letter.
4. A What did Joe buy Mary and Judy?
   B Joe bought Mary and Judy a cake.
5. A What did Joe give Eva?
   B Joe gave Eva roses.
6. A What did Joe send Paul?
   B Joe sent Paul an invitation.

Lesson D: Reading

Page 128, Exercise 2 – CD 2, Track 33

Celia had a graduation party last Friday. Her husband sent invitations to Celia's teacher and to their relatives and friends. They all came to the party! Some guests brought gifts for Celia. Her teacher Mrs. Campbell gave her a card. Her Aunt Ana brought her flowers. Her friend Sue gave her some perfume. Her classmate Ruth brought her some cookies. After the party, Celia wrote them thank-you notes. Tomorrow, she is going to mail the thank-you notes at the post office.

Page 129, Exercise 4A – CD 2, Track 34

1. Thanksgiving
2. Independence Day
3. a wedding
4. a housewarming
5. New Year's Eve
6. Mother's Day
7. Halloween
8. a baby shower
9. Valentine's Day

Review: Units 9 and 10

Page 134, Exercise 1 – CD 2, Track 35

A Did you move to your new apartment yet, Ramona?
B Yes, I moved last week. And I want to have a party to celebrate. I hope you'll come, Fabio.
A Sure. When is it?
B I don't know. Maybe next month.
A Next month? Why are you waiting so long?
B Well, my apartment is really nice, but it isn't ready yet. I want to paint the rooms. Do you know any good painters?
A Yes, I know two good painters.
B Which one do you recommend?
A Well, the first painter is Walter Hewitt. He's good, but very expensive. The second painter is free. I recommend the second one.
B The second painter is free?
A Yes, because I'm the second painter. I'm very good, and you don't have to pay me. What do you think?
B That's great. You're a good friend, Fabio!

Page 135, Exercise 3A – CD 2, Track 36

Could you
Could you help me?
Could you paint the wall, please?
Would you
Would you like some water?
Would you repair the refrigerator, please?

Page 135, Exercise 3B – CD 2, Track 37

Could you
Could you send someone to help?
Could you recommend a painter?
Could you please fix this?
Would you
Would you turn on the light, please?
Would you unclog the sink?
Would you like a piece of cake?

Page 135, Exercise 3C – CD 2, Track 38

1. Could you wash the floor?
2. Would you please fix the light?
3. Would you call the painter for me?
4. Would you send a plumber right away, please?
5. Could you fix the washing machine?
6. Would you like a cup of coffee?

Tests

Overview

The unit tests, midterm test, and final test help teachers assess students' mastery of the material in the *Ventures 2* Student's Book.

- Each of the ten unit tests covers one unit.
- The midterm test covers Units 1–5.
- The final test covers Units 6–10.
- Each test assesses listening, grammar, reading, and writing, with real-life documents incorporated into the reading and writing sections.

Students' performance on the tests helps to determine what has been successfully learned and what may need more attention. Successful completion of a test can also give students a sense of accomplishment.

Getting ready for a test

- Plan to give a unit test shortly after students have completed a unit and have had time for a review. The midterm should follow completion of Unit 5 and the review lesson for Units 5 and 6. The final test should follow completion of Unit 10 and the review lesson for Units 9 and 10. Tell students when the test will be given. Encourage students to study together and to ask you for help if needed.
- Explain the purpose of the test and how students' scores will be used.
- Prepare one test for each student. The tests may be photocopied from the Teacher's Edition, starting on page T-165, or printed from the *Teacher's Toolkit Audio CD/CD-ROM*.
- Schedule approximately 30 minutes for each unit test and 1 hour for the midterm and final tests. Allow more time if needed.
- Locate the audio program for each test's listening section on the *Teacher's Toolkit Audio CD/CD-ROM*. The CD is a hybrid. It will work in both a stereo and a computer CD-ROM drive.

Giving a test

- During the test, have students use a pencil and an eraser. Tell students to put away their Student's Books and dictionaries before the test.
- Hand out one copy of the test to each student.
- Encourage students to take a few minutes to look through the test without answering any of the items. Go through the instructions to make sure students understand them.
- Tell students that approximately 5 minutes of the unit test (10 minutes of the midterm and final tests) will be used for the listening section.
- When playing the listening section of the test, you may choose to pause or repeat the audio program if you feel that students require more time to answer. The audio script appears in the Teacher's Edition on page T-193. The script can also be printed from the *Teacher's Toolkit Audio CD/CD-ROM* and read aloud in class.

Scoring

- You can collect the tests and grade them on your own. Alternatively, you can have students correct their own tests by going over the answers in class or by having students exchange tests with a partner and correcting each other's answers. The answer key is located in the Teacher's Edition on page T-195. It can also be printed from the *Teacher's Toolkit Audio CD/CD-ROM* Tests menu or the "View" button.
- Each test has a total score of 100 points. Each unit test has five sections worth 20 points each. The midterm and final tests have eight sections worth 10 or 15 points each.

Track list for test audio program

Track 1: Introduction
Track 2: Unit 1 Test
Track 3: Unit 2 Test
Track 4: Unit 3 Test
Track 5: Unit 4 Test
Track 6: Unit 5 Test
Track 7: Midterm Test, Section A
Track 8: Midterm Test, Section B
Track 9: Unit 6 Test
Track 10: Unit 7 Test
Track 11: Unit 8 Test
Track 12: Unit 9 Test
Track 13: Unit 10 Test
Track 14: Final Test, Section A
Track 15: Final Test, Section B

Name: _____

Date: _____

Score: _____

TEST UNIT 1 — Personal information

A Listening

Listen. Circle the words you hear.

1. a checked shirt   a striped skirt
2. new blue jeans   a short green dress
3. uniform   watches
4. a long black and white coat   small brown and white boots
5. today   Tuesday

B Grammar

Write the correct word.

1. I'm _____ TV now.
   (watch / watching)

2. What _____ Mike do every Friday?
   (do / does)

3. What are they _____ today?
   (do / doing)

4. They usually _____ every night.
   (studies / study)

5. What _____ you doing right now?
   (are / do)

C Grammar

Write the words in the correct order.

1. Sam has _____ _____ hair.
   (brown / curly)

2. She's wearing a _____ _____ skirt.
   (plaid / short)

3. Linda is taking her _____ _____ backpack.
   (black / small)

4. Steve is wearing a _____ _____ shirt.
   (red and white / striped)

5. Ms. Thomas is wearing a _____ _____ scarf.
   (long / white)

© Cambridge University Press 2008 Photocopiable   Ventures 2 Test Unit 1   T-165

D Reading

Complete the paragraph. Use the words in the box.

| green | large | usually | wearing | wears |

Antonio's Good News

Antonio looks different today. He usually _____ blue
                                              1.
jeans and a big shirt. Today he's _____ a new gray
                                     2.
uniform. He _____ carries a small _____
              3.   4.
backpack. Today he's carrying a _____ black bag. Antonio
                                   5.
has a new job. He's an electrician.

E Writing

Write a paragraph about the picture.

_____
_____
_____
_____
_____
_____

TEST UNIT 2 — At school

A Listening

Listen. Circle the words you hear.

1. computers   instructors
2. accounting   nursing
3. college   language
4. business   citizen
5. counseling   keyboarding

B Grammar

Write the correct word.

1. I need _____ a computer class.
   (take / to take)
2. He won't _____ on Wednesday.
   (to work / work)
3. Linda wants _____ a citizen.
   (become / to become)
4. Steve will _____ more money.
   (make / makes)
5. _____ probably take a GED class.
   (She / She'll)

C Grammar

Match the questions with the answers.

1. What do you need to do? ____
2. What will you do tomorrow? ____
3. What does Celia want to do? ____
4. What will Bill and Ali do? ____
5. What does Joseph need to do? ____

a. He needs to study.
b. I need to finish my homework.
c. They'll take a vocational course.
d. Maybe I'll go to the party.
e. She wants to learn Spanish.

© Cambridge University Press 2008 Photocopiable   Ventures 2 Test Unit 2   T-167

Name: _____

Date: _____

D Reading

Read the paragraph. Read the sentences. Are they correct? Circle *Yes* or *No*.

Mary's Goal

Mary has a new goal. She wants to become a home health care assistant. She wants to help people, and she wants to make more money. First, she needs to learn more English. Second, she needs to take vocational classes. Third, she'll probably need to take computer classes. Maybe Mary will be ready to reach her goal in a few years.

1. Mary is working as a home health care assistant.   Yes   No
2. She'll work at her home.   Yes   No
3. She'll probably study English.   Yes   No
4. She'll need to take vocational classes.   Yes   No
5. She'll probably be a home health care assistant in a few months.   Yes   No

E Writing

Write a paragraph about your goal. Use the paragraph in Section D as a model.

_____
_____
_____
_____
_____
_____
_____
_____
_____
_____
_____
_____
_____
_____

TEST UNIT 3 Friends and family

Name: _____

Date: _____

Score: _____

A Listening

Listen. Circle the words you hear.

1. nap   shop
2. groceries   movies
3. make the beds take a bath
4. cell phone   fix the engine
5. laundry   lunch

B Grammar

Complete the conversations. Use the simple present or the simple past.

1. **A** When do they usually eat dinner?
   B They usually _____ dinner at 7:00.

2. **A** What time did he meet his friends?
   B He _____ them at noon.

3. **A** What time did you get up this morning?
   B I _____ up at 8:00.

4. **A** When does she usually clean her apartment?
   B She usually _____ her apartment on Saturday.

5. **A** What did they do last weekend?
   B They _____ to the movies.

C Grammar

Write the correct word.

1. He _____ the movie last night.
   (watch / watched)

2. They didn't _____ soccer yesterday.
   (play / played)

3. She _____ usually study after work.
   (doesn't / don't)

4. Mike and Rosa _____ work last night.
   (didn't / doesn't)

5. I didn't _____ shopping last week.
   (go / went)

Name: _____

Date: _____

D Reading

Read the paragraph. Read the sentences. Are they correct? Circle *Yes* or *No*.

Last Saturday

Last Saturday was a special day for me. My son usually gets up at noon on Saturday. Last Saturday, he didn't sleep late. He got up at 7:00, and he did the laundry. My daughter doesn't usually clean the house. Last Saturday, she made the beds, cleaned the kitchen, and cleaned the bathroom. My husband usually watches soccer on Saturday. But last Saturday, he went to the supermarket and bought groceries. Then he drove us to a restaurant for a special dinner. I had a wonderful birthday!

---

1. Her son got up early last Saturday.   Yes   No
2. Her daughter usually cleans the house on Saturday.   Yes   No
3. Her husband watched TV last Saturday.   Yes   No
4. Her husband went shopping.   Yes   No
5. The family ate dinner at a restaurant.   Yes   No

E Writing

Write a paragraph about a special day in your life. Use the paragraph in Section D as a model.

_____
_____
_____
_____
_____
_____
_____
_____
_____
_____
_____
_____

TEST UNIT 4 Health

A Listening

Listen. Circle the words you hear.

1. dentist   rest
2. aspirin   medicine
3. accident   X-ray
4. crutches   stomachaches
5. aspirin and rest   sprained wrist

B Grammar

Write the correct word.

1. What does Tony _____ do?
   (has to / have to)

2. They _____ fill out a report.
   (has to / have to)

3. Layla _____ get a prescription.
   (has to / have to)

4. What do the children _____ do?
   (has to / have to)

5. He _____ take some medicine.
   (has to / have to)

C Grammar

What should he do? Match the problems with the best advice.

1. He has asthma. ____   a. He shouldn't carry heavy equipment.
2. He hurt his leg. ____   b. He should take his medicine.
3. His tooth hurts. ____   c. He should see a dentist.
4. His eyes hurt. ____   d. He should get a pair of crutches.
5. He hurt his back. ____   e. He shouldn't read.

Name: _____

Date: _____

D Reading

Read the accident report. Read the sentences. Are they correct? Circle *Yes* or *No*.

ACCIDENT REPORT FORM

Employee name: Pam Hunt

Date of accident: July 30, 2008   Time: 11:00 a.m.

Type of injury: Sprained wrist

How did the accident happen? I climbed the ladder with a lot of equipment and heavy tools. In the afternoon, my wrist was swollen. I went to Dr. Brown's office yesterday and had an X-ray.

Signature: Pam Hunt   Date: July 31, 2008

---

1. Pam Hunt had an accident at work.   Yes   No
2. Her accident happened on July 31.   Yes   No
3. She hurt her wrist.   Yes   No
4. The injury happened at the doctor's office.   Yes   No
5. She completed the form on July 31.   Yes   No

E Writing

Complete the accident report form. Use your imagination or write about a real accident.

ACCIDENT REPORT FORM

Employee name: _____

Date of accident: _____   Time: _____

Type of injury: _____

How did the accident happen? _____
_____
_____
_____
_____

Signature: _____   Date: _____

T-172   *Ventures 2 Test Unit 4*   © Cambridge University Press 2008 **Photocopiable**

TEST UNIT 5 Around town

A Listening

Listen. Circle the words you hear.

1. once a year   twice a year
2. rarely   really
3. always   often
4. buy souvenirs   stay with relatives
5. a half hour   an hour

B Grammar

Write the correct word.

1. How _____ do you drive to work?
   (long / often)
2. It takes _____ hour to get to work.
   (once / one)
3. How often _____ trains go to York?
   (do / does)
4. How _____ does it take?
   (long / often)
5. How often _____ the bus come?
   (do / does)

C Grammar

Write the correct words.

1. Keiko _____ her bike.
   (rarely rides / rides rarely)
2. I _____ late.
   (always am / am always)
3. He _____ a taxi.
   (never takes / takes never)
4. She _____ tired.
   (often is / is often)
5. I _____ to school.
   (sometimes walk / walk sometimes)

D Reading

Read the bus schedule. Read the sentences. Are they correct? Circle *Yes* or *No*.

US Bus Schedule

Springfield to New York City			Springfield to Capital Airport		
Departs	Arrives	Duration	Departs	Arrives	Duration
6:30 a.m.	9:00 a.m.	2h 30m	5:30 a.m.	6:50 a.m.	1h 20m
11:00 a.m.	1:30 p.m.	2h 30m	9:00 a.m.	10:20 a.m.	1h 20m
2:00 p.m.	4:30 p.m.	2h 30m	3:00 p.m.	4:20 p.m.	1h 20m
6:30 p.m.	9:00 p.m.	2h 30m	5:00 p.m.	6:20 p.m.	1h 20m
			6:00 p.m.	7:20 p.m.	1h 20m

Springfield to Boston			Springfield to Washington, D.C.		
Departs	Arrives	Duration	Departs	Arrives	Duration
8:00 a.m.	4:15 p.m.	8h 15m	7:45 a.m.	11:15 a.m.	3h 30m
9:30 a.m.	5:45 p.m.	8h 15m	9:45 a.m.	1:15 p.m.	3h 30m
11:00 a.m.	7:15 p.m.	8h 15m	11:00 a.m.	2:30 p.m.	3h 30m
			1:00 p.m.	4:30 p.m.	3h 30m

h = hour   m = minute

1. Buses go eight times a day to Boston.   Yes   No
2. It takes three and a half hours to get from Springfield to Washington, D.C.   Yes   No
3. It takes about 30 hours to get to New York City.   Yes   No
4. Buses depart twice a day to Capital Airport.   Yes   No
5. Buses to Boston always leave in the morning.   Yes   No

E Writing

Write a letter to a friend about a trip.

_____
_____
_____
_____
_____
_____
_____
_____
_____

Name: _____

Date: _____

Score: _____

MIDTERM TEST Units 1–5

A 🔘 Listening

Listen. Circle the words you hear.

1. boots   suit
2. athletic   headache
3. rarely   usually
4. 20 minutes   twice a month
5. driving   riding

B 🔘 Listening

Listen. Circle the sentences you hear.

1. She's leaving.   She's reading.
2. I'll go today.   I'll go Tuesday.
3. They took a walk.   They went to the park.
4. He has a new injury.   He needs to buy a new engine.
5. She has chills.   She has three children.

C Grammar

Write the correct word.

1. What _____ you doing right now?
          (are / do)

2. _____ Sara wearing?
   (What / What's)

3. What _____ you do tomorrow?
          (do / will)

4. What does Isaac _____ to do?
                    (need / needs)

5. What _____ Ed do last weekend?
          (did / does)

© Cambridge University Press 2008 **Photocopiable**   Ventures 2 Midterm Test   T-175

Name: _____
Date: _____

D Grammar

Match the questions with the answers.

1. What should they do? ____
2. Did they go to the beach? ____
3. What will they do tonight? ____
4. How often do they go? ____
5. What do they do at night? ____

a. They study.
b. They'll probably work.
c. They should take a class.
d. Yes, they did.
e. Twice a year.

E Reading

Read the questions. Look at the course catalog. Circle the answers.

COURSE CATALOG

General Equivalency Diploma (GED)

Do you want to get your GED? Then you need to practice your reading, writing, and math skills. Classes are in English or Spanish. No fee.

Instructor: Mr. Chen (English)
　　　　　　Ms. Lopez (Spanish)
Days/Times: Mon, Wed 6:00 p.m.–8:00 p.m.

TV and DVD Repair

This class will teach you how to repair TVs and DVD players. You will also learn about opening your own repair shop. Fee: $85

Instructor: Mr. Stern
Days/Times: Mon, Tues 6:00 p.m. – 8:00 p.m.

Introduction to Computers

This class is for adults who want to learn about computers and the Internet. You will learn about keyboarding, e-mail, and computer jobs. Fee: $75

Instructor: Mrs. Gates
Days/Times: Mon, Wed 7:00 p.m.–9:00 p.m.

Citizenship

Do you want to be an American citizen? First, you need to learn about American history and civics. This class will prepare you for the U.S. citizenship test. Requirements: Legal resident. No fee.

Instructor: Ms. Cuevas
Days/Times: Thurs 7:00 p.m.–9:00 p.m.

1. How often does the computer class meet?
   a. once a week
   b. twice a week
   c. three times a week
   d. twice a month

2. What should you do in Mr. Chen's class?
   a. pay a fee
   b. speak English
   c. use a computer
   d. speak Spanish

3. What will you learn in Mr. Stern's class?
   a. American history
   b. computer repair
   c. TV repair
   d. math skills

4. What do you have to do in the citizenship class?
   a. become a citizen
   b. learn U.S. civics
   c. pay a fee
   d. get a GED

5. How long is each class?
   a. one hour
   b. two hours
   c. twice a night
   d. two times a night

Name: _____

Date: _____

F Reading

Read the paragraph. Read the sentences. Are they correct? Circle *Yes* or *No*.

> ### My Aunt Victoria
>
> This morning, I went to visit my Aunt Victoria. I usually visit her at her home, but I went to see her in the hospital. She fell down and hurt her head yesterday. She didn't want to leave her home, but her children drove her to the hospital. She's staying for three days. She's not happy! She wants to go home right now. She says that the food in the hospital is very, very bad. She says that she'll never get better with bad food!

1. Aunt Victoria is staying at home now.   Yes   No
2. Aunt Victoria had an accident at home.   Yes   No
3. Aunt Victoria wanted to go to the hospital.   Yes   No
4. Aunt Victoria has to stay in the hospital for three days.   Yes   No
5. Aunt Victoria likes the food in the hospital.   Yes   No

G Writing

Complete the postcard. Use the words in the box.

| go | having | should | staying | went |

Dear Rita,

We're _____(1) a good time in New York City! We're _____(2) at a hotel in the city. Last night, we _____(3) to the theater. This afternoon, we'll _____(4) to the zoo. Next time, you _____(5) come with us!

Your friend,
Eliza

Name: _____

Date: _____

H Writing

Write a paragraph about what you did yesterday.

_____
_____
_____
_____
_____
_____
_____
_____
_____
_____
_____
_____
_____
_____
_____
_____
_____
_____
_____
_____
_____
_____
_____
_____

Name: _____

Date: _____

Score: _____

TEST UNIT 6 Time

A Listening

Listen. Circle the words you hear.

1. started a business   became citizens
2. on December 15th   on September 13th
3. after 2:00   at 10:00
4. eight weeks ago   four weeks ago
5. at 4:00 p.m.   before June 10th

B Grammar

Write the correct word.

1. When did they _____?
   (meet / met)
2. She _____ school in August.
   (start / started)
3. I _____ Korea in 2003.
   (leave / left)
4. When _____ Angela move?
   (did / do)
5. He _____ from Japan one year ago.
   (came / come)

C Grammar

Complete the sentences. Write the correct letter.

1. She got promoted on ____   a. noon.
2. He moved to the United States in ____   b. last week.
3. They took the citizenship exam ____   c. October 13th.
4. They got married at ____   d. hour ago.
5. I registered for the class an ____   e. May.

© Cambridge University Press 2008 **Photocopiable**

Ventures 2 Test Unit 6   T-179

D Reading

Read the paragraph. Read the sentences. Are they correct? Circle *Yes* or *No*.

COMPUTER SYSTEMS INC.

A New Employee: Bo-Hai Cheng

I was born in 1983 in Beijing. I started university in 2001. I studied civil engineering. In 2004, I moved to Miami. After I moved, I bought a car. I also got engaged. Then I studied computers at a vocational school. I graduated on July 3rd. Three weeks ago, I found a computer job. In October, I'm going to get married!

1. Bo-Hai began university in 2001.   Yes   No
2. Bo-Hai moved to the United States in 2004. Yes   No
3. Bo-Hai bought a car in 2001.   Yes   No
4. Bo-Hai got engaged before he moved to Miami. Yes No
5. Bo-Hai got married on July 3rd.   Yes   No

E Writing

Write a paragraph about your time line. Use the paragraph in Section D as a model.

_____
_____
_____
_____
_____
_____
_____
_____
_____
_____

Name: _____

Date: _____

Score: _____

Shopping

A 🔘 Listening

Listen. Circle the words you hear.

1. better   bigger
2. more beautiful   the most beautiful
3. the newest   the nicest
4. comfortable   customer
5. the best   the cheapest

B Grammar

Complete the sentences. Use comparatives.

1. Which TV is _____ ?
                    (small)
2. Which bed is _____ ?
                 (comfortable)
3. Which table is _____ ?
                     (big)
4. Which stove is _____ ?
                  (expensive)
5. Which desk is _____ ?
                   (heavy)

C Grammar

Complete the sentences. Use superlatives.

1. The salespeople are _____ in the mall.
                         (friendly)
2. It's always _____ restaurant in the city.
                 (crowded)
3. That sofa is _____ in the store.
                  (cheap)
4. It's _____ university in the country.
          (old)
5. Cleo's Boutique is having _____ sale of the year!
                                (long)

© Cambridge University Press 2008 Photocopiable   Ventures 2 Test Unit 7   T-181

Name: _____

Date: _____

D Reading

Complete the paragraph. Use the words in the box.

| bought | have | last | lowest | read |

My New Computer

The best thing I ever bought was my computer. I _____ 1.
it from a friend _____ 2. week. Yesterday, I went on the
Internet. I _____ 3. newspapers from my native country. I
wrote letters to my family. Then I used it to find the _____ 4.
prices for plane tickets to my country. Now I _____ 5. to save
money for the trip!

E Writing

Write a paragraph about the oldest thing you have. Use the paragraph in Section D as a model.

_____
_____
_____
_____
_____
_____
_____
_____
_____
_____
_____
_____

TEST UNIT 8 *Work*

Name: _____
Date: _____
Score: _____

A Listening

Listen. Circle the words you hear.

1. Linda   linens
2. walked   worked
3. cleared   delivered
4. Rachel   schedule
5. day shifts   patients

B Grammar

Write the correct word.

1. _____ did they meet?
   (What / Where)

2. What did Leo _____ last night?
   (did / do)

3. _____ you clear the tables?
   (Are / Did)

4. She _____ her friends after work.
   (meet / met)

5. They didn't _____ patients this morning.
   (help / helped)

C Grammar

Write the correct word.

1. Kate cleaned the furniture, _____ she didn't clean the carpet.
   (and / but)

2. They went to the meeting, _____ they wrote a report.
   (and / but)

3. I study at home _____ in the library.
   (but / or)

4. He checked e-mail _____ watched TV.
   (and / but)

5. She works at the store, _____ she doesn't like to handle money.
   (but / or)

© Cambridge University Press 2008 **Photocopiable**   Ventures 2 Test Unit 8   T-183

Name: _____

Date: _____

D Reading

Read the time sheet. Read the sentences. Are they correct? Circle *Yes* or *No*.

```
LARRY'S DISCOUNT STORE – WEEKLY TIME SHEET
```

Employee: *Iara da Silva*   Social Security Number: *000-99-0531*
Rate: *$9.00/hour*

DAY	DATE	TIME IN	TIME OUT	TIME IN	TIME OUT	HOURS
MONDAY	8/7	9:00 A.M.	12:00 NOON	1:00 P.M.	4:00 P.M.	6
TUESDAY	8/8	8:30 A.M.	12:30 P.M.	1:30 P.M.	5:30 P.M.	8
WEDNESDAY	8/9	9:00 A.M.	2:00 P.M.	3:00 P.M.	7:00 P.M.	9
THURSDAY	8/10	7:30 A.M.	12:30 P.M.	1:30 P.M.	3:30 P.M.	7
FRIDAY	8/11	9:00 A.M.	12:00 NOON	1:00 P.M.	5:00 P.M.	7
TOTAL HOURS						37

I have worked these hours. I understand that false information will result in my termination with the company.

Employee's signature *Iara da Silva*   Date: *8/15*

Supervisor's signature *Helen Wilson*   Date: *8/15*

1. Iara started work every day at 9:00 a.m.   Yes   No
2. Iara worked 6 hours on Monday and 7 hours on Friday.   Yes   No
3. Her schedule was always the same every day.   Yes   No
4. She left work at 4:00 p.m. every day.   Yes   No
5. She worked 37 hours.   Yes   No

E Writing

Write a paragraph about your work history.

_____
_____
_____
_____
_____
_____
_____
_____

TEST UNIT 9 Daily living

A Listening

Listen. Circle the words you hear.

1. department store   drugstore
2. fully insured   fully licensed
3. the door   the floor
4. electrician   gas station
5. customer   plumber

B Grammar

Write the correct word.

1. Which bank does he _____?
   (recommend / recommends)
2. Which carpenter _____ the tenant like?
   (do / does)
3. The landlord _____ Midway Electric.
   (suggest / suggests)
4. Which restaurants do they _____?
   (like / likes)
5. I recommend SaveMore Supermarket. _____ open 24 hours a day.
   (It / It's)

C Grammar

Complete the questions. Write the correct letter.

1. Can you unclog the ____   a. lock?
2. Will you change the ____   b. plumber?
3. Would you call a ____   c. lightbulb?
4. Can you fix the ____   d. electrician?
5. Could you call an ____   e. sink?

D Reading

Complete the letter of complaint. Use the words in the box.

| ceiling | fix | lights | send | tenant |

Dear Building Manager:

I am a _____(1)_____ at 812 Valley Street. I am writing to you about some problems in the apartment. First, the _____(2)_____ is leaking. Second, there are no _____(3)_____ in the hallway. Could you please _____(4)_____ a repair person to _____(5)_____ these things?

You can contact me in Apartment 3A. Thank you.

Sincerely,

Daniel Brown

Daniel Brown

E Writing

Write a letter of complaint. Name two problems. Use the letter in Section D as a model.

Name: _____

Date: _____

Score: _____

 **Leisure**

A Listening

Listen. Circle the words you hear.

1. wedding   housewarming
2. books   cookies
3. card   cake
4. balloon   perfume
5. Valentine's   a piece of pie

B Grammar

Complete the sentences. Write the correct word.

1. _____ like some salad.
   (They / They'd)

2. Would _____ like something to eat?
   (you / you'd)

3. _____ you like a cup of tea?
   (What / Would)

4. She'd _____ some fruit.
   (like / likes)

5. Yes, _____ would.
   (he / he'd)

C Grammar

Complete the sentences. Write the correct word.

1. I _____ a letter to Eva this morning.
   (write / wrote)

2. They gave _____ her.
   (cookies to / to cookies)

3. Nick gave _____ a gift.
   (Pam / to Pam)

4. She sent some books _____.
   (him / to him)

5. Judy brought flowers _____ mother.
   (my to / to my)

Name: _____

Date: _____

D Reading

Read the paragraph. Read the sentences. Are they correct? Circle *Yes* or *No*.

Mrs. Taylor's Party

Mrs. Taylor retired from her job last week. Her co-workers had a party for her. They sent invitations to her friends and family. One co-worker bought a card, and everyone wrote a special message to her. She likes to read, so her co-workers bought her a lot of books. Now she has a lot of time to relax and read all those new books!

1. Mrs. Taylor's co-workers had a graduation party for her.   Yes   No
2. Her co-workers invited her family and friends.   Yes   No
3. Mrs. Taylor wrote a special message to her co-workers.   Yes   No
4. Mrs. Taylor likes to read.   Yes   No
5. She'd like to give the books to her co-workers.   Yes   No

E Writing

Write a thank-you note to a friend for a gift.

_____
_____
_____
_____
_____
_____
_____
_____
_____
_____
_____
_____

FINAL TEST Units 6–10

Name: _____
Date: _____
Score: _____

A Listening

Listen. Circle the words you hear.

1. customer   plumber
2. lab   lamp
3. graduate   immigrate
4. appliances supplies
5. prepare   repair

B Listening

Listen. Write the letter of the conversation.

1. ____

2. ____

3. ____

4. ____

5. ____

C Grammar

Write the correct word.

1. Angie _____ a nice present to Eva.
   (gave / give)

2. Mega Mall has _____ lowest prices.
   (some / the)

3. She took the test three weeks _____.
   (ago / last)

4. They brought flowers, _____ they brought a cake, too.
   (and / but)

5. Denise is more _____ than her sister.
   (beautiful / pretty)

© Cambridge University Press 2008 **Photocopiable**   *Ventures 2* Final Test   T-189

Name: _____

Date: _____

D Grammar

Match the questions with the answers.

1. Where did you go? ____
2. Would you like some tea? ____
3. What did you do? ____
4. Which restaurant do you like? ____
5. Could you repair the dryer? ____

a. I like Nick's Pizzeria.
b. I'd be happy to.
c. Yes, I would.
d. I got married.
e. I went to a party.

E Reading

Read the letter. Read the sentences. Are they correct? Circle *Yes* or *No*.

ACME OFFICES, INC.
1378 N. RIVERDALE DRIVE • PLIMPTON, NY 10036

Dear Mr. Stephens:

    I am happy to write a letter of recommendation for Lily Lee. I met Lily in 2004. She began to work for us part-time, but she got promoted to full-time after she graduated in 2005. She has many job duties in our office. She prepares reports, takes notes at meetings, handles money, and deals with customers. She does all her jobs very well. Her co-workers like her very much.

    Lily wants to move to Chicago with her new husband. We are happy for Lily, but we are sad to lose her!

    I recommend Lily very highly.

Sincerely,

Victoria Banks
Victoria Banks
Human Resource Assistant

---

1. Lily was promoted in 2005.   Yes   No
2. Victoria Banks met Lily after she graduated.   Yes   No
3. Lily worked full-time before she graduated.   Yes   No
4. Lily handles money and deals with customers.   Yes   No
5. Lily got married.   Yes   No

Name: _____

Date: _____

F Reading

Read the questions. Look at the invoice. Circle the answers.

BROWN'S PLUMBING SERVICE
654 Darby Drive • Dallas, Texas 75227

CUSTOMER INVOICE

Customer name: *Russell Taylor*

Customer address: *5672 Kings Ave. Apt 3A*
Dallas, TX 75227

Service Technician: *Binh*

DESCRIPTION OF PROBLEM	ACTUAL COST
Washing machine overflowed	40.00
Dishwasher leaking	45.00
Toilet overflowed	30.00
TOTAL:	115.00

---

1. Who did the repairs?
   a. Binh
   b. Mr. Brown
   c. Mr. Taylor
   d. Russell

2. Which repair was the cheapest?
   a. the dishwasher
   b. the dryer
   c. the toilet
   d. the washing machine

3. What is the total cost of the repairs?
   a. $30.00
   b. $40.00
   c. $45.00
   d. $115.00

4. What was the most expensive repair?
   a. the dishwasher
   b. the dryer
   c. the toilet
   d. the washing machine

5. What did it cost to repair the washing machine?
   a. $30.00
   b. $40.00
   c. $45.00
   d. $115.00

G Writing

Read about Yana. Then fill out the bride's section of the marriage license application.

This is Yana Viktorovna Romanova. Her address is 13524 Coral Drive, Miami, Florida. Her zip code is 33175. She was born in Moscow, Russia, on September 18, 1981. She got married in 2004, but she got divorced on April 26, 2007. Now, she wants to get married again.

APPLICATION FOR MARRIAGE LICENSE

Bride's Personal Data

Name of Bride (First)	(Middle)	(Last)	Birthdate (Mo / Day / Yr)
1.			2.

Residence (Street & Number)	City	State	Zip Code	Place of Birth
3.	4.	5.	6.	7.

Number of Previous Marriages	Last Marriage Ended by	Date (Mo / Day / Yr)
8.	9.	10.

H Writing

Write about the best day in your life. What was the date? What happened?

_____
_____
_____
_____
_____
_____
_____
_____
_____
_____
_____

Tests audio script

This audio script contains the listening portions of the *Ventures 2* unit tests, midterm test, and final test. A printable copy is available on the *Teacher's Toolkit Audio CD / CD-ROM*. You can play the audio program using the *Teacher's Toolkit Audio CD / CD-ROM* in a computer or a stereo, or you can read the script aloud.

Unit 1: Personal information
Track 2

A Listening
Listen. Circle the words you hear.

1 A What's he wearing?
  B He's wearing a checked shirt.
2 A What do you usually wear?
  B I usually wear a short green dress.
3 A What does he do every Saturday?
  B He washes his uniform.
4 A What's Shoko wearing?
  B She's wearing a long black and white coat.
5 A What's he doing today?
  B He's studying.

Unit 2: At school
Track 3

A Listening
Listen. Circle the words you hear.

1 A What does Bill want to do?
  B He wants to learn about computers.
2 A What does she need to do?
  B She needs to take an accounting course.
3 A What will Lisa probably do?
  B She'll probably go to college.
4 A What's Nick's goal?
  B He wants to open a business.
5 A What will they study?
  B They'll probably study keyboarding.

Unit 3: Friends and family
Track 4

A Listening
Listen. Circle the words you hear.

1 A What did you do this morning?
  B I took my car to the shop.
2 A What did Mike do last night?
  B He bought groceries.
3 A When do they make the beds?
  B They make the beds at 10:00.
4 A Did she have a cell phone?
  B Yes, she did.
5 A When did she do the laundry?
  B She did it in the afternoon.

Unit 4: Health
Track 5

A Listening
Listen. Circle the words you hear.

1 A What should I do?
  B You should see a dentist.
2 A What do you have to do?
  B I have to take some medicine.
3 A What should Amy do?
  B She should get an X-ray.
4 A What does Tom have to do?
  B He has to get a pair of crutches.
5 A What does he have to do?
  B He has to take aspirin and rest.

Unit 5: Around town
Track 6

A Listening
Listen. Circle the words you hear.

1 A How often does your son go to Boston?
  B He goes once a year.
2 A How often does your daughter ride her bike to school?
  B She rarely rides to school.
3 A What does your wife do in the morning?
  B She often studies in the morning.
4 A Will you stay with relatives on your trip?
  B Yes, I will.
5 A How long does it take to get to school?
  B It usually takes a half hour.

Midterm Test Units 1–5
Track 7

A Listening
Listen. Circle the words you hear.

1 A What does she need to buy?
  B She needs to buy black shoes and a black suit.
2 A Do you like sports?
  B Yes. I'm very athletic!
3 A When does she usually study?
  B She usually studies at night.
4 A How long does it take to get to the beach?
  B It takes 20 minutes.
5 A What's he doing now?
  B He's driving to the airport.

Track 8

B Listening
Listen. Circle the sentences you hear.

1 A What's your daughter doing right now?
  B She's reading.
2 A When will you get the prescription?
  B I'll go Tuesday.
3 A Where did your relatives go?
  B They went to the park.
4 A What does he need to do?
  B He needs to buy a new engine.
5 A Why did Susan stay home today?
  B She has chills.

Unit 6: Time
Track 9

A Listening
Listen. Circle the words you hear.

1 A When did they become citizens?
  B They became citizens in 1995.
2 A When did she have a baby?
  B She had a baby on September 13th.

3 A When will she start her new class?
　B She'll start her new class at 10:00 today.
4 A When did Anna and Marco graduate?
　B They graduated four weeks ago.
5 A When will Marie retire from her job?
　B She'll retire before June 10th.

Unit 7: Shopping
Track 10

A Listening
Listen. Circle the words you hear.
1 A Which piano is better?
　B The black piano is better.
2 A Which place has the most beautiful clothes?
　B The new boutique has the most beautiful clothes.
3 A Where should I go for furniture?
　B Mega Store has the nicest furniture.
4 A Which sofa should I buy?
　B You should buy the most comfortable sofa.
5 A Where did she go shopping?
　B She went to Mega Mart. It has the best prices.

Unit 8: Work
Track 11

A Listening
Listen. Circle the words you hear.
1 A What did he do this morning?
　B He picked up linens.
2 A Where did Amy go?
　B She walked to the new boutique.
3 A What did Jill do?
　B She delivered X-rays to the third floor.
4 A What were her job duties?
　B She prepared the work schedule.
5 A What did Brian do this morning?
　B He met with patients.

Unit 9: Daily living
Track 12

A Listening
Listen. Circle the words you hear.
1 A Which department store do you recommend?
　B I like the department store on Main Street.
2 A Which plumber is better?
　B Brown's Plumbing Service. It's fully licensed.
3 A Would you repair the door, please?
　B Sorry, I can't right now.
4 A Which electrician did he call?
　B He called XYZ Electric.
5 A Can you unclog the sink?
　B Yes, of course. I'm a plumber.

Unit 10: Leisure
Track 13

A Listening
Listen. Circle the words you hear.
1 A Did you go to the party?
　B Yes, I did. It was a housewarming.
2 A What would the children like?
　B They'd like some books.
3 A What did Lisa bring Hamid?
　B She brought him a cake.
4 A Would she like a balloon?
　B Yes, she would.
5 A Would you like a piece of pie?
　B Yes, please.

Final Test Units 6–10
Track 14

A Listening
Listen. Circle the words you hear.
1 A What did Marco do?
　B He helped a customer.
2 A Where did Suzanne go?
　B She went to the lab.
3 A When did Tim graduate?
　B He graduated a year ago.
4 A Would you like some supplies?
　B Yes, I would.
5 A Can you repair the lamp?
　B Yes, of course.

Track 15

B Listening
Listen. Write the letter of the conversation.

Conversation A
　A What did Shawn do this morning?
　B He took a patient to the lab.
Conversation B
　A What did Joseph do at work?
　B He prepared food.
Conversation C
　A What did Daniel do last week?
　B He operated large machines.
Conversation D
　A What did Michelle do yesterday?
　B She handled money.
Conversation E
　A What did Nick do?
　B He pumped gas.

Tests answer key

Each unit test item is 4 points. Unit test sections have five items; therefore, each section is worth 20 points, for a total of 100 points per unit test.

Unit 1: Personal information
A Listening
1. a checked shirt
2. a short green dress
3. uniform
4. a long black and white coat
5. today

B Grammar
1. watching
2. does
3. doing
4. study
5. are

C Grammar
1. curly brown
2. short plaid
3. small black
4. red and white striped
5. long white

D Reading
1. wears
2. wearing
3. usually
4. green
5. large

E Writing
Answers will vary. This section is worth 20 points. Score for accuracy, grammar, punctuation, and spelling.

Unit 2: At school
A Listening
1. computers
2. accounting
3. college
4. business
5. keyboarding

B Grammar
1. to take
2. work
3. to become
4. make
5. She'll

C Grammar
1. b 2. d 3. e 4. c 5. a

D Reading
1. No
2. No
3. Yes
4. Yes
5. No

E Writing
Answers will vary. This section is worth 20 points. Score for accuracy, grammar, punctuation, and spelling.

Unit 3: Friends and famiily
A Listening
1. shop
2. groceries
3. make the beds
4. cell phone
5. laundry

B Grammar
1. eat
2. met
3. got
4. cleans
5. went

C Grammar
1. watched
2. play
3. doesn't
4. didn't
5. go

D Reading
1. Yes
2. No
3. No
4. Yes
5. Yes

E Writing
Answers will vary. This section is worth 20 points. Score for accuracy, grammar, punctuation, and spelling.

Unit 4: Health
A Listening
1. dentist
2. medicine
3. X-ray
4. crutches
5. aspirin and rest

B Grammar
1. have to
2. have to
3. has to
4. have to
5. has to

C Grammar
1. b 2. d 3. c 4. e 5. a

D Reading
1. Yes
2. No
3. Yes
4. No
5. Yes

E Writing
Answers will vary. This section is worth 20 points. Score for accuracy, grammar, punctuation, and spelling.

Unit 5: Around town
A Listening
1. once a year
2. rarely
3. often
4. stay with relatives
5. a half hour

B Grammar
1. often
2. one
3. do
4. long
5. does

C Grammar
1. rarely rides
2. am always
3. never takes
4. is often
5. sometimes walk

D Reading
1. No
2. Yes
3. No
4. No
5. Yes

E Writing
Answers will vary. This section is worth 20 points. Score for accuracy, grammar, punctuation, and spelling.

Midterm Test Units 1–5
A Listening
(2 points per item)
1. suit
2. athletic
3. usually
4. 20 minutes
5. driving

B Listening
(3 points per item)
1. She's reading.
2. I'll go Tuesday.
3. They went to the park.
4. He needs to buy a new engine.
5. She has chills.

C Grammar
(2 points per item)
1. are
2. What's
3. will
4. need
5. did

D Grammar
(3 points per item)
1. c 2. d 3. b 4. e 5. a

E Reading
(2 points per item)
1. b 2. b 3. c 4. b 5. b

F Reading
(3 points per item)
1. No
2. Yes
3. No
4. Yes
5. No

G Writing
(2 points per item)
1. having
2. staying
3. went
4. go
5. should

H Writing
Answers will vary. This section is worth 15 points. Score for accuracy, grammar, punctuation, and spelling.

Unit 6: Time

A Listening
1. became citizens
2. on September 13th
3. at 10:00
4. four weeks ago
5. before June 10th

B Grammar
1. meet
2. started
3. left
4. did
5. came

C Grammar
1. c 2. e 3. b 4. a 5. d

D Reading
1. Yes
2. Yes
3. No
4. No
5. No

E Writing
Answers will vary. This section is worth 20 points. Score for accuracy, grammar, punctuation, and spelling.

Unit 7: Shopping

A Listening
1. better
2. the most beautiful
3. the nicest
4. comfortable
5. the best

B Grammar
1. smaller
2. more comfortable
3. bigger
4. more expensive
5. heavier

C Grammar
1. the friendliest
2. the most crowded
3. the cheapest
4. the oldest
5. the longest

D Reading
1. bought
2. last
3. read
4. lowest
5. have

E Writing
Answers will vary. This section is worth 20 points. Score for accuracy, grammar, punctuation, and spelling.

Unit 8: Work

A Listening
1. linens
2. walked
3. delivered
4. schedule
5. patients

B Grammar
1. Where
2. do
3. Did
4. met
5. help

C Grammar
1. but
2. and
3. or
4. and
5. but

D Reading
1. No
2. Yes
3. No
4. No
5. Yes

E Writing
Answers will vary. This section is worth 20 points. Score for accuracy, grammar, punctuation, and spelling.

Unit 9: Daily living

A Listening
1. department store
2. fully licensed
3. the door
4. electrician
5. plumber

B Grammar
1. recommend
2. does
3. suggests
4. like
5. It's

C Grammar
1. e 2. c 3. b 4. a 5. d

D Reading
1. tenant
2. ceiling
3. lights
4. send
5. fix

E Writing
Answers will vary. This section is worth 20 points. Score for accuracy, grammar, punctuation, and spelling.

Unit 10: Leisure

A Listening
1. housewarming
2. books
3. cake
4. balloon
5. a piece of pie

B Grammar
1. They'd
2. you
3. Would
4. like
5. he

C Grammar
1. wrote
2. cookies to
3. Pam
4. to him
5. to my

D Reading
1. No
2. Yes
3. No
4. Yes
5. No

E Writing
Answers will vary. This section is worth 20 points. Score for accuracy, grammar, punctuation, and spelling.

Final Test Units 6–10

A Listening
(2 points per item)
1. customer
2. lab
3. graduate
4. supplies
5. repair

B Listening
(3 points per item)
1. B
2. A
3. E
4. D
5. C

C Grammar
(2 points per item)
1. gave
2. the
3. ago
4. and
5. beautiful

D Grammar
(3 points per item)
1. e 2. c 3. d 4. a 5. b

E Reading
(2 points per item)
1. Yes
2. No
3. No
4. Yes
5. Yes

F Reading
(3 points per item)
1. a 2. c 3. d 4. a 5. b

G Writing
(1 point per item)
1. Viktorovna
2. 9/18/81
3. 13524 Coral Drive
4. Miami
5. Florida
6. 33175
7. Moscow, Russia
8. 1
9. divorce
10. 4/26/07

H Writing
Answers will vary. This section is worth 15 points. Score for accuracy, grammar, punctuation, and spelling.

Teacher's Toolkit Audio CD/CD-ROM

Overview

The *Teacher's Toolkit Audio CD/CD-ROM* is an additional resource for teachers using the *Ventures 2* Student's Book. The *Teacher's Toolkit Audio CD/CD-ROM* provides reproducible, supplementary materials for use during in-class assessment, whole-class activities, and group work. It provides more than 200 pages of additional material.

What's included in the *Teacher's Toolkit Audio CD/CD-ROM*:

- **Unit tests**, a **midterm test**, and a **final test** with corresponding **answer keys**, **audio scripts**, **audio program**, and instructions for administering and scoring the tests. When browsing the tests, a pop-up window can be opened that shows that test's audio script and answer key. The tests can be reproduced from the *Teacher's Toolkit Audio CD/CD-ROM* or from the printed test pages in the Teacher's Edition. Use a compact disc player or your computer's audio software to access the test audio program on the CD-ROM.
- The **self-assessments** from the *Ventures 2* Student's Book. Each unit self-assessment can be duplicated from the CD-ROM, completed by students, and saved as a portfolio assessment tool.
- **Collaborative Activity Worksheets**. For each lesson in the *Ventures 2* Student's Book, there is a reproducible activity worksheet to encourage collaborative pair and group work in class. On each worksheet screen, there is a pop-up window that can be opened to show the instructions for using the worksheet in class.
- Reproducible **Picture Dictionary Cards**. The **Picture Dictionary Cards** display each vocabulary item from the *Ventures 2* Student's Book Picture Dictionary pages. In addition, there are **Picture Dictionary Worksheets**, **Picture Dictionary Card indexes**, and **Teaching tips**. The Picture Dictionary Cards and Worksheets offer additional unit-by-unit practice of all the vocabulary introduced on the Picture dictionary, Lesson D, Reading pages. For instructions on how to print multiple Picture dictionary cards on one sheet of paper, please log on to the *Ventures* Teacher Support Site: http://www.cambridge.org/us/esl/teacher.
- **Real-life Documents**. Forms and documents introduced in *Ventures 2* Student's Book can be reproduced and completed by students to reinforce necessary life skills.
- A **vocabulary list**. All key vocabulary in *Ventures 2* Student's Book is listed alphabetically, with first occurrence page numbers included for easy reference.
- A **certificate of completion**. To recognize students for satisfactory completion of *Ventures 2,* a printable certificate is included.

Overview

Games provide practice and reinforcement of skills, but in a fun and engaging manner. Students love to play games. Games raise motivation and enjoyment for learning. They can be used as a warm-up, practice, or review activity. The games described below can be adjusted and adapted to the skill level of the class.

1. Stand By

Skills: speaking, listening, writing
Objective: to practice asking and answering questions
Preparation: Write the question and answers on the board. Prepare grids.

- Write a question on the board, for example: *When do you usually eat dinner?*
- Write possible answers (*5:00, 6:00, 7:00 . . .*) scattered on the board or taped around the room.
- Ss copy the question and write their answer to the question.
- When students have finished writing, they stand next to the answer that corresponds to their own answer.
- Ss discuss their answer with others who have the same answer, using questions such as *Why do you eat dinner at _____?*
- Then Ss mingle with the rest of the class, asking the initial question and recording each S's name and response on the grid.
- Use the completed grids to ask Ss questions about the responses. For example, *Why does Maria eat at 7:00? How many other students eat at 7:00?*
- The questions can be made easier or more difficult, depending on the level of the Ss.

Sample Grid:

Question:	
Student's Name	Answer

2. Match the Leader

Skills: speaking, listening, writing
Objective: to practice giving and following directions
Preparation: Prepare grids with boxes – 3 x 3, 3 x 4, or 3 x 5.

- Ss form groups of four or five and designate one S as the leader.
- Provide the leader with a list of words / items (for example, vocabulary words, shapes, telephone numbers) to be reviewed.
- The leader selects an item from the list and tells group members where to write / draw that item on their grids. (For example, *Write X-ray in the box in the top right corner.*)
- The leader enters the item in the same location on his / her own grid (behind an opened file folder so others can't see it).
- The leader continues through all items until the grid is full.
- The leader then shows his / her grid to the group to use to check their own grids.

Adaptation: Spaces on the grids may be numbered for lower-level Ss. For higher-level Ss, teach location words such as *top, bottom, left, right, next to, between,* and *under.*

3. Round Table

Skills: speaking, listening, writing
Objective: to review vocabulary from a unit
Preparation: none

- Ss form groups of four or five. Each group has a blank sheet of paper.
- Announce the topic, usually the unit topic just completed.
- The first S says a word related to the topic, writes the word on the paper, and passes the paper to the next S.
- That S says a new word related to the topic, enters the word on the paper, and passes the paper to the third S, who continues the process.
- Ss can ask for help from their teammates when they cannot think of a new word to add to the list.
- The paper continues to pass around the table until no one can think of another related word.
- A unique way of scoring is to have one group read its first word. If no other group has that word, the first group receives three points. If any other group has that word, the first group receives one point. The first group continues through its list, one word at a time.

- The other groups mark off the words on their lists as they are heard and record one point for each of those words as they know another group has the same word.
- When the first group finishes reading its list, the second group reads only those words that have not already been mentioned. Again, if other groups have the word, they each score one point; if no other group has the word, the first group scores three points.
- Continue until all groups have accounted for all their words.

4. Bingo

Skills: listening, writing
Objective: to review vocabulary
Preparation: Bingo grids (3 x 3, 3 x 4, 4 x 4 . . .)

- Select enough words to fill a Bingo grid. Read and spell each new word and use it in a sentence.
- Ss write each word randomly on their bingo grids. Lower-level Ss may need to copy the words from the board.
- When the grids are filled, play Bingo.
- The S who shouts "Bingo" first calls the next game.

Adaptation: Depending on the Ss' familiarity with the words, call the words by saying the word, spelling the word, providing a definition or an example, or giving a synonym or an antonym.

5. Picture It

Skill: speaking
Objective: to review vocabulary
Preparation: sets of vocabulary cards (one per group)

- Ss form groups of three or four. Give each group one set of vocabulary cards.
- One S chooses a card but does not tell the group members the word.
- On a piece of paper, this S draws a picture or pictures representing the word. Point out that the S drawing the picture cannot talk or make gestures.
- The other Ss try to guess the word, using the drawings as clues.
- Ss take turns choosing and drawing words until all words are chosen.

Adaptation: Instead of drawing the words, Ss can act out the words for group members to guess.

6. Prediction Bingo

Skills: reading or listening
Objective: to develop the prereading or prelistening strategy of predicting
Preparation: Bingo grids (3 x 3, 3 x 4, 4 x 4 . . .)

- Provide Ss with the title or topic of a selection to be read or heard from an audio recording.
- In each square of the Bingo grid, Ss enter a word related to that topic that they think will appear in the reading or audio.
- Ss listen to the audio or read the text. When they hear or see a word that is on their Bingo grid, they circle it.
- Ss discuss in small groups their choices, both correct and incorrect, and how they relate to the topic.

7. Disappearing Dialog

Skills: speaking, listening, reading, writing
Objective: to practice learning dialogs
Preparation: none

- Write a dialog on the board.
- Go over the dialog with the whole class, then have selected groups say the dialog.
- Next, have Ss practice the dialog in pairs.
- Erase one word from each line of the dialog each time pairs practice, until all words are gone.
- Have volunteers recite the dialog without support from words on the board.
- Then have Ss add words back to the board until all words are again in place.

8. Moving Dialog

Skills: speaking, listening
Objective: to practice using dialogs
Preparation: none

- Ss stand in two lines (A and B), facing each other as partners.
- Ss in line A have one side of a conversation. Ss in line B have the other side. At a signal, Ss in line A begin the dialog, with Ss in line B responding. The dialog may be two or several lines long, depending on the level of the Ss.
- When Ss have completed the dialog, Ss in line A move one (or more) people to the left and practice the dialog again with a new partner.
- Ss at the end of the line will move to the beginning of the line to find their new partners.

Adaptation: This exchange may be a simple question and answer (**A:** *What is your name?* **B:** *My name is _____.*) for lower-level Ss.

If necessary, Ss can have a card with the dialog printed on it, but encourage Ss to look up and face their partner when they are speaking.

9. Hear Ye, Hear Ye

Skills: listening or reading
Objective: to refine listening skills
Preparation: a reading text or an audio clip; a file card with a word or phrase from the clip on it (one word or phrase for each S or, if not enough words, use the same word multiple times)

- Select an audio clip or a reading segment.
- Provide each S with a file card containing a word or phrase that occurs one or more times in the clip or reading segment.
- Play or read the segment.
- Ss listen, paying particular attention for their word or phrase. They raise, then lower, their file card each time they hear the word.

Adaptation: The audio may be a song, a lecture, or a dialog. Ss can listen for things other than specific words, such as past tense verbs, numbers, or three-syllable words.

Alternatively, Ss can stand up or sit down when they hear their word, rather than raise their cards.

10. Treasure Hunt

Skills: reading, writing
Objective: to develop the reading skill of scanning
Preparation: Enlarge a reading selection from the Student's Book and cut it into paragraphs. Number each one. Create a handout with questions/items to be found in the reading.

- Post the pieces of the reading around the room.
- Ss, individually or in pairs, go around the room and locate specific information to enter into their handout. For example: *Write the words that begin with st*, or *Where did Olga go to university?*
- Ss check their answers by reading or reviewing the completed text in their books and sharing their answers as a class.

Adaptation: A short reading selection can be cut into sentences for lower-level Ss.

Multilevel classroom management

All classrooms are multilevel in some sense. No two students will ever be exactly the same. Learners vary in demographic factors such as culture and ethnicity, personal factors such as a willingness to take risks and differing learning styles, and experiential factors such as background knowledge and previous education. With all these differences, it will always be a challenge to provide useful learning activities for all members of the class. Yet there are some techniques that make working with a multilevel class more manageable.

1. Group work is one of the best ways of working with a multilevel class. Some tasks, such as watching a video, going on a field trip, or describing a picture, can be performed as a whole group. What will change in a multilevel class is the level of expectation of responses following the shared experience. Other tasks can be performed as a whole group, but the tasks are adapted for the students' levels. This could include interviews with varying difficulty of questions or a project such as a class newspaper, where students of differing levels contribute through activities appropriate to their abilities.

   Smaller, homogeneous groups allow students of the same level the opportunity to work together on activities such as a problem-solving task or a group writing activity. Smaller, heterogeneous groups are good for board games or jigsaw activities where the difficulty of the material can be controlled. In *Ventures 2,* the picture cards on the *Teacher's Toolkit Audio CD / CD-ROM* are excellent resources for working with heterogeneous or homogeneous groups. Ideas for how to use the picture cards are also on the CD-ROM.

2. Varying the materials or activities is another help in addressing the issue of multiple levels in the classroom. *Add Ventures,* the multilevel component of *Ventures,* provides activities for learners at differing levels. These can be used in the classroom with heterogeneous or homogeneous groups because the answers are the same for all three levels of worksheets.

3. Self-access centers are another kind of classroom management technique. These centers would be located in corners of the classroom and would provide opportunities for learners to work at varying levels. By providing a variety of materials, which can be color-coded for levels of difficulty, students have the opportunity to make choices as to the level they feel comfortable working on. Students can self-correct with answer keys. In this way, students are working towards more learner autonomy, which is a valuable assistant in a multilevel classroom, and a good start towards promoting lifelong learning skills.

4. Computer-assisted learning, using computers located within the classroom, can provide self-directed learning through software programs geared to a student's individual ability. Most programs provide immediate feedback to students to correct errors and build in a level of difficulty as a student progresses. Like-ability groups of students can rotate their time on the computer, working in pairs, or students can work individually at their own level.

A multilevel classroom, while challenging to the teacher, should offer each learner appropriate levels of instruction according to the learner's abilities, interests, needs, and experiences, and it should be designed to maximize each learner's educational gains. Good management techniques call for the teacher to provide a mixture of whole class, small group, and individual activities, create a learner-centered class by establishing self-access materials, use computers, and incorporate variety in the difficulty of the tasks and materials given to each student.

Authors' acknowledgments

The authors would like to acknowledge and thank focus group participants and reviewers for their insightful comments, as well as CUP editorial, marketing, and production staffs, whose thorough research and attention to detail have resulted in a quality product.

The publishers would also like to extend their particular thanks to the following reviewers and consultants for their valuable insights and suggestions:

Francesca Armendaris, North Orange County Community College District, Anaheim, California; **Alex A. Baez**, The Texas Professional Development Group, Austin, Texas; **Kit Bell**, LAUSD Division of Adult and Career Education, Los Angeles, California; **Rose Anne Cleary**, Catholic Migration Office, Diocese of Brooklyn, Brooklyn, New York; **Inga Cristi**, Pima Community College Adult Education, Tucson, Arizona; **Kay De Gennaro**, West Valley Occupational Center, Woodland Hills, California; **Patricia DeJesus-Lopez**, Illinois Community College Board, Springfield, Illinois; **Magali Apareaida Morais Duignan**, Augusta State University, Augusta, Georgia; **Gayle Fagan**, Harris County Department of Education, Houston, Texas; **Lisa A. Fears**, Inglewood Community Adult School, Inglewood, California; **Jas Gill**, English Language Institute at the University of British Columbia, Vancouver, British Columbia, Canada; **Elisabeth Goodwin**, Pima Community College Adult Education, Tucson, Arizona; **Carolyn Grimaldi**, Center for Immigrant Education and Training, LaGuardia Community College, Long Island City, New York; **Masha Gromyko**, Pima Community College Adult Education, Tucson, Arizona; **Jennifer M. Herrin**, Albuquerque TVI Community College, Albuquerque, New Mexico; **Giang T. Hoang**, Evans Community Adult School, Los Angeles, California; **Karen Hribar**, LAUSD West Valley Occupational Center, Los Angeles, California; **Patricia Ishill**, Union County College, Union County, New Jersey; **Dr. Stephen G. Karel**, McKinley Community School for Adults, Honolulu, Hawaii; **Aaron Kelly**, North Orange County Community College District, Anaheim, California; **Dan Kiernan**, Metro Skills Center, LAUSD, Los Angeles, California; **Kirsten Kilcup**, Green River Community College, Auburn, Washington; **Tom Knutson**, New York Association for New Americans, Inc., New York, New York; **Liz Koenig-Golombek**, LAUSD, Los Angeles, California; **Anita Lemonis**, West Valley Occupational Center, Los Angeles, California; **Lia Lerner**, Burbank Adult School, Burbank, California; **Susan Lundquist**, Pima Community College Adult Education, Tucson, Arizona; **Dr. Amal Mahmoud**, Highline Community College, Des Moines, Washington; **Fatiha Makloufi**, Hostos Community College, Bronx, New York; **Judith Martin-Hall**, Indian River Community College, Fort Pierce, Florida; **Gwen Mayer**, Van Nuys Community Adult School, Los Angeles, California; **Lois Miller**, Pima Community College, Tucson, Arizona; **Vicki Moore**, El Monte-Rosemead Adult School, El Monte, California; **Jeanne Petrus-Rivera**, Cuyahoga Community College, Cleveland, Ohio; **Pearl W. Pigott**, Houston Community College, Houston, Texas; **Catherine Porter**, Adult Learning Resource Center, Des Plaines, Illinois; **Planaria Price**, Evans Community Adult School, Los Angeles, California; **James P. Regan**, NYC Board of Education, New York, New York; **Catherine M. Rifkin**, Florida Community College at Jacksonville, Jacksonville, Florida; **Amy Schneider**, Pacoima Skills Center, Los Angeles, California; **Bonnie Sherman**, Green River Community College, Auburn, Washington; **Julie Singer**, Garfield Community Adult School, Los Angeles, California; **Yilin Sun**, Seattle Central Community College, Seattle, Washington; **André Sutton**, Belmont Community Adult School, Los Angeles, California; **Deborah Thompson**, El Camino Real Community Adult School, Los Angeles, California; **Evelyn Trottier**, Basic Studies Division, Seattle Central Community College, Seattle, Washington; **Debra Un**, New York University, American Language Institute, New York, New York; **Jodie Morgan Vargas**, Orange County Public Schools, Orlando, Florida; **Christopher Wahl**, Hudson County Community College, Jersey City, New Jersey; **Ethel S. Watson**, Evans Community Adult School, Los Angeles, California; **Barbara Williams**; **Mimi Yang**, Belmont Community Adult School, Los Angeles, California; **Adèle Youmans**, Pima Community College Adult Education, Tucson, Arizona.

Ventures Student's Book 2
Illustration credits

Ken Batelman: 86, 87, 88, 119
Travis Foster: 46, 47 (bottom), 107
Chuck Gonzales: 9, 29, 48, 49, 52, 81, 124
Brad Hamann: 11, 21, 35, 89, 114
Ben Kirchner: 2, 4, 6, 7, 12, 18, 19, 24, 32, 33, 38, 44, 45, 50, 58, 59, 64, 70, 71, 76, 84, 85, 90, 96, 97, 102, 110, 111, 116, 122, 123, 128

Jim Kopp: 13, 25, 39, 51, 65, 77, 91, 103, 117, 129
Monika Roe: 17, 36, 37, 62, 75, 115, 127
Lucy Truman: 47 (top), 72, 101

Photography credits

14 ©Punchstock

23 *(clockwise from top left)* ©Jupiter Images; ©Alamy; ©Punchstock; ©Don Mason/Corbis; ©Jupiter Images; ©Livia Corona/Getty Images

29 *(clockwise from top left)* ©Photos.com; ©Alamy; ©Alamy; ©Alamy; ©Michael Kelley/Getty Images; ©Photos.com

34 ©Jupiter Images

42 ©Punchstock

55 ©Larry Williams/Corbis

63 *(top to bottom)* ©Punchstock; ©Getty Images

66 *(top to bottom)* ©Istock Photos; ©Jupiter Images

73 *(top to bottom)* ©Jupiter Images; ©Alamy

74 ©Jupiter Images

78 ©Michael Cogliantry/Getty Images

87 *(left to right)* ©Punchstock; ©Hemera; ©Photos.com; ©Istock Photos

88 *(left to right)* ©Istock Photos; ©Alamy; ©Punchstock; *(inset)* ©Shutterstock

93 ©Shutterstock

98 ©Age Fotostock

121 *(top to bottom)* ©Age Fotostock; ©Jupiter Images; ©Photo Library; ©Billy Hustace/Getty Images; ©Alamy

125 *(clockwise from top left)* ©Alamy; ©Alamy; ©Alamy; ©Istock Photos; ©Age Fotostock; ©Jupiter Images; ©Jupiter Images; ©Alamy; ©Stock Xpert

133 ©Istock Photos

Ventures Teacher's Edition 2 tests
Illustration credits

William Waitzman: T-166

Photography credits

T-180: Michael Cogliantry/Getty Images
T-189: *(clockwise from top left)* ©Shutterstock; ©Jupiter Images; ©Alamy; ©Shutterstock; ©Jupiter Images
T-192: ©Michael Speers

Collaborative Activities
Illustration credits

Kathy Baxendale: 30, 66
Ron Carboni: 58, 71
Laurie Conley: 5, 47, 89

Monika Roe: 1, 2, 9, 10, 34, 35, 43, 82, 83
William Waitzman: 18, 19, 26, 54, 55, 62

Picture Dictionary Cards
Illustration credits

Jim Kopp: all illustrations

Ventures 2 Teacher's Toolkit Audio CD / CD-ROM

Minimum System Requirements

Windows 2000, XP, Vista

- Intel Pentium processor – minimum 400 MHz
- 128 MB RAM minimum
- Sound card. Speakers or headphones.

Macintosh

- PowerPC processor – minimum 300 MHz
- MacOS OSX
- 64 MB free RAM minimum
- Sound card. Speakers or headphones.

Browsers & Plug-ins

- Flash Player 8 or higher
- Mac: Microsoft Internet Explorer 5.2 or a comparable browser
- Windows: Microsoft Internet Explorer 6.0 or a comparable browser

Audio

To play the audio CD portion of the *Teacher's Toolkit* on a computer, follow these instructions:

Insert the disc into the CD-ROM drive. Open a media player such as Windows Media Player or iTunes. Click "Play."

You can also play the audio CD portion of the *Teacher's Toolkit* in a conventional audio CD player.